Yamada-kun and the Seven Witches

14

MIKI YOSHIKAWA

ムス
SULK

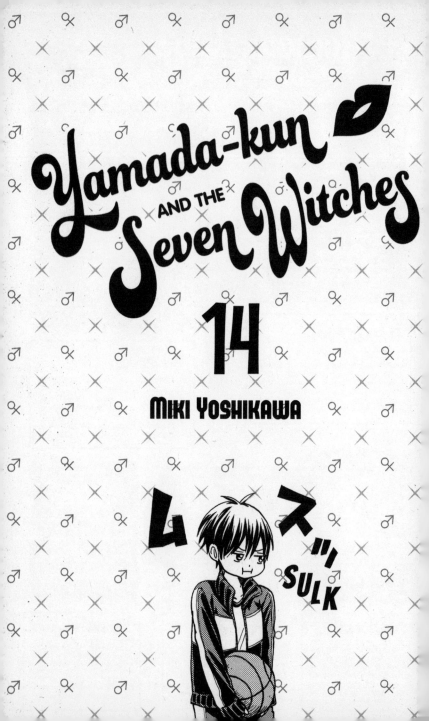

Yamada-kun and the Seven Witches

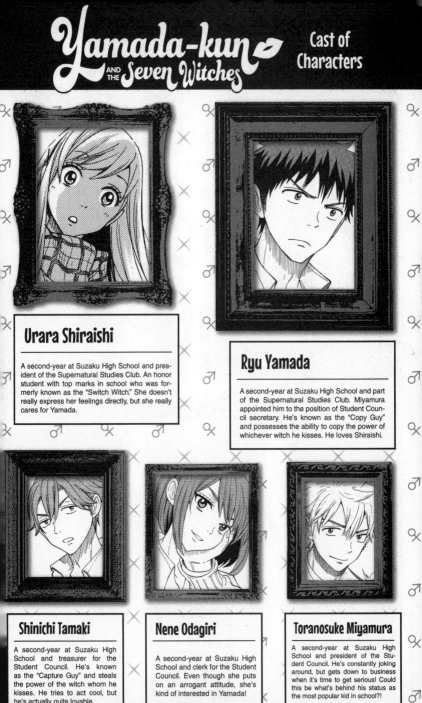

Cast of Characters

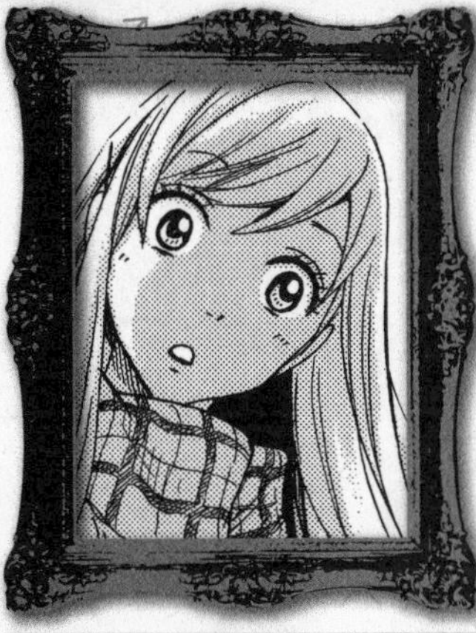

Urara Shiraishi

A second-year at Suzaku High School and president of the Supernatural Studies Club. An honor student with top marks in school who was formerly known as the "Switch Witch." She doesn't really express her feelings directly, but she really cares for Yamada.

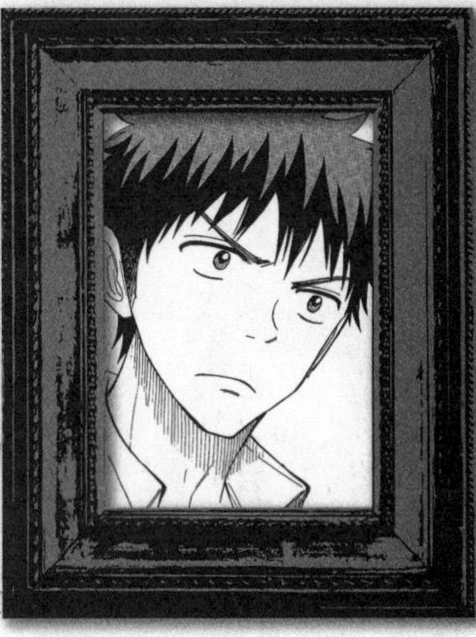

Ryu Yamada

A second-year at Suzaku High School and part of the Supernatural Studies Club. Miyamura appointed him to the position of Student Council secretary. He's known as the "Copy Guy" and possesses the ability to copy the power of whichever witch he kisses. He loves Shiraishi.

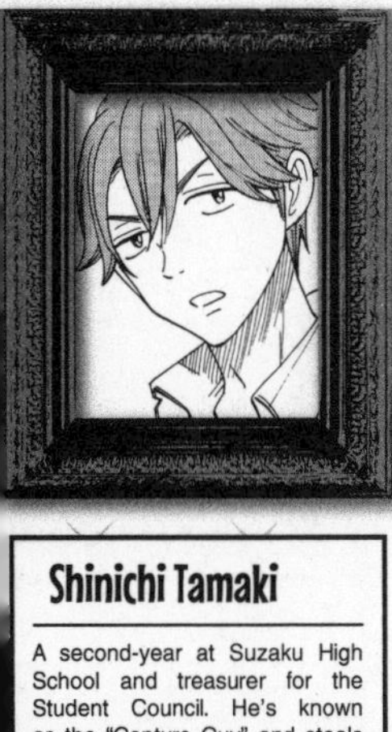

Shinichi Tamaki

A second-year at Suzaku High School and treasurer for the Student Council. He's known as the "Capture Guy" and steals the power of the witch whom he kisses. He tries to act cool, but he's actually quite lovable.

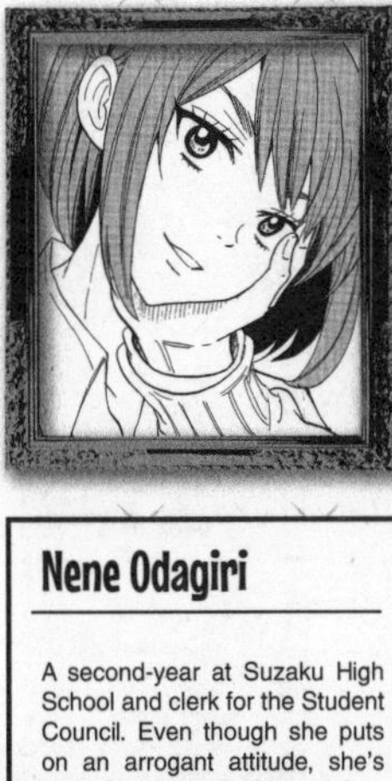

Nene Odagiri

A second-year at Suzaku High School and clerk for the Student Council. Even though she puts on an arrogant attitude, she's kind of interested in Yamada!

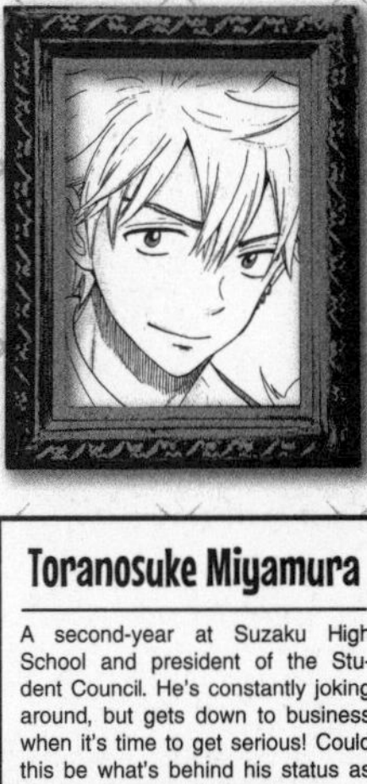

Toranosuke Miyamura

A second-year at Suzaku High School and president of the Student Council. He's constantly joking around, but gets down to business when it's time to get serious! Could this be what's behind his status as the most popular kid in school?!

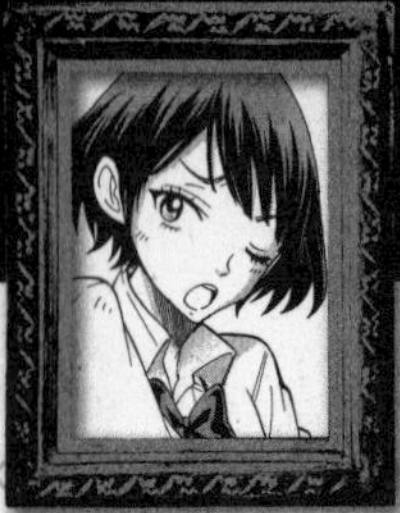

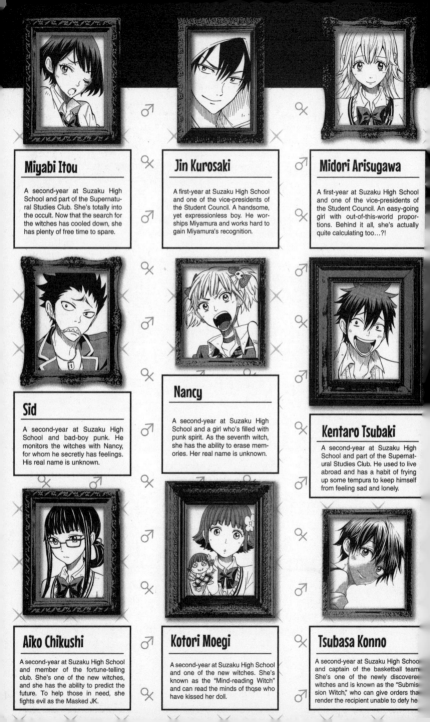

Miyabi Itou

A second-year at Suzaku High School and part of the Supernatural Studies Club. She's totally into the occult. Now that the search for the witches has cooled down, she has plenty of free time to spare.

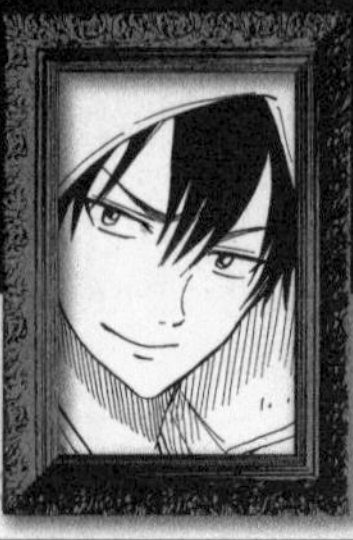

Jin Kurosaki

A first-year at Suzaku High School and one of the vice-presidents of the Student Council. A handsome, yet expressionless boy. He worships Miyamura and works hard to gain Miyamura's recognition.

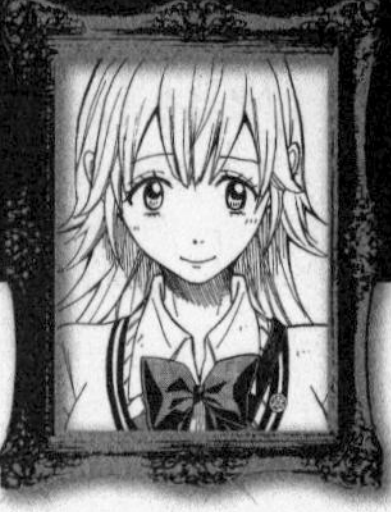

Midori Arisugawa

A first-year at Suzaku High School and one of the vice-presidents of the Student Council. An easy-going girl with out-of-this-world proportions. Behind it all, she's actually quite calculating too…?!

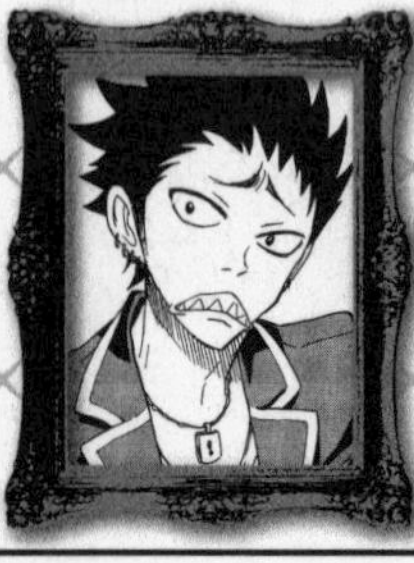

Sid

A second-year at Suzaku High School and bad-boy punk. He monitors the witches with Nancy, for whom he secretly has feelings. His real name is unknown.

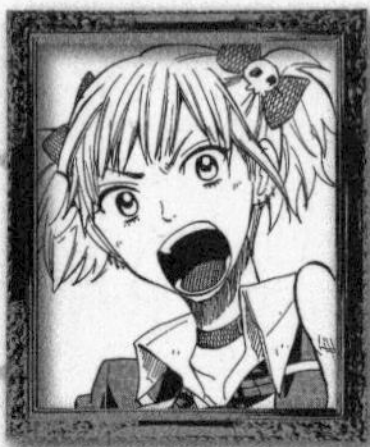

Nancy

A second-year at Suzaku High School and a girl who's filled with punk spirit. As the seventh witch, she has the ability to erase memories. Her real name is unknown.

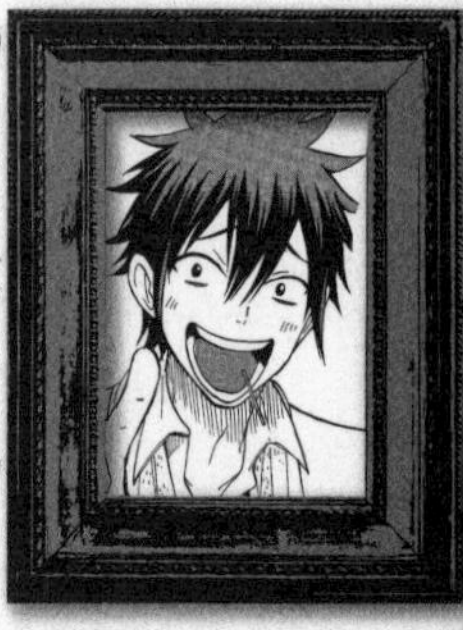

Kentaro Tsubaki

A second-year at Suzaku High School and part of the Supernatural Studies Club. He used to live abroad and has a habit of frying up some tempura to keep himself from feeling sad and lonely.

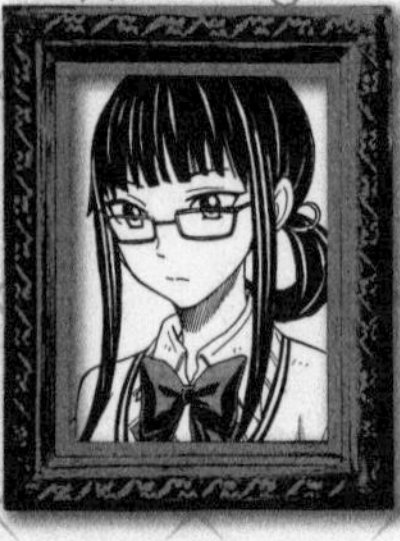

Aiko Chikushi

A second-year at Suzaku High School and member of the fortune-telling club. She's one of the new witches, and she has the ability to predict the future. To help those in need, she fights evil as the Masked JK.

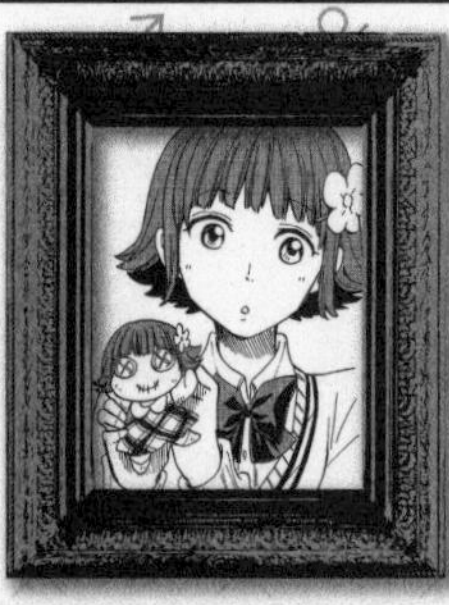

Kotori Moegi

A second-year at Suzaku High School and one of the new witches. She's known as the "Mind-reading Witch" and can read the minds of those who have kissed her doll.

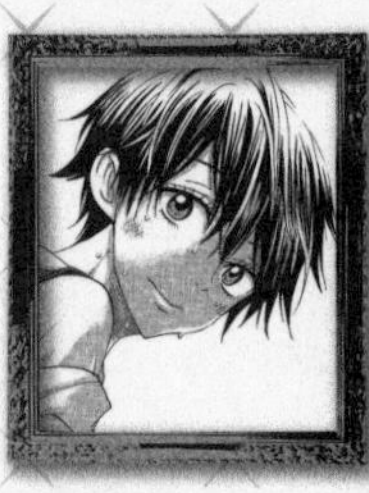

Tsubasa Konno

A second-year at Suzaku High Schoo and captain of the basketball team She's one of the newly discovere witches and is known as the "Submis sion Witch," who can give orders tha render the recipient unable to defy he

CONTENTS

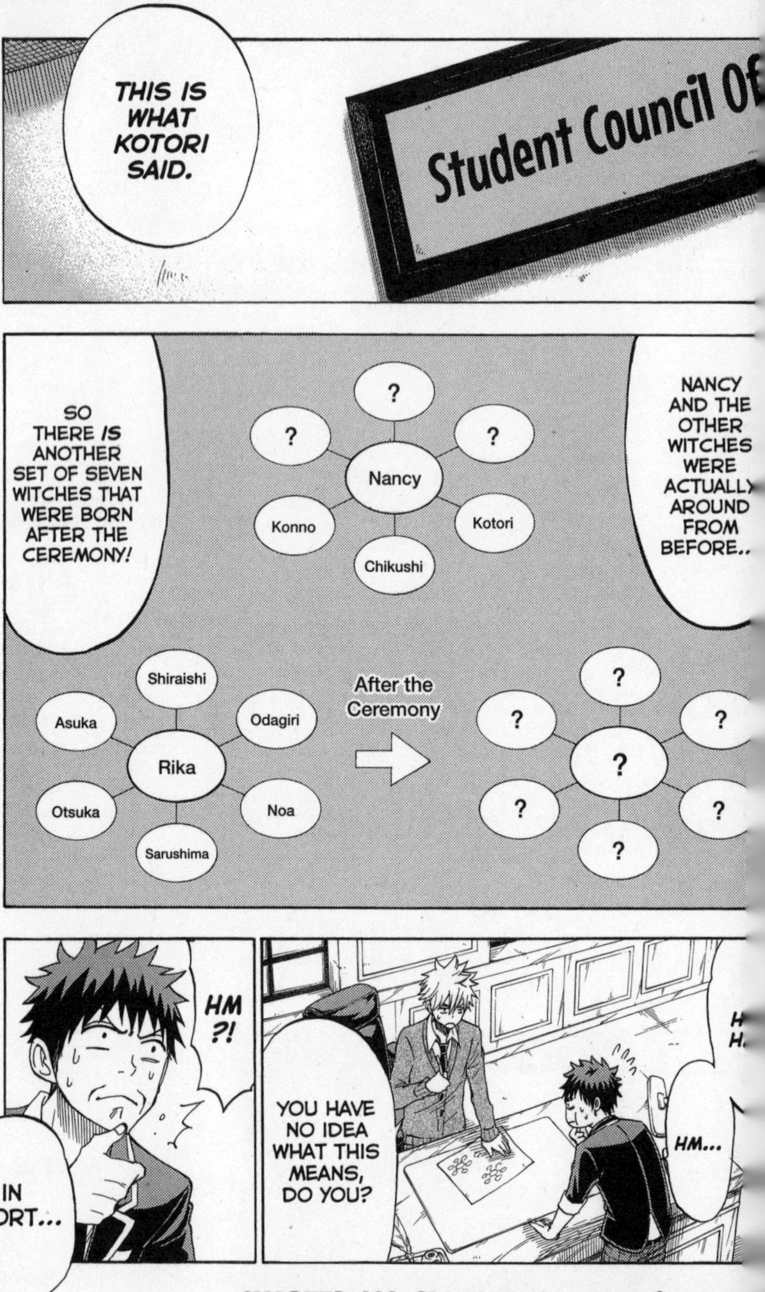
THIS IS WHAT KOTORI SAID.
Student Council Of
NANCY AND THE OTHER WITCHES WERE ACTUALL AROUND FROM BEFORE..
?
?
?
Nancy
Konno
Kotori
Chikushi
SO THERE *IS* ANOTHER SET OF SEVEN WITCHES THAT WERE BORN AFTER THE CEREMONY!
Shiraishi
Asuka
Odagiri
Rika
Otsuka
Noa
Sarushima
After the Ceremony
?
?
?
?
?
?
?
?
HM...
YOU HAVE NO IDEA WHAT THIS MEANS, DO YOU?
HM ?!
IN SHORT...

CHAPTER 111: She does have a nice bo

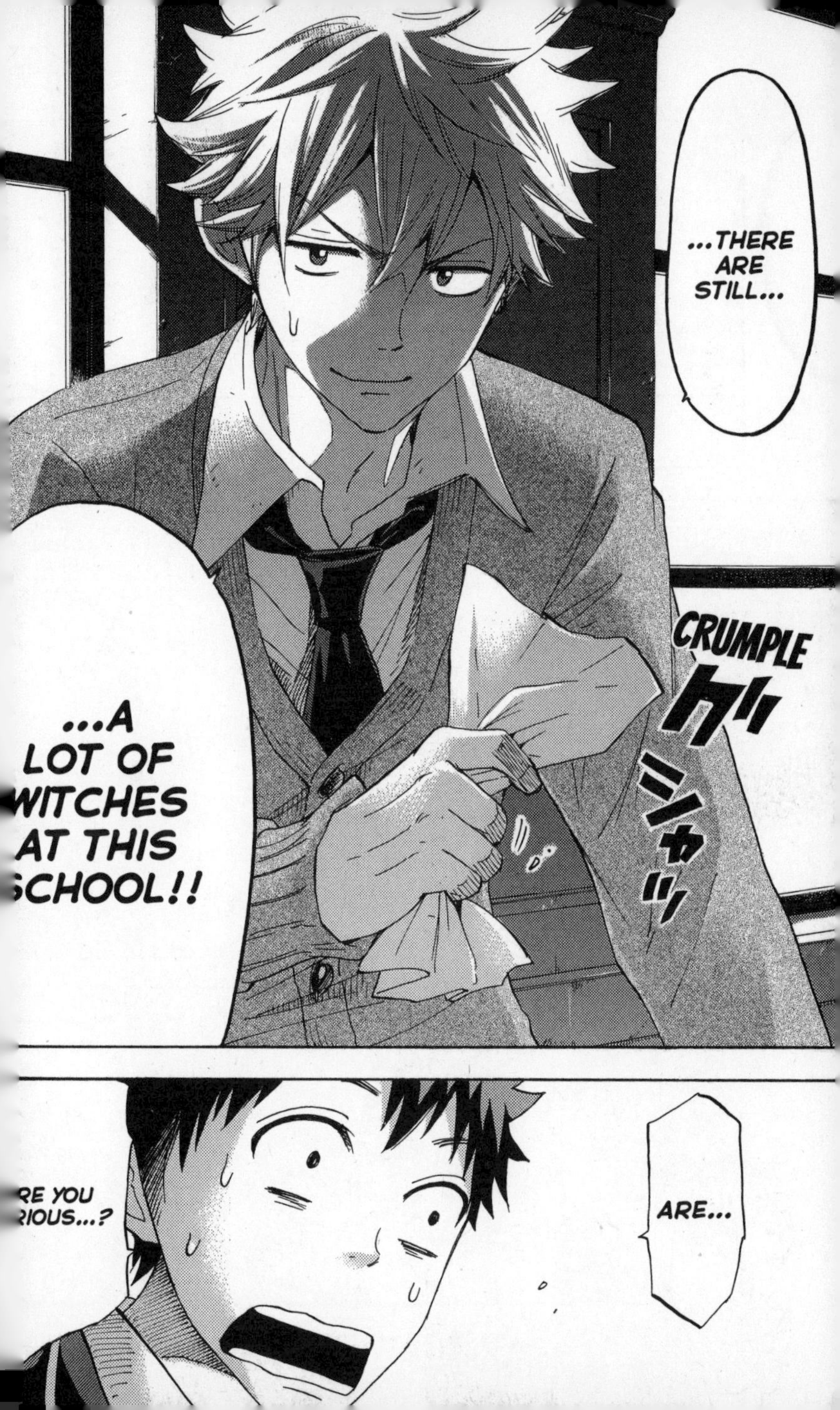
...THERE ARE STILL...
CRUMPLE
グシャッ
...A LOT OF WITCHES AT THIS SCHOOL!!
ARE...
RE YOU RIOUS...?

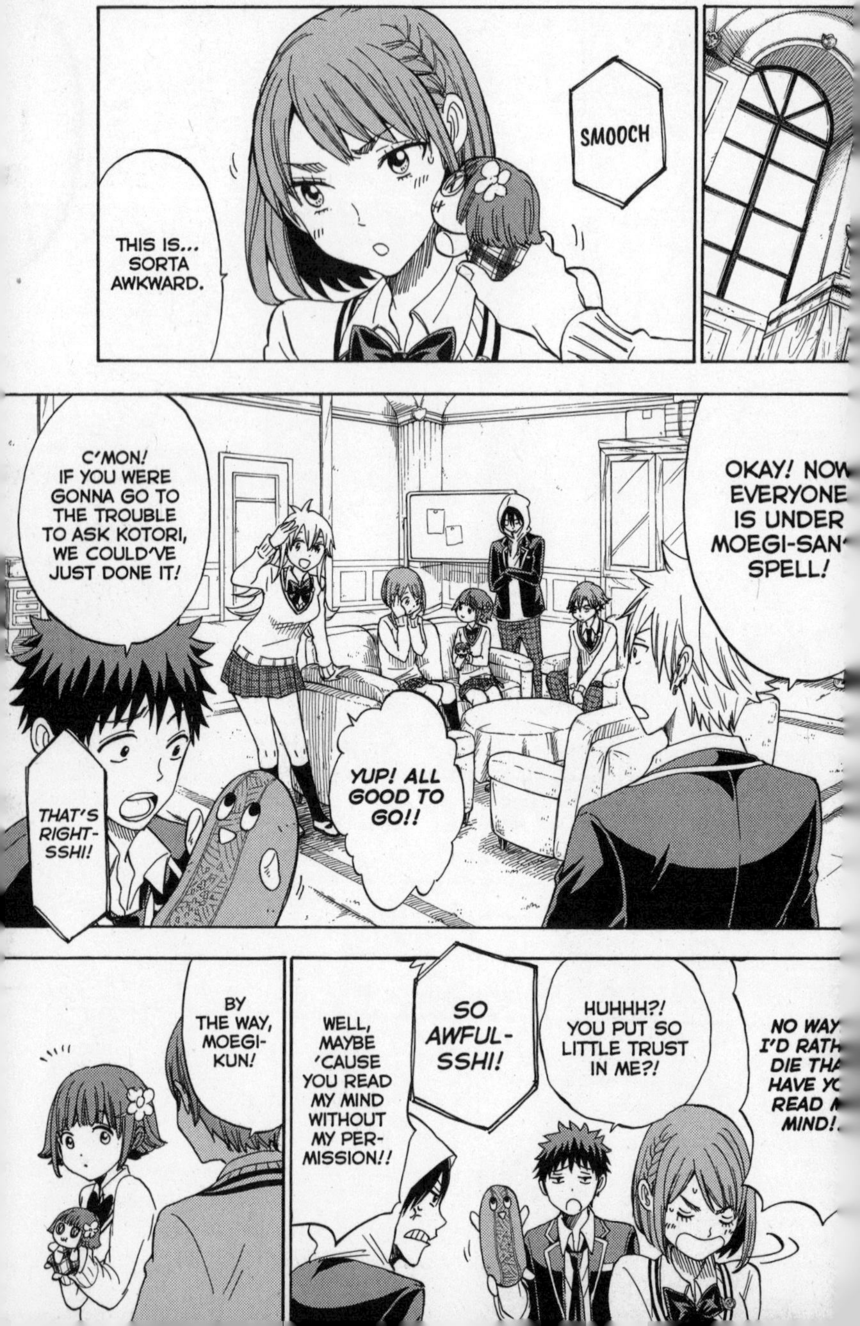
SMOOCH
THIS IS... SORTA AWKWARD.
OKAY! NOW EVERYONE IS UNDER MOEGI-SAN SPELL!
C'MON! IF YOU WERE GONNA GO TO THE TROUBLE TO ASK KOTORI, WE COULD'VE JUST DONE IT!
YUP! ALL GOOD TO GO!!
THAT'S RIGHT-SSHI!
NO WAY I'D RATH DIE THA HAVE YO READ M MIND!!
HUHHH?! YOU PUT SO LITTLE TRUST IN ME?!
SO AWFUL-SSHI!
WELL, MAYBE 'CAUSE YOU READ MY MIND WITHOUT MY PER-MISSION!!
BY THE WAY, MOEGI-KUN!

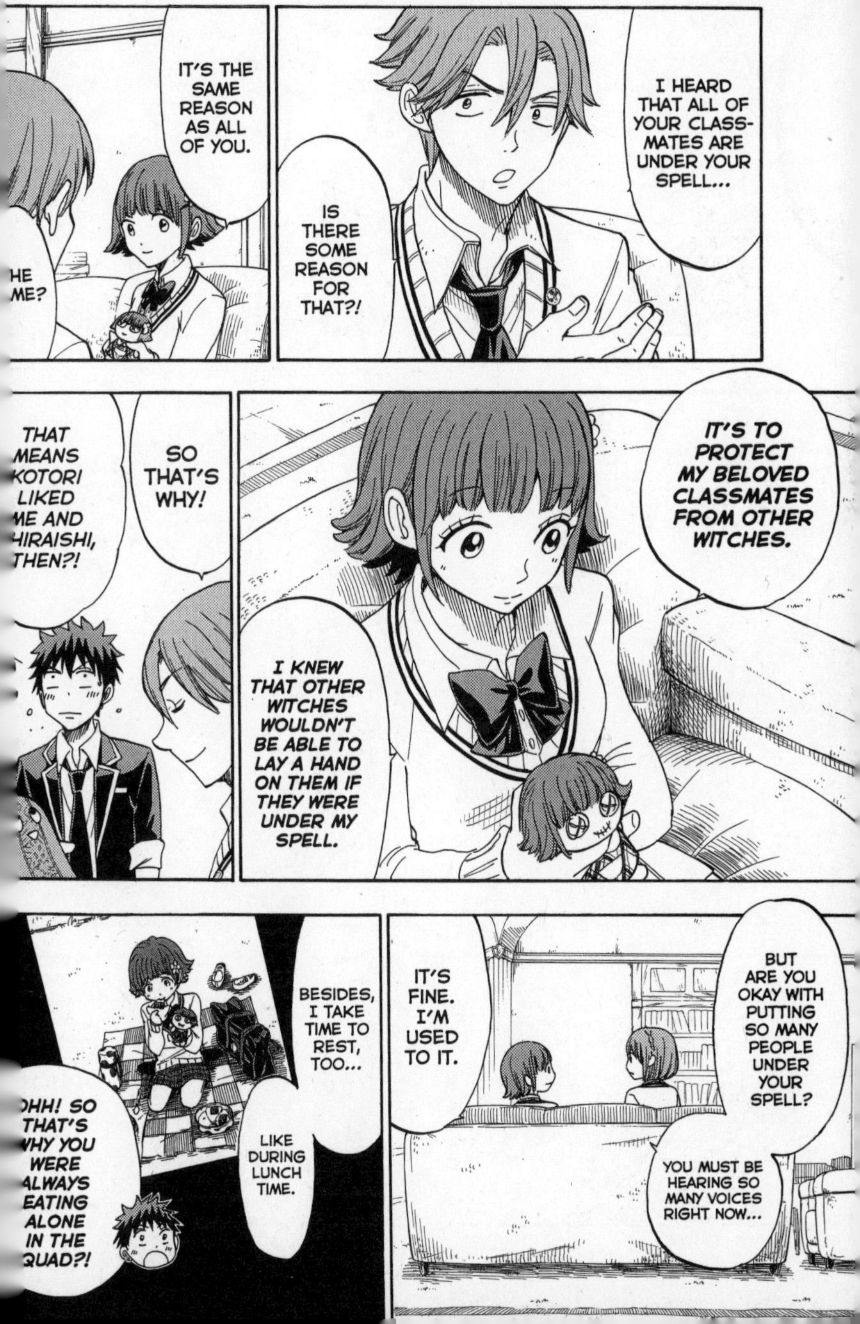
I HEARD THAT ALL OF YOUR CLASSMATES ARE UNDER YOUR SPELL...
IS THERE SOME REASON FOR THAT?!
IT'S THE SAME REASON AS ALL OF YOU.
IT'S TO PROTECT MY BELOVED CLASSMATES FROM OTHER WITCHES.
I KNEW THAT OTHER WITCHES WOULDN'T BE ABLE TO LAY A HAND ON THEM IF THEY WERE UNDER MY SPELL.
SO THAT'S WHY!
THAT MEANS KOTORI LIKED ME AND HIRAISHI, THEN?!
BUT ARE YOU OKAY WITH PUTTING SO MANY PEOPLE UNDER YOUR SPELL?
YOU MUST BE HEARING SO MANY VOICES RIGHT NOW...
IT'S FINE. I'M USED TO IT.
BESIDES, I TAKE TIME TO REST, TOO...
LIKE DURING LUNCH TIME.
OHH! SO THAT'S WHY YOU WERE ALWAYS EATING ALONE IN THE QUAD?!

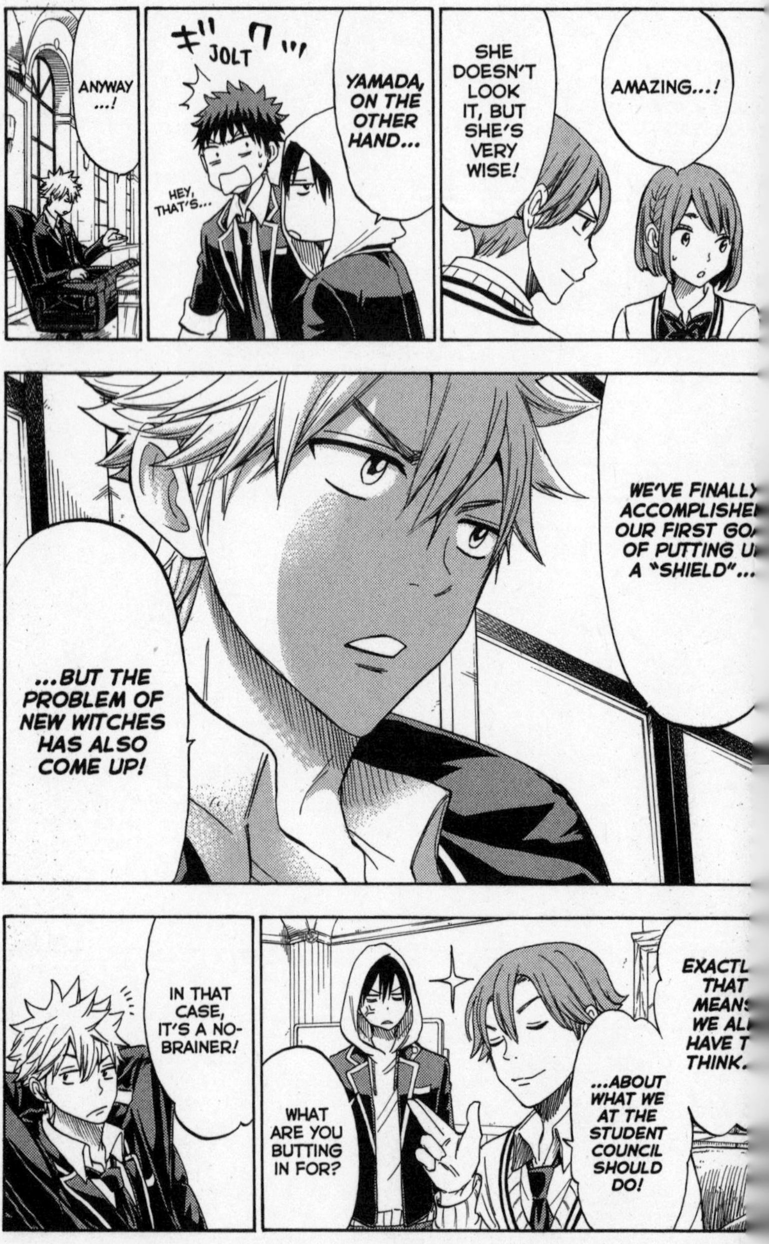
AMAZING...!
SHE DOESN'T LOOK IT, BUT SHE'S VERY WISE!
YAMADA, ON THE OTHER HAND...
ギクッ JOLT
HEY, THAT'S...
ANYWAY ...!
WE'VE FINALLY ACCOMPLISHE OUR FIRST GOA OF PUTTING U A "SHIELD"...
...BUT THE PROBLEM OF NEW WITCHES HAS ALSO COME UP!
EXACTL THAT MEANS WE AL HAVE T THINK...
...ABOUT WHAT WE AT THE STUDENT COUNCIL SHOULD DO!
WHAT ARE YOU BUTTING IN FOR?
IN THAT CASE, IT'S A NO-BRAINER!

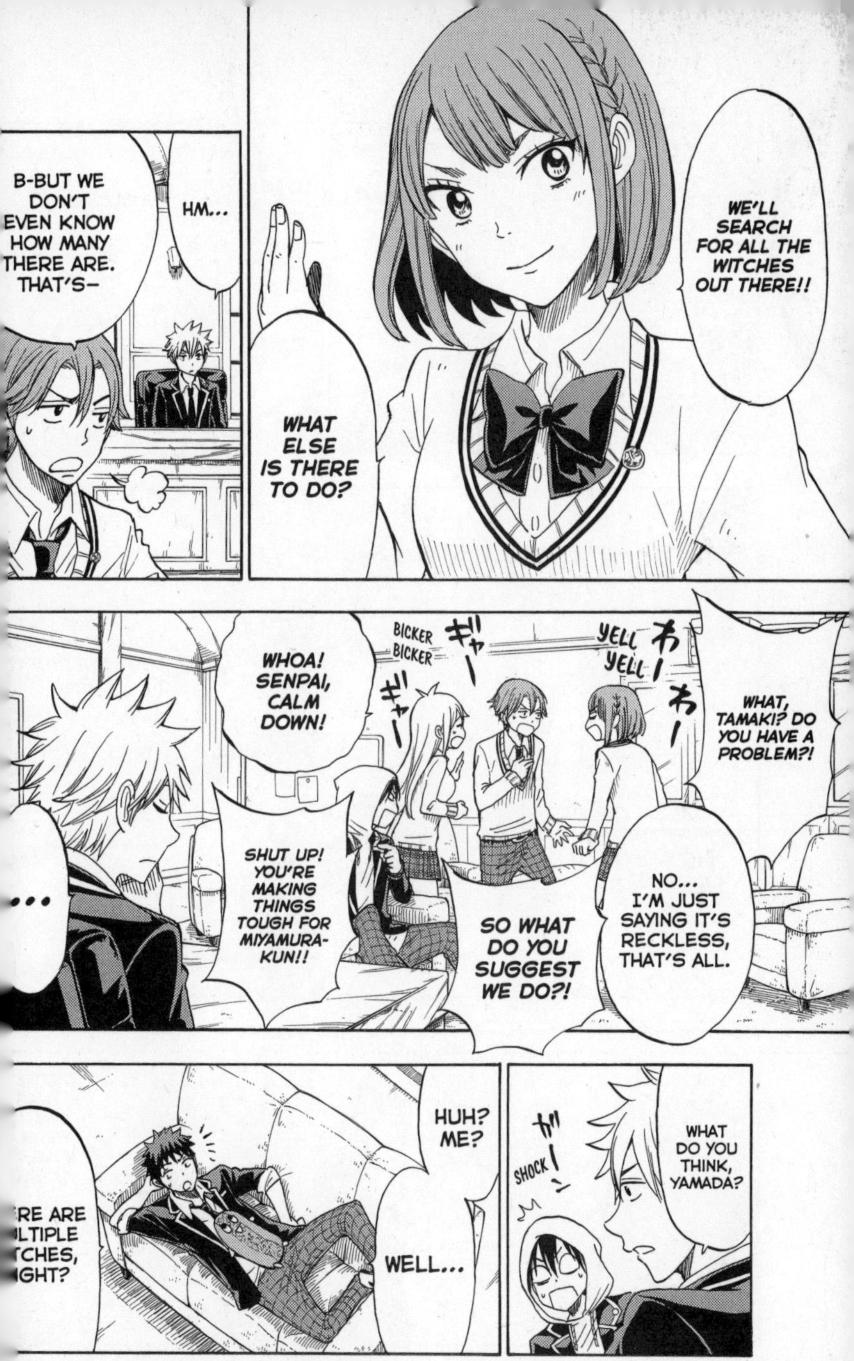
WE'LL SEARCH FOR ALL THE WITCHES OUT THERE!!
WHAT ELSE IS THERE TO DO?
HM...
B-BUT WE DON'T EVEN KNOW HOW MANY THERE ARE. THAT'S—
WHAT, TAMAKI? DO YOU HAVE A PROBLEM?!
YELL YELL
BICKER BICKER
NO... I'M JUST SAYING IT'S RECKLESS, THAT'S ALL.
WHOA! SENPAI, CALM DOWN!
SO WHAT DO YOU SUGGEST WE DO?!
SHUT UP! YOU'RE MAKING THINGS TOUGH FOR MIYAMURA-KUN!!
...
WHAT DO YOU THINK, YAMADA?
SHOCK
HUH? ME?
WELL...
ERE ARE LTIPLE TCHES, GHT?

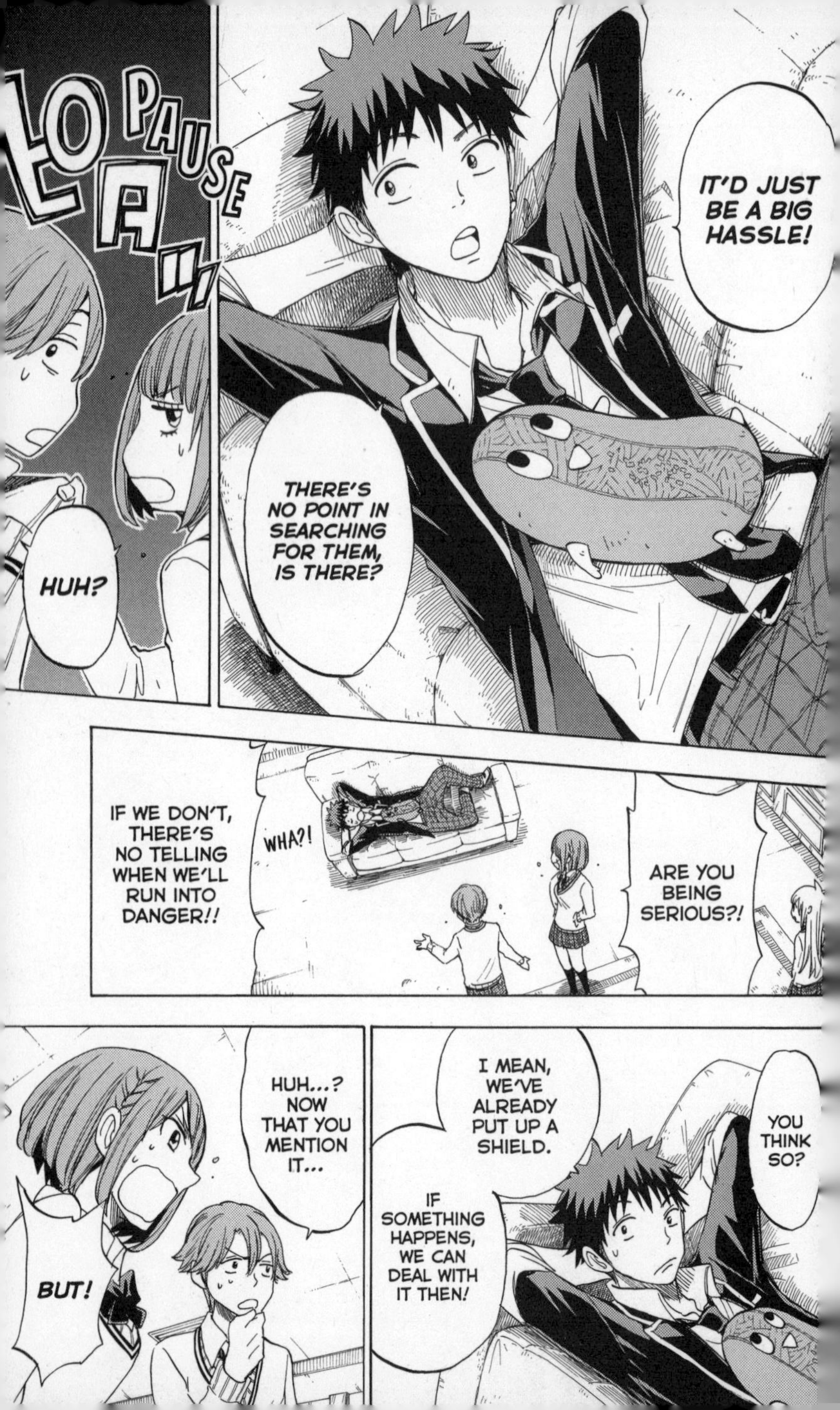
IT'D JUST BE A BIG HASSLE!
THERE'S NO POINT IN SEARCHING FOR THEM, IS THERE?
PAUSE
HUH?
ARE YOU BEING SERIOUS?!
WHA?!
IF WE DON'T, THERE'S NO TELLING WHEN WE'LL RUN INTO DANGER!!
YOU THINK SO?
I MEAN, WE'VE ALREADY PUT UP A SHIELD.
IF SOMETHING HAPPENS, WE CAN DEAL WITH IT THEN!
HUH...? NOW THAT YOU MENTION IT...
BUT!

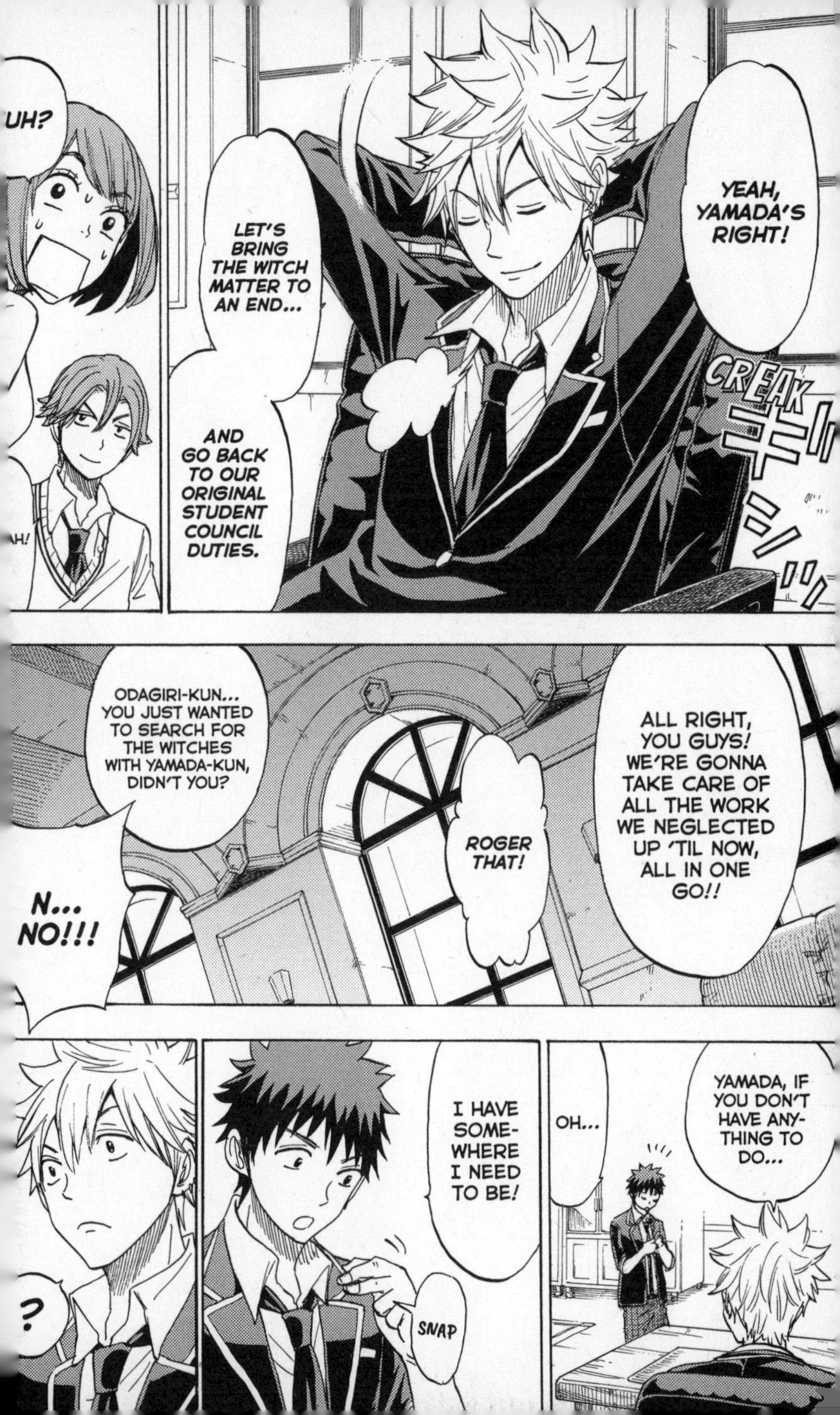
YEAH, YAMADA'S RIGHT!
CREAK
LET'S BRING THE WITCH MATTER TO AN END...
AND GO BACK TO OUR ORIGINAL STUDENT COUNCIL DUTIES.
UH?
AH!
ALL RIGHT, YOU GUYS! WE'RE GONNA TAKE CARE OF ALL THE WORK WE NEGLECTED UP 'TIL NOW, ALL IN ONE GO!!
ROGER THAT!
ODAGIRI-KUN... YOU JUST WANTED TO SEARCH FOR THE WITCHES WITH YAMADA-KUN, DIDN'T YOU?
N... NO!!!
YAMADA, IF YOU DON'T HAVE ANY-THING TO DO...
OH...
I HAVE SOME-WHERE I NEED TO BE!
SNAP
?

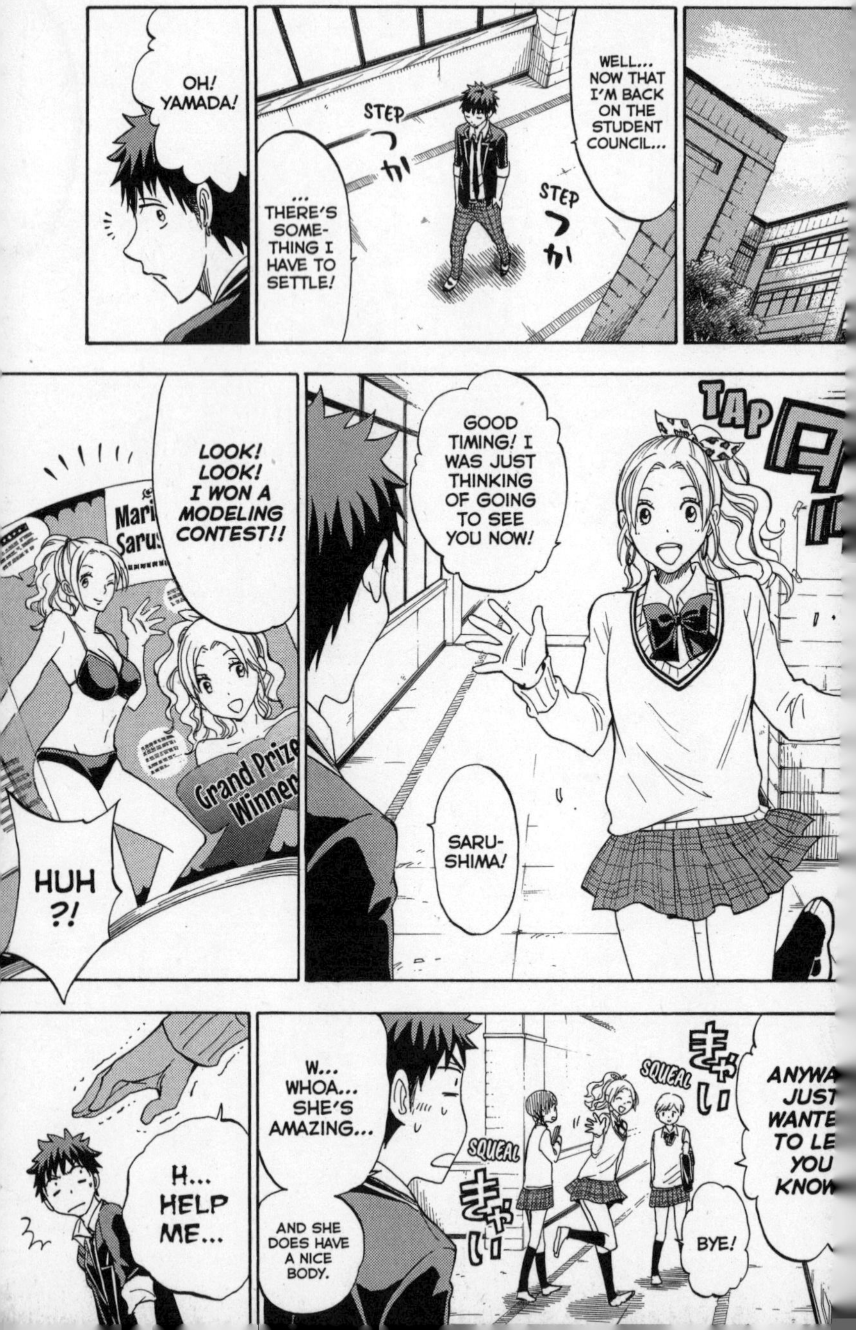
WELL... NOW THAT I'M BACK ON THE STUDENT COUNCIL...
STEP
つか
STEP
つか
... THERE'S SOME-THING I HAVE TO SETTLE!
OH! YAMADA!
TAP
GOOD TIMING! I WAS JUST THINKING OF GOING TO SEE YOU NOW!
SARU-SHIMA!
LOOK! LOOK! I WON A MODELING CONTEST!!
Mari
Sarus
Grand Prize Winner
HUH ?!
ANYWA JUST WANTE TO LE YOU KNOW
SQUEAL
きゃー
BYE!
W... WHOA... SHE'S AMAZING...
SQUEAL
きゃー
AND SHE DOES HAVE A NICE BODY.
H... HELP ME...

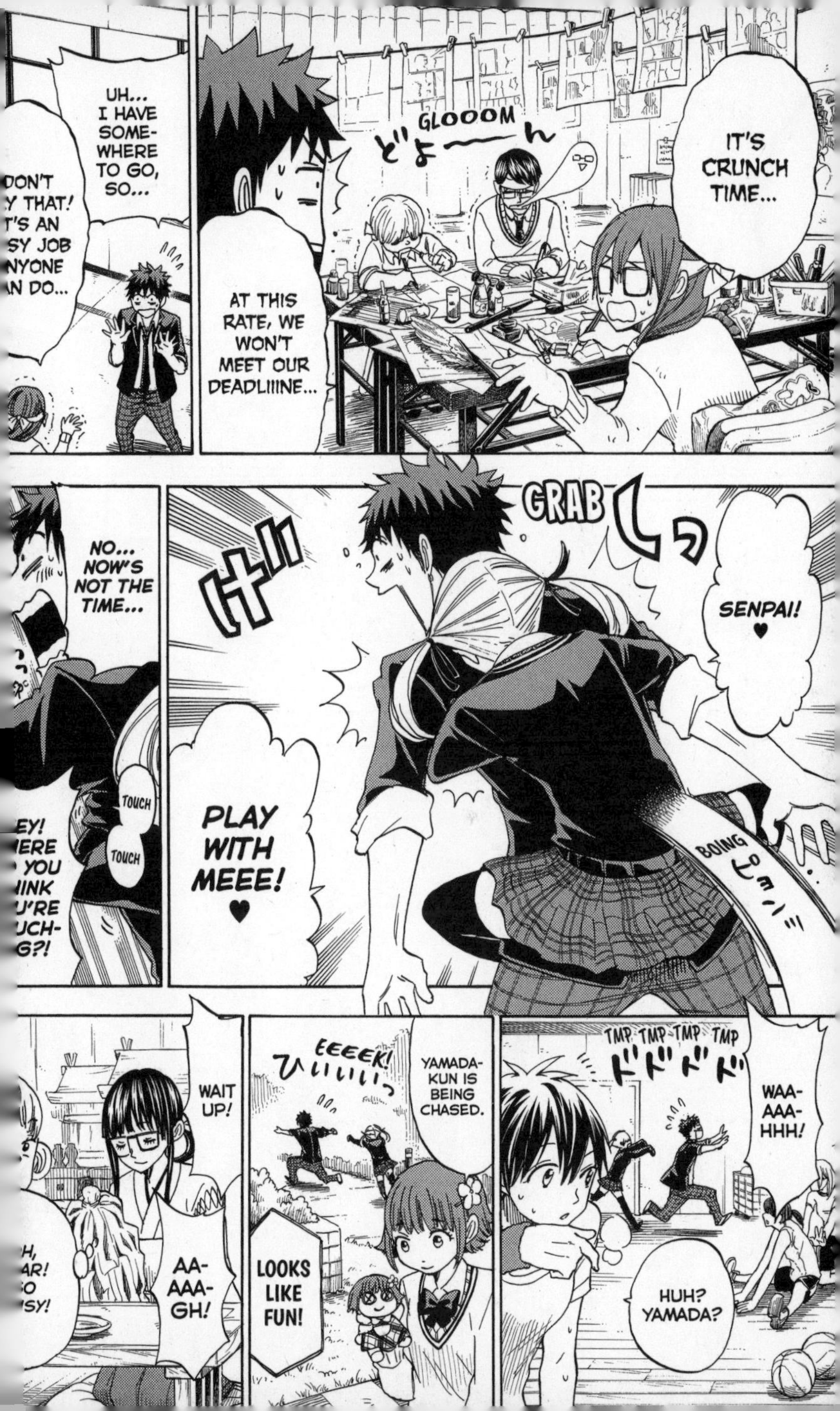

IT'S CRUNCH TIME...
GLOOOM
どよ〜〜ん
AT THIS RATE, WE WON'T MEET OUR DEADLIIINE...
UH... I HAVE SOMEWHERE TO GO, SO...
GRAB
しっ
SENPAI! ♥
はっ
PLAY WITH MEEE! ♥
BOING
ピョーン
NO... NOW'S NOT THE TIME...
TOUCH
TOUCH
TMP TMP TMP TMP
ドドドド
WAA-AAA-HHH!
HUH? YAMADA?
YAMADA-KUN IS BEING CHASED.
EEEEK!
ひいいいっ
LOOKS LIKE FUN!
WAIT UP!
AA-AAA-GH!

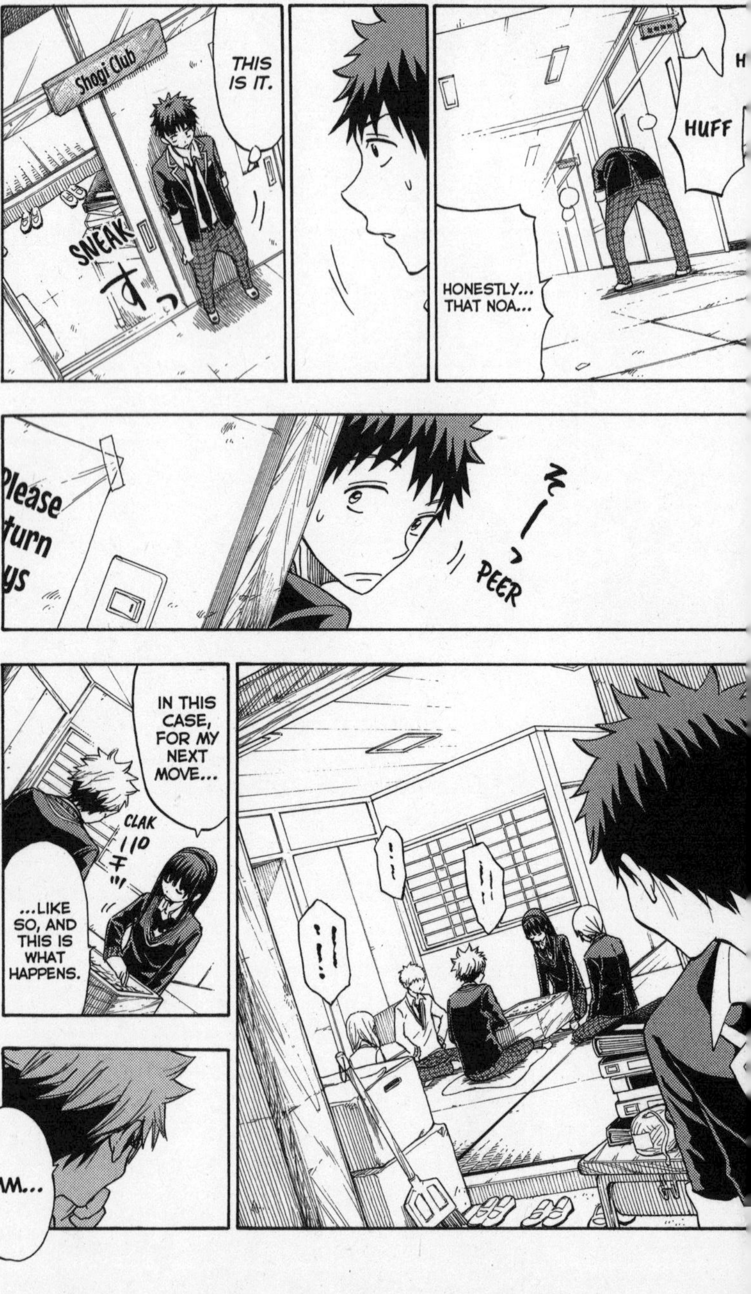
HUFF
HONESTLY... THAT NOA...
THIS IS IT.
Shogi Club
SNEAK
すっ
PEER
Please
turn
ys
IN THIS CASE, FOR MY NEXT MOVE...
CLAK
...LIKE SO, AND THIS IS WHAT HAPPENS.
HMM...

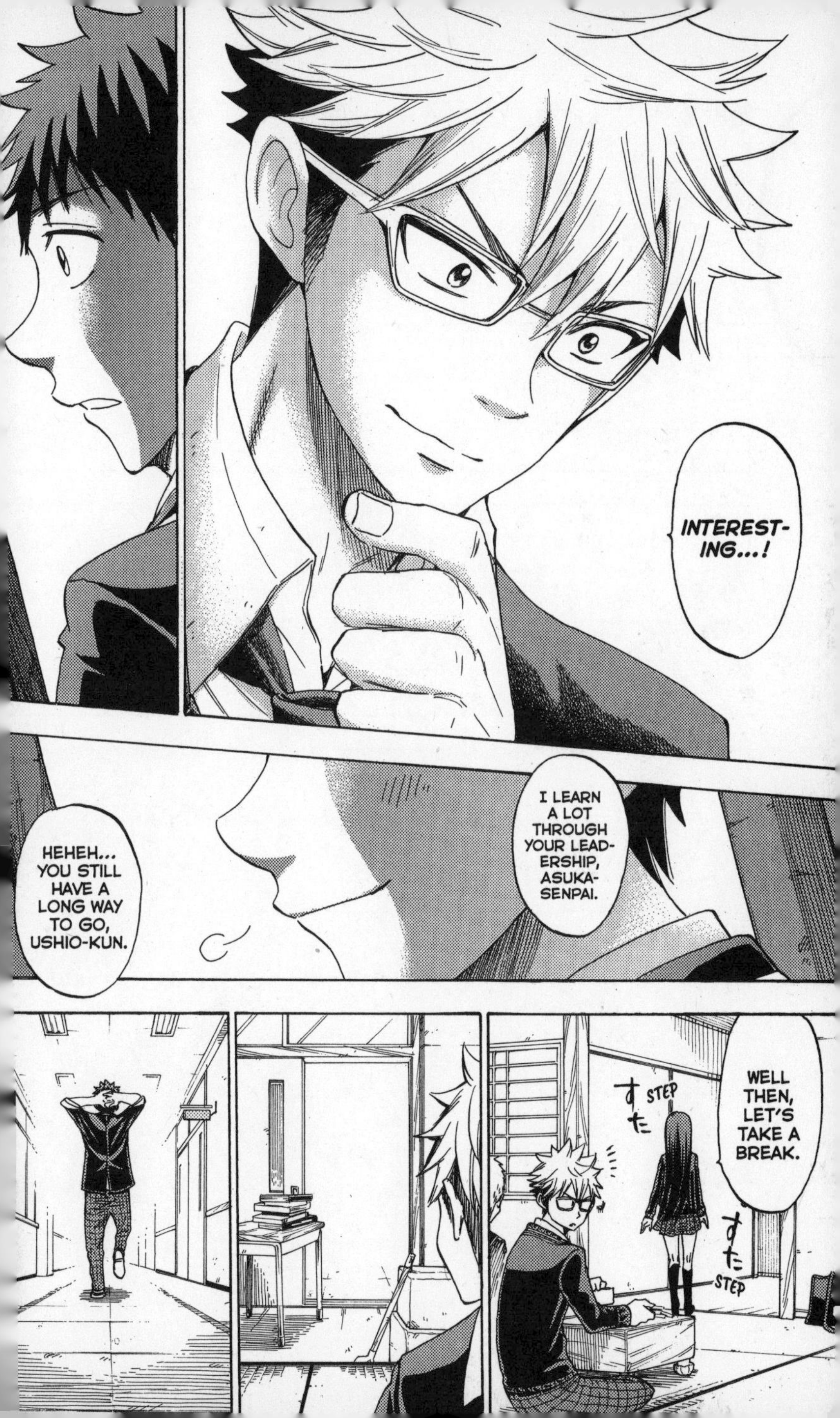
INTEREST-ING...!
I LEARN A LOT THROUGH YOUR LEAD-ERSHIP, ASUKA-SENPAI.
HEHEH... YOU STILL HAVE A LONG WAY TO GO, USHIO-KUN.
WELL THEN, LET'S TAKE A BREAK.
すた STEP
すた STEP

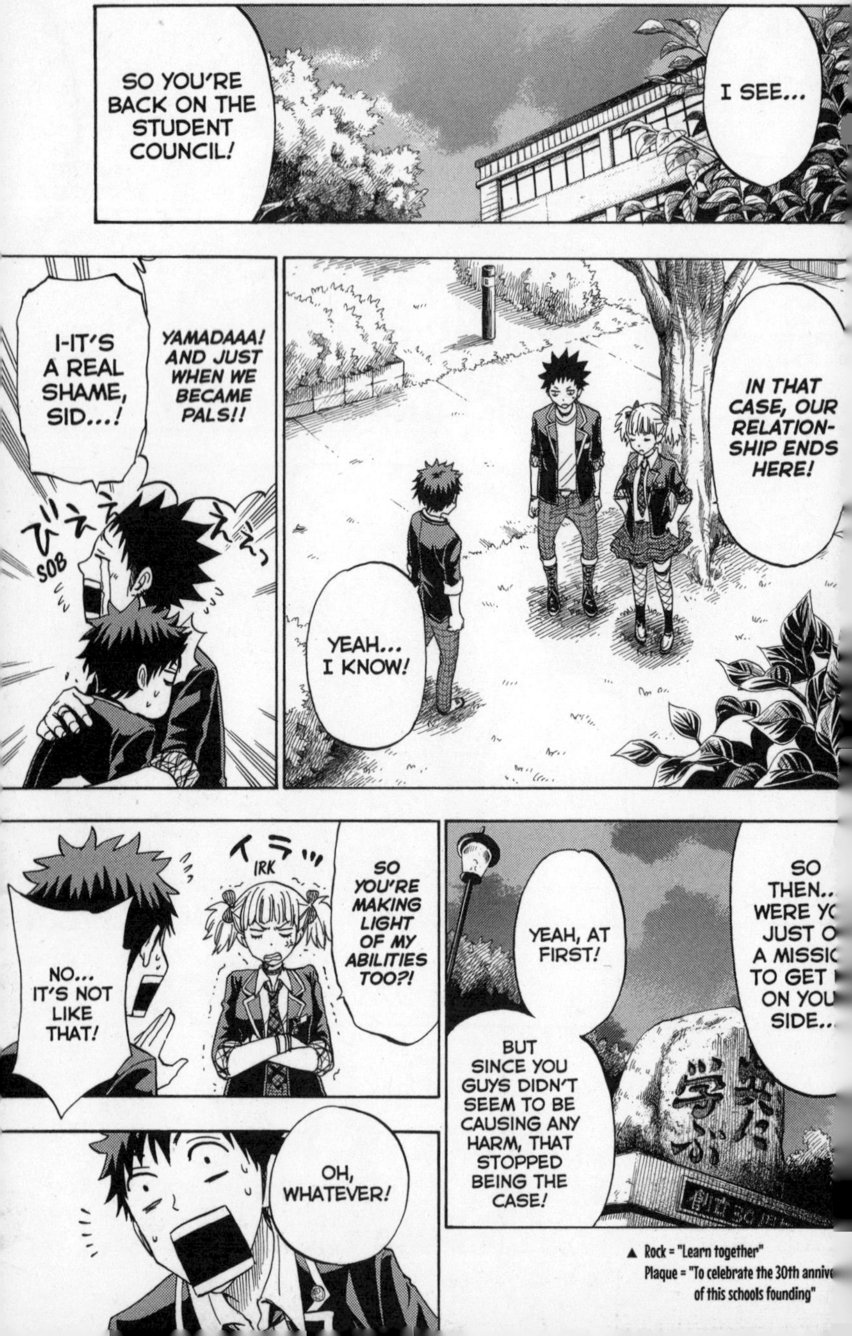
I SEE...
SO YOU'RE BACK ON THE STUDENT COUNCIL!
IN THAT CASE, OUR RELATIONSHIP ENDS HERE!
YEAH... I KNOW!
YAMADAAA! AND JUST WHEN WE BECAME PALS!!
I-IT'S A REAL SHAME, SID...!
SOB
SO THEN... WERE YO JUST O A MISSIC TO GET ON YOU SIDE...
YEAH, AT FIRST!
BUT SINCE YOU GUYS DIDN'T SEEM TO BE CAUSING ANY HARM, THAT STOPPED BEING THE CASE!
IRK
SO YOU'RE MAKING LIGHT OF MY ABILITIES TOO?!
NO... IT'S NOT LIKE THAT!
OH, WHATEVER!

▲ Rock = "Learn together"
Plaque = "To celebrate the 30th annive of this schools founding"

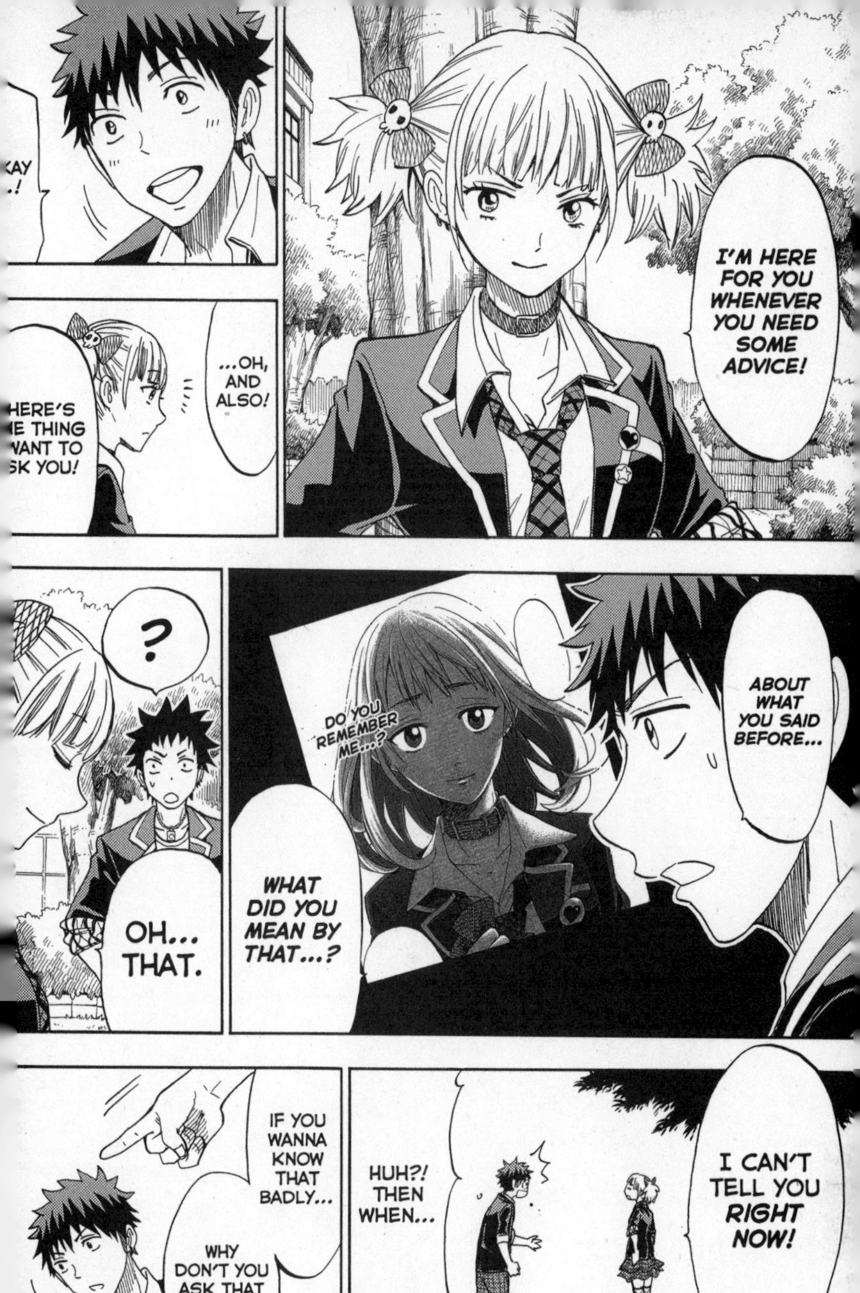
I'M HERE FOR YOU WHENEVER YOU NEED SOME ADVICE!
KAY .!
...OH, AND ALSO!
HERE'S E THING VANT TO SK YOU!
ABOUT WHAT YOU SAID BEFORE...
DO YOU REMEMBER ME...?
WHAT DID YOU MEAN BY THAT...?
?
OH... THAT.
I CAN'T TELL YOU RIGHT NOW!
HUH?! THEN WHEN...
IF YOU WANNA KNOW THAT BADLY...
WHY DON'T YOU ASK THAT GUY OVER THERE?

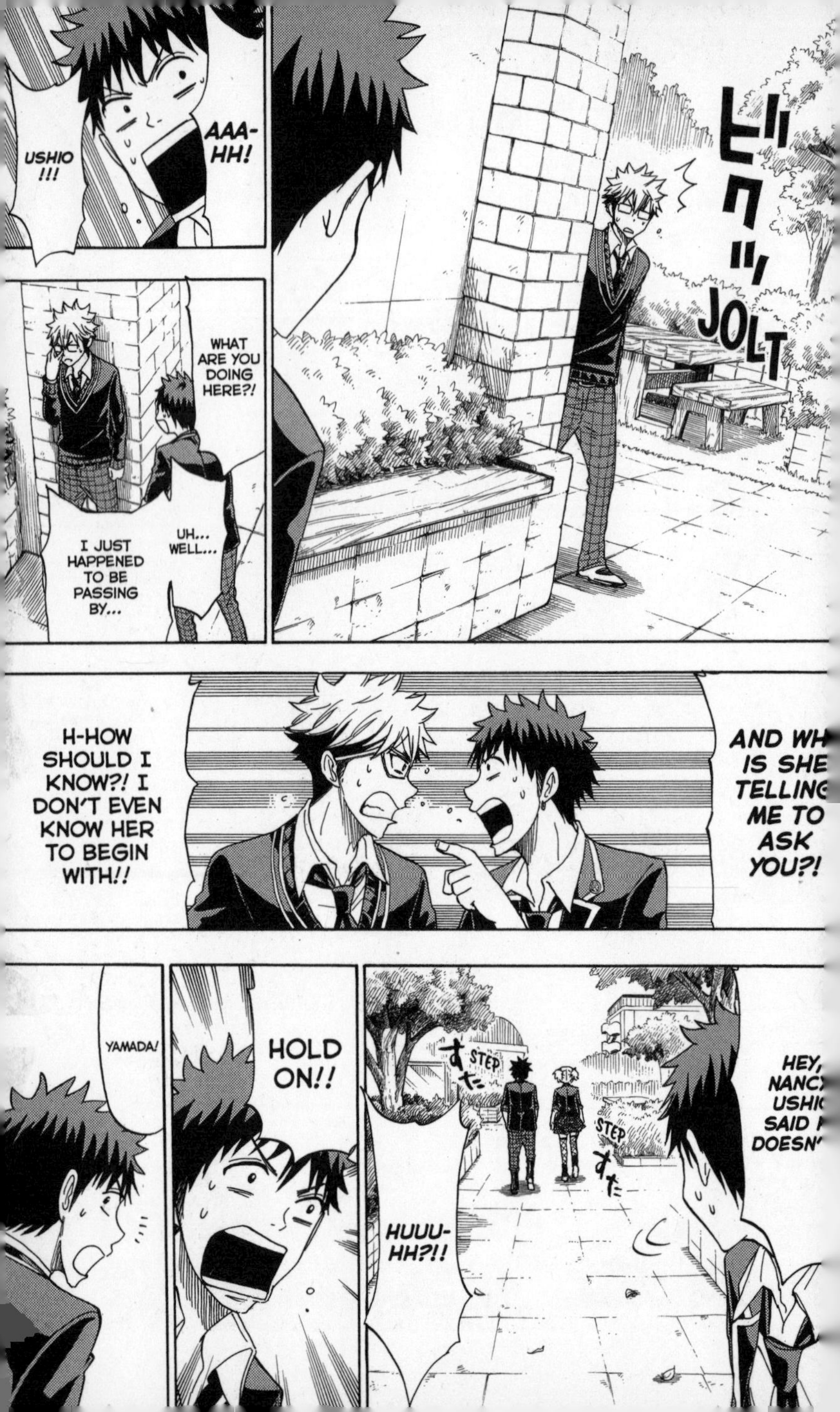

ビクッ
JOLT
AAA-HH!
USHIO !!!
WHAT ARE YOU DOING HERE?!
UH... WELL...
I JUST HAPPENED TO BE PASSING BY...
AND WH IS SHE TELLING ME TO ASK YOU?!
H-HOW SHOULD I KNOW?! I DON'T EVEN KNOW HER TO BEGIN WITH!!
HEY, NANC USHIO SAID DOESN'
すた STEP
すた STEP
HUUU-HH?!!
HOLD ON!!
YAMADA!

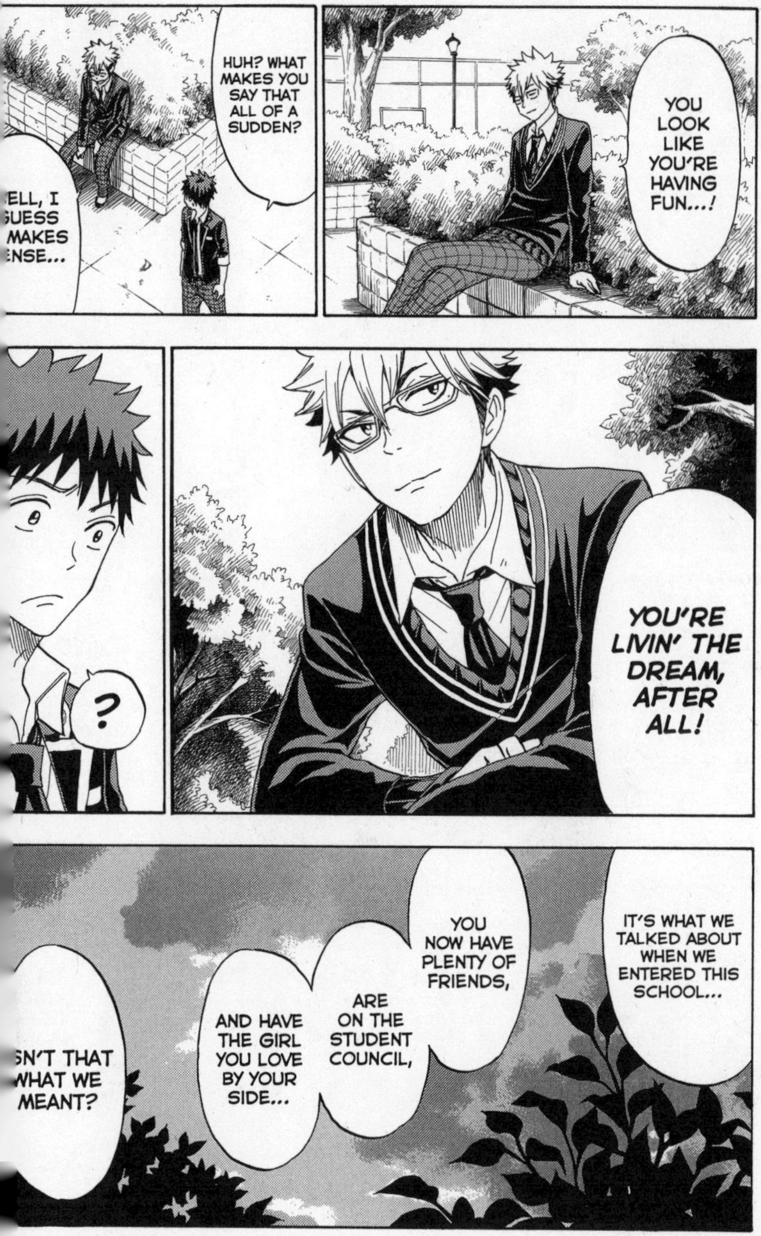

YOU LOOK LIKE YOU'RE HAVING FUN...!
HUH? WHAT MAKES YOU SAY THAT ALL OF A SUDDEN?
ELL, I UESS MAKES NSE...
YOU'RE LIVIN' THE DREAM, AFTER ALL!
?
IT'S WHAT WE TALKED ABOUT WHEN WE ENTERED THIS SCHOOL...
YOU NOW HAVE PLENTY OF FRIENDS,
ARE ON THE STUDENT COUNCIL,
AND HAVE THE GIRL YOU LOVE BY YOUR SIDE...
SN'T THAT WHAT WE MEANT?

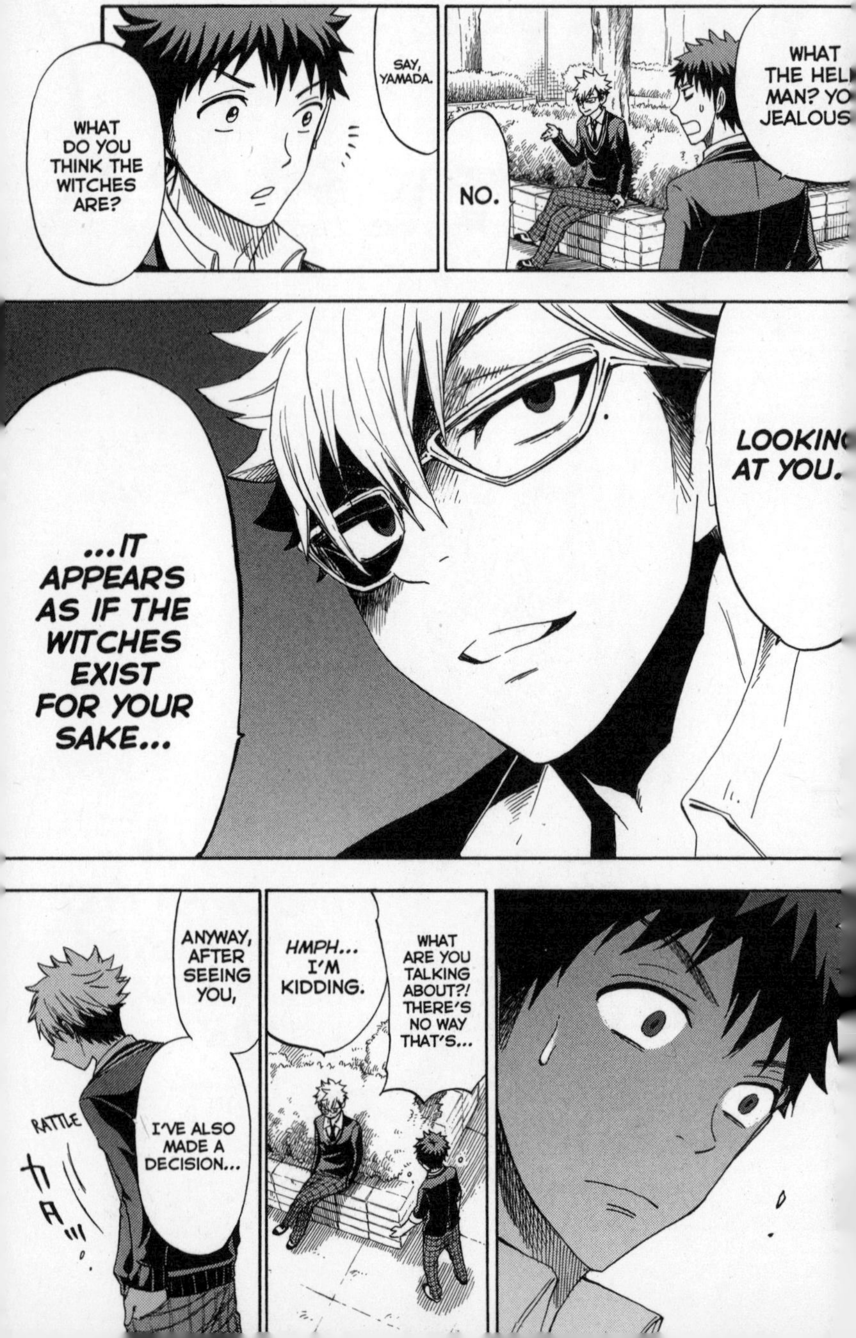
WHAT THE HEL MAN? YO JEALOUS
NO.
SAY, YAMADA.
WHAT DO YOU THINK THE WITCHES ARE?
LOOKIN AT YOU.
...IT APPEARS AS IF THE WITCHES EXIST FOR YOUR SAKE...
WHAT ARE YOU TALKING ABOUT?! THERE'S NO WAY THAT'S...
HMPH... I'M KIDDING.
ANYWAY, AFTER SEEING YOU,
I'VE ALSO MADE A DECISION...
RATTLE

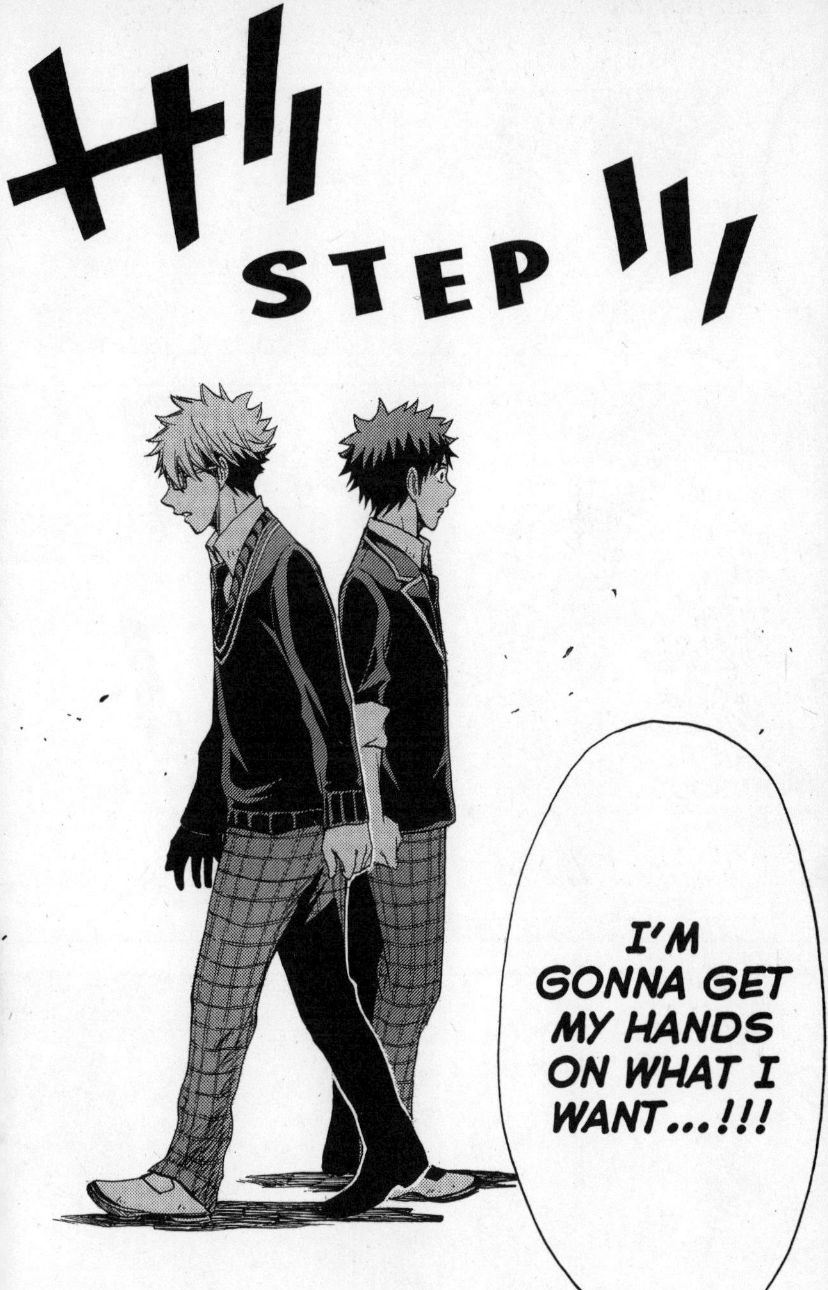
STEP
I'M GONNA GET MY HANDS ON WHAT I WANT...!!!

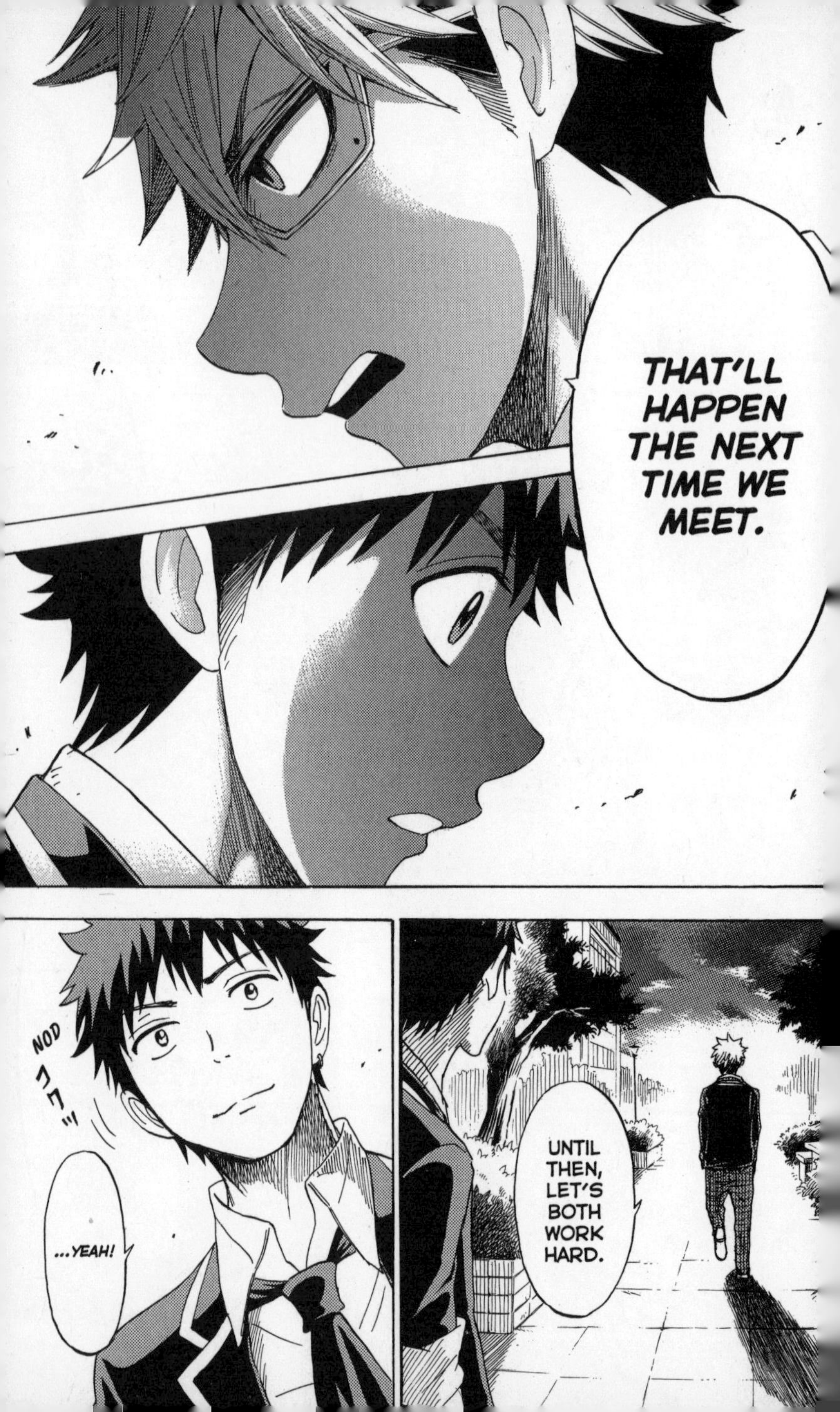
THAT'LL HAPPEN THE NEXT TIME WE MEET.
UNTIL THEN, LET'S BOTH WORK HARD.
NOD
コクッ
...YEAH!

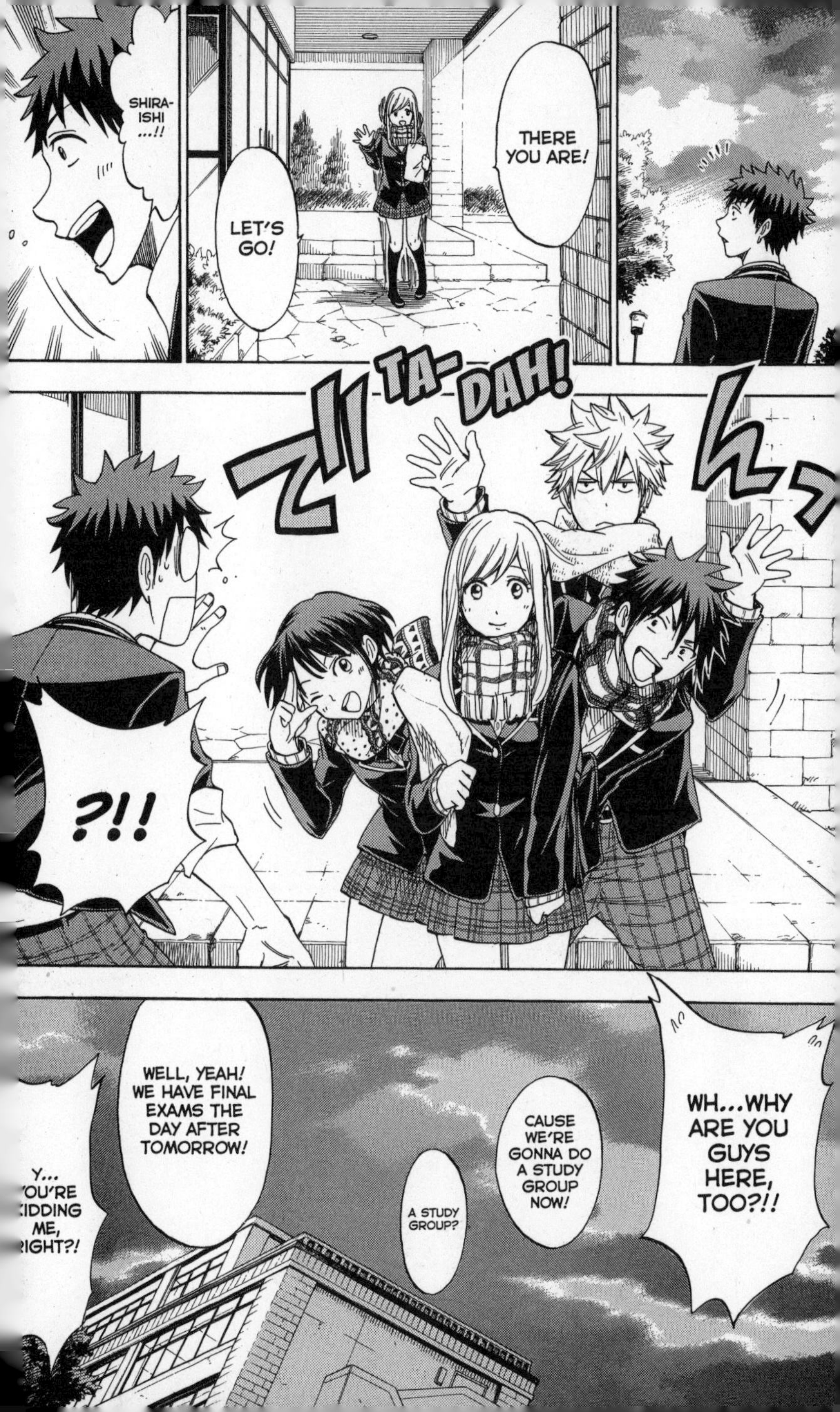
THERE YOU ARE!
LET'S GO!
SHIRA-ISHI ...!!
TA-DAH!
?!!
WH...WHY ARE YOU GUYS HERE, TOO?!!
CAUSE WE'RE GONNA DO A STUDY GROUP NOW!
A STUDY GROUP?
WELL, YEAH! WE HAVE FINAL EXAMS THE DAY AFTER TOMORROW!
Y... YOU'RE KIDDING ME, RIGHT?!

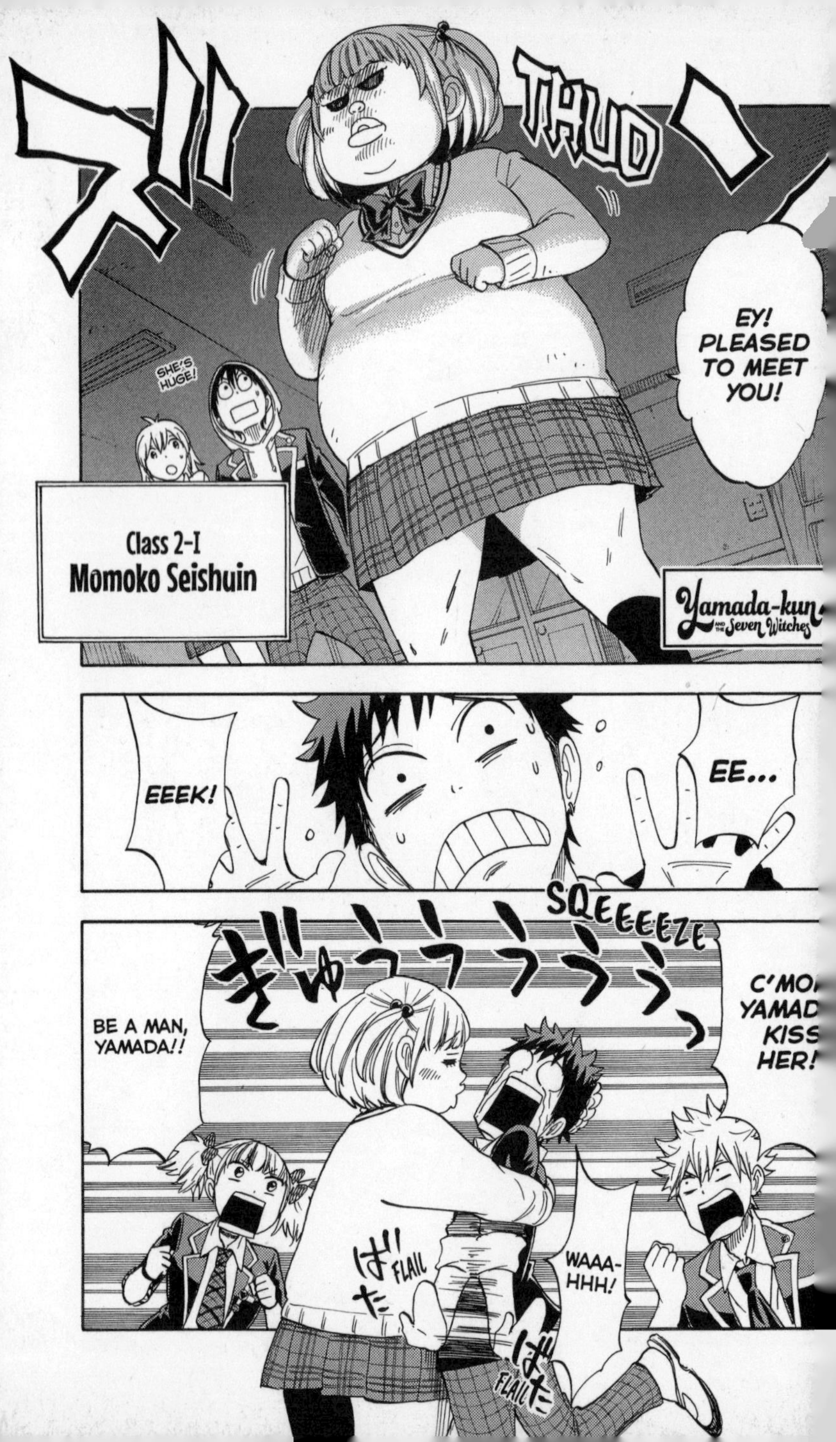
THUD
EY! PLEASED TO MEET YOU!
SHE'S HUGE!
Class 2-I
Momoko Seishuin
Yamada-kun and the Seven Witches
EE...
EEEK!
SQEEEEZE
C'MO YAMAD KISS HER!
BE A MAN, YAMADA!!
WAAA-HHH!
FLAIL
FLAIL

APTER 112: In the abyss.

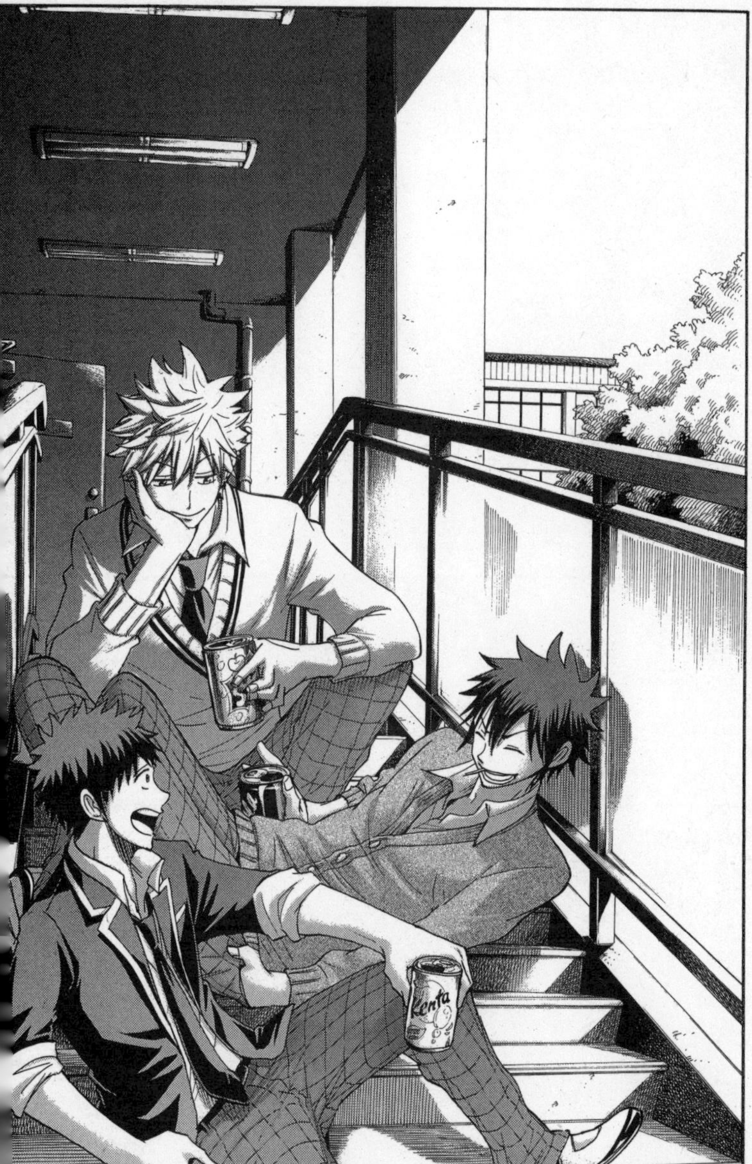
Kenta

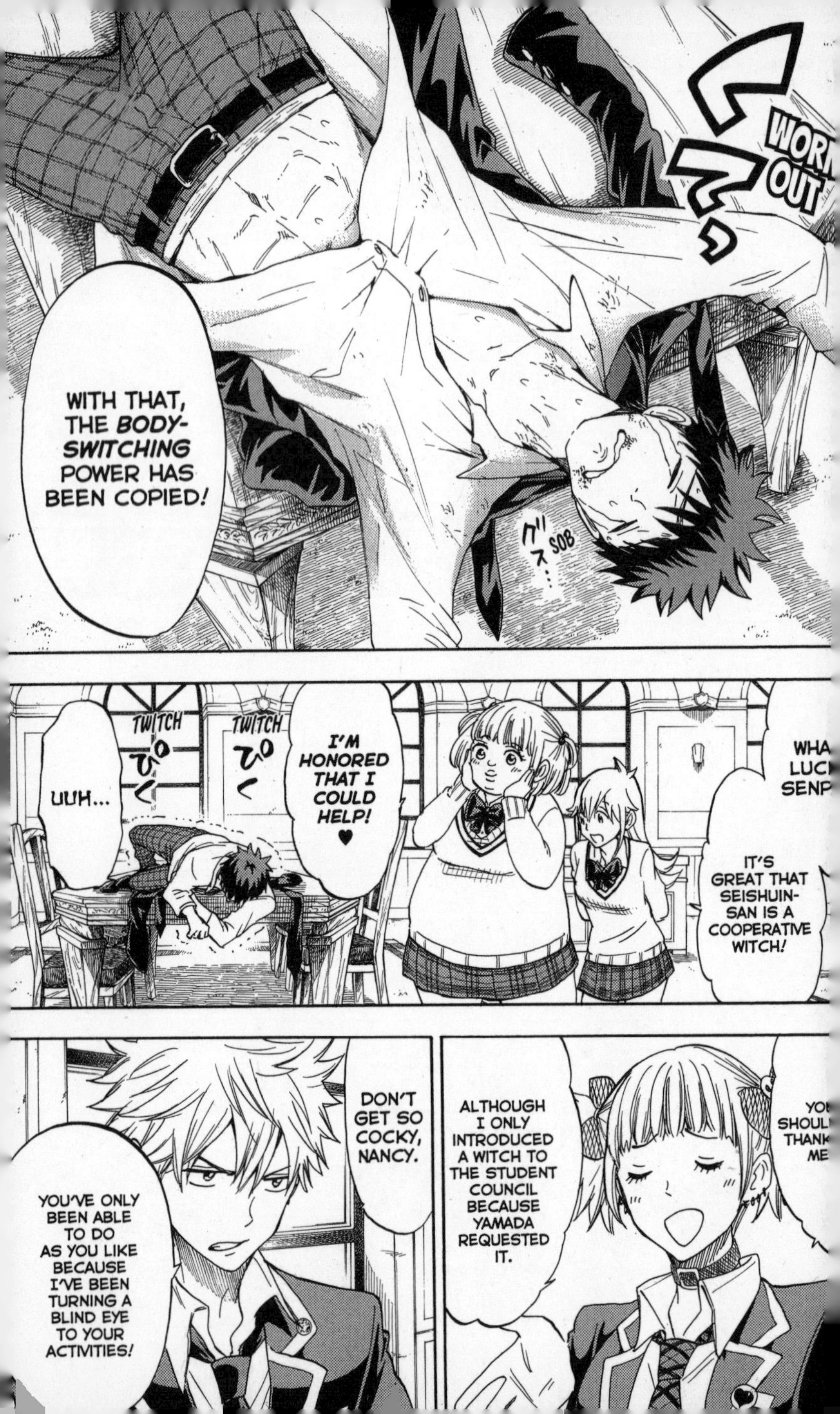
WORK OUT
グス SOB
WITH THAT, THE *BODY-SWITCHING* POWER HAS BEEN COPIED!
WHA LUCK SENP
IT'S GREAT THAT SEISHUIN-SAN IS A COOPERATIVE WITCH!
I'M HONORED THAT I COULD HELP! ♥
TWITCH ぴく
TWITCH ぴく
UUH...
YO SHOUL THANK ME
ALTHOUGH I ONLY INTRODUCED A WITCH TO THE STUDENT COUNCIL BECAUSE YAMADA REQUESTED IT.
DON'T GET SO COCKY, NANCY.
YOU'VE ONLY BEEN ABLE TO DO AS YOU LIKE BECAUSE I'VE BEEN TURNING A BLIND EYE TO YOUR ACTIVITIES!

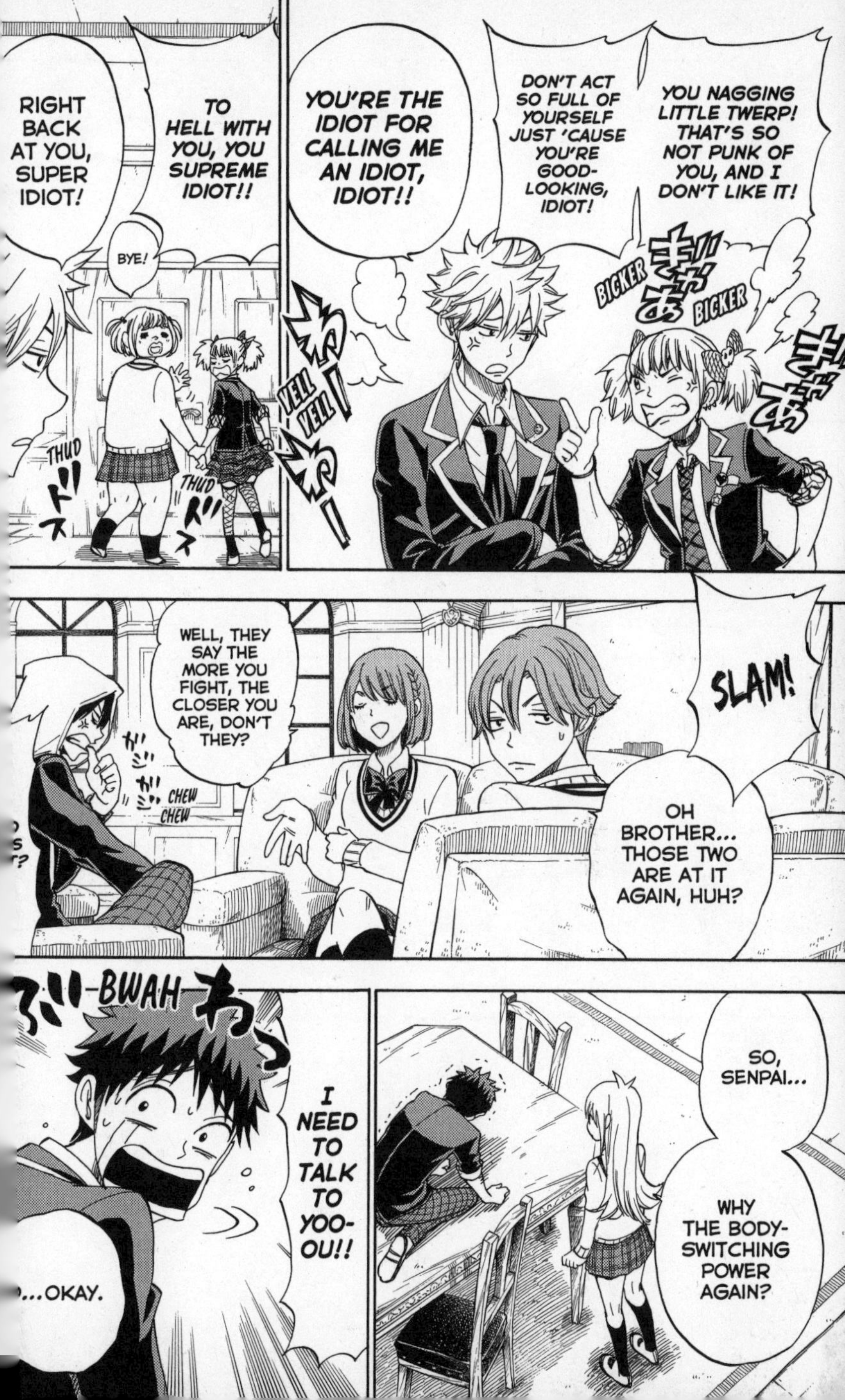
YOU NAGGING LITTLE TWERP! THAT'S SO NOT PUNK OF YOU, AND I DON'T LIKE IT!
DON'T ACT SO FULL OF YOURSELF JUST 'CAUSE YOU'RE GOOD-LOOKING, IDIOT!
BICKER
BICKER
YOU'RE THE IDIOT FOR CALLING ME AN IDIOT, IDIOT!!
YELL
YELL
TO HELL WITH YOU, YOU SUPREME IDIOT!!
RIGHT BACK AT YOU, SUPER IDIOT!
BYE!
THUD
THUD
SLAM!
OH BROTHER... THOSE TWO ARE AT IT AGAIN, HUH?
WELL, THEY SAY THE MORE YOU FIGHT, THE CLOSER YOU ARE, DON'T THEY?
CHEW
CHEW
SO, SENPAI...
WHY THE BODY-SWITCHING POWER AGAIN?
I NEED TO TALK TO YOO-OU!!
-BWAH
...OKAY.

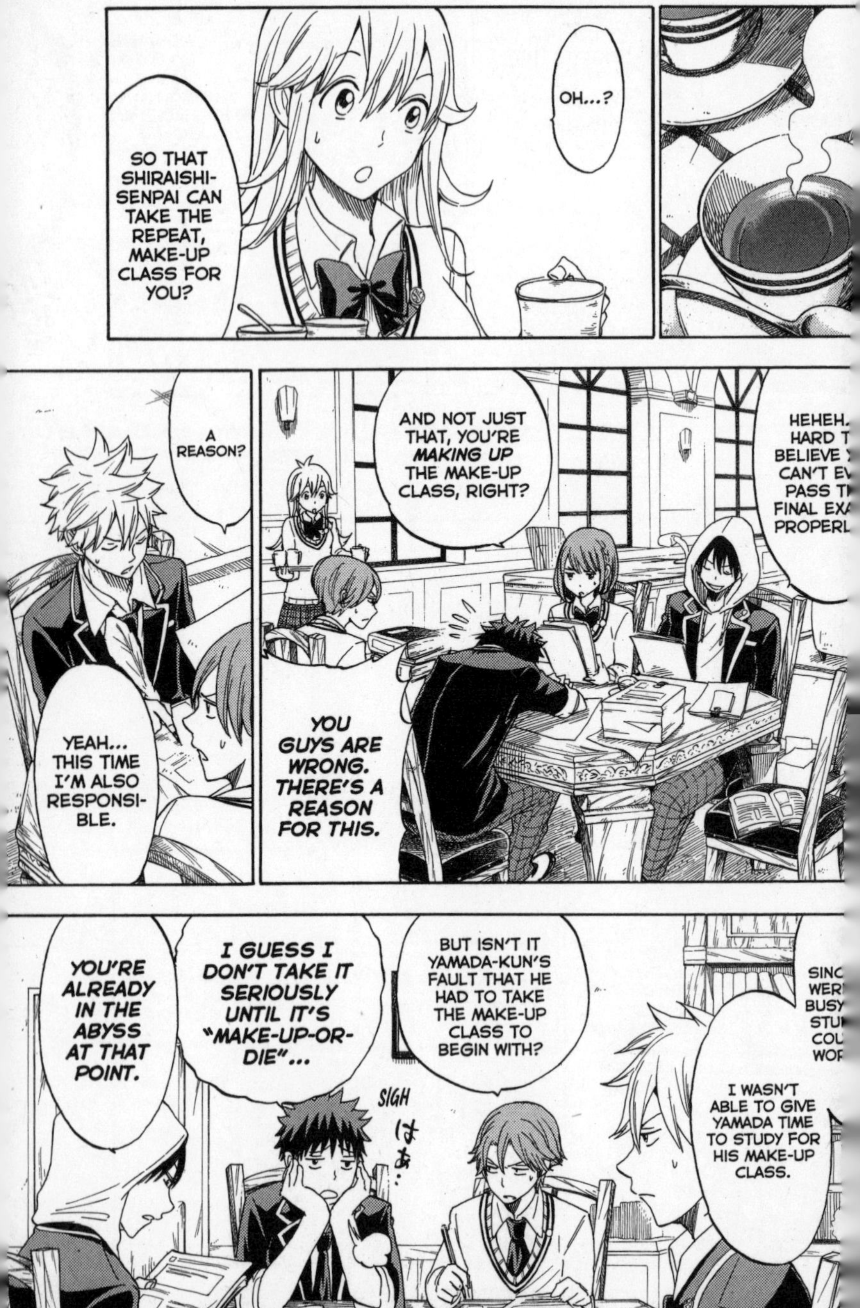
OH...?
SO THAT SHIRAISHI-SENPAI CAN TAKE THE REPEAT, MAKE-UP CLASS FOR YOU?
AND NOT JUST THAT, YOU'RE *MAKING UP* THE MAKE-UP CLASS, RIGHT?
YOU GUYS ARE WRONG. THERE'S A REASON FOR THIS.
A REASON?
YEAH... THIS TIME I'M ALSO RESPONSIBLE.
I WASN'T ABLE TO GIVE YAMADA TIME TO STUDY FOR HIS MAKE-UP CLASS.
BUT ISN'T IT YAMADA-KUN'S FAULT THAT HE HAD TO TAKE THE MAKE-UP CLASS TO BEGIN WITH?
SIGH
はぁ
I GUESS I DON'T TAKE IT SERIOUSLY UNTIL IT'S "MAKE-UP-OR-DIE"...
YOU'RE ALREADY IN THE ABYSS AT THAT POINT.

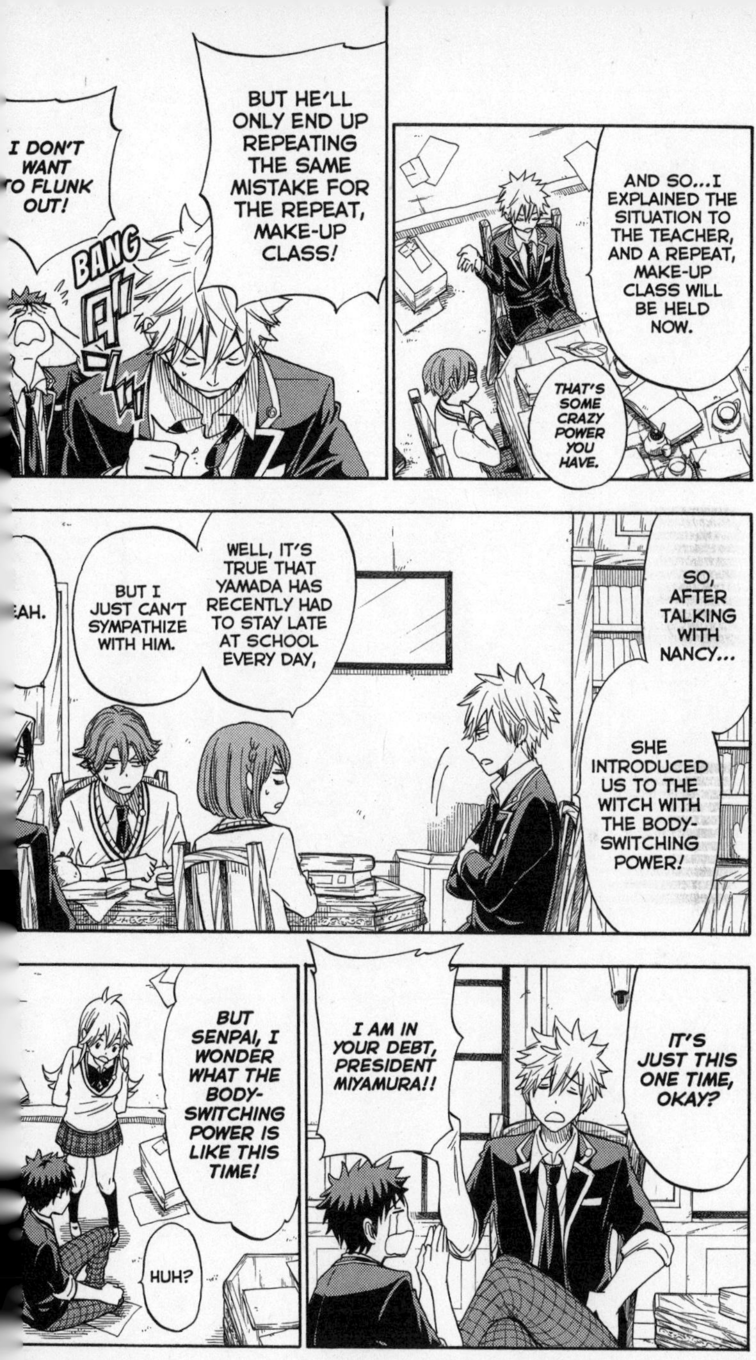
AND SO...I EXPLAINED THE SITUATION TO THE TEACHER, AND A REPEAT, MAKE-UP CLASS WILL BE HELD NOW.
THAT'S SOME CRAZY POWER YOU HAVE.
BUT HE'LL ONLY END UP REPEATING THE SAME MISTAKE FOR THE REPEAT, MAKE-UP CLASS!
I DON'T WANT TO FLUNK OUT!
BANG
SO, AFTER TALKING WITH NANCY...
SHE INTRODUCED US TO THE WITCH WITH THE BODY-SWITCHING POWER!
WELL, IT'S TRUE THAT YAMADA HAS RECENTLY HAD TO STAY LATE AT SCHOOL EVERY DAY,
BUT I JUST CAN'T SYMPATHIZE WITH HIM.
EAH.
IT'S JUST THIS ONE TIME, OKAY?
I AM IN YOUR DEBT, PRESIDENT MIYAMURA!!
BUT SENPAI, I WONDER WHAT THE BODY-SWITCHING POWER IS LIKE THIS TIME!
HUH?

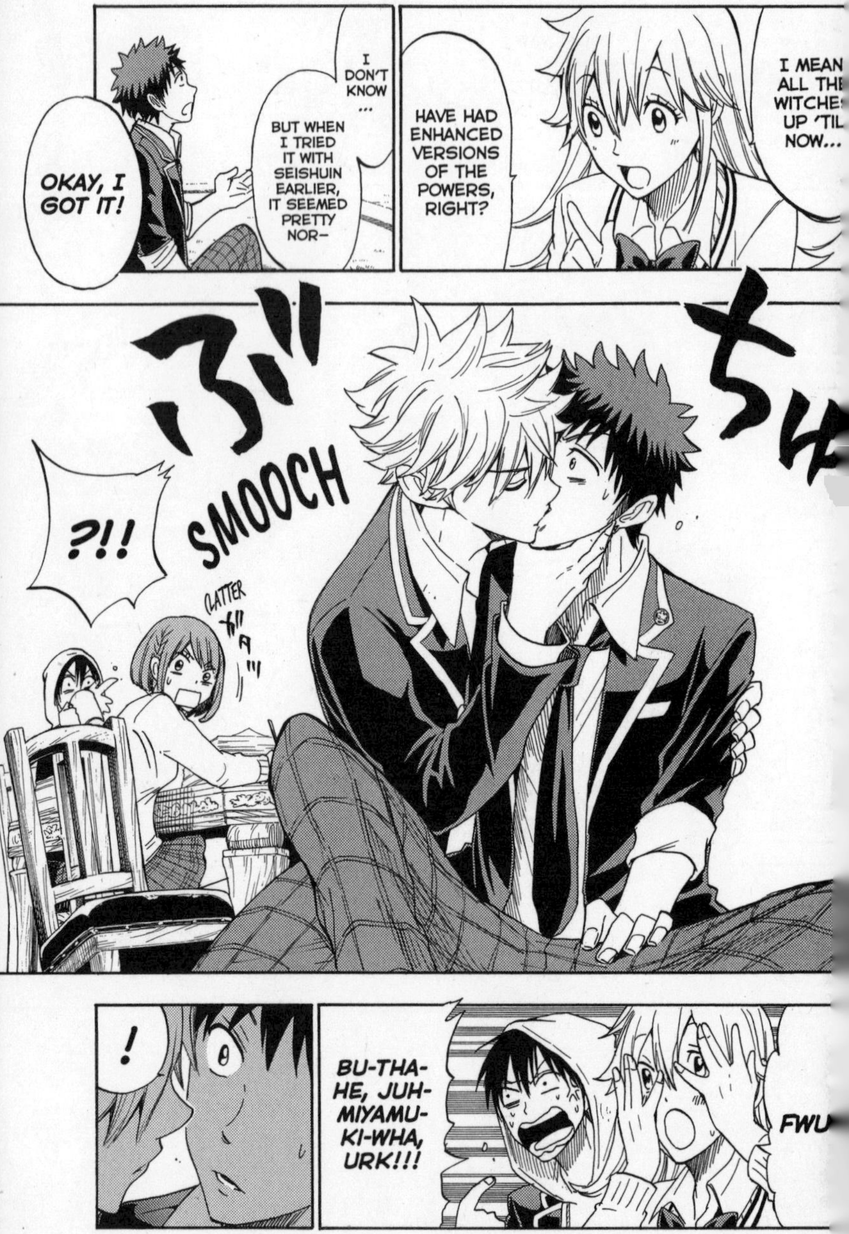
I MEAN ALL THE WITCHES UP 'TIL NOW...
HAVE HAD ENHANCED VERSIONS OF THE POWERS, RIGHT?
I DON'T KNOW ...
BUT WHEN I TRIED IT WITH SEISHUIN EARLIER, IT SEEMED PRETTY NOR–
OKAY, I GOT IT!
ぶちゅ
SMOOCH
?!!
CLATTER
ガタ
FWU
BU-THA-HE, JUH-MIYAMU-KI-WHA, URK!!!
!

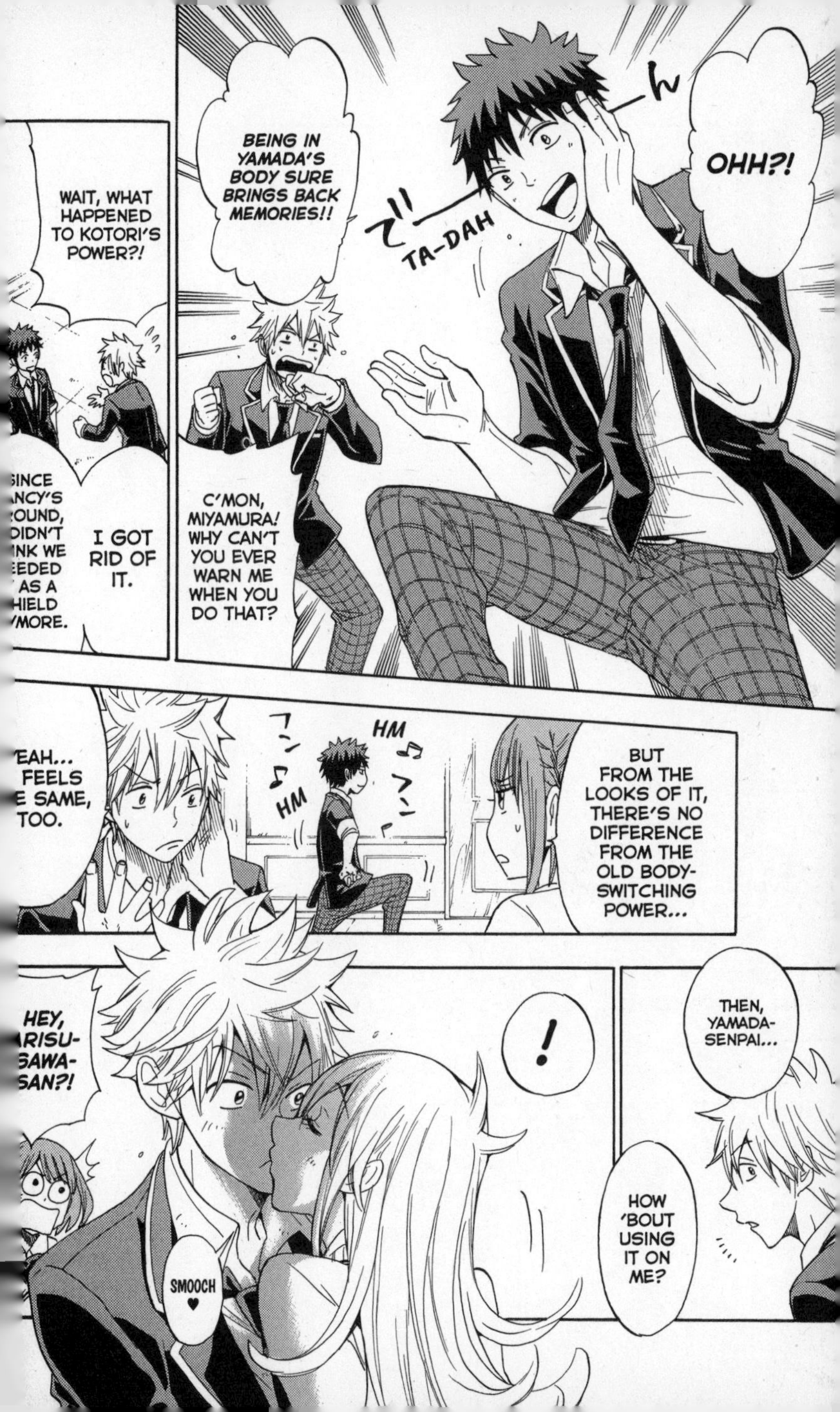
OHH?!
TA-DAH
BEING IN YAMADA'S BODY SURE BRINGS BACK MEMORIES!!
C'MON, MIYAMURA! WHY CAN'T YOU EVER WARN ME WHEN YOU DO THAT?
WAIT, WHAT HAPPENED TO KOTORI'S POWER?!
I GOT RID OF IT.
SINCE ANCY'S ROUND, DIDN'T INK WE EEDED AS A HIELD YMORE.
BUT FROM THE LOOKS OF IT, THERE'S NO DIFFERENCE FROM THE OLD BODY-SWITCHING POWER...
HM
HM
YEAH... FEELS E SAME, TOO.
THEN, YAMADA-SENPAI...
HOW 'BOUT USING IT ON ME?
!
SMOOCH ♥
HEY, ARISU-SAWA-SAN?!

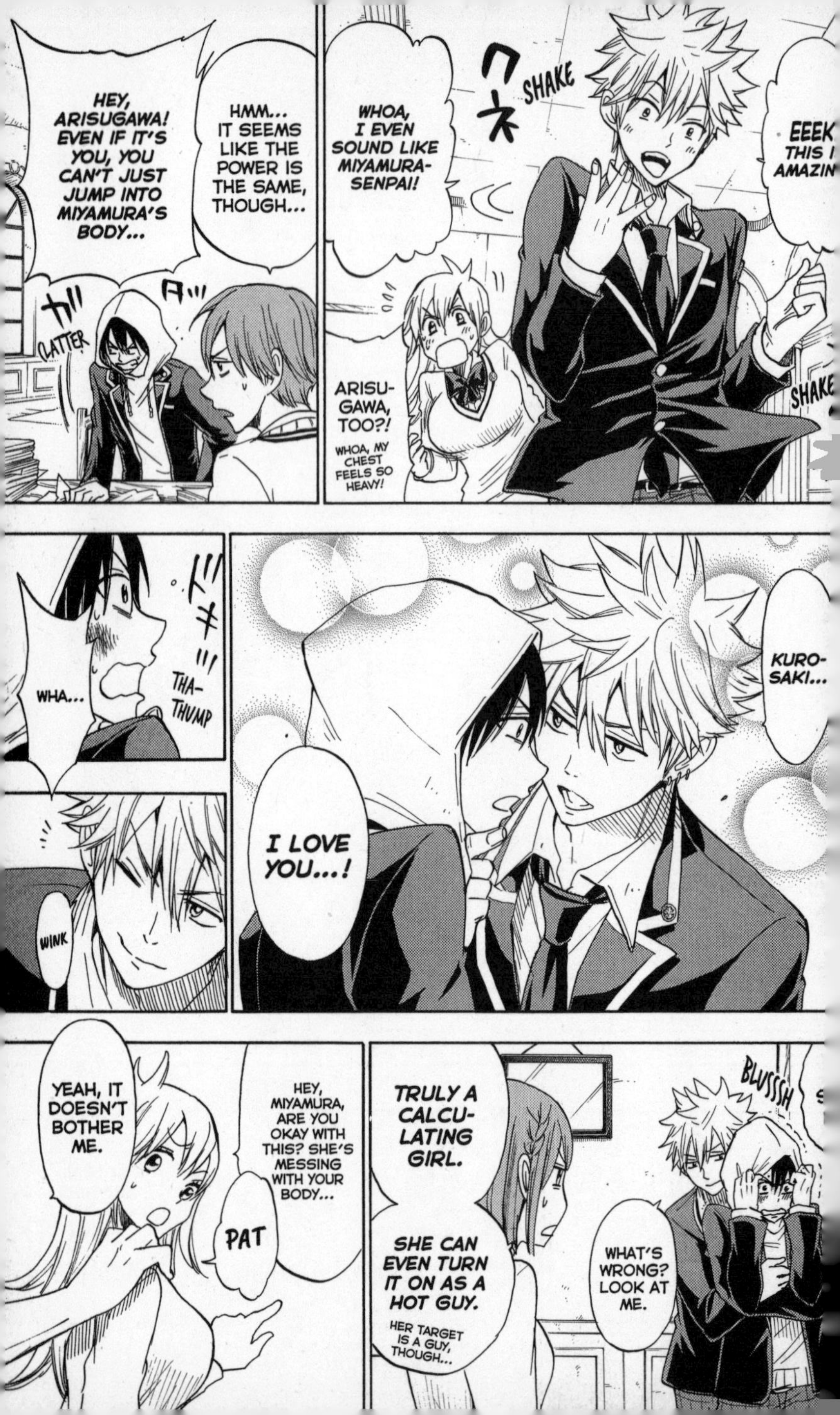
EEEK THIS I AMAZIN
SHAKE
WHOA, I EVEN SOUND LIKE MIYAMURA-SENPAI!
SHAKE
ARISUGAWA, TOO?!
WHOA, MY CHEST FEELS SO HEAVY!
HMM... IT SEEMS LIKE THE POWER IS THE SAME, THOUGH...
HEY, ARISUGAWA! EVEN IF IT'S YOU, YOU CAN'T JUST JUMP INTO MIYAMURA'S BODY...
CLATTER
KURO-SAKI...
I LOVE YOU...!
THA-THUMP
WHA...
WINK
BLUSSSH
WHAT'S WRONG? LOOK AT ME.
TRULY A CALCU-LATING GIRL.
SHE CAN EVEN TURN IT ON AS A HOT GUY.
HER TARGET IS A GUY, THOUGH...
HEY, MIYAMURA, ARE YOU OKAY WITH THIS? SHE'S MESSING WITH YOUR BODY...
YEAH, IT DOESN'T BOTHER ME.
PAT

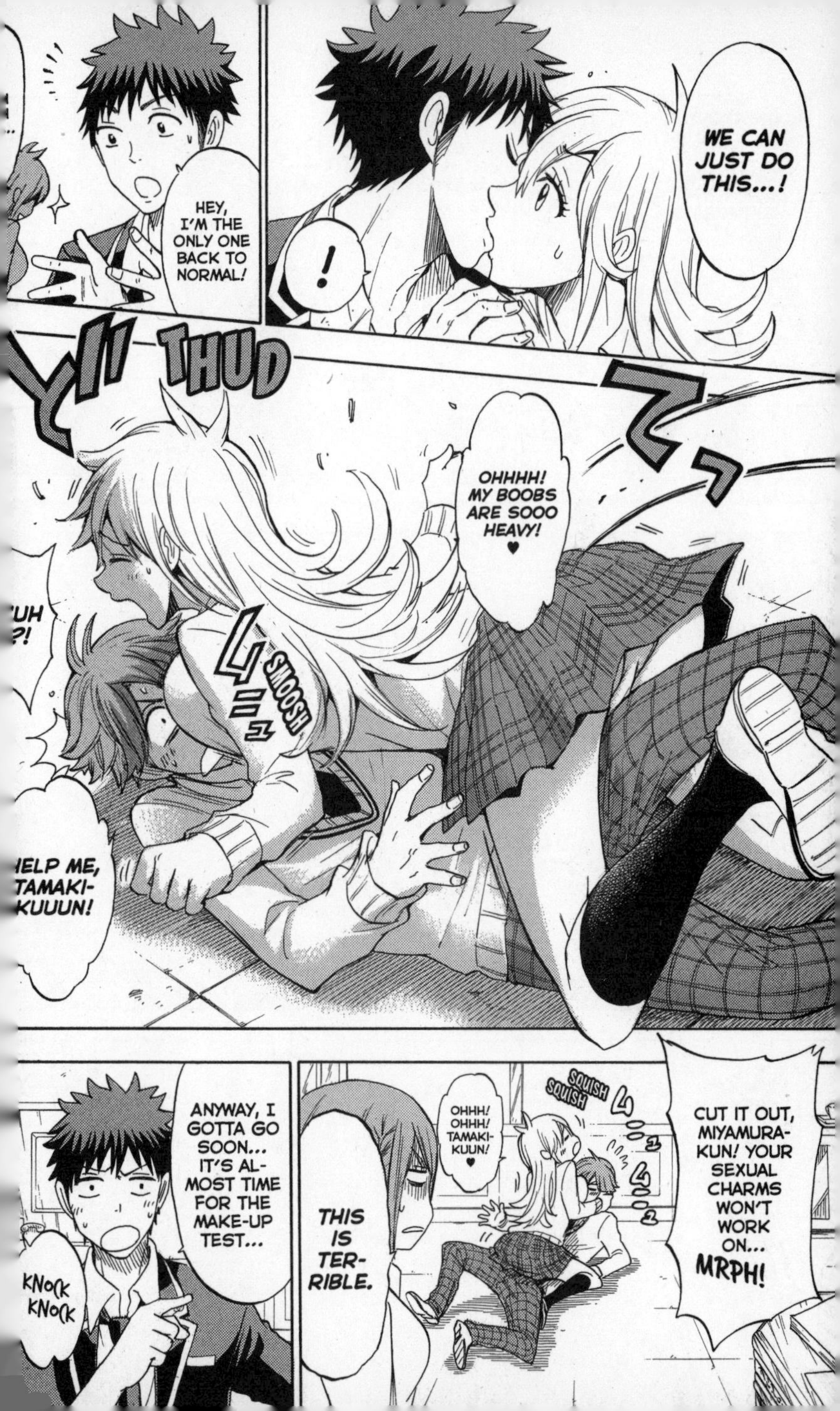
WE CAN JUST DO THIS...!
!
HEY, I'M THE ONLY ONE BACK TO NORMAL!
THUD
OHHHH! MY BOOBS ARE SOOO HEAVY! ♥
SMOOSH
HELP ME, TAMAKI-KUUUN!
CUT IT OUT, MIYAMURA-KUN! YOUR SEXUAL CHARMS WON'T WORK ON... MRPH!
SQUISH SQUISH
OHHH! OHHH! TAMAKI-KUUN! ♥
THIS IS TERRIBLE.
ANYWAY, I GOTTA GO SOON... IT'S AL-MOST TIME FOR THE MAKE-UP TEST...
KNOCK KNOCK

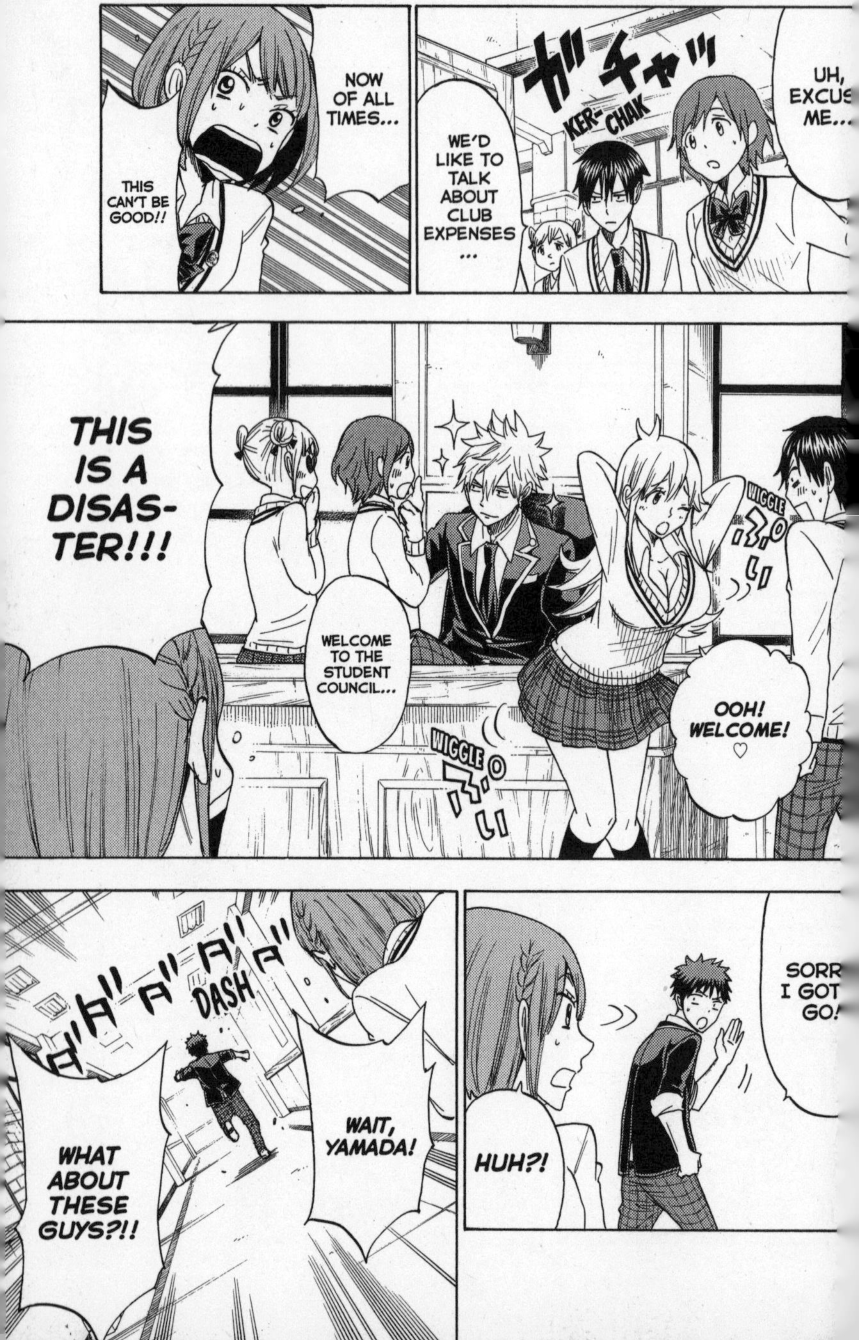
UH, EXCUS ME...
ガチャッ
KER-CHAK
WE'D LIKE TO TALK ABOUT CLUB EXPENSES...
NOW OF ALL TIMES...
THIS CAN'T BE GOOD!!
OOH! WELCOME! ♡
WIGGLE
WIGGLE
WELCOME TO THE STUDENT COUNCIL...
THIS IS A DISASTER!!!
SORR I GOT GO!
HUH?!
WAIT, YAMADA!
ダダダダダ
DASH
WHAT ABOUT THESE GUYS?!!

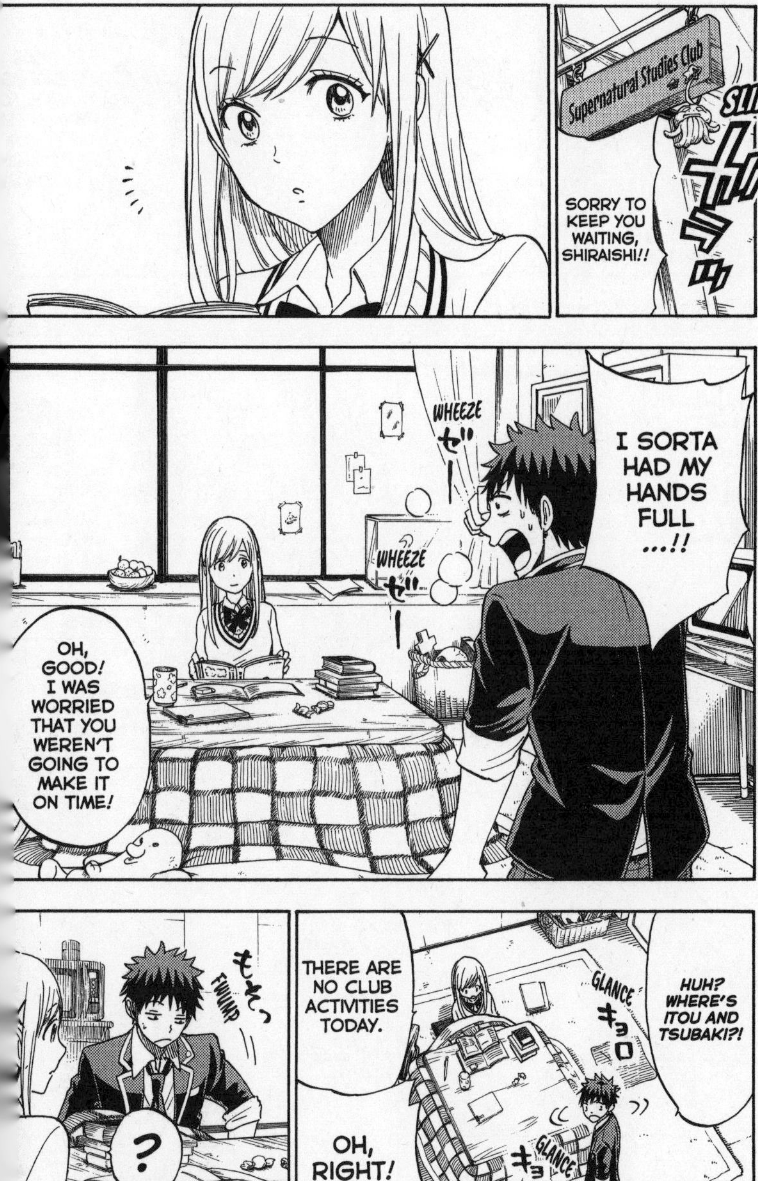
Supernatural Studies Club
SLIDE
SORRY TO KEEP YOU WAITING, SHIRAISHI!!
I SORTA HAD MY HANDS FULL ...!!
WHEEZE
ゼー
WHEEZE
ゼー
OH, GOOD! I WAS WORRIED THAT YOU WEREN'T GOING TO MAKE IT ON TIME!
HUH? WHERE'S ITOU AND TSUBAKI?!
GLANCE
キョロ
GLANCE
キョロ
THERE ARE NO CLUB ACTIVITIES TODAY.
OH, RIGHT!
もそっ
FWUMP
?

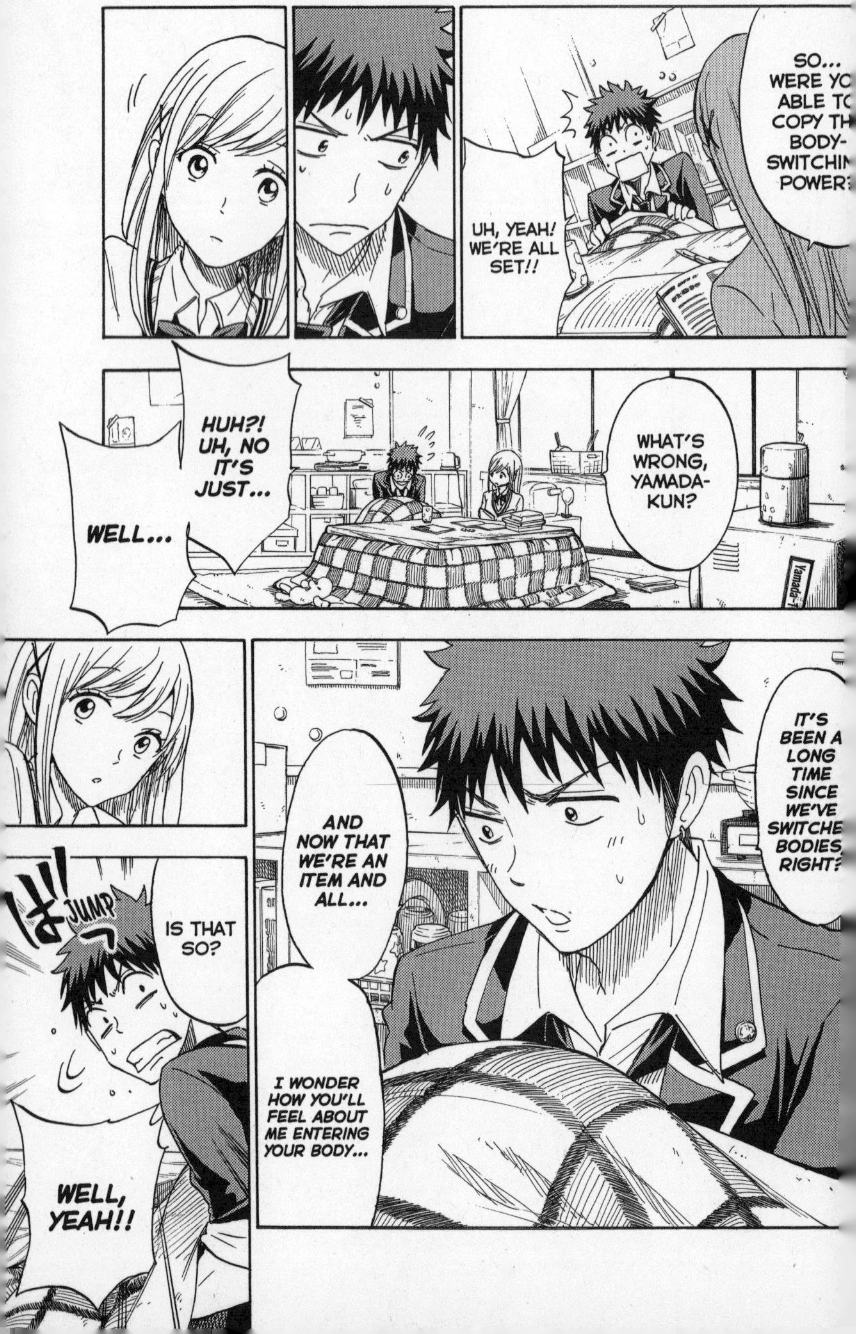
SO... WERE YO ABLE TO COPY TH BODY-SWITCHIN POWER?
UH, YEAH! WE'RE ALL SET!!
WHAT'S WRONG, YAMADA-KUN?
HUH?! UH, NO IT'S JUST...
WELL...
IT'S BEEN A LONG TIME SINCE WE'VE SWITCHE BODIES, RIGHT?
AND NOW THAT WE'RE AN ITEM AND ALL...
I WONDER HOW YOU'LL FEEL ABOUT ME ENTERING YOUR BODY...
は
JUMP
IS THAT SO?
WELL, YEAH!!

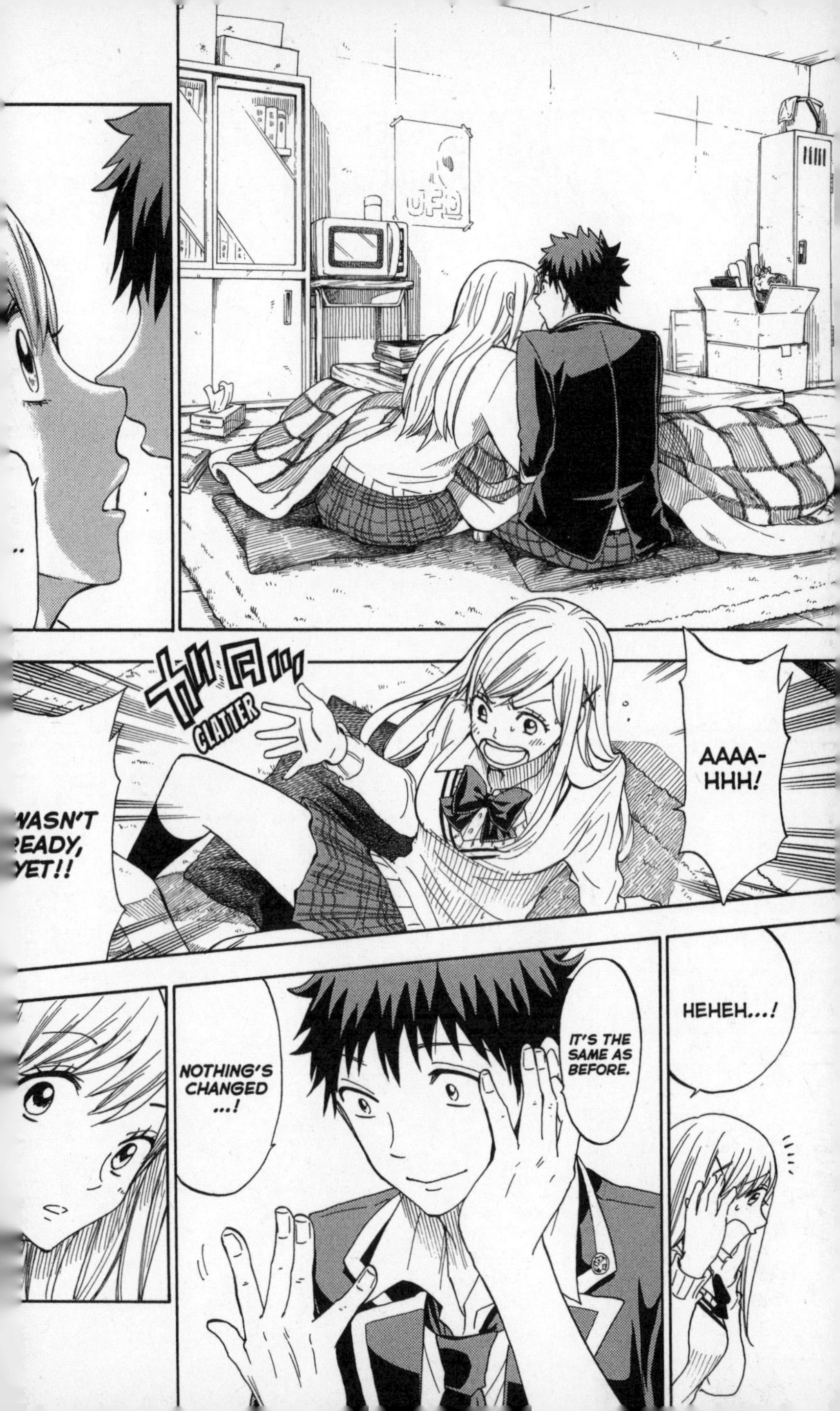
AAAA-HHH!
CLATTER
WASN'T READY, YET!!
HEHEH...!
IT'S THE SAME AS BEFORE.
NOTHING'S CHANGED ...!

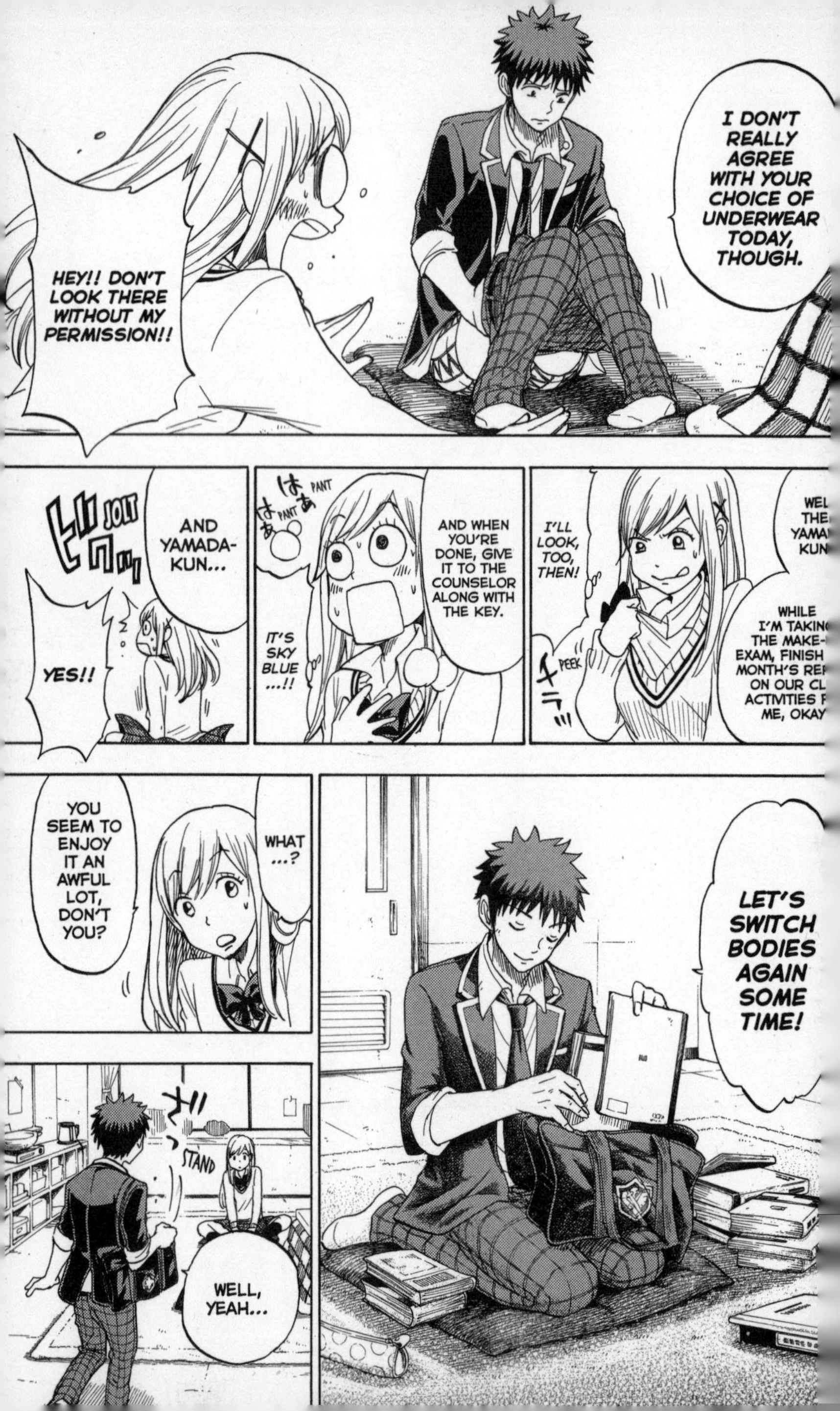
I DON'T REALLY AGREE WITH YOUR CHOICE OF UNDERWEAR TODAY, THOUGH.
HEY!! DON'T LOOK THERE WITHOUT MY PERMISSION!!
WEL THE YAMA KUN
WHILE I'M TAKIN THE MAKE- EXAM, FINISH MONTH'S REP ON OUR CL ACTIVITIES F ME, OKAY
I'LL LOOK, TOO, THEN!
PEEK
PANT
PANT
AND WHEN YOU'RE DONE, GIVE IT TO THE COUNSELOR ALONG WITH THE KEY.
IT'S SKY BLUE ...!!
JOLT
AND YAMADA-KUN...
YES!!
LET'S SWITCH BODIES AGAIN SOME TIME!
WHAT ...?
YOU SEEM TO ENJOY IT AN AWFUL LOT, DON'T YOU?
STAND
WELL, YEAH...

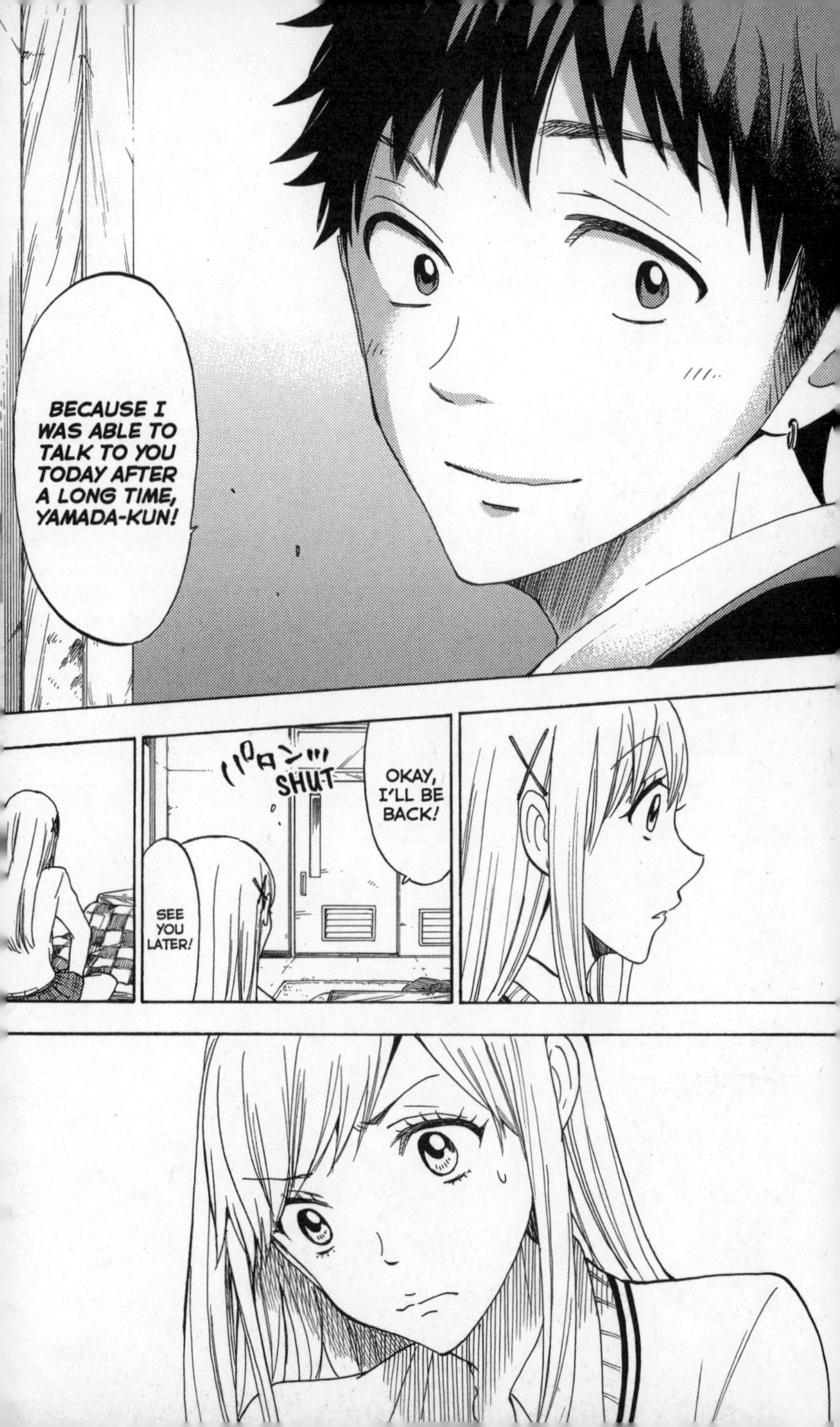
BECAUSE I WAS ABLE TO TALK TO YOU TODAY AFTER A LONG TIME, YAMADA-KUN!
OKAY, I'LL BE BACK!
SHUT
SEE YOU LATER!

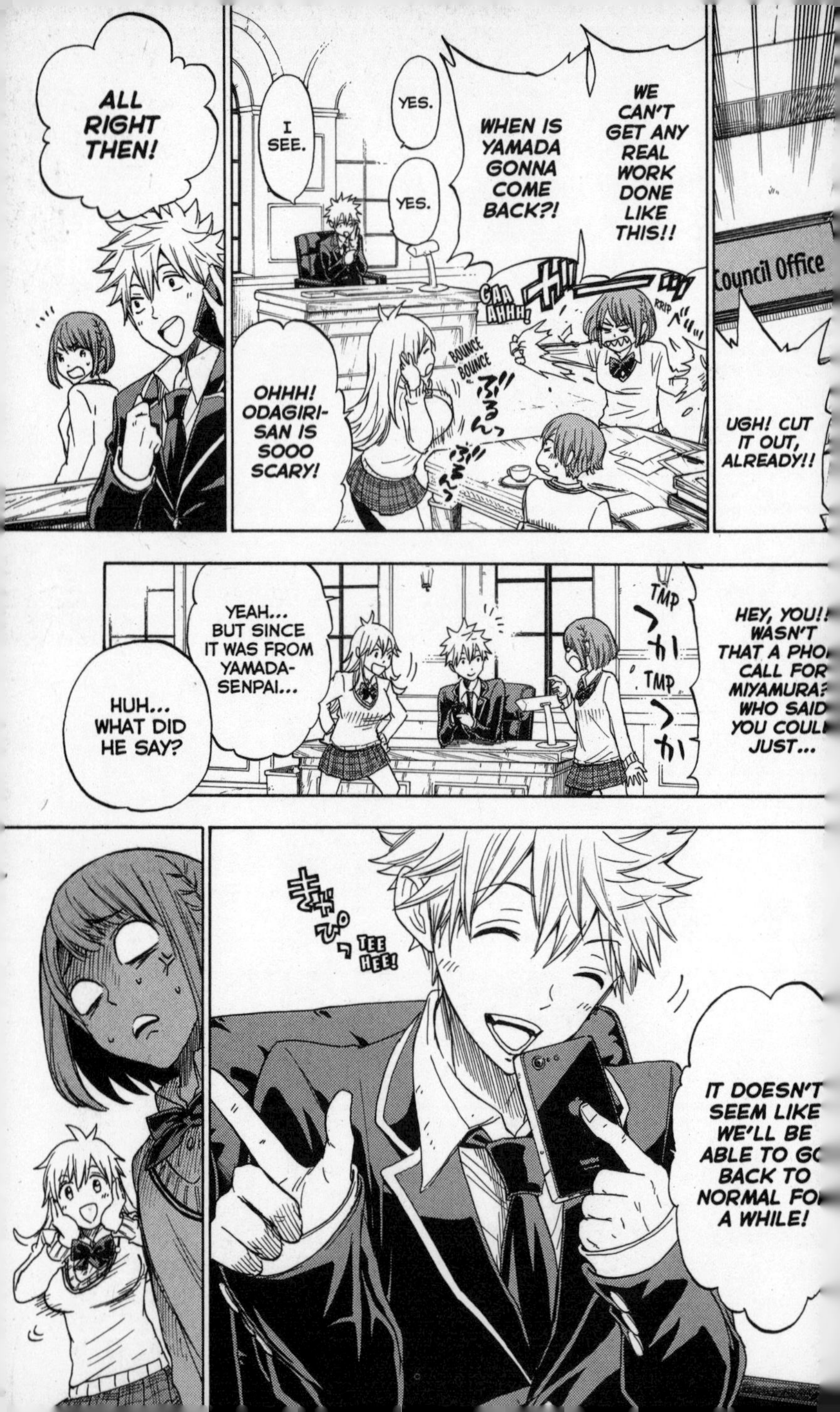
Council Office
UGH! CUT IT OUT, ALREADY!!
WE CAN'T GET ANY REAL WORK DONE LIKE THIS!!
WHEN IS YAMADA GONNA COME BACK?!
YES.
YES.
I SEE.
GAAAHHH!
RRIP
BOUNCE BOUNCE
OHHH! ODAGIRI-SAN IS SOOO SCARY!
ALL RIGHT THEN!
HEY, YOU!! WASN'T THAT A PHO CALL FOR MIYAMURA? WHO SAID YOU COUL JUST...
TMP
TMP
YEAH... BUT SINCE IT WAS FROM YAMADA-SENPAI...
HUH... WHAT DID HE SAY?
IT DOESN'T SEEM LIKE WE'LL BE ABLE TO GO BACK TO NORMAL FO A WHILE!
TEE HEE!

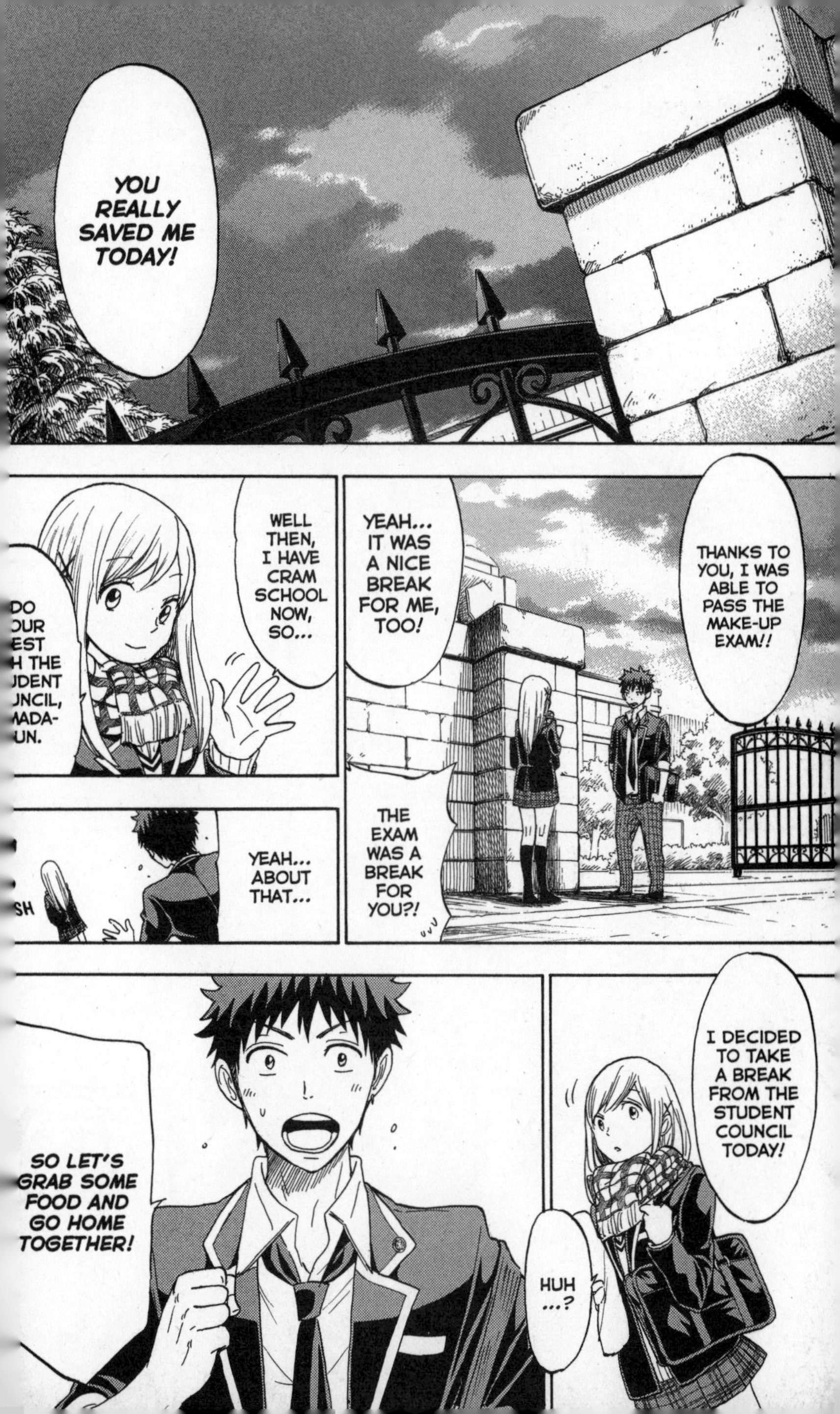
YOU REALLY SAVED ME TODAY!
THANKS TO YOU, I WAS ABLE TO PASS THE MAKE-UP EXAM!!
YEAH... IT WAS A NICE BREAK FOR ME, TOO!
THE EXAM WAS A BREAK FOR YOU?!
WELL THEN, I HAVE CRAM SCHOOL NOW, SO...
DO OUR EST H THE UDENT UNCIL, MADA- UN.
YEAH... ABOUT THAT...
SH
I DECIDED TO TAKE A BREAK FROM THE STUDENT COUNCIL TODAY!
HUH ...?
SO LET'S GRAB SOME FOOD AND GO HOME TOGETHER!

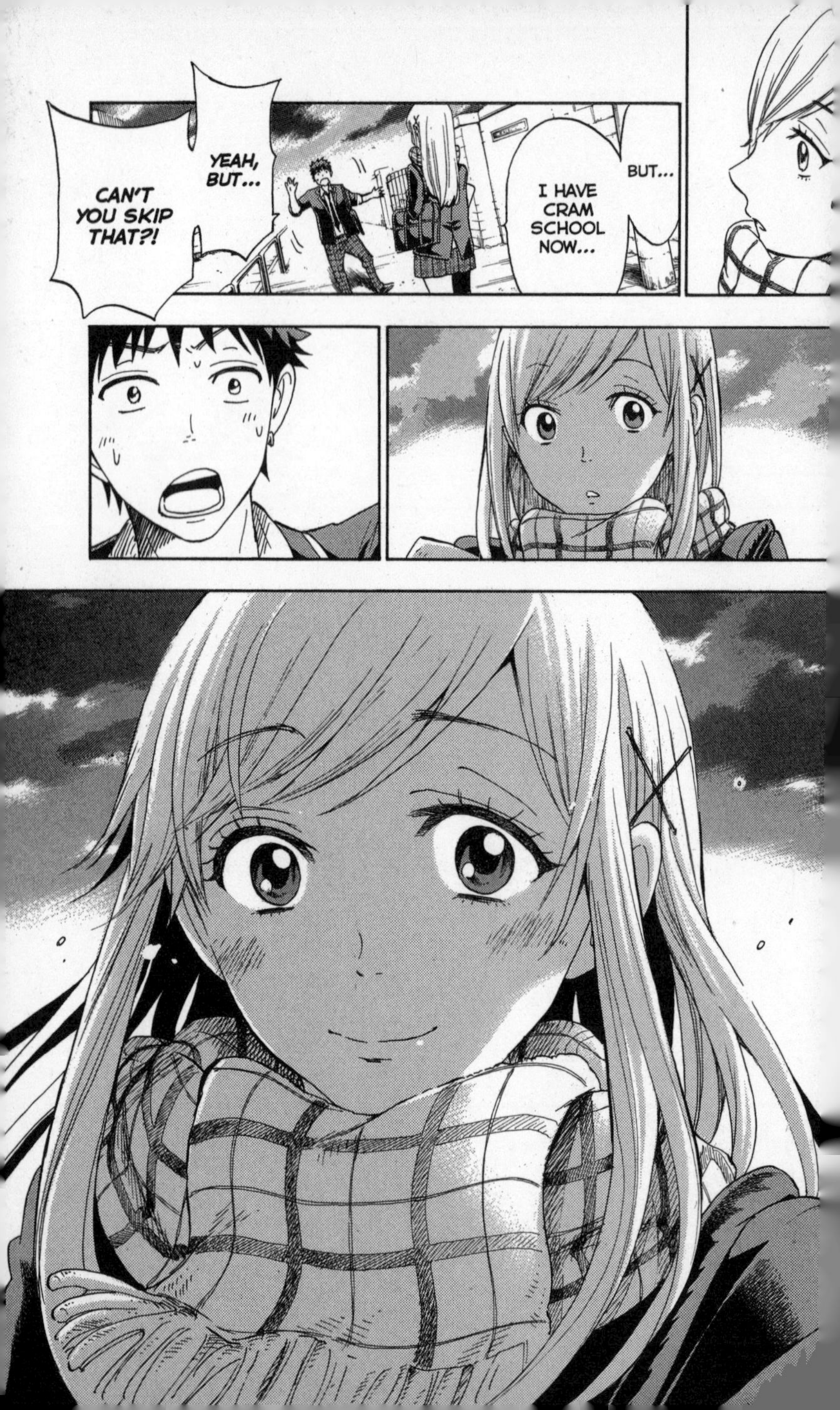
BUT...
I HAVE CRAM SCHOOL NOW...
YEAH, BUT...
CAN'T YOU SKIP THAT?!

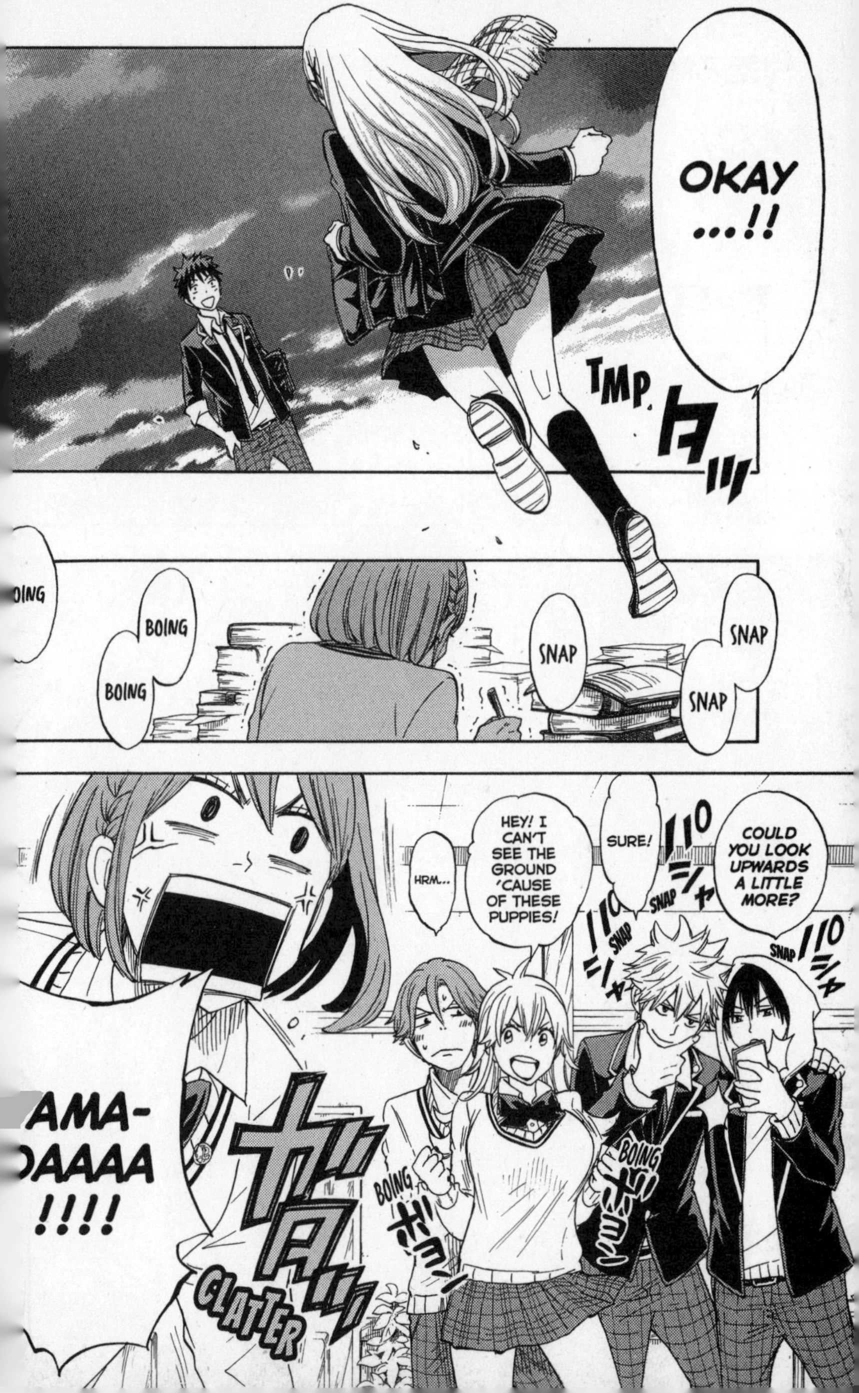
OKAY ...!!
TMP.
SNAP
SNAP
SNAP
BOING
BOING
BOING
COULD YOU LOOK UPWARDS A LITTLE MORE?
SNAP
SURE!
SNAP
HEY! I CAN'T SEE THE GROUND 'CAUSE OF THESE PUPPIES!
HRM...
SNAP
BOING
BOING
CLATTER
AMA-DAAAA !!!!

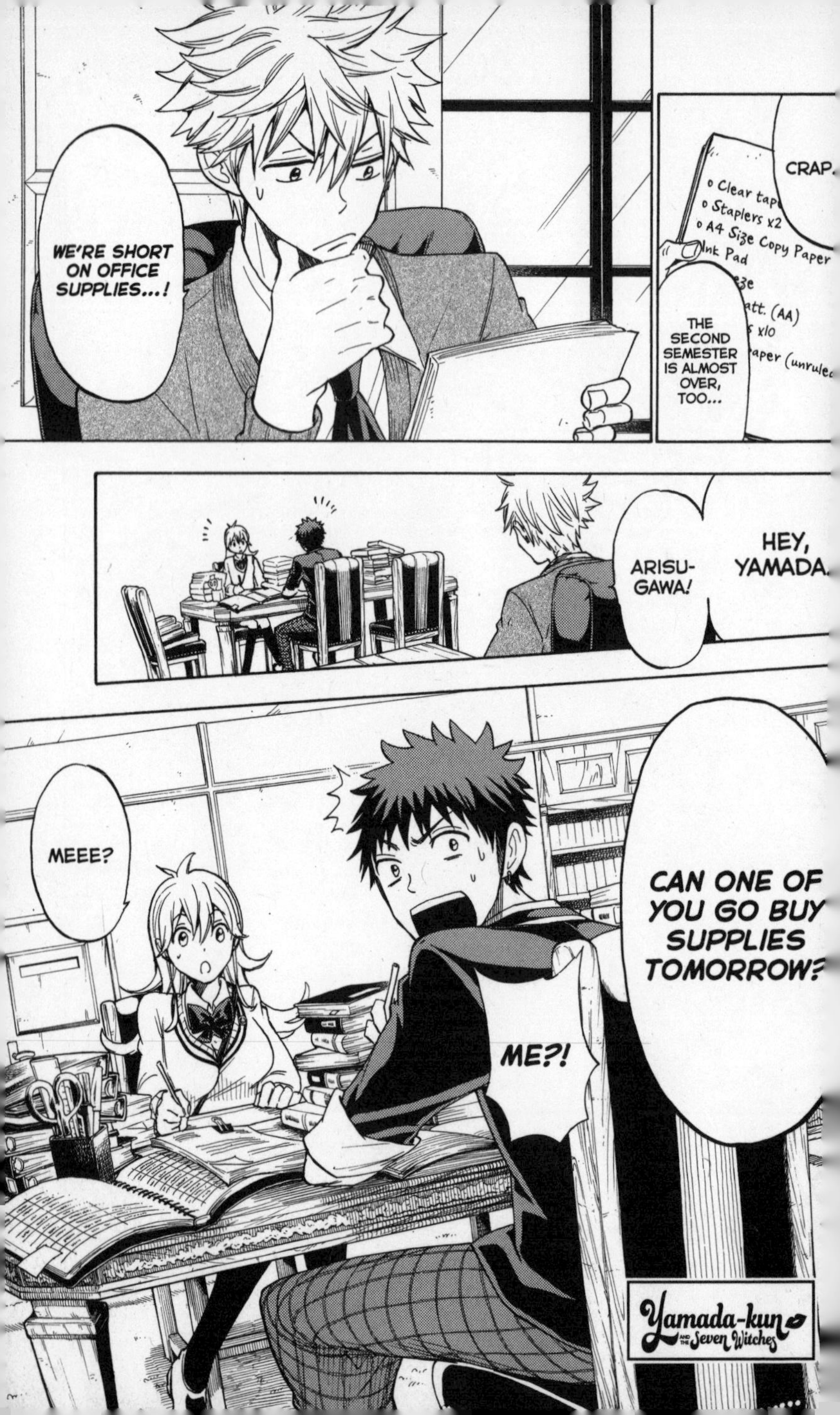
CRAP.
o Clear tap
o Staplers x2
o A4 Size Copy Paper
Ink Pad
THE SECOND SEMESTER IS ALMOST OVER, TOO...
WE'RE SHORT ON OFFICE SUPPLIES...!
HEY, YAMADA.
ARISU-GAWA!
CAN ONE OF YOU GO BUY SUPPLIES TOMORROW?
ME?!
MEEE?
Yamada-kun and the Seven Witches

CHAPTER 113: Ten years too early.

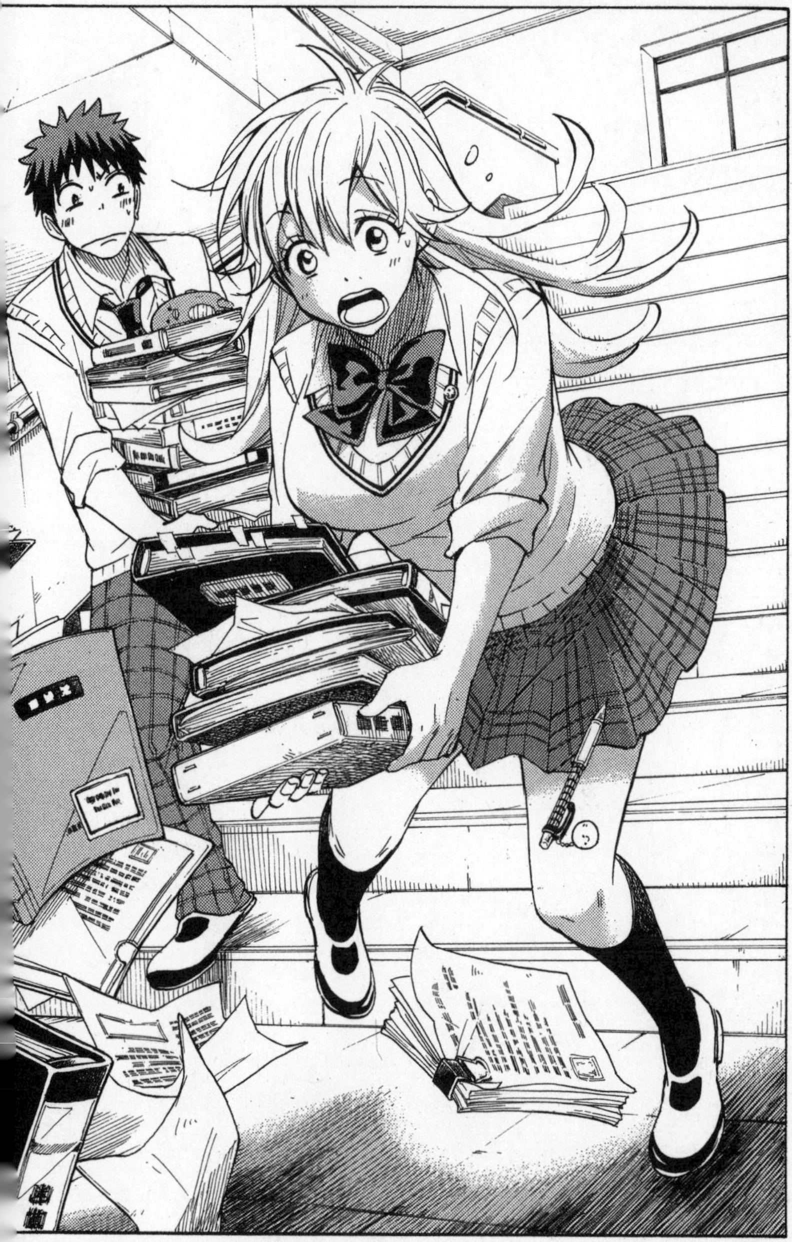

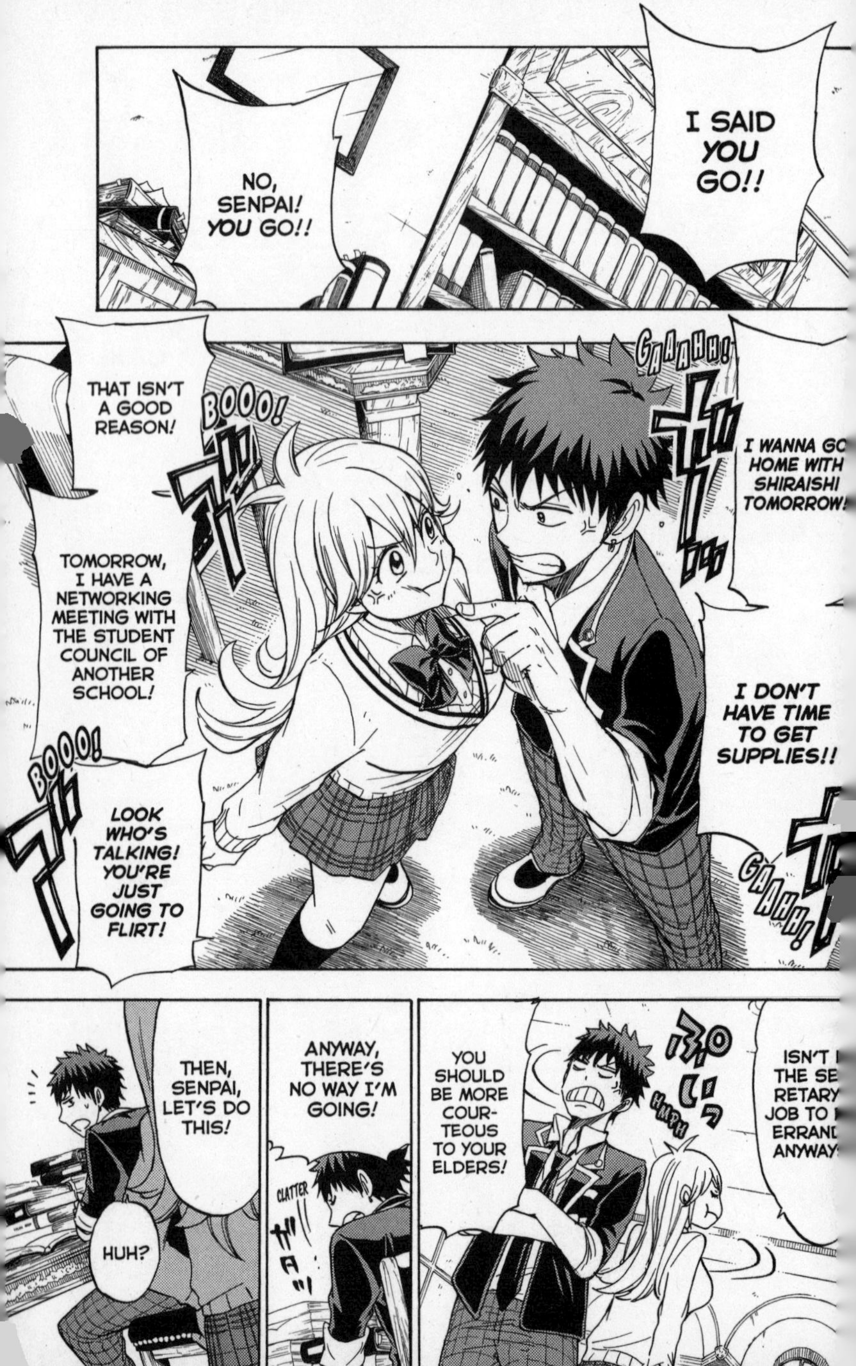
I SAID YOU GO!!
NO, SENPAI! YOU GO!!
GAAAHH!
I WANNA GO HOME WITH SHIRAISHI TOMORROW!
I DON'T HAVE TIME TO GET SUPPLIES!!
GAAHH!
BOOO!
THAT ISN'T A GOOD REASON!
TOMORROW, I HAVE A NETWORKING MEETING WITH THE STUDENT COUNCIL OF ANOTHER SCHOOL!
BOOO!
LOOK WHO'S TALKING! YOU'RE JUST GOING TO FLIRT!
ISN'T I THE SE RETARY JOB TO ERRAND ANYWAY
HMPH
YOU SHOULD BE MORE COUR- TEOUS TO YOUR ELDERS!
ANYWAY, THERE'S NO WAY I'M GOING!
CLATTER
THEN, SENPAI, LET'S DO THIS!
HUH?

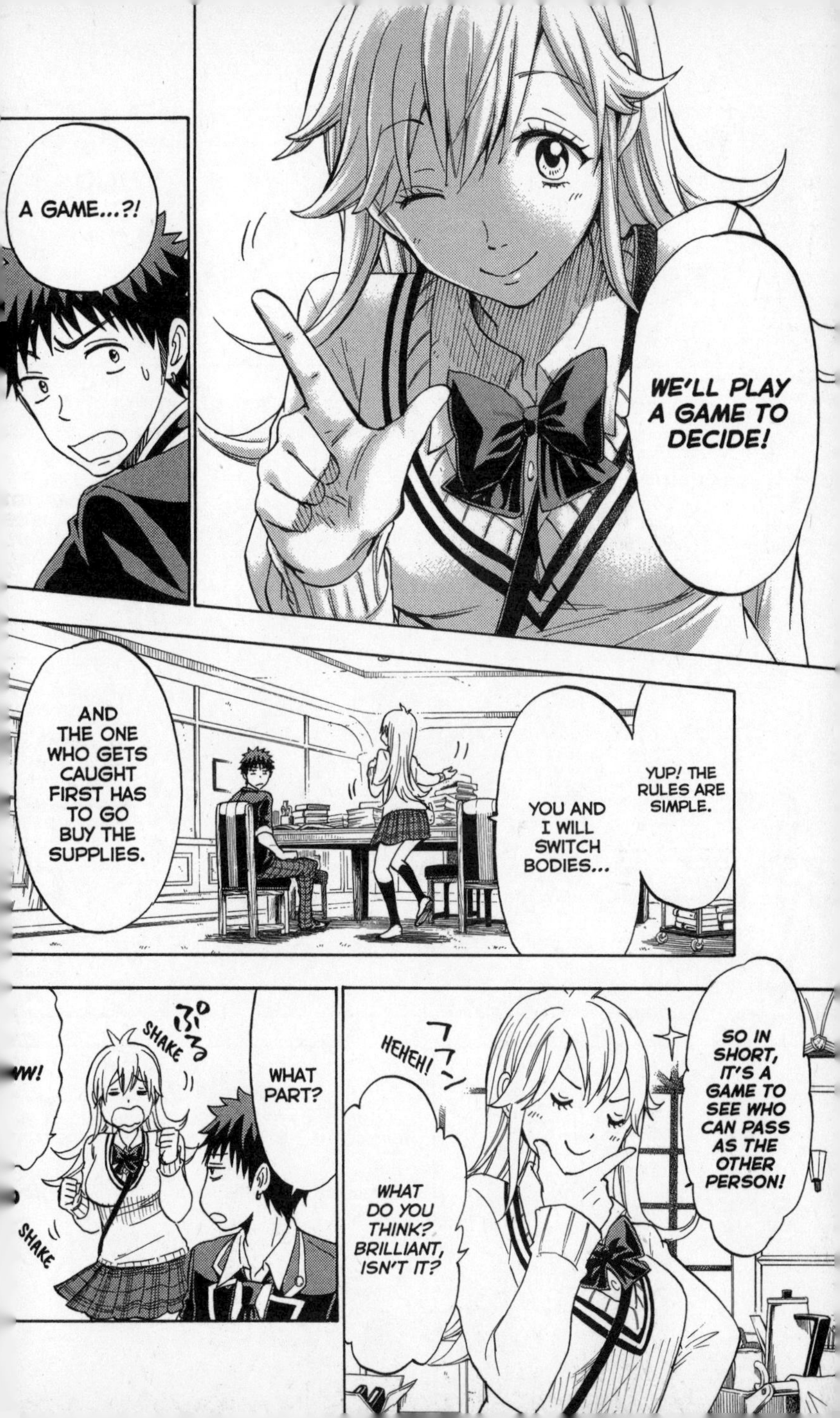

WE'LL PLAY A GAME TO DECIDE!
A GAME...?!
YUP! THE RULES ARE SIMPLE.
YOU AND I WILL SWITCH BODIES...
AND THE ONE WHO GETS CAUGHT FIRST HAS TO GO BUY THE SUPPLIES.
SO IN SHORT, IT'S A GAME TO SEE WHO CAN PASS AS THE OTHER PERSON!
フフ〜
HEHEH!
WHAT DO YOU THINK? BRILLIANT, ISN'T IT?
WHAT PART?
ぷる
SHAKE
SHAKE

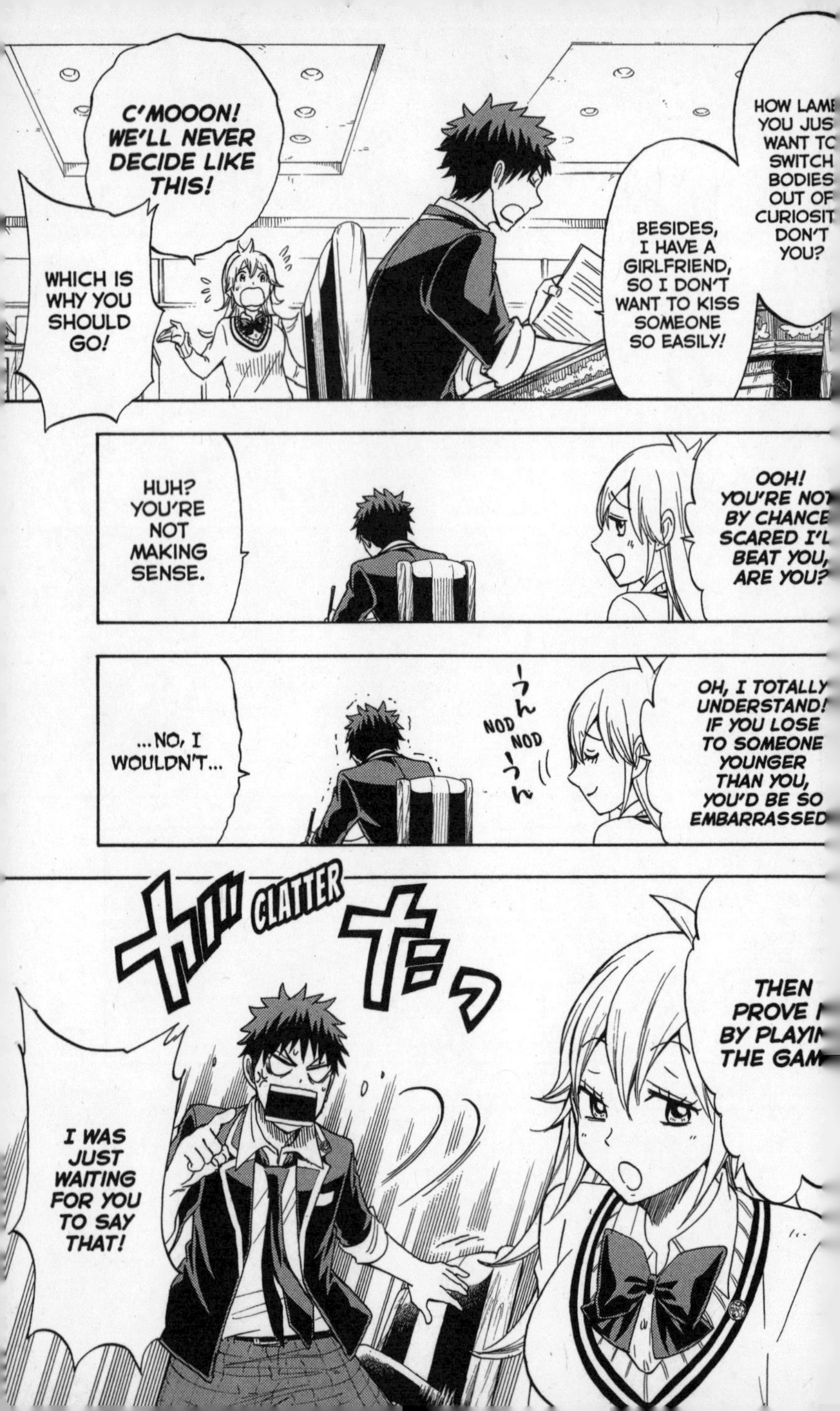
HOW LAME YOU JUS WANT TO SWITCH BODIES OUT OF CURIOSIT DON'T YOU?
BESIDES, I HAVE A GIRLFRIEND, SO I DON'T WANT TO KISS SOMEONE SO EASILY!
C'MOOON! WE'LL NEVER DECIDE LIKE THIS!
WHICH IS WHY YOU SHOULD GO!
OOH! YOU'RE NOT BY CHANCE SCARED I'L BEAT YOU, ARE YOU?
HUH? YOU'RE NOT MAKING SENSE.
OH, I TOTALLY UNDERSTAND! IF YOU LOSE TO SOMEONE YOUNGER THAN YOU, YOU'D BE SO EMBARRASSED
うん NOD NOD うん
...NO, I WOULDN'T...
THEN PROVE I BY PLAYIN THE GAM
CLATTER
I WAS JUST WAITING FOR YOU TO SAY THAT!

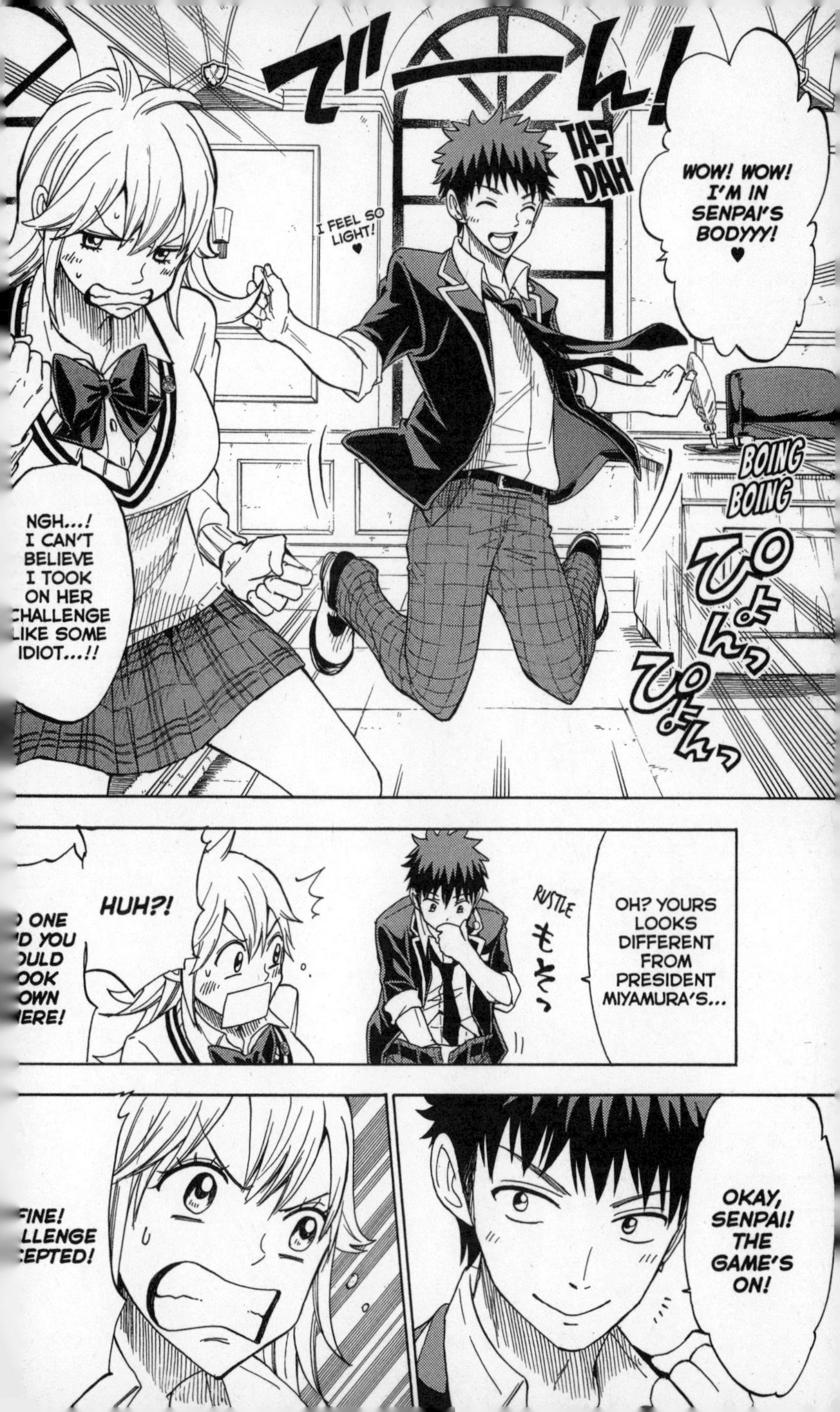
でーん!
TA-DAH
WOW! WOW! I'M IN SENPAI'S BODYYY! ♥
I FEEL SO LIGHT! ♥
BOING BOING
ぴょんっぴょんっ
NGH...! I CAN'T BELIEVE I TOOK ON HER CHALLENGE LIKE SOME IDIOT...!!
OH? YOURS LOOKS DIFFERENT FROM PRESIDENT MIYAMURA'S...
RUSTLE
もぞっ
HUH?!
OKAY, SENPAI! THE GAME'S ON!
FINE!

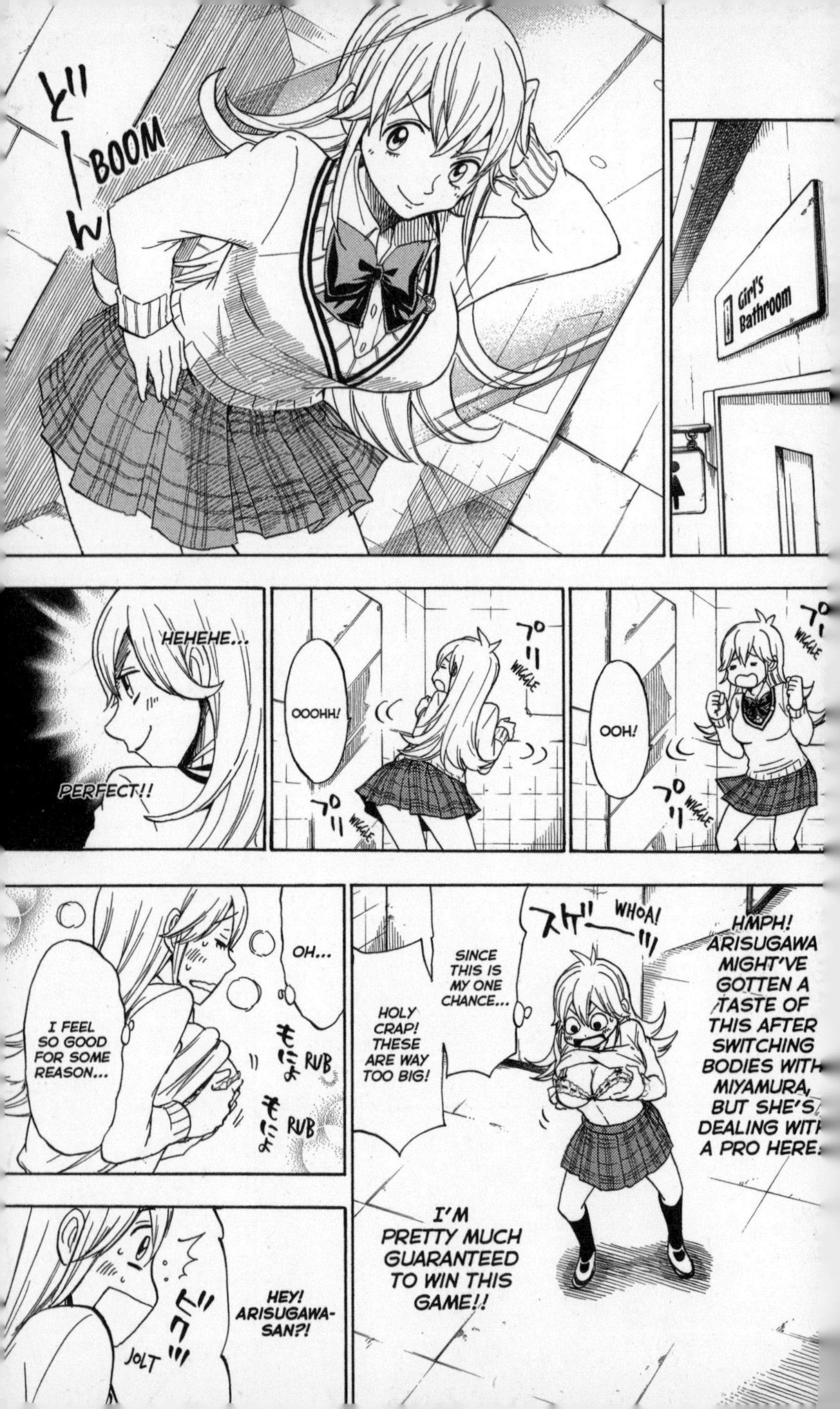

Girl's Bathroom
どーん
BOOM
プリ
WIGGLE
OOH!
プリ
WIGGLE
プリ
WIGGLE
OOOHH!
プリ
WIGGLE
HEHEHE...
PERFECT!!
HMPH! ARISUGAWA MIGHT'VE GOTTEN A TASTE OF THIS AFTER SWITCHING BODIES WITH MIYAMURA, BUT SHE'S DEALING WITH A PRO HERE!
スゲー
WHOA!
SINCE THIS IS MY ONE CHANCE...
HOLY CRAP! THESE ARE WAY TOO BIG!
I'M PRETTY MUCH GUARANTEED TO WIN THIS GAME!!
OH...
もにょ
RUB
もにょ
RUB
I FEEL SO GOOD FOR SOME REASON...
HEY! ARISUGAWA-SAN?!
ビクッ
JOLT

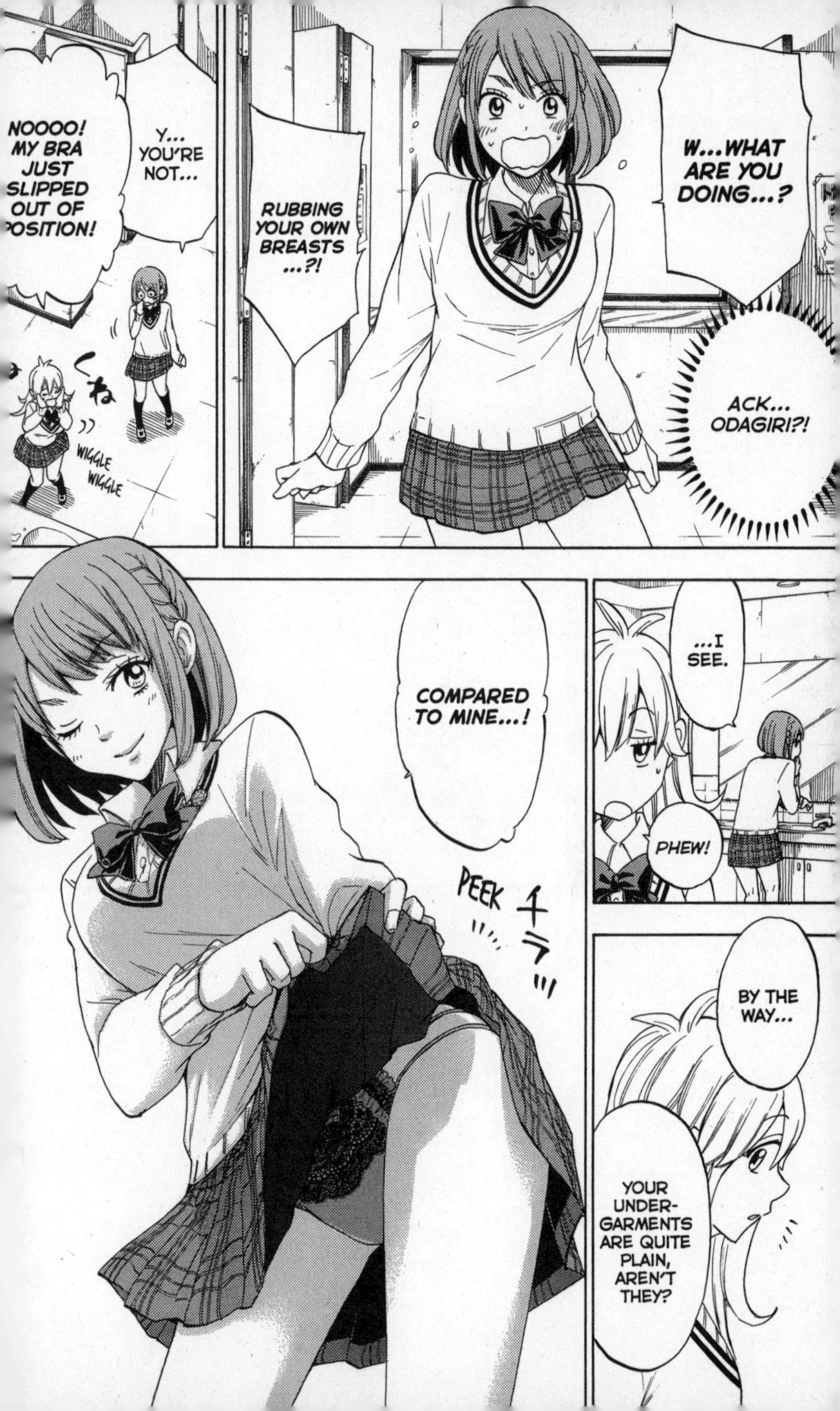
W...WHAT ARE YOU DOING...?
ACK... ODAGIRI?!
RUBBING YOUR OWN BREASTS ...?!
Y... YOU'RE NOT...
NOOOO! MY BRA JUST SLIPPED OUT OF POSITION!
くね
WIGGLE WIGGLE
...I SEE.
PHEW!
BY THE WAY...
YOUR UNDER-GARMENTS ARE QUITE PLAIN, AREN'T THEY?
COMPARED TO MINE...!
PEEK チラ

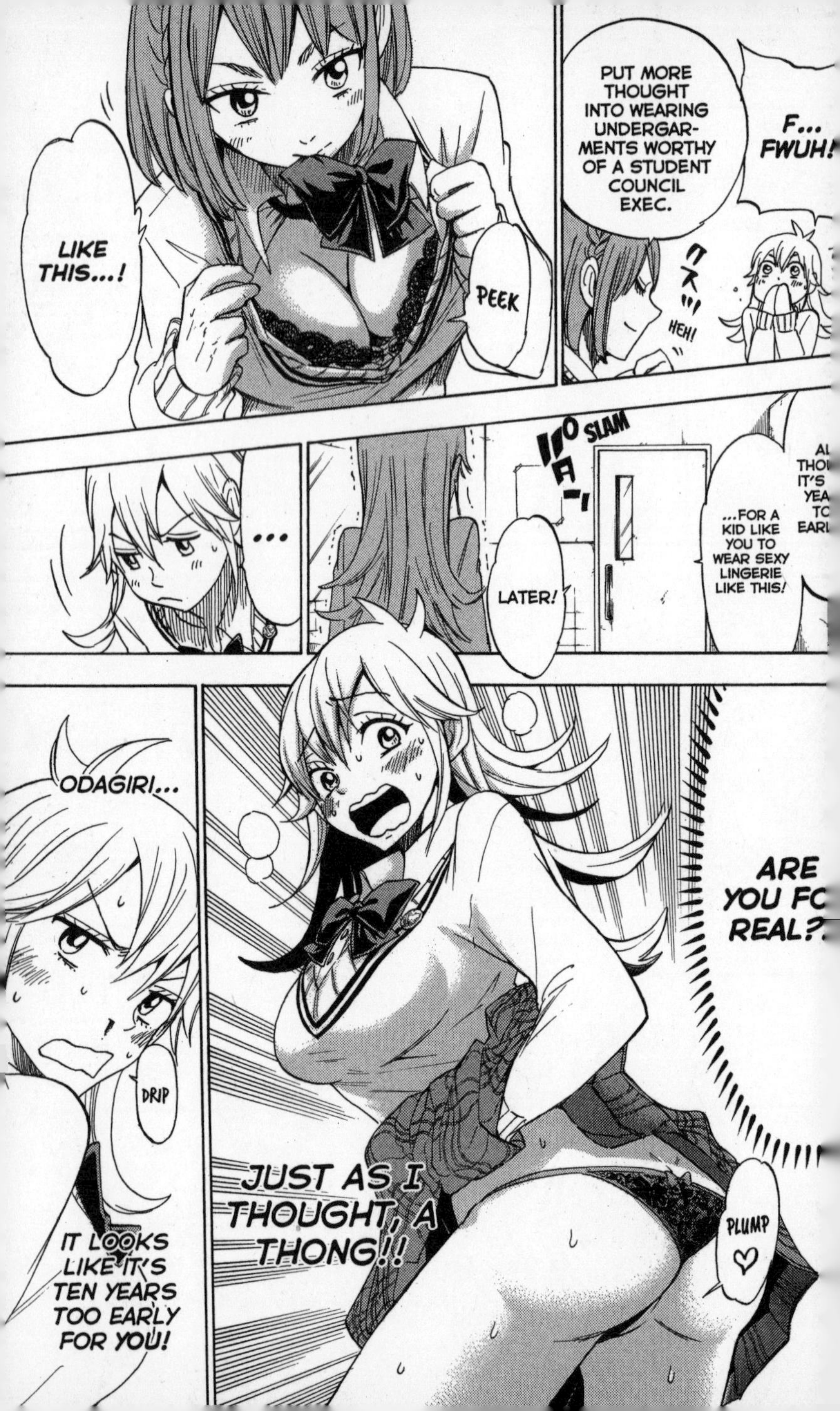
F... FWUH!
PUT MORE THOUGHT INTO WEARING UNDERGARMENTS WORTHY OF A STUDENT COUNCIL EXEC.
クス!!
HEH!
PEEK
LIKE THIS...!
AL THO IT'S YEA TO EARL
...FOR A KID LIKE YOU TO WEAR SEXY LINGERIE LIKE THIS!
SLAM
LATER!
...
ARE YOU FO REAL?!
PLUMP ♥
JUST AS I THOUGHT, A THONG!!
ODAGIRI...
DRIP
IT LOOKS LIKE IT'S TEN YEARS TOO EARLY FOR YOU!

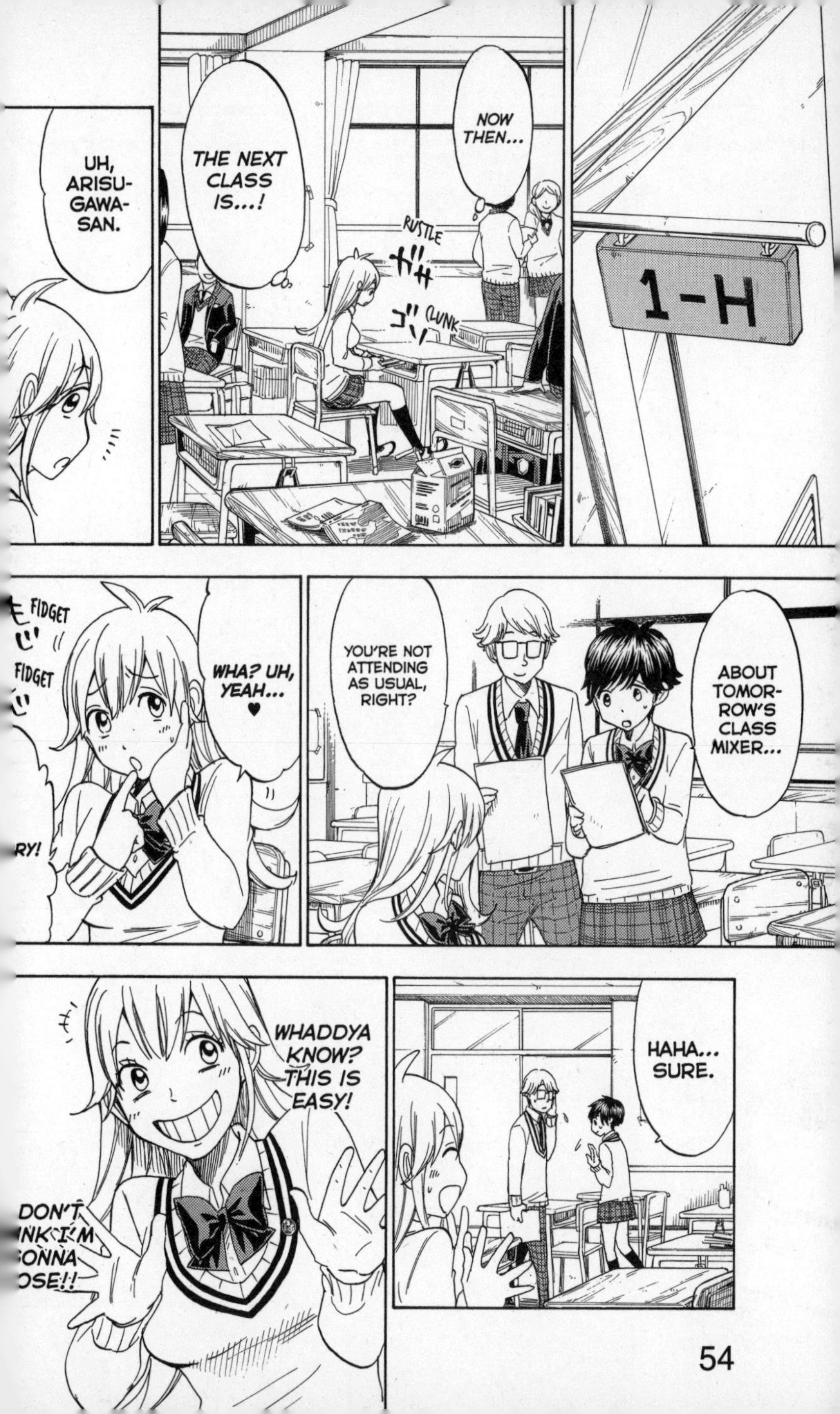
1-H
NOW THEN...
THE NEXT CLASS IS...!
RUSTLE
CLUNK
UH, ARISU-GAWA-SAN.
ABOUT TOMOR-ROW'S CLASS MIXER...
YOU'RE NOT ATTENDING AS USUAL, RIGHT?
WHA? UH, YEAH... ♥
FIDGET
FIDGET
RY!
HAHA... SURE.
WHADDYA KNOW? THIS IS EASY!
DON'T
NK I'M
ONNA
OSE!!

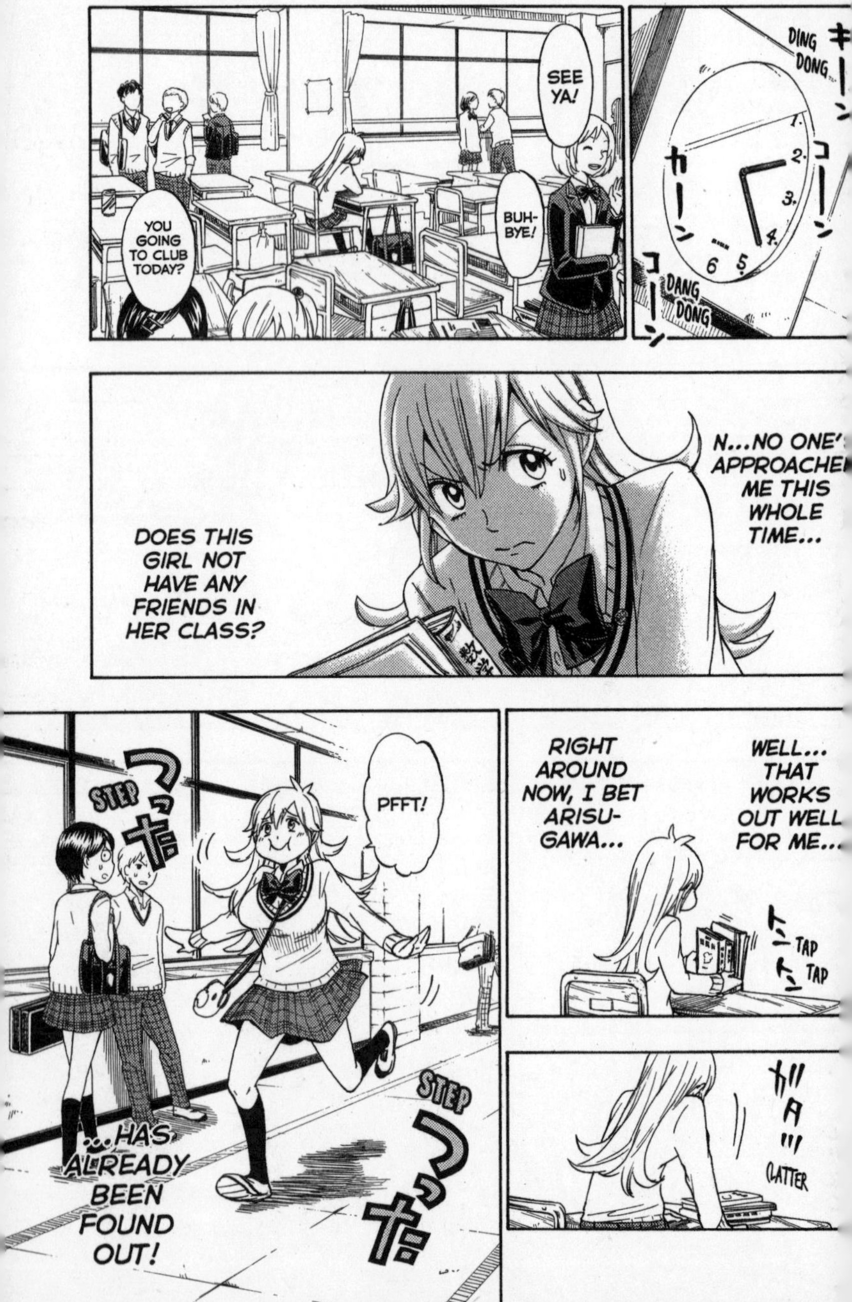
DING DONG
DANG DONG
SEE YA!
BUH-BYE!
YOU GOING TO CLUB TODAY?
N...NO ONE' APPROACHE ME THIS WHOLE TIME...
DOES THIS GIRL NOT HAVE ANY FRIENDS IN HER CLASS?
WELL... THAT WORKS OUT WELL FOR ME...
RIGHT AROUND NOW, I BET ARISU-GAWA...
TAP TAP
CLATTER
STEP
PFFT!
STEP
...HAS ALREADY BEEN FOUND OUT!

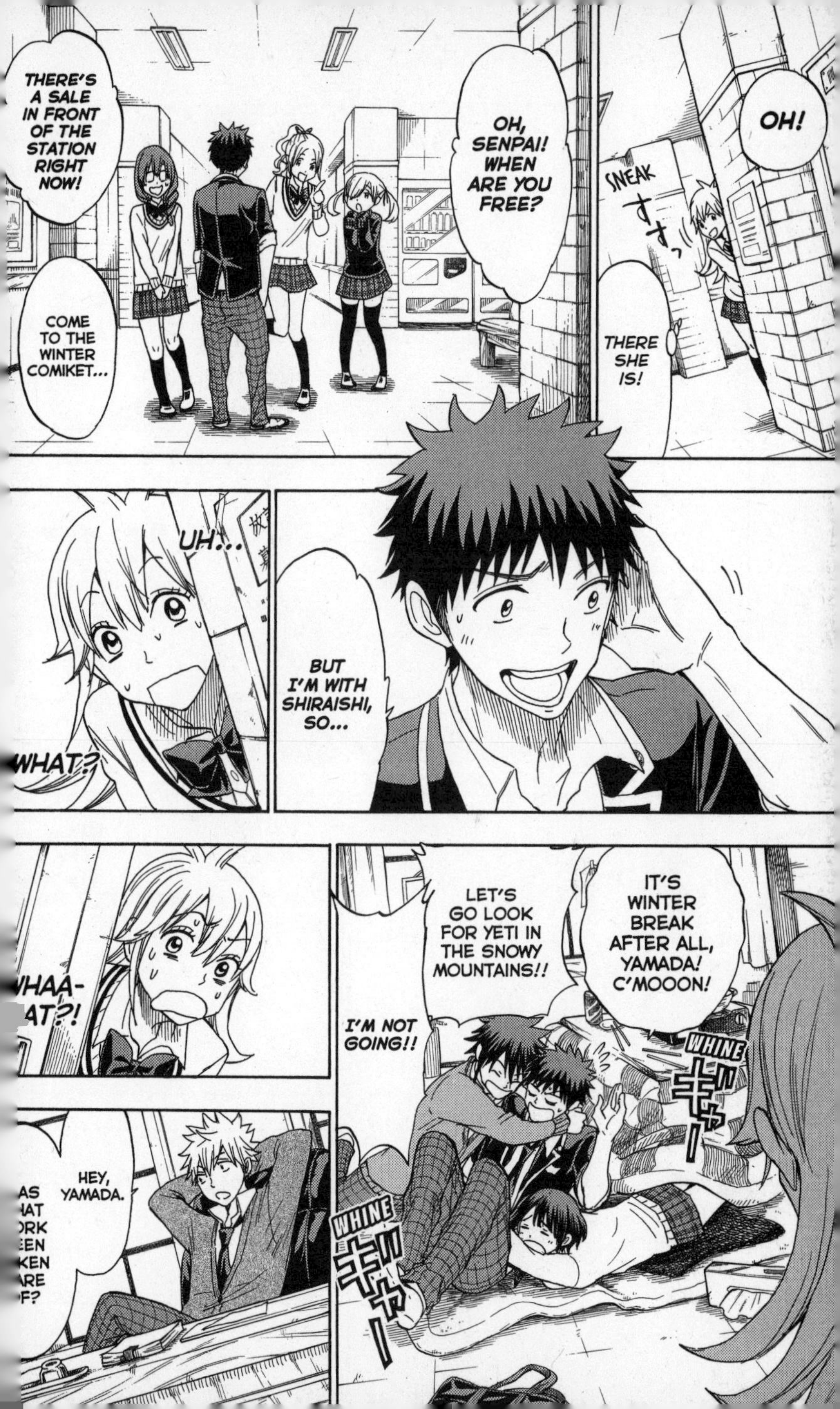
OH!
SNEAK
すすっ
THERE SHE IS!
OH, SENPAI! WHEN ARE YOU FREE?
THERE'S A SALE IN FRONT OF THE STATION RIGHT NOW!
COME TO THE WINTER COMIKET...
BUT I'M WITH SHIRAISHI, SO...
UH...
WHAT?
IT'S WINTER BREAK AFTER ALL, YAMADA! C'MOOON!
LET'S GO LOOK FOR YETI IN THE SNOWY MOUNTAINS!!
I'M NOT GOING!!
WHINE
WHINE
WHAA-AT?!
HEY, YAMADA.

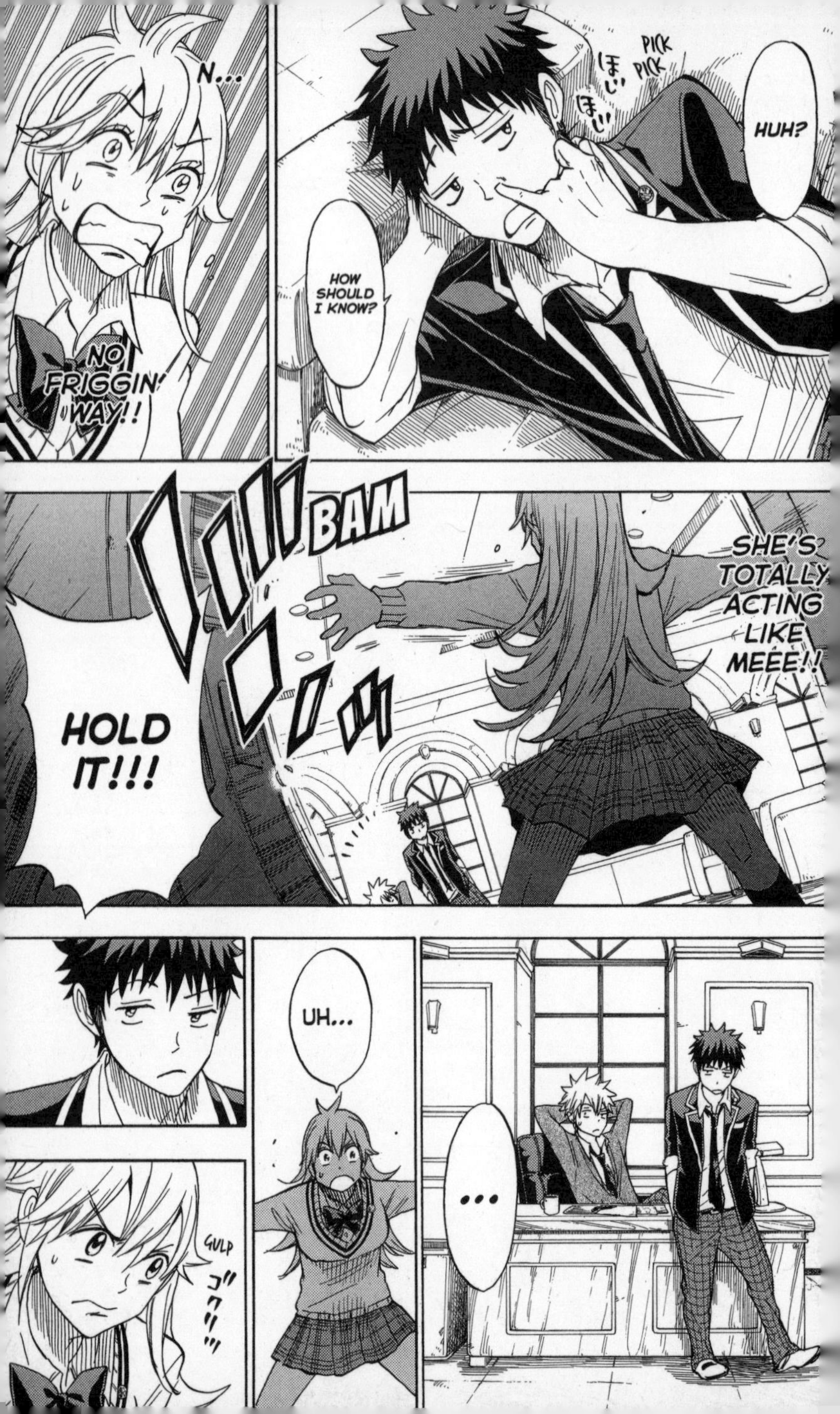
HUH?
PICK PICK
ほじ ほじ
HOW SHOULD I KNOW?
N...
NO FRIGGIN' WAY!!
SHE'S TOTALLY ACTING LIKE MEEE!!
BAM
HOLD IT!!!
...
UH...
GULP

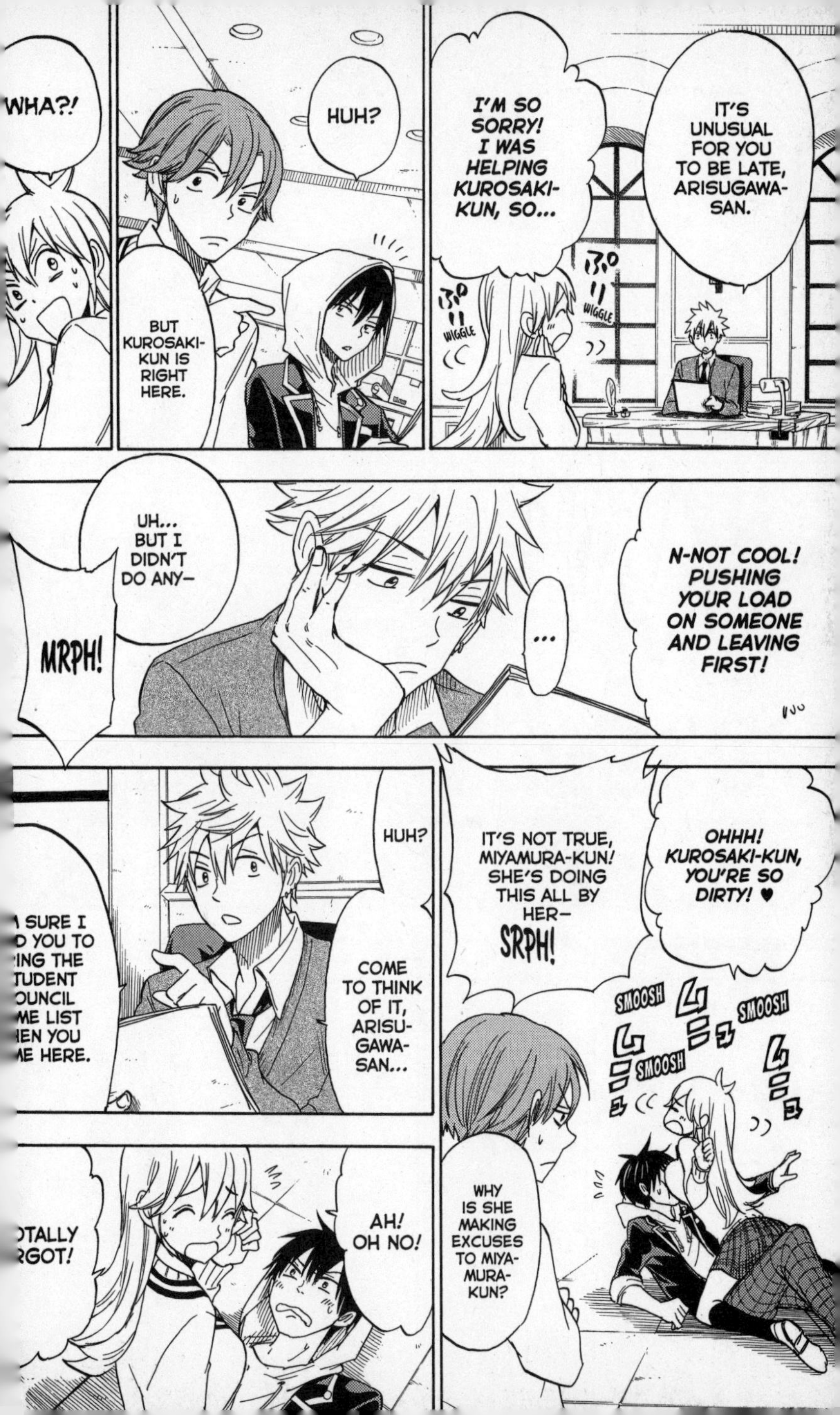
IT'S UNUSUAL FOR YOU TO BE LATE, ARISUGAWA-SAN.
I'M SO SORRY! I WAS HELPING KUROSAKI-KUN, SO...
WIGGLE
WIGGLE
HUH?
BUT KUROSAKI-KUN IS RIGHT HERE.
WHA?!
N-NOT COOL! PUSHING YOUR LOAD ON SOMEONE AND LEAVING FIRST!
...
UH... BUT I DIDN'T DO ANY—
MRPH!
OHHH! KUROSAKI-KUN, YOU'RE SO DIRTY! ♥
IT'S NOT TRUE, MIYAMURA-KUN! SHE'S DOING THIS ALL BY HER—
SRPH!
SMOOSH
SMOOSH
SMOOSH
WHY IS SHE MAKING EXCUSES TO MIYAMURA-KUN?
HUH?
COME TO THINK OF IT, ARISUGAWA-SAN...
SURE I D YOU TO ING THE TUDENT OUNCIL ME LIST HEN YOU ME HERE.
AH! OH NO!
OTALLY RGOT!

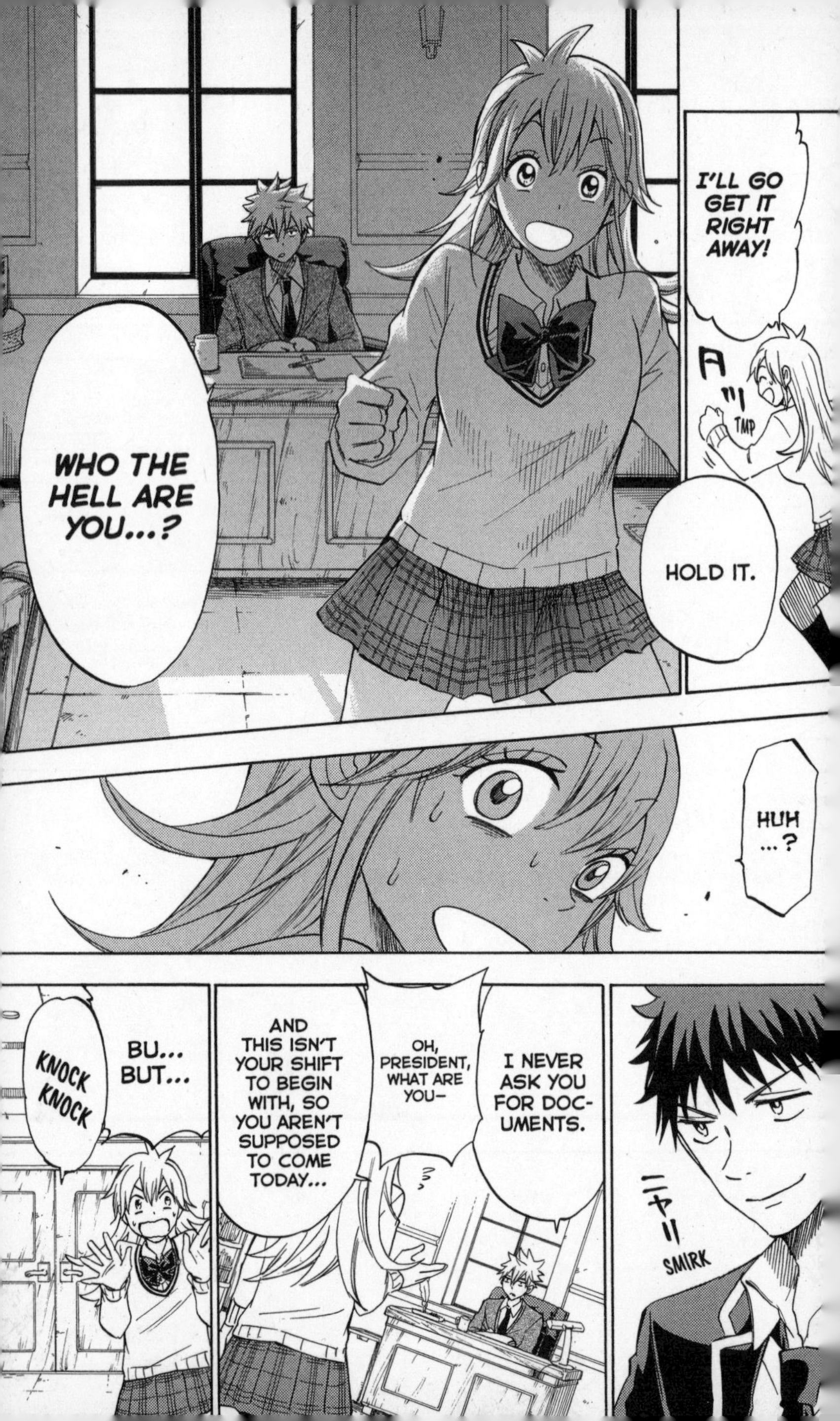
I'LL GO GET IT RIGHT AWAY!
TMP
HOLD IT.
WHO THE HELL ARE YOU...?
HUH ...?
I NEVER ASK YOU FOR DOCUMENTS.
SMIRK
OH, PRESIDENT, WHAT ARE YOU–
AND THIS ISN'T YOUR SHIFT TO BEGIN WITH, SO YOU AREN'T SUPPOSED TO COME TODAY...
BU... BUT...
KNOCK KNOCK

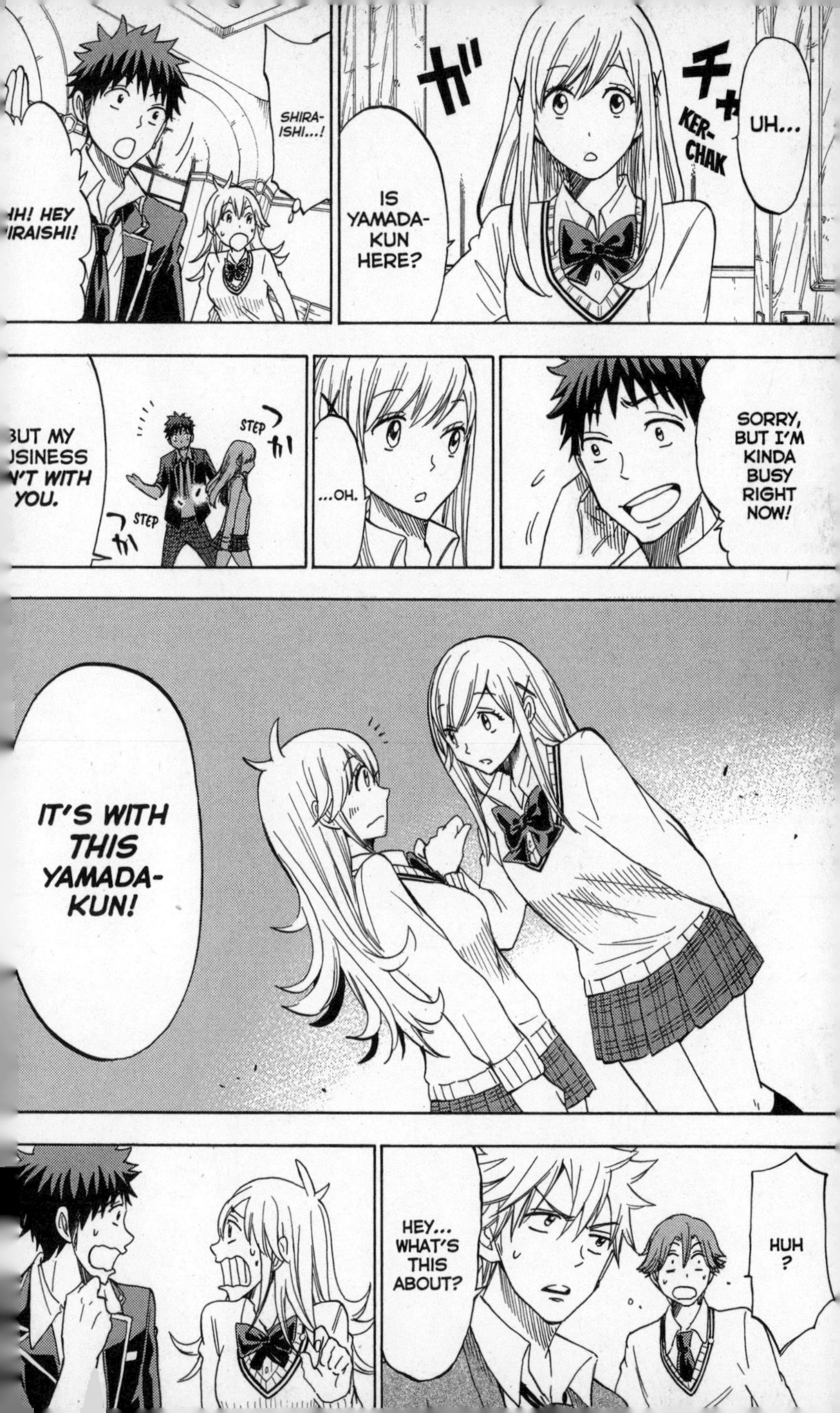
UH...
ガチャ
KER-CHAK
IS YAMADA-KUN HERE?
SHIRA-ISHI...!
HH! HEY IRAISHI!
SORRY, BUT I'M KINDA BUSY RIGHT NOW!
...OH.
STEP
STEP
BUT MY USINESS N'T WITH YOU.
IT'S WITH THIS YAMADA-KUN!
HUH?
HEY... WHAT'S THIS ABOUT?

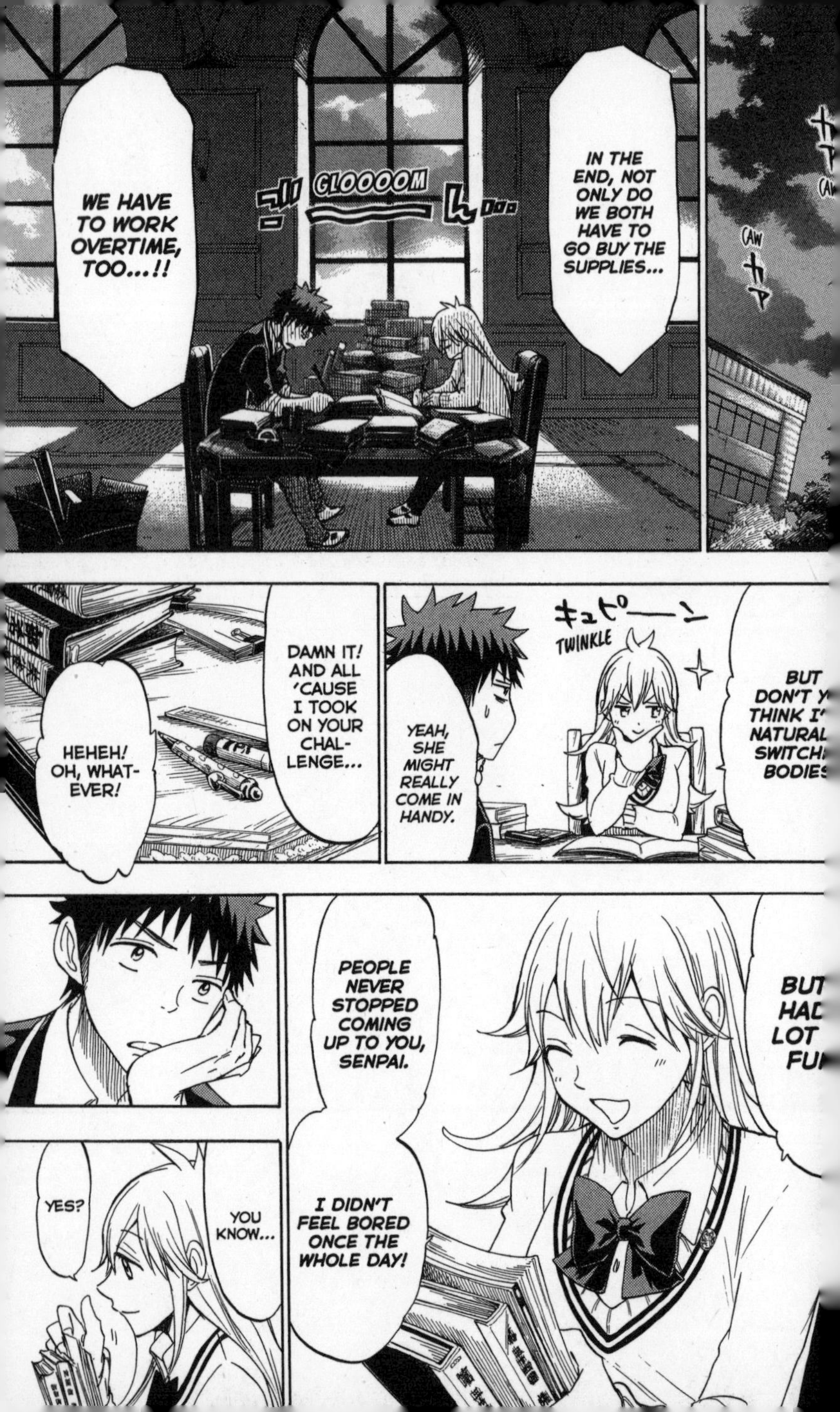
カァ
CAW
CAW
カァ
IN THE END, NOT ONLY DO WE BOTH HAVE TO GO BUY THE SUPPLIES...
GLOOOOM
WE HAVE TO WORK OVERTIME, TOO...!!
BUT DON'T Y
THINK I'
NATURAL
SWITCH
BODIES
キュピーン
TWINKLE
YEAH, SHE MIGHT REALLY COME IN HANDY.
DAMN IT! AND ALL 'CAUSE I TOOK ON YOUR CHAL-LENGE...
HEHEH! OH, WHAT-EVER!
BUT
HAD
LOT
FU
PEOPLE NEVER STOPPED COMING UP TO YOU, SENPAI.
I DIDN'T FEEL BORED ONCE THE WHOLE DAY!
YOU KNOW...
YES?

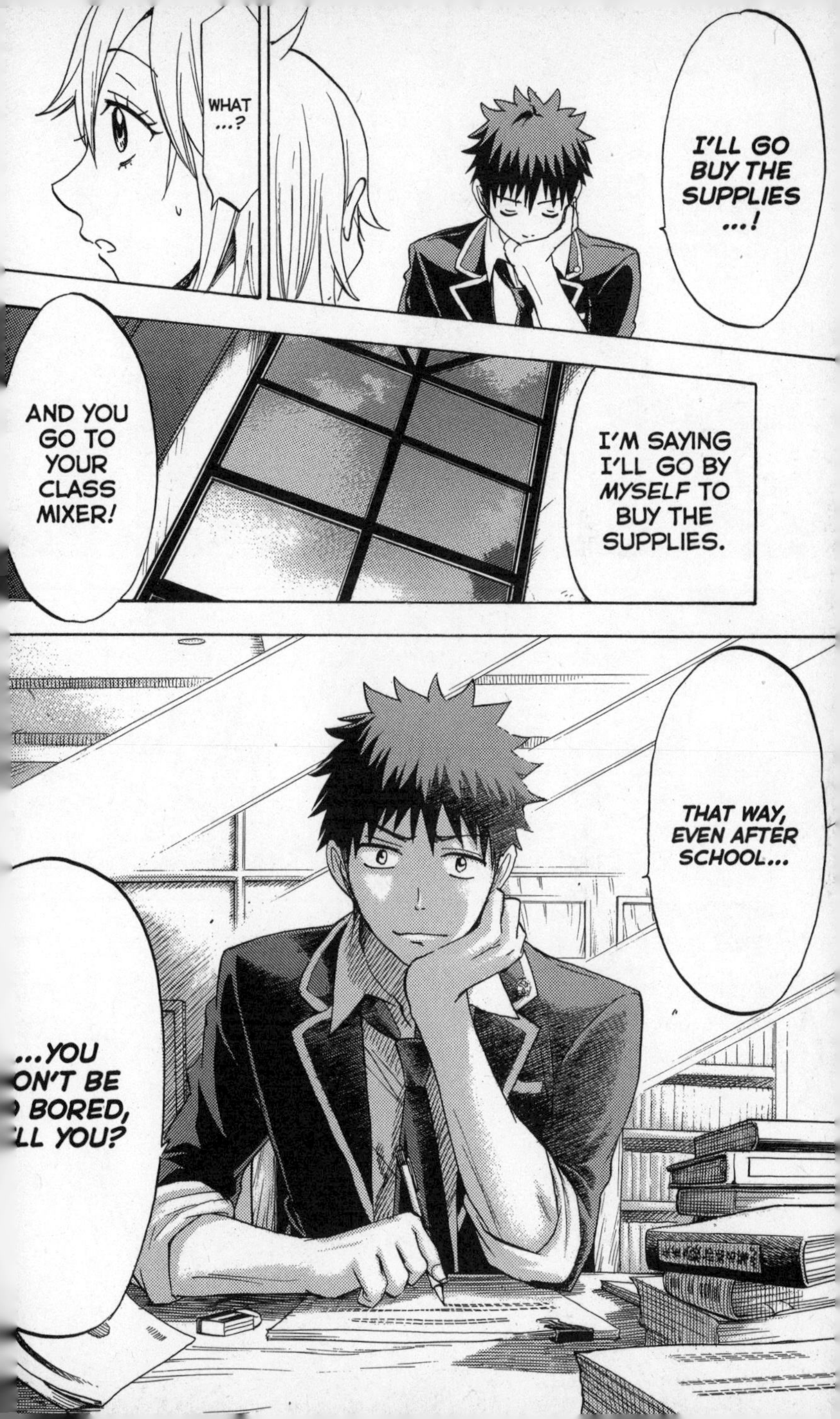
I'LL GO BUY THE SUPPLIES ...!
WHAT ...?
I'M SAYING I'LL GO BY *MYSELF* TO BUY THE SUPPLIES.
AND YOU GO TO YOUR CLASS MIXER!
THAT WAY, EVEN AFTER SCHOOL...
...YOU ON'T BE BORED, LL YOU?

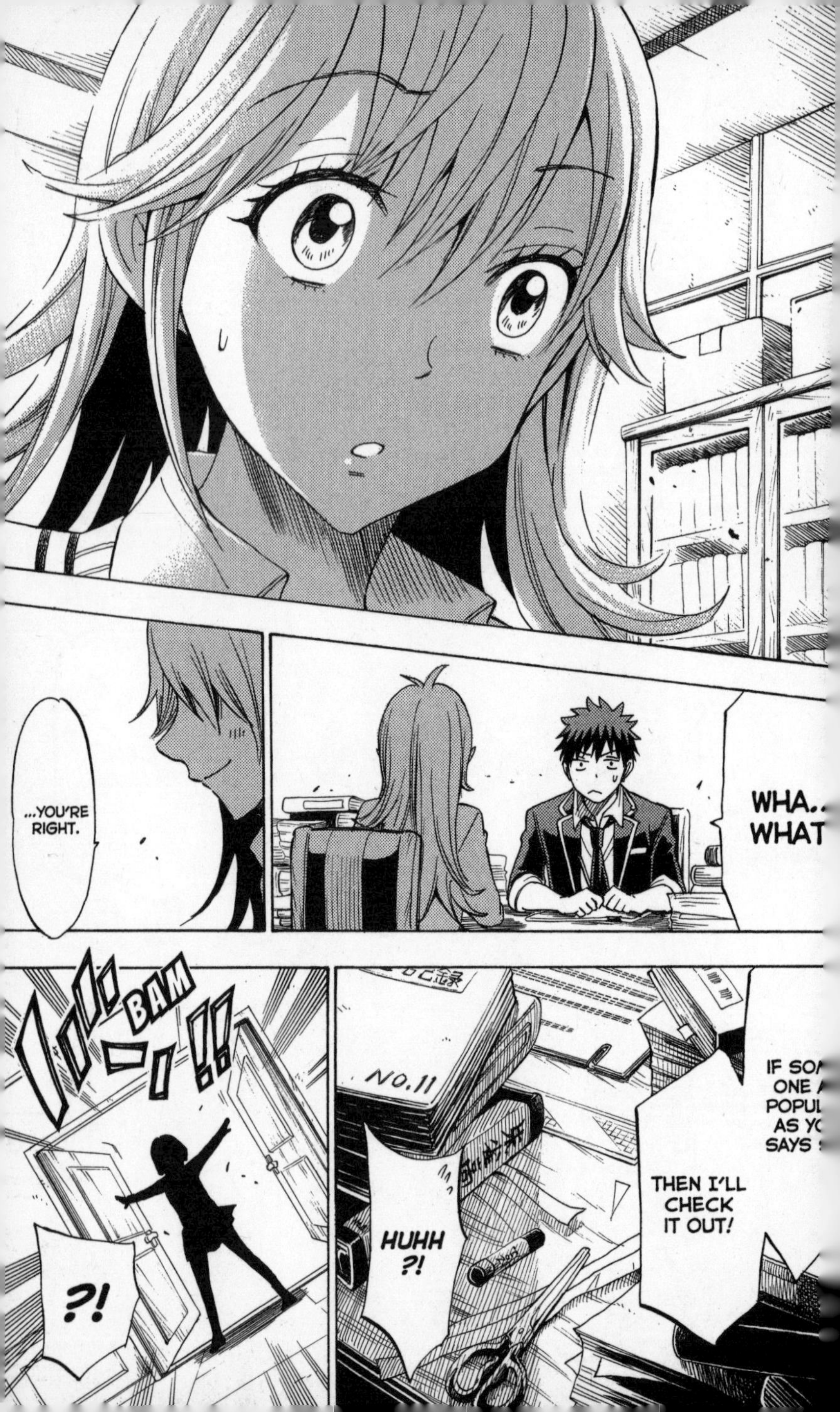
WHA.. WHAT
...YOU'RE RIGHT.
IF SOM ONE A POPUL AS YO SAYS
THEN I'LL CHECK IT OUT!
NO.11
HUHH ?!
BAM
?!

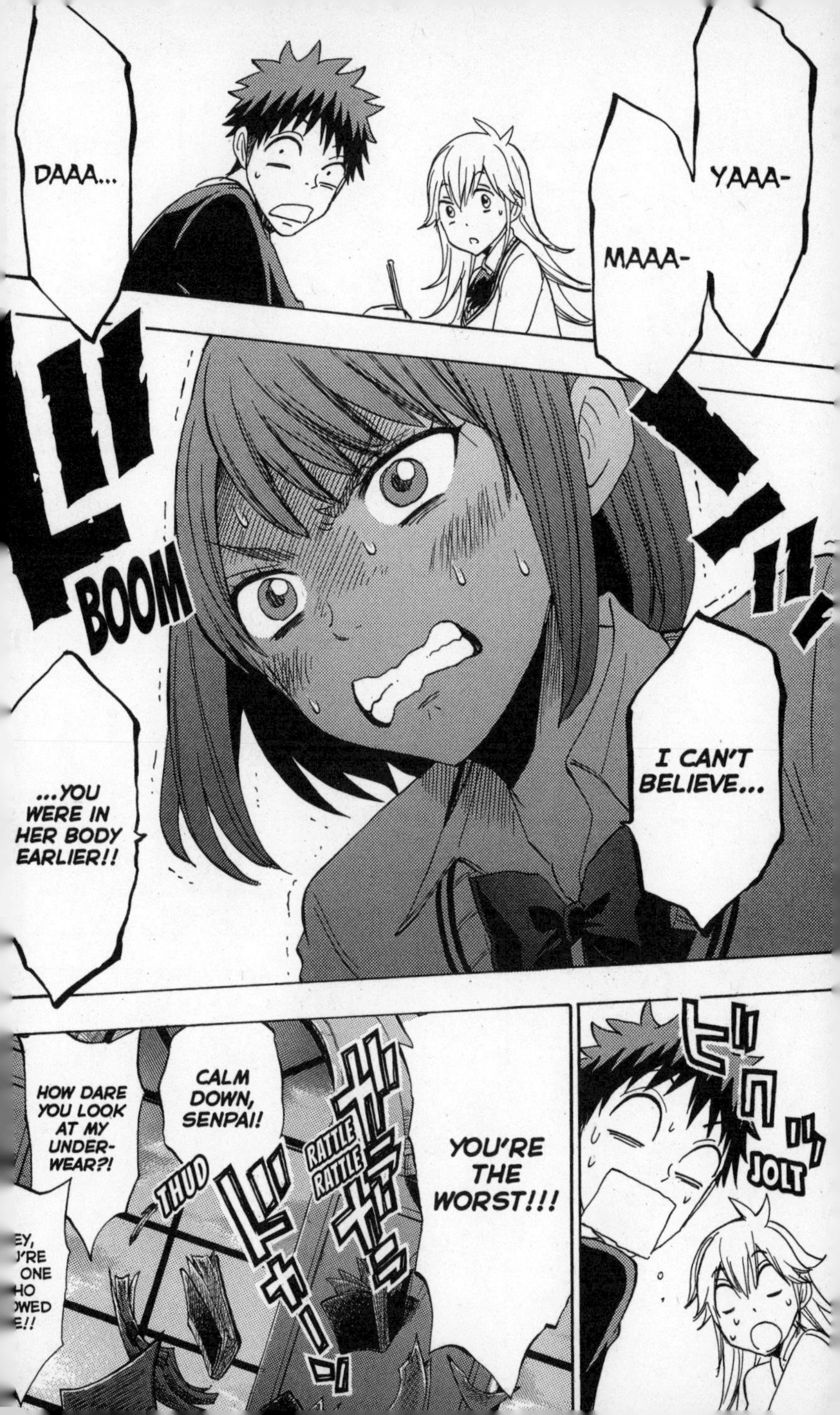
YAAA-
MAAA-
DAAA...
BOOM
I CAN'T BELIEVE...
...YOU WERE IN HER BODY EARLIER!!
JOLT
YOU'RE THE WORST!!!
RATTLE RATTLE
CALM DOWN, SENPAI!
THUD
HOW DARE YOU LOOK AT MY UNDER-WEAR?!

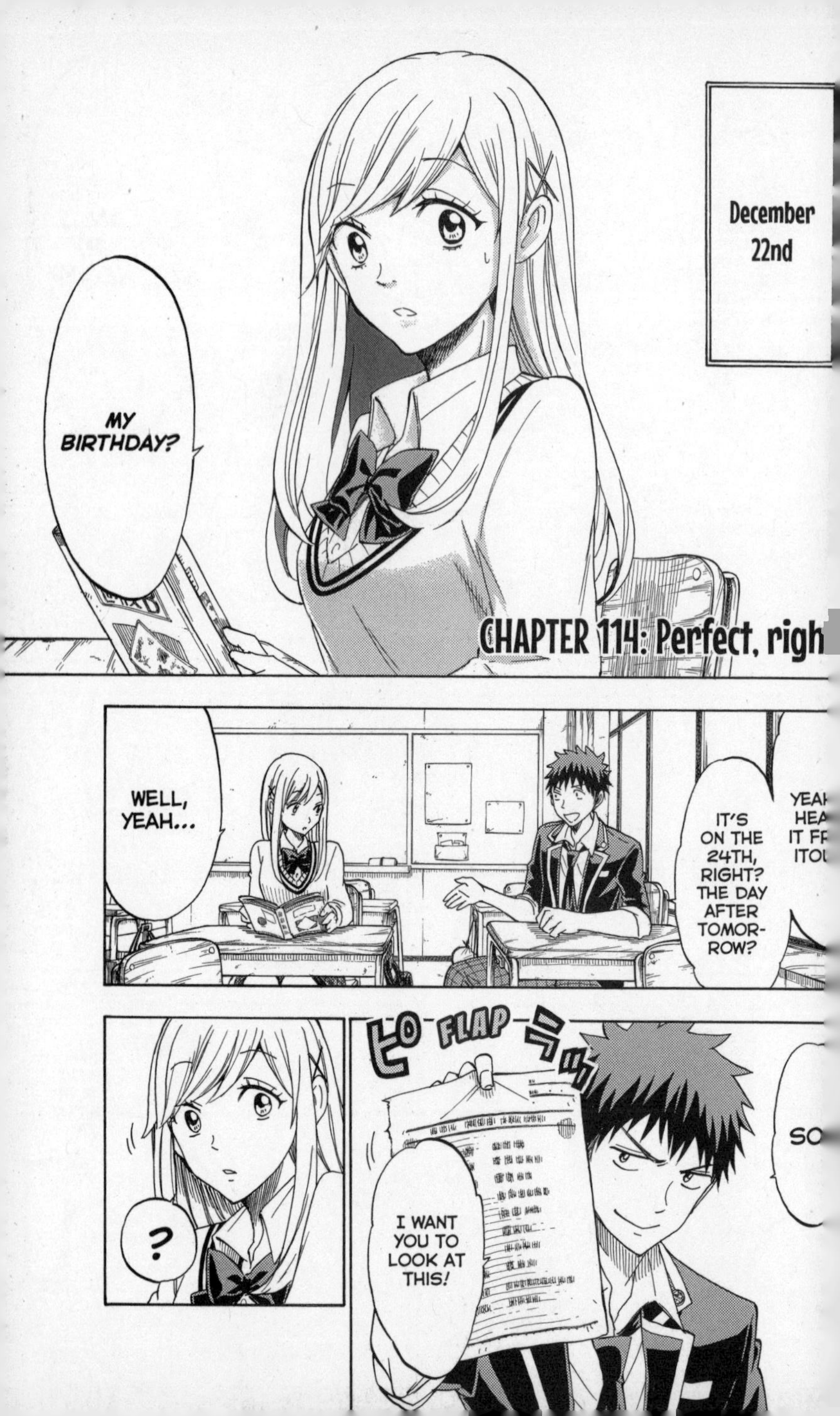
December 22nd
MY BIRTHDAY?
CHAPTER 114: Perfect, righ
YEA HEA IT F ITOU
IT'S ON THE 24TH, RIGHT? THE DAY AFTER TOMOR-ROW?
WELL, YEAH...
SO
FLAP
I WANT YOU TO LOOK AT THIS!
?

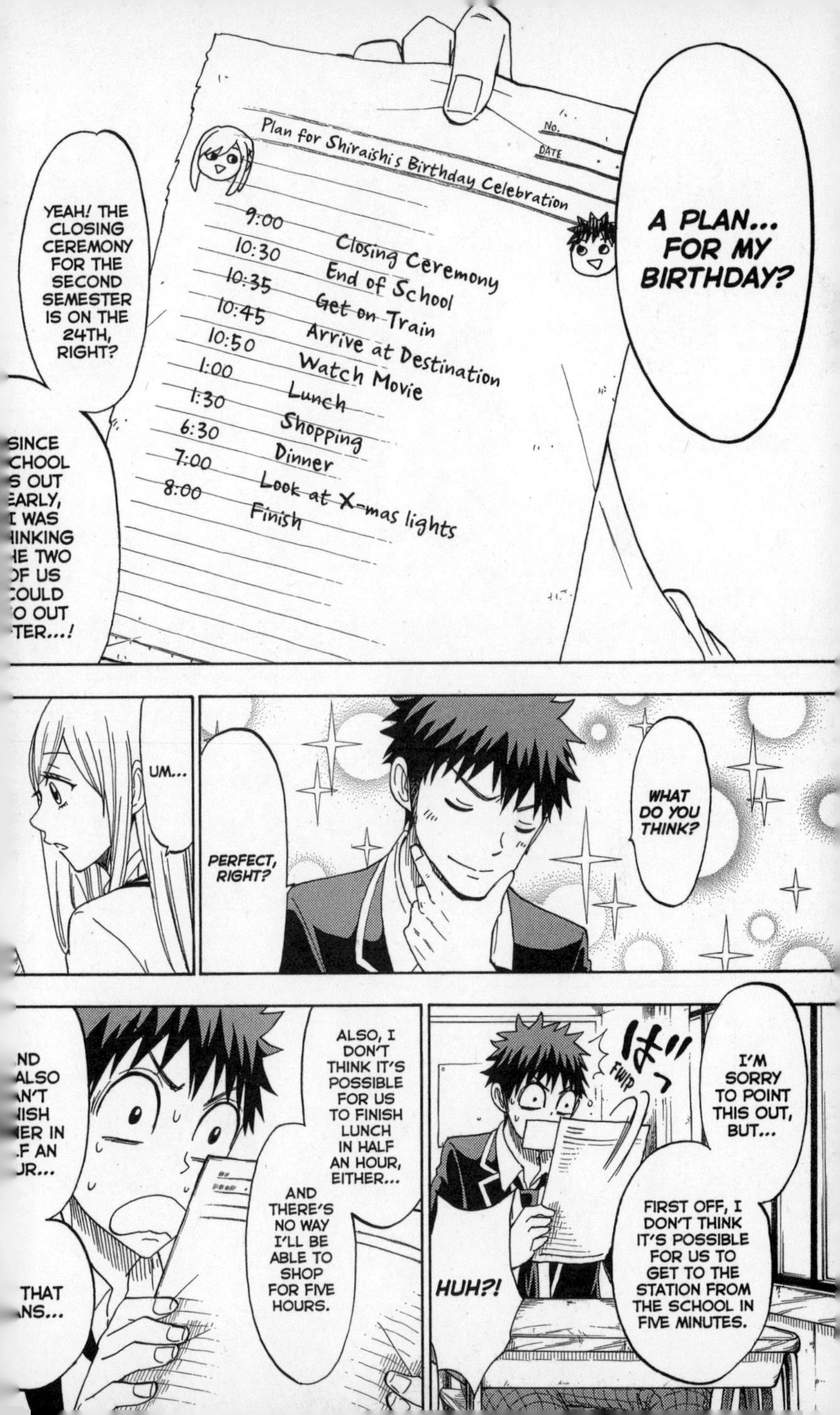

YEAH! THE CLOSING CEREMONY FOR THE SECOND SEMESTER IS ON THE 24TH, RIGHT?

SINCE SCHOOL IS OUT EARLY, I WAS THINKING THE TWO OF US COULD GO OUT TER...!

Plan for Shiraishi's Birthday Celebration

9:00	Closing Ceremony
10:30	End of School
10:35	Get on Train
10:45	Arrive at Destination
10:50	Watch Movie
1:00	Lunch
1:30	Shopping
6:30	Dinner
7:00	Look at X-mas lights
8:00	Finish

A PLAN... FOR MY BIRTHDAY?

UM...

PERFECT, RIGHT?

WHAT DO YOU THINK?

ND ALSO AN'T NISH NER IN .F AN UR...

THAT NS...

ALSO, I DON'T THINK IT'S POSSIBLE FOR US TO FINISH LUNCH IN HALF AN HOUR, EITHER...

AND THERE'S NO WAY I'LL BE ABLE TO SHOP FOR FIVE HOURS.

HUH?!

FWIP

I'M SORRY TO POINT THIS OUT, BUT...

FIRST OFF, I DON'T THINK IT'S POSSIBLE FOR US TO GET TO THE STATION FROM THE SCHOOL IN FIVE MINUTES.

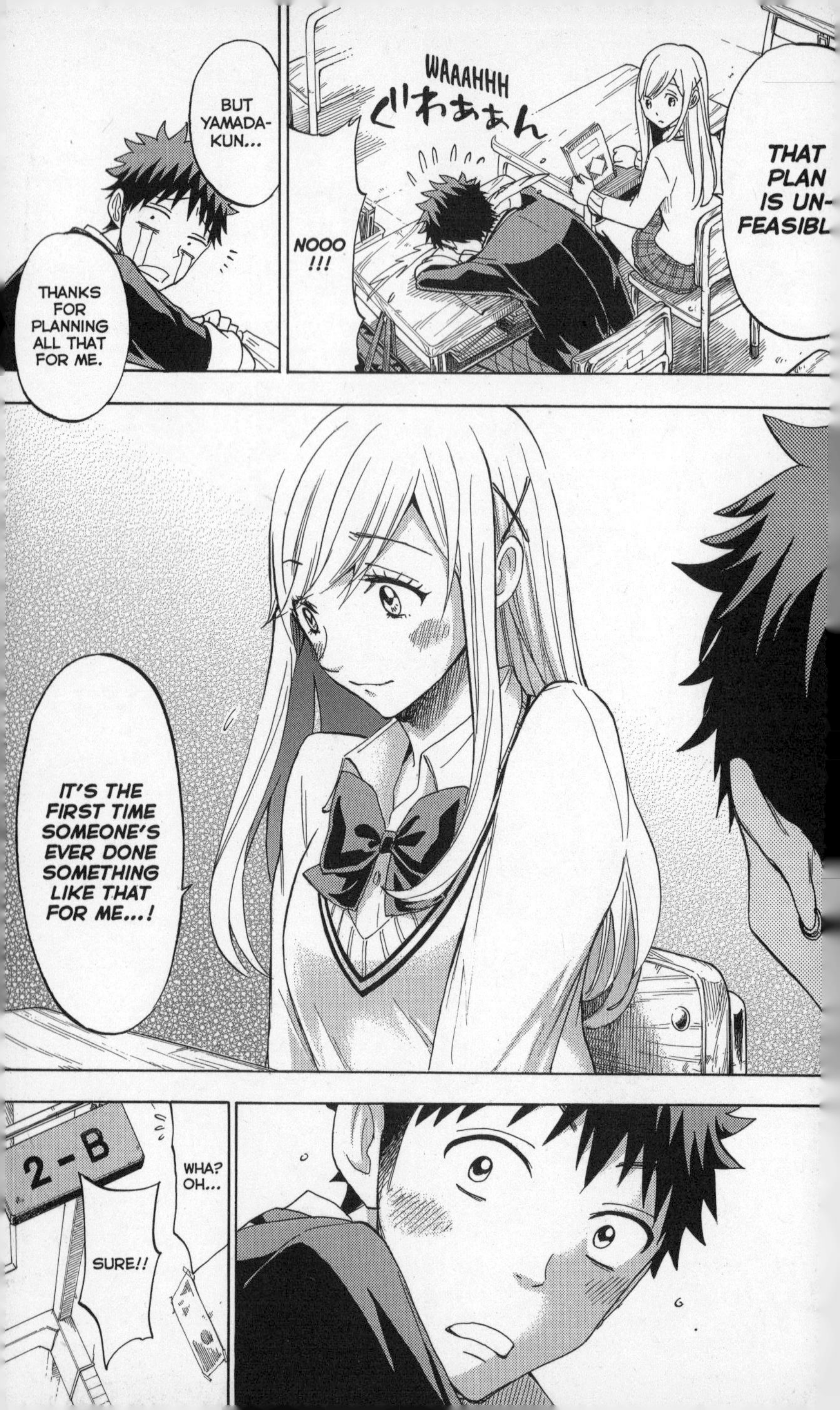
THAT PLAN IS UN-FEASIBL
WAAAHHH
ぐわぁぁん
NOOO !!!
BUT YAMADA-KUN...
THANKS FOR PLANNING ALL THAT FOR ME.
IT'S THE FIRST TIME SOMEONE'S EVER DONE SOMETHING LIKE THAT FOR ME...!
WHA? OH...
SURE!!
2-B

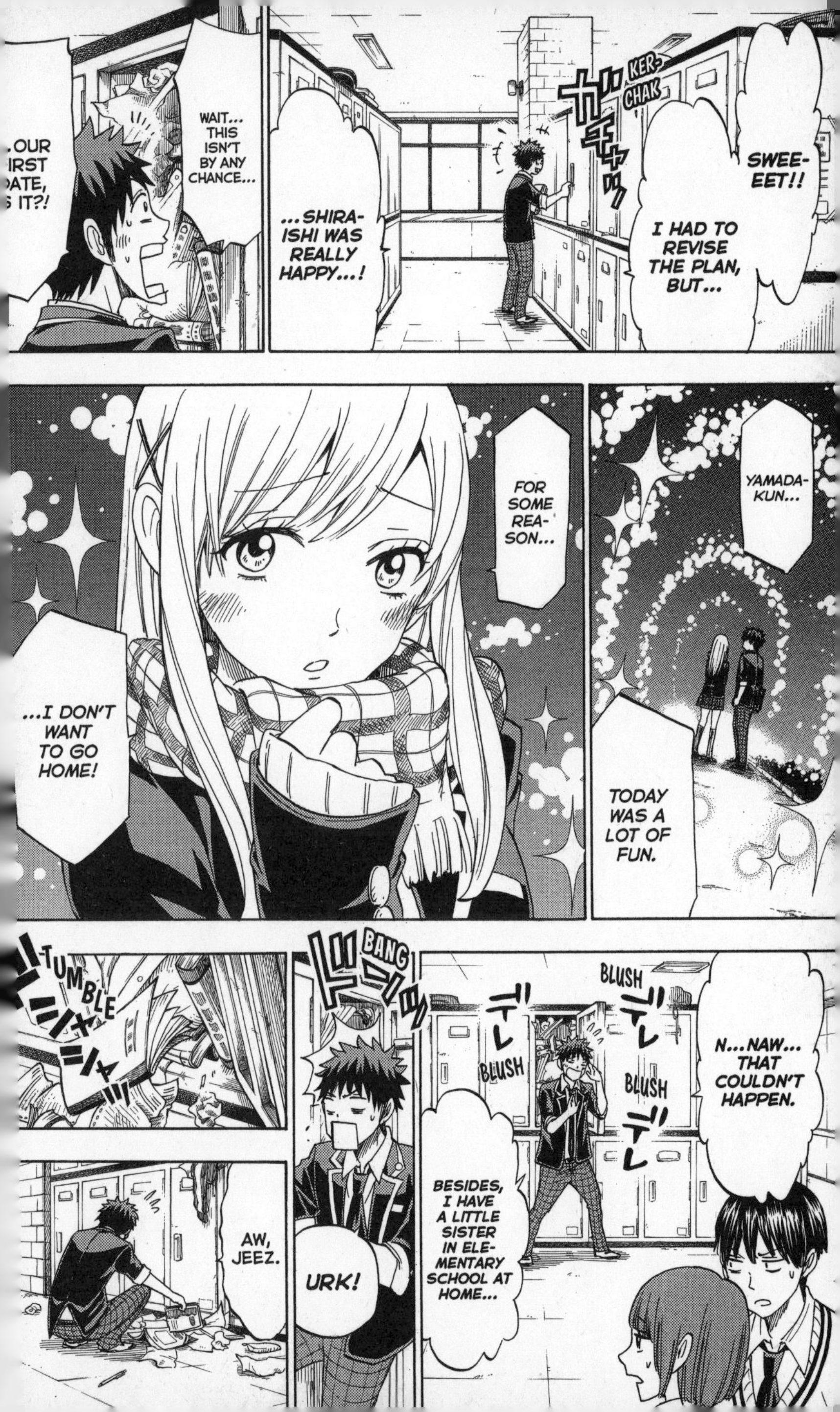
KER-CHAK
SWEEE-EET!!
I HAD TO REVISE THE PLAN, BUT...
...SHIRAISHI WAS REALLY HAPPY...!
WAIT... THIS ISN'T BY ANY CHANCE...
.OUR IRST DATE, S IT?!
YAMADA-KUN...
TODAY WAS A LOT OF FUN.
FOR SOME REASON...
...I DON'T WANT TO GO HOME!
N...NAW... THAT COULDN'T HAPPEN.
BLUSH
BLUSH
BLUSH
BESIDES, I HAVE A LITTLE SISTER IN ELEMENTARY SCHOOL AT HOME...
BANG
URK!
TUMBLE
AW, JEEZ.

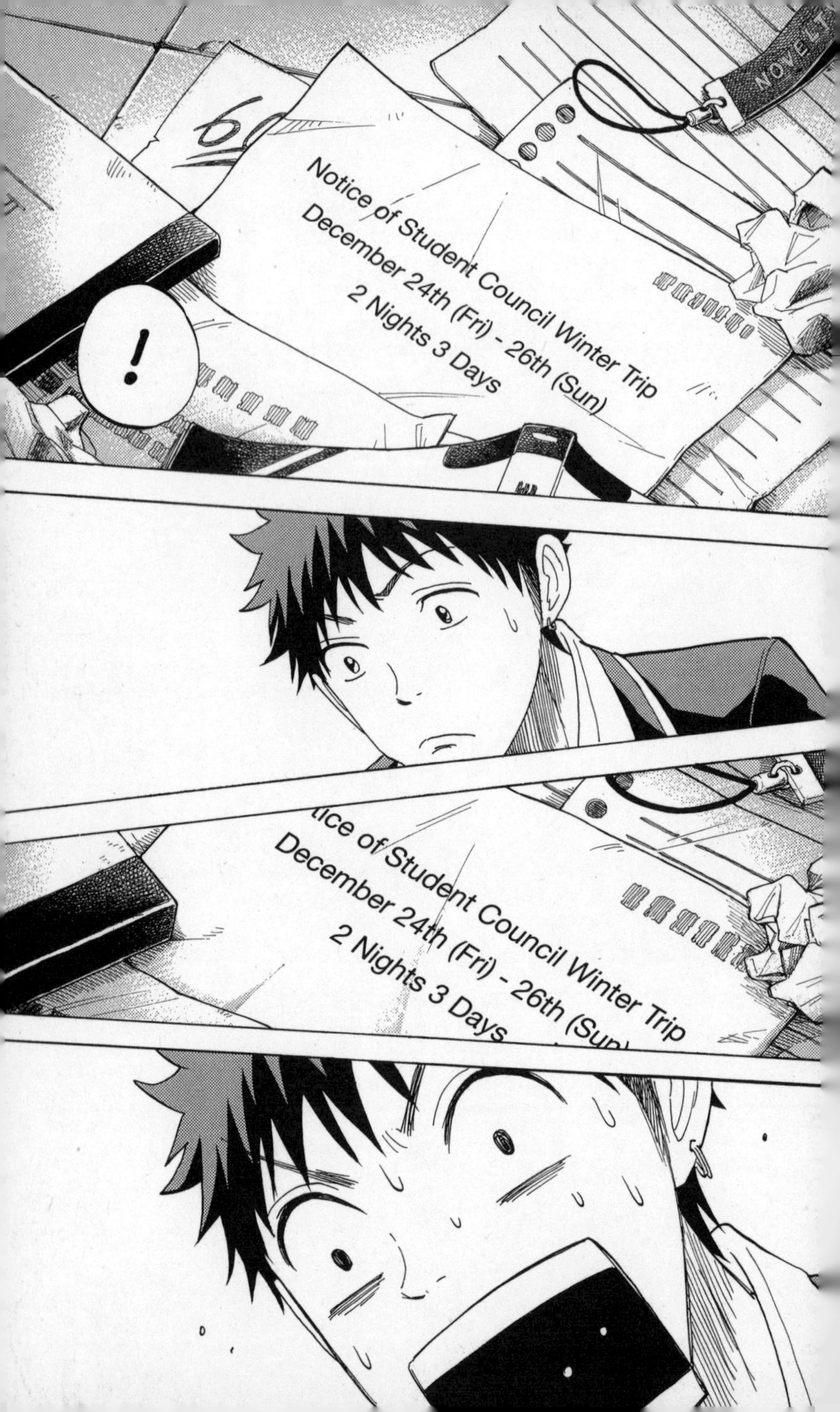
NOVELT
Notice of Student Council Winter Trip
December 24th (Fri) - 26th (Sun)
2 Nights 3 Days
!
tice of Student Council Winter Trip
December 24th (Fri) - 26th (Sun
2 Nights 3 Days

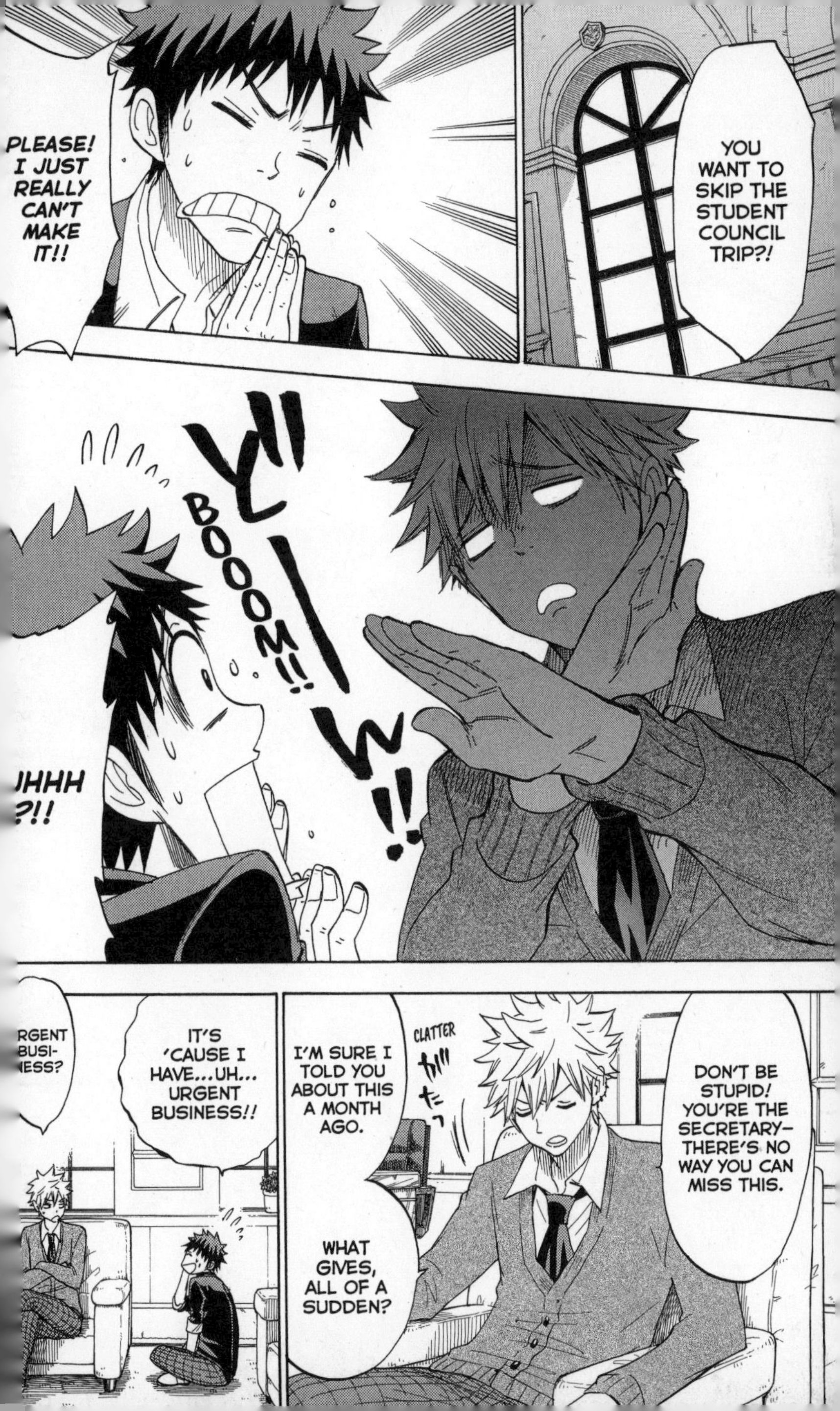
YOU WANT TO SKIP THE STUDENT COUNCIL TRIP?!
PLEASE! I JUST REALLY CAN'T MAKE IT!!
BOOOOM!!
HHH ?!!
DON'T BE STUPID! YOU'RE THE SECRETARY—THERE'S NO WAY YOU CAN MISS THIS.
CLATTER
I'M SURE I TOLD YOU ABOUT THIS A MONTH AGO.
WHAT GIVES, ALL OF A SUDDEN?
IT'S 'CAUSE I HAVE...UH... URGENT BUSINESS!!
RGENT BUSI-NESS?

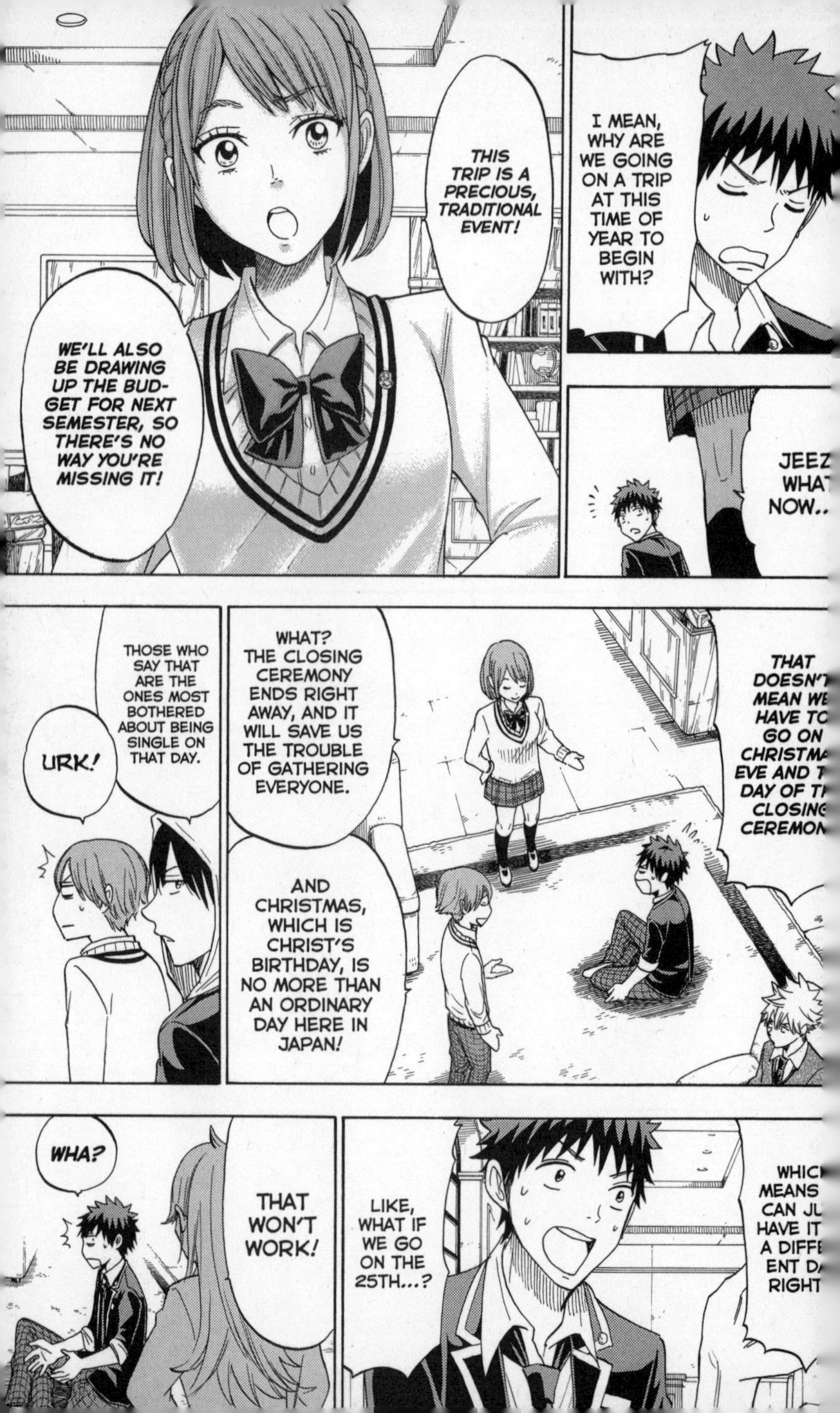
I MEAN, WHY ARE WE GOING ON A TRIP AT THIS TIME OF YEAR TO BEGIN WITH?
JEEZ WHAT NOW..
THIS TRIP IS A PRECIOUS, TRADITIONAL EVENT!
WE'LL ALSO BE DRAWING UP THE BUD-GET FOR NEXT SEMESTER, SO THERE'S NO WAY YOU'RE MISSING IT!
THAT DOESN'T MEAN WE HAVE TO GO ON CHRISTMAS EVE AND T DAY OF TH CLOSING CEREMON
WHAT? THE CLOSING CEREMONY ENDS RIGHT AWAY, AND IT WILL SAVE US THE TROUBLE OF GATHERING EVERYONE.
AND CHRISTMAS, WHICH IS CHRIST'S BIRTHDAY, IS NO MORE THAN AN ORDINARY DAY HERE IN JAPAN!
THOSE WHO SAY THAT ARE THE ONES MOST BOTHERED ABOUT BEING SINGLE ON THAT DAY.
URK!
WHICH MEANS CAN JU HAVE IT A DIFFE ENT DA RIGHT
LIKE, WHAT IF WE GO ON THE 25TH...?
THAT WON'T WORK!
WHA?

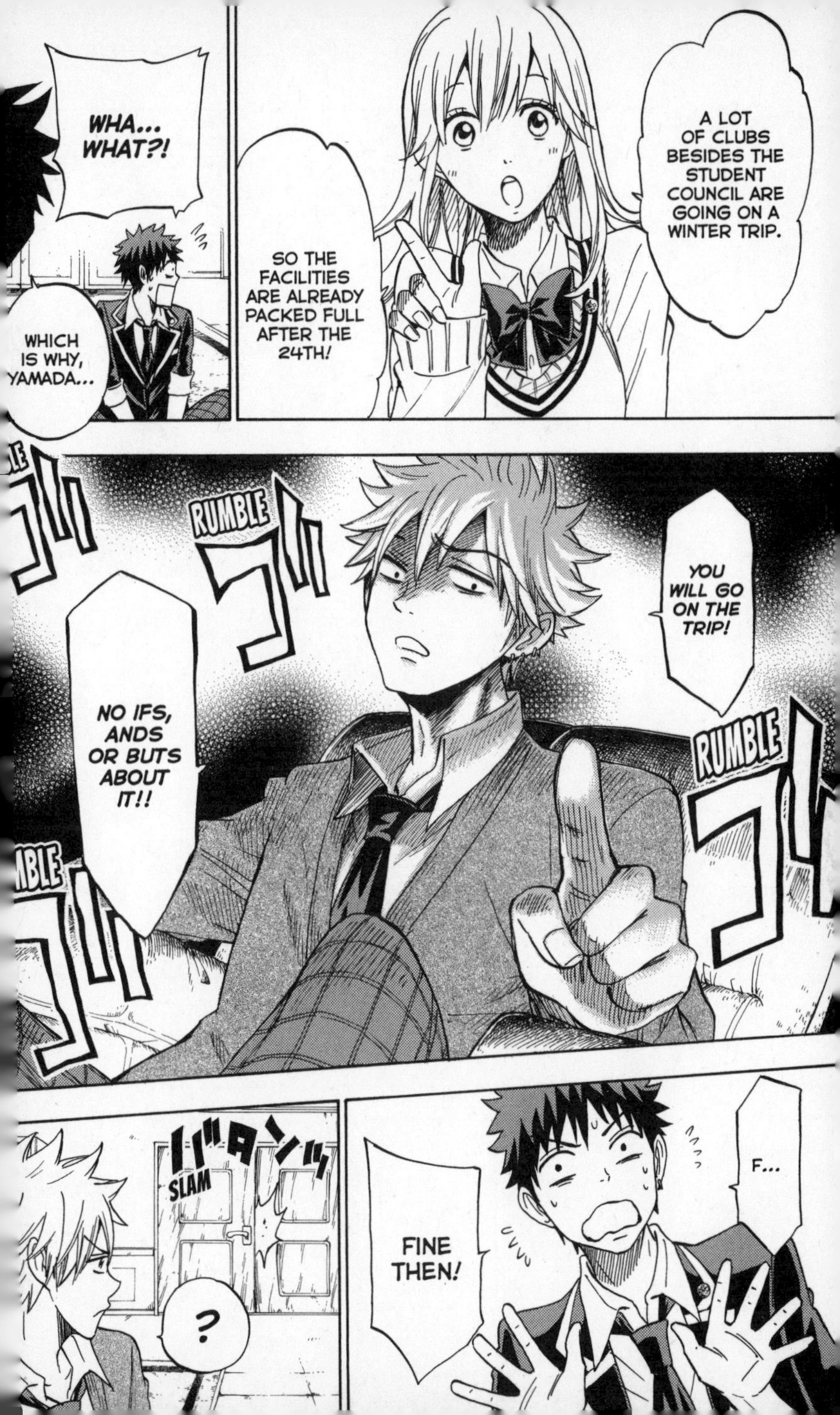
A LOT OF CLUBS BESIDES THE STUDENT COUNCIL ARE GOING ON A WINTER TRIP.
SO THE FACILITIES ARE ALREADY PACKED FULL AFTER THE 24TH!
WHA... WHAT?!
WHICH IS WHY, YAMADA...
RUMBLE
YOU WILL GO ON THE TRIP!
RUMBLE
NO IFS, ANDS OR BUTS ABOUT IT!!
RUMBLE
F...
FINE THEN!
SLAM
?

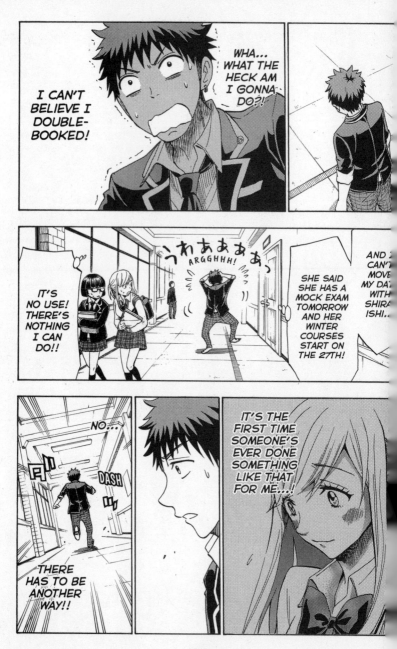

WHA... WHAT THE HECK AM I GONNA DO?!
I CAN'T BELIEVE I DOUBLE-BOOKED!
AND I CAN'T MOVE MY DA WITH SHIRA ISHI..
SHE SAID SHE HAS A MOCK EXAM TOMORROW AND HER WINTER COURSES START ON THE 27TH!
うわあああああ
ARGGHHH!
IT'S NO USE! THERE'S NOTHING I CAN DO!!
IT'S THE FIRST TIME SOMEONE'S EVER DONE SOMETHING LIKE THAT FOR ME...!
NO...
DASH
THERE HAS TO BE ANOTHER WAY!!

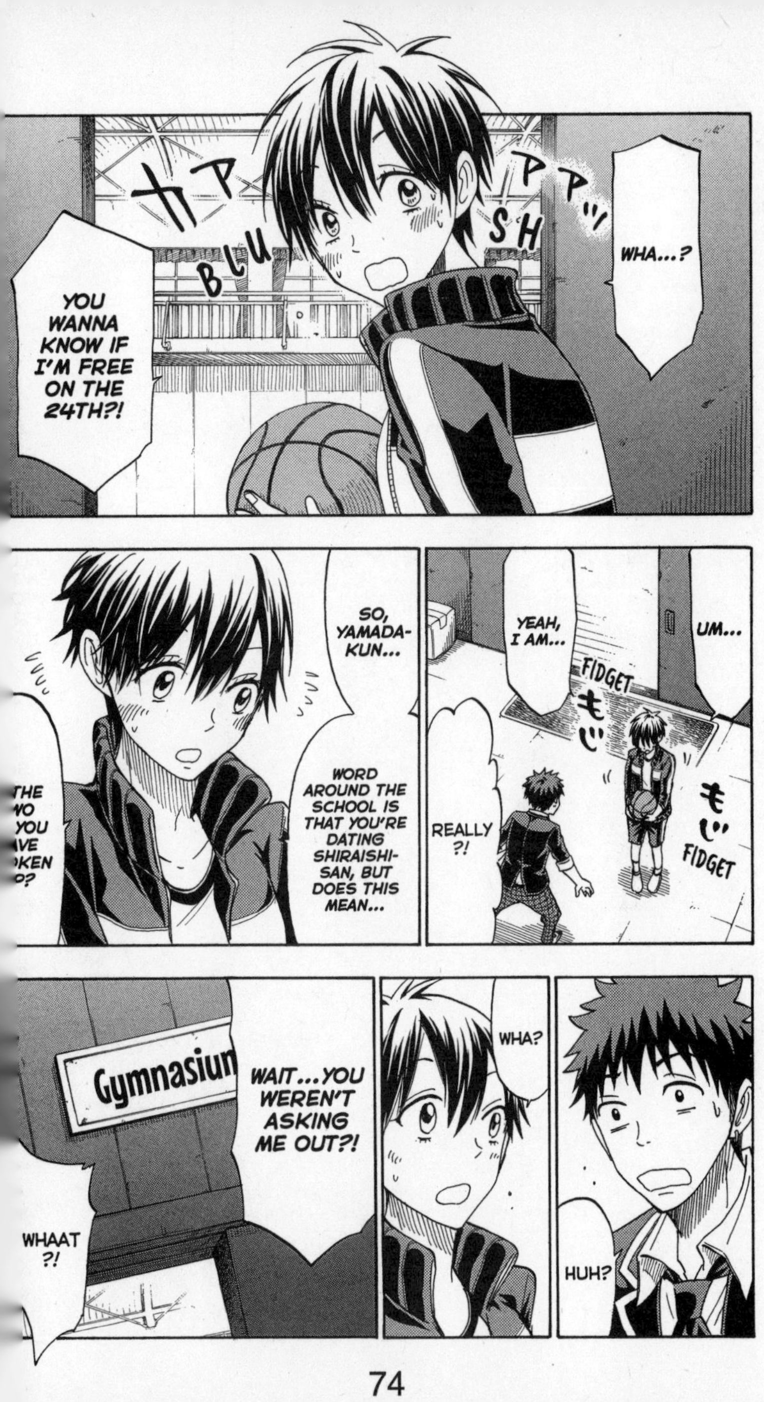
WHA...?
BLUSH
カァッ
YOU WANNA KNOW IF I'M FREE ON THE 24TH?!
UM...
YEAH, I AM...
FIDGET
もじ
もじ
FIDGET
REALLY?!
SO, YAMADA-KUN...
WORD AROUND THE SCHOOL IS THAT YOU'RE DATING SHIRAISHI-SAN, BUT DOES THIS MEAN...
THE WO YOU AVE OKEN ?
HUH?
WHA?
WAIT...YOU WEREN'T ASKING ME OUT?!
Gymnasiun
WHAAT?!

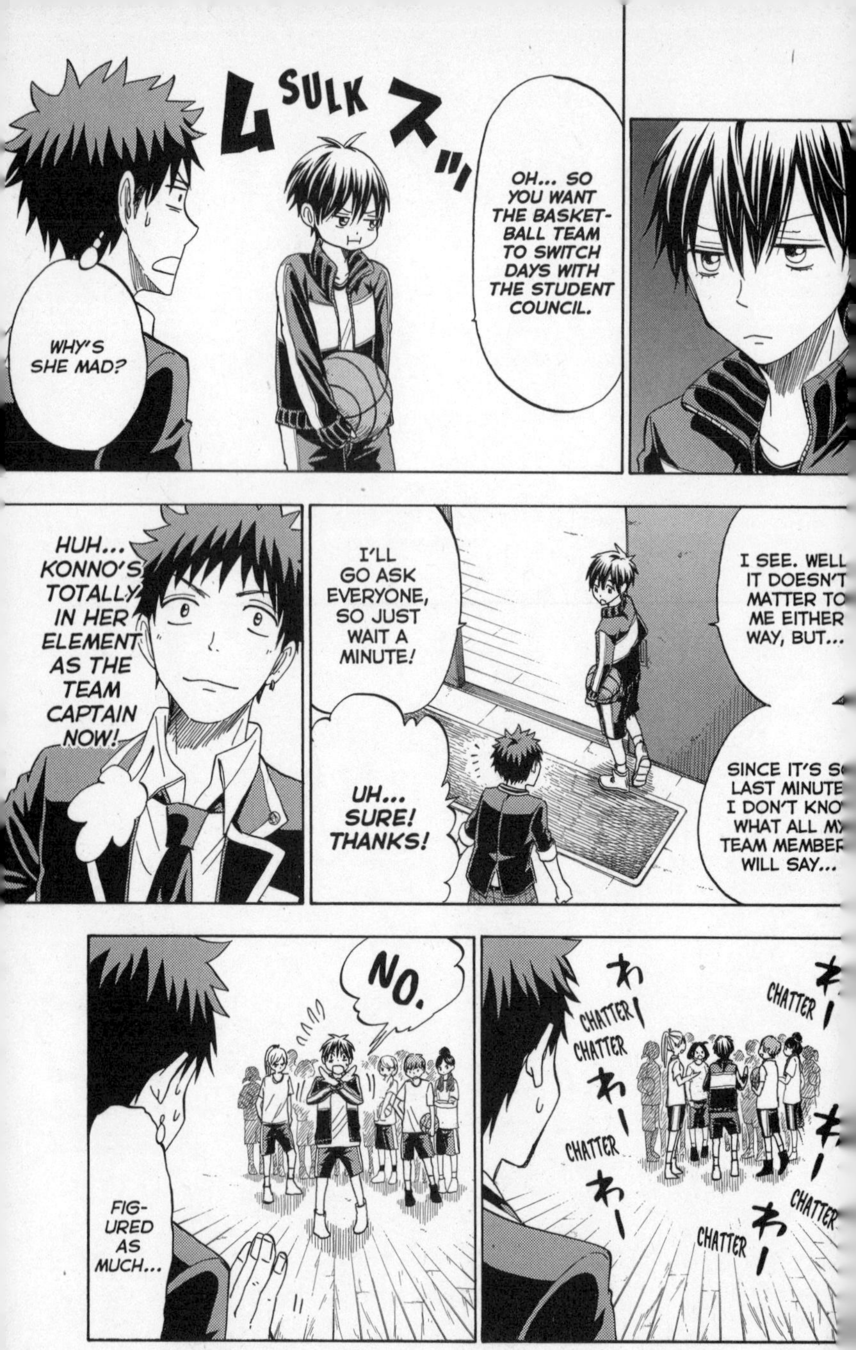
OH... SO YOU WANT THE BASKET-BALL TEAM TO SWITCH DAYS WITH THE STUDENT COUNCIL.
ムスッ
SULK
WHY'S SHE MAD?
I SEE. WELL IT DOESN'T MATTER TO ME EITHER WAY, BUT...
SINCE IT'S S LAST MINUTE I DON'T KNO WHAT ALL MY TEAM MEMBER WILL SAY...
I'LL GO ASK EVERYONE, SO JUST WAIT A MINUTE!
UH... SURE! THANKS!
HUH... KONNO'S TOTALLY IN HER ELEMENT AS THE TEAM CAPTAIN NOW!
CHATTER
CHATTER
CHATTER
CHATTER
CHATTER
CHATTER
NO.
FIG-URED AS MUCH...

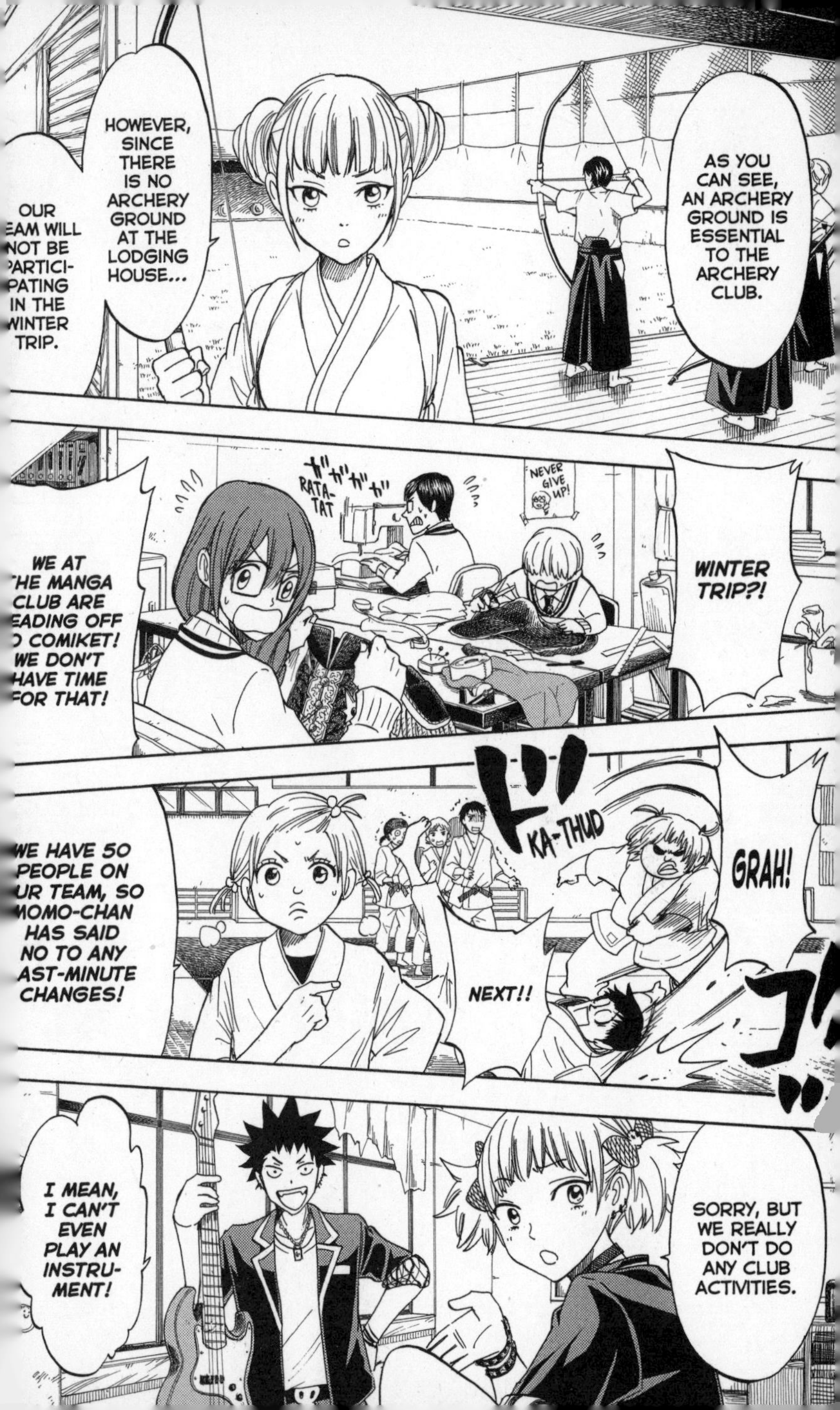
AS YOU CAN SEE, AN ARCHERY GROUND IS ESSENTIAL TO THE ARCHERY CLUB.
HOWEVER, SINCE THERE IS NO ARCHERY GROUND AT THE LODGING HOUSE...
OUR EAM WILL NOT BE PARTICI- PATING IN THE WINTER TRIP.
WINTER TRIP?!
NEVER GIVE UP!
RATA-TAT
WE AT HE MANGA CLUB ARE EADING OFF O COMIKET! WE DON'T HAVE TIME FOR THAT!
GRAH!
KA-THUD
NEXT!!
WE HAVE 50 PEOPLE ON UR TEAM, SO MOMO-CHAN HAS SAID NO TO ANY AST-MINUTE CHANGES!
SORRY, BUT WE REALLY DON'T DO ANY CLUB ACTIVITIES.
I MEAN, I CAN'T EVEN PLAY AN INSTRU- MENT!

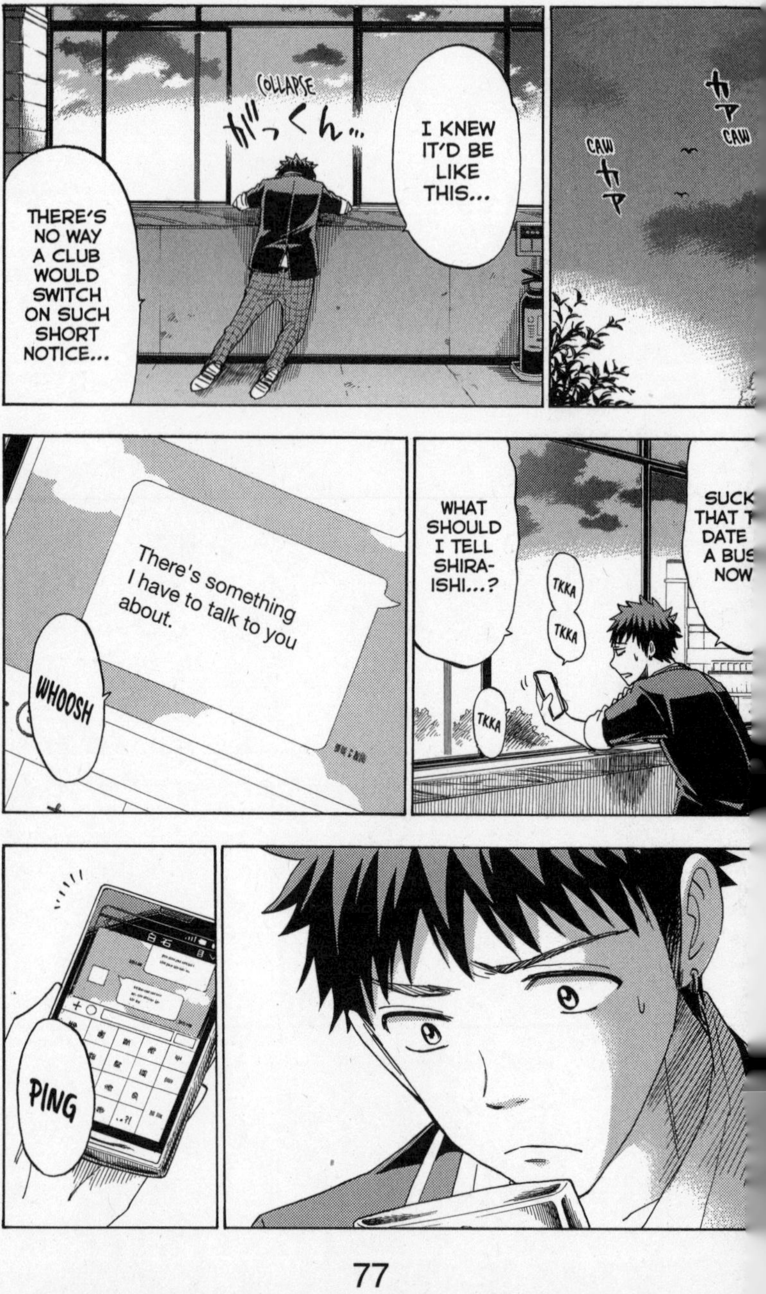
カァ CAW
CAW カァ
I KNEW IT'D BE LIKE THIS...
COLLAPSE
がっくん…
THERE'S NO WAY A CLUB WOULD SWITCH ON SUCH SHORT NOTICE...
SUCK THAT T DATE A BUS NOW
WHAT SHOULD I TELL SHIRA-ISHI...?
TKKA
TKKA
TKKA
There's something I have to talk to you about.
WHOOSH
PING

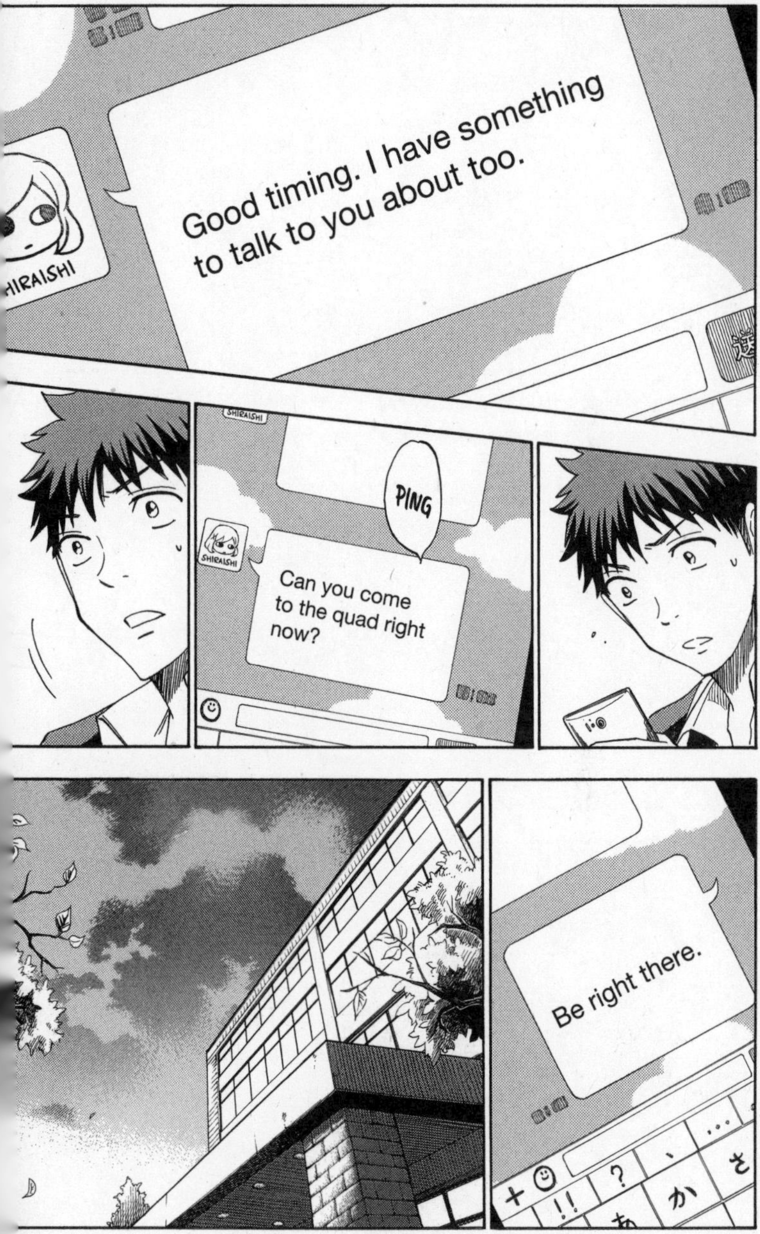
SHIRAISHI
Good timing. I have something to talk to you about too.
SHIRAISHI
PING
Can you come to the quad right now?
Be right there.

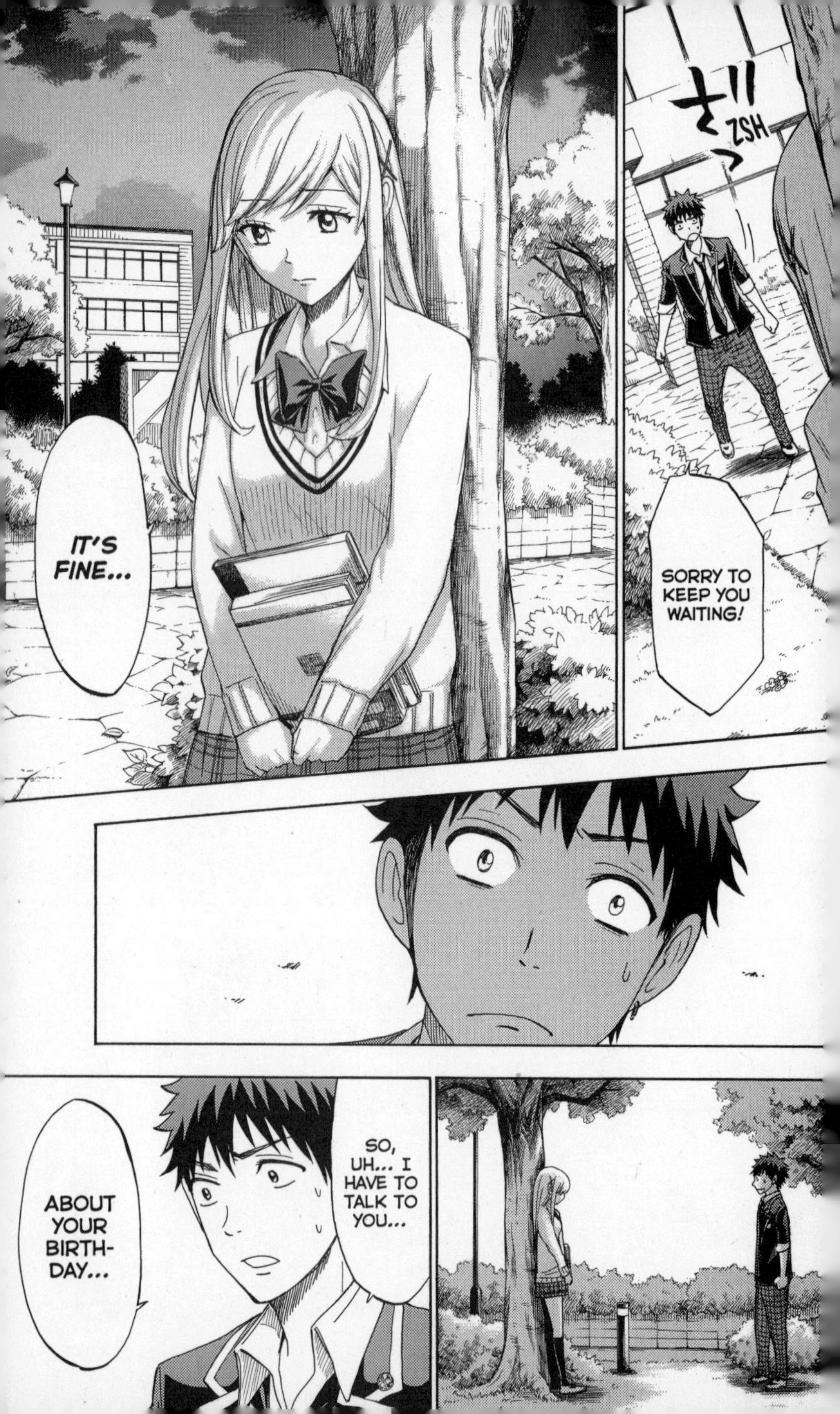
ZSH
SORRY TO KEEP YOU WAITING!
IT'S FINE...
SO, UH... I HAVE TO TALK TO YOU...
ABOUT YOUR BIRTH-DAY...

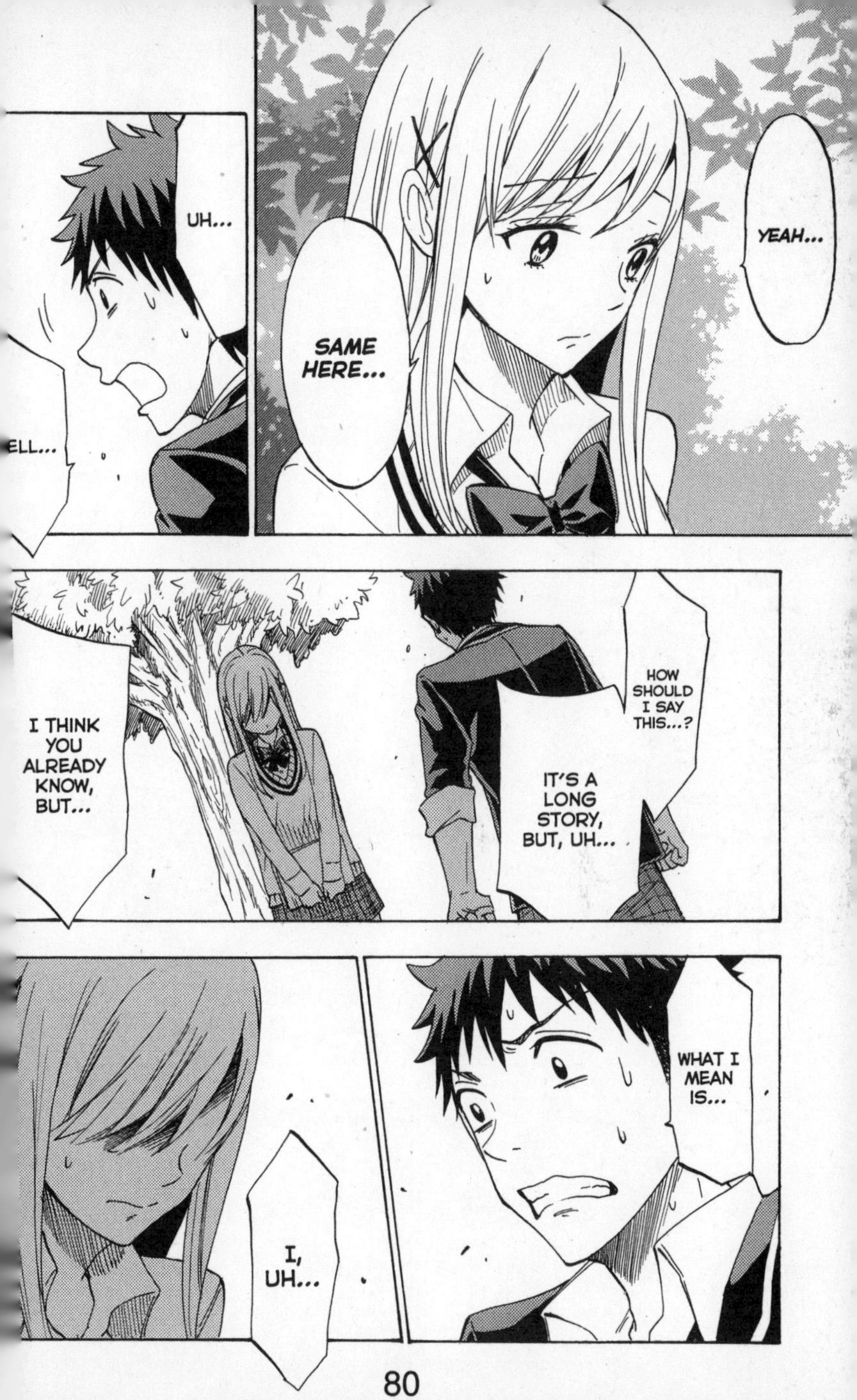
YEAH...
SAME HERE...
UH...
ELL...
HOW SHOULD I SAY THIS...?
IT'S A LONG STORY, BUT, UH...
I THINK YOU ALREADY KNOW, BUT...
WHAT I MEAN IS...
I, UH...

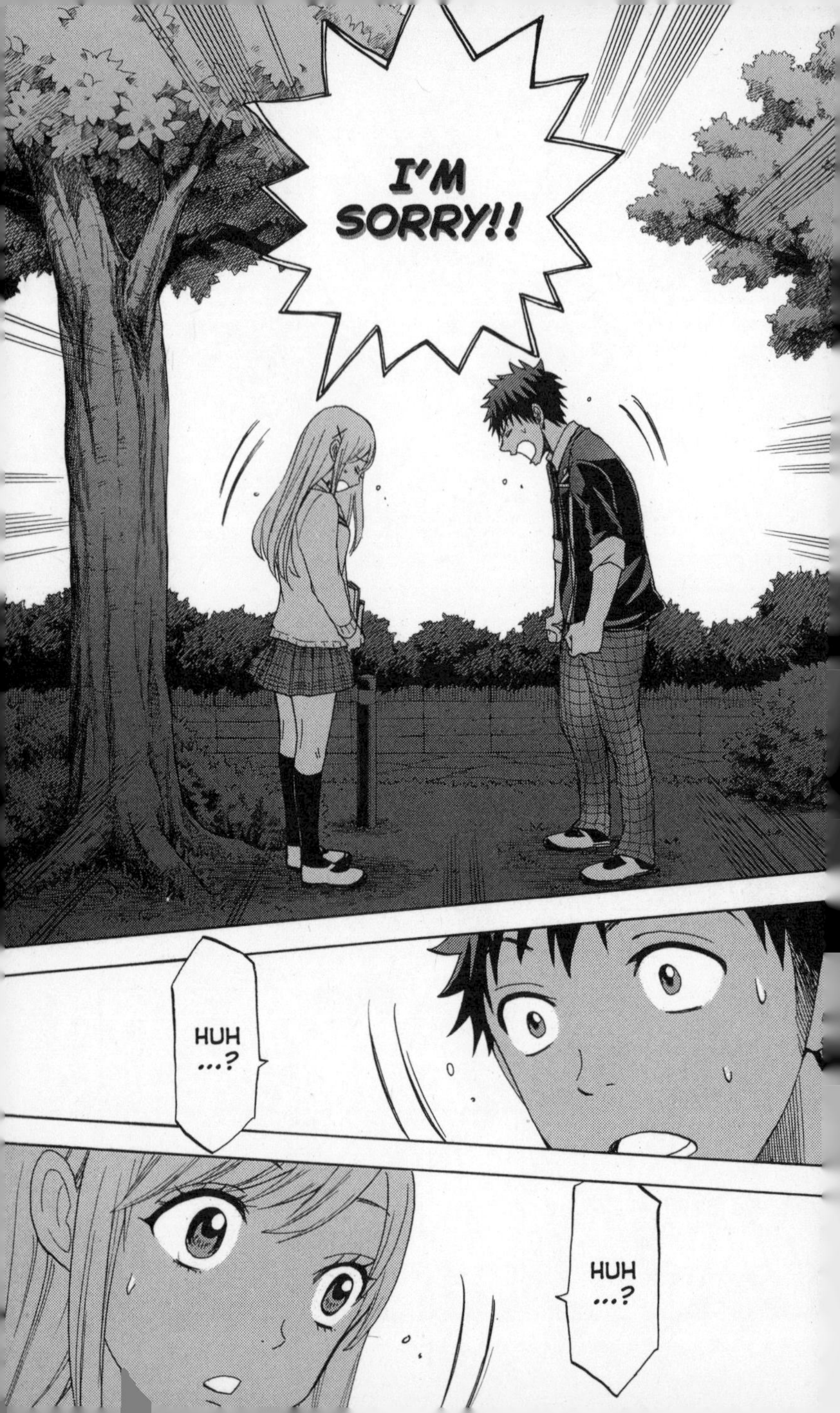
I'M SORRY!!
HUH ...?
HUH ...?

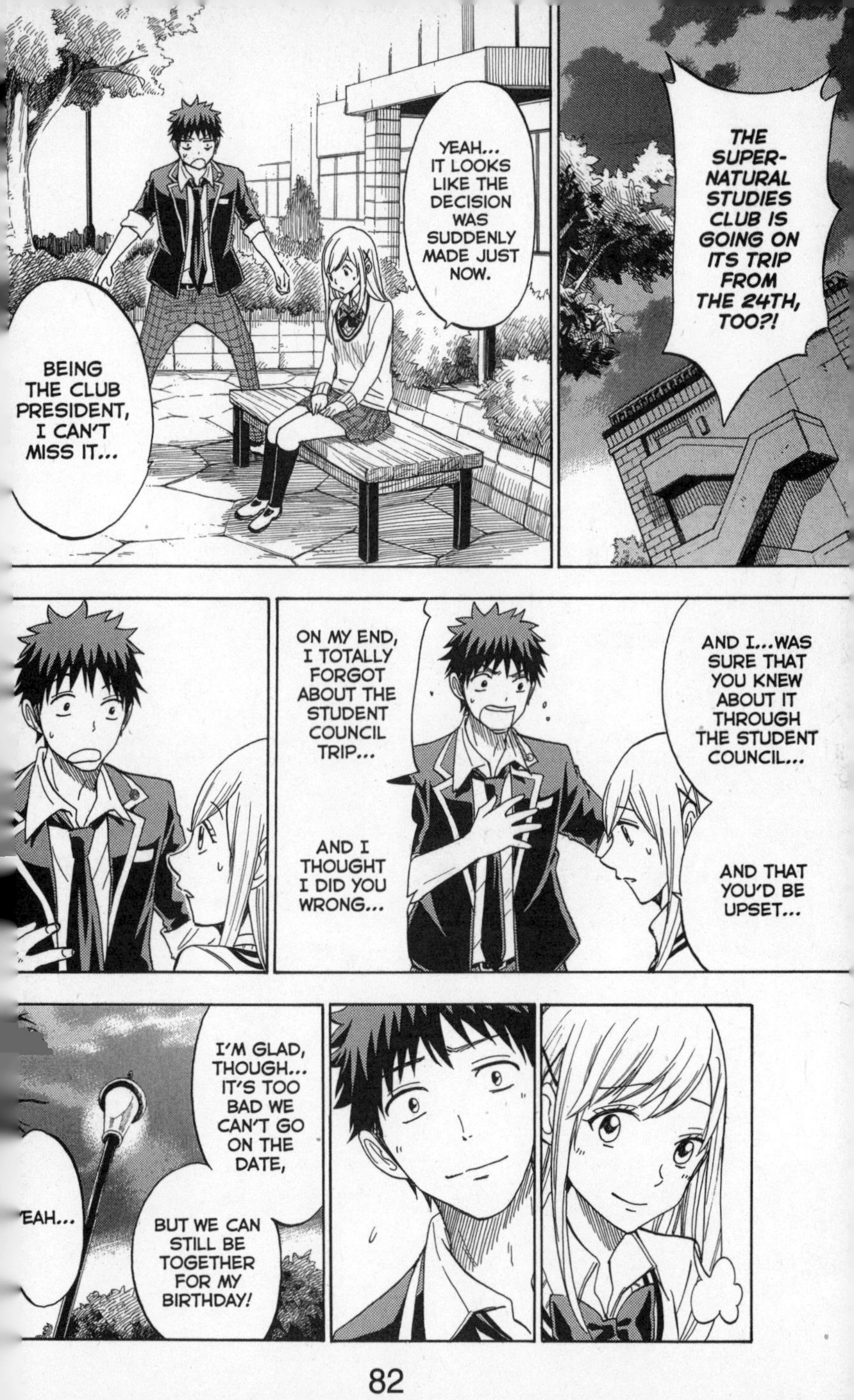
THE SUPER-NATURAL STUDIES CLUB IS GOING ON ITS TRIP FROM THE 24TH, TOO?!
YEAH... IT LOOKS LIKE THE DECISION WAS SUDDENLY MADE JUST NOW.
BEING THE CLUB PRESIDENT, I CAN'T MISS IT...
AND I...WAS SURE THAT YOU KNEW ABOUT IT THROUGH THE STUDENT COUNCIL...
AND THAT YOU'D BE UPSET...
ON MY END, I TOTALLY FORGOT ABOUT THE STUDENT COUNCIL TRIP...
AND I THOUGHT I DID YOU WRONG...
I'M GLAD, THOUGH... IT'S TOO BAD WE CAN'T GO ON THE DATE,
BUT WE CAN STILL BE TOGETHER FOR MY BIRTHDAY!
EAH...

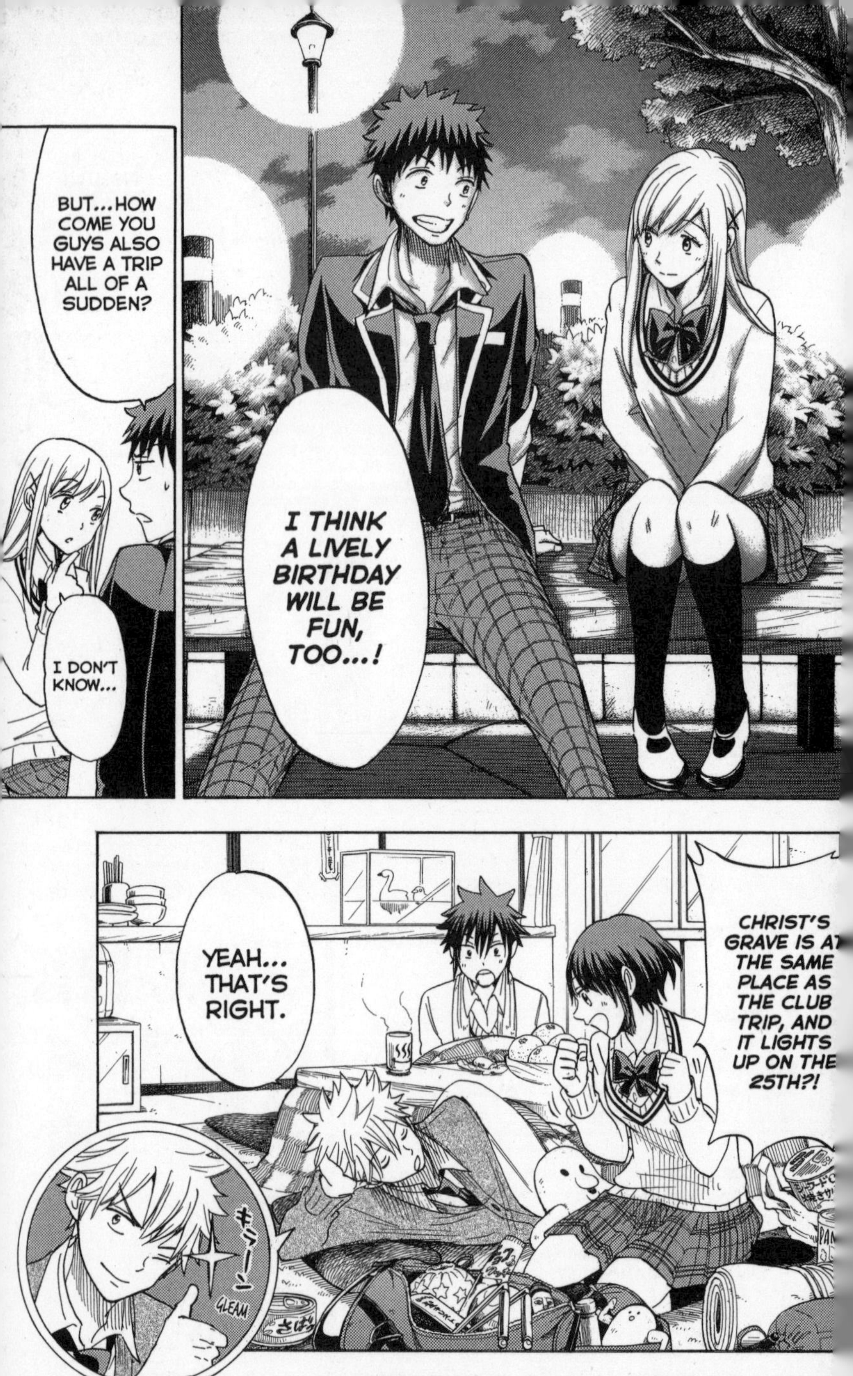
I THINK A LIVELY BIRTHDAY WILL BE FUN, TOO...!
BUT...HOW COME YOU GUYS ALSO HAVE A TRIP ALL OF A SUDDEN?
I DON'T KNOW...
CHRIST'S GRAVE IS A THE SAME PLACE AS THE CLUB TRIP, AND IT LIGHTS UP ON THE 25TH?!
YEAH... THAT'S RIGHT.
キラーン
GLEAM

Suzaku Gallery

This is where we'll introduce illustrations that we've received from all of you!

Selected artists will receive a signed shikishi from the series creator! When you make a submission, please make sure to clearly write your address, name, and phone number! If you don't, we won't be able to send you a prize even if you're selected! Looking forward to all your submissions!

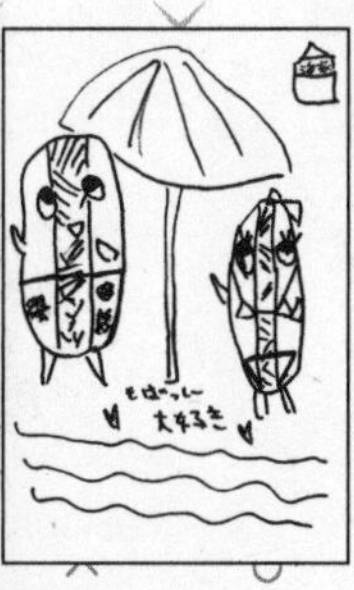

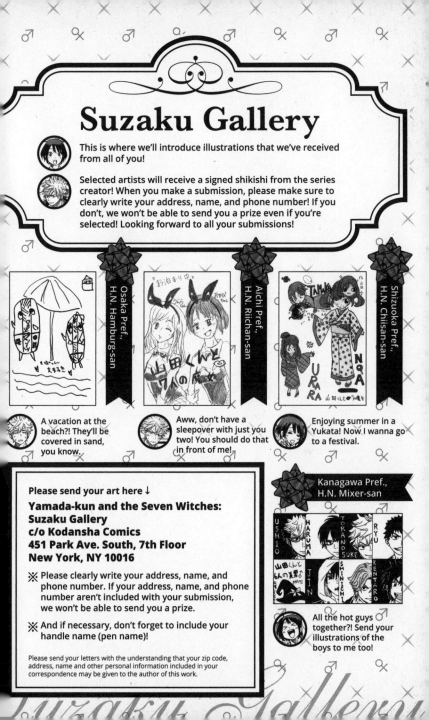

Osaka Pref.,
H.N. Hamburg-san

A vacation at the beach?! They'll be covered in sand, you know.

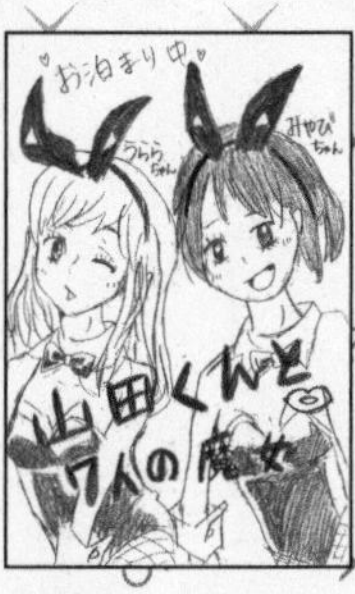
お泊まり中
山田くんと7人の魔女

Aichi Pref.,
H.N. Riichan-san

Aww, don't have a sleepover with just you two! You should do that in front of me!

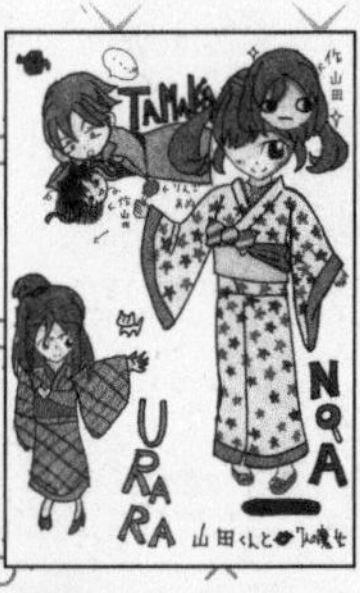
URARA
NOA
山田くんと7人の魔女

Shizuoka Pref.,
H.N. Chiisan-san

Enjoying summer in a Yukata! Now I wanna go to a festival.

Please send your art here ↓

Yamada-kun and the Seven Witches:
Suzaku Gallery
c/o Kodansha Comics
451 Park Ave. South, 7th Floor
New York, NY 10016

※ Please clearly write your address, name, and phone number. If your address, name, and phone number aren't included with your submission, we won't be able to send you a prize.

※ And if necessary, don't forget to include your handle name (pen name)!

Please send your letters with the understanding that your zip code, address, name and other personal information included in your correspondence may be given to the author of this work.

Kanagawa Pref.,
H.N. Mixer-san

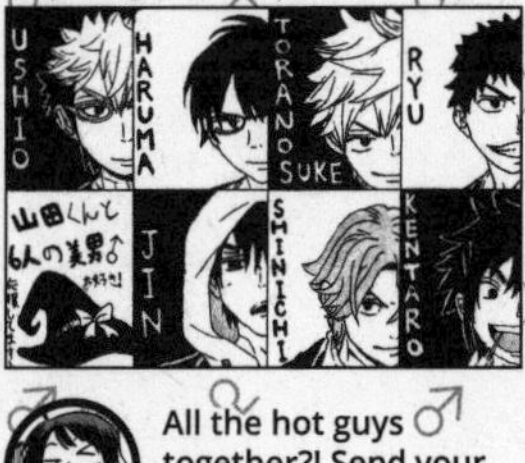
USHIO
HARUMA
TORANOSUKE
RYU
JIN
SHINICHI
KENTARO

All the hot guys together?! Send your illustrations of the boys to me too!

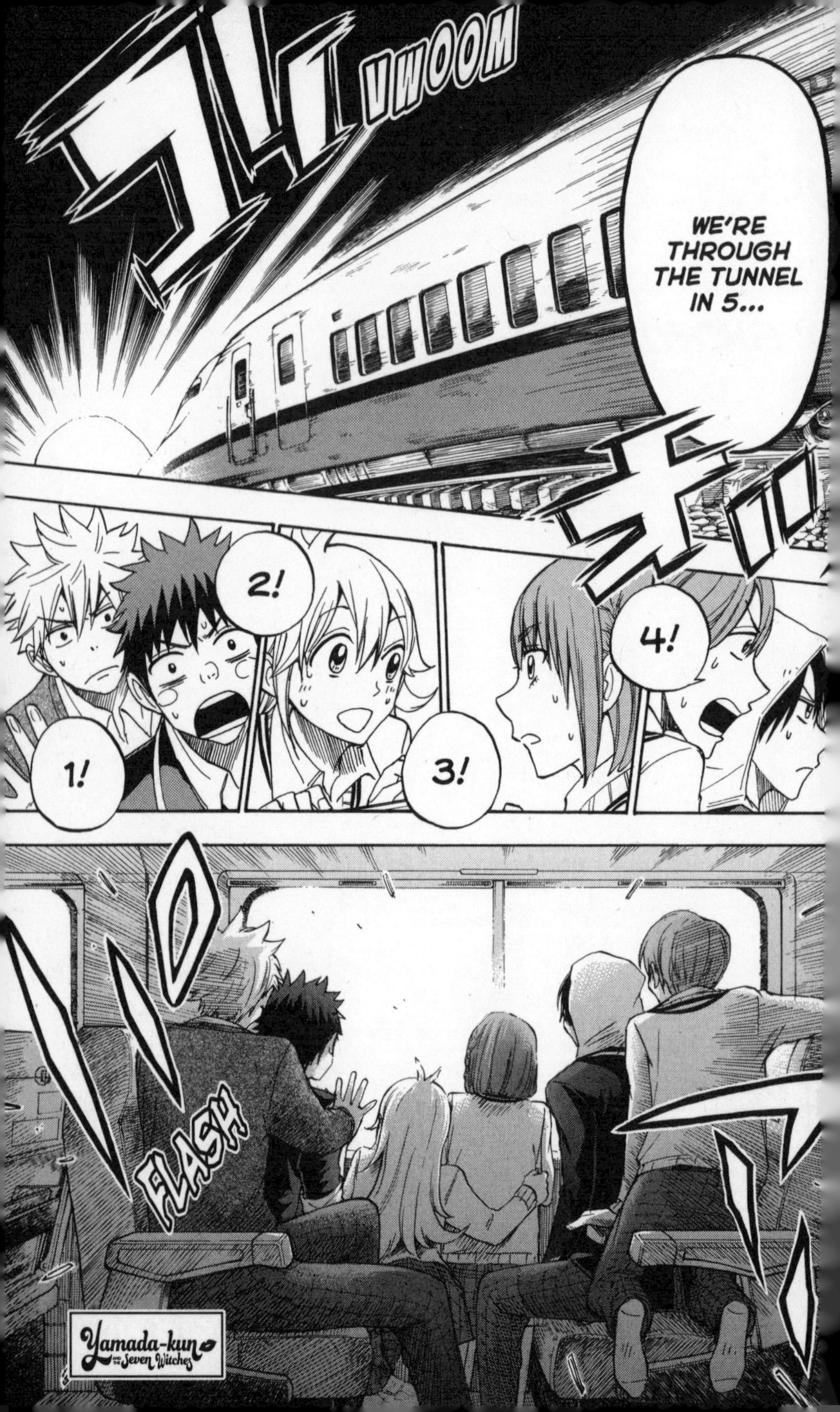
VWOOM
WE'RE THROUGH THE TUNNEL IN 5...
4!
3!
2!
1!
FLASH
Yamada-kun and the Seven Witches

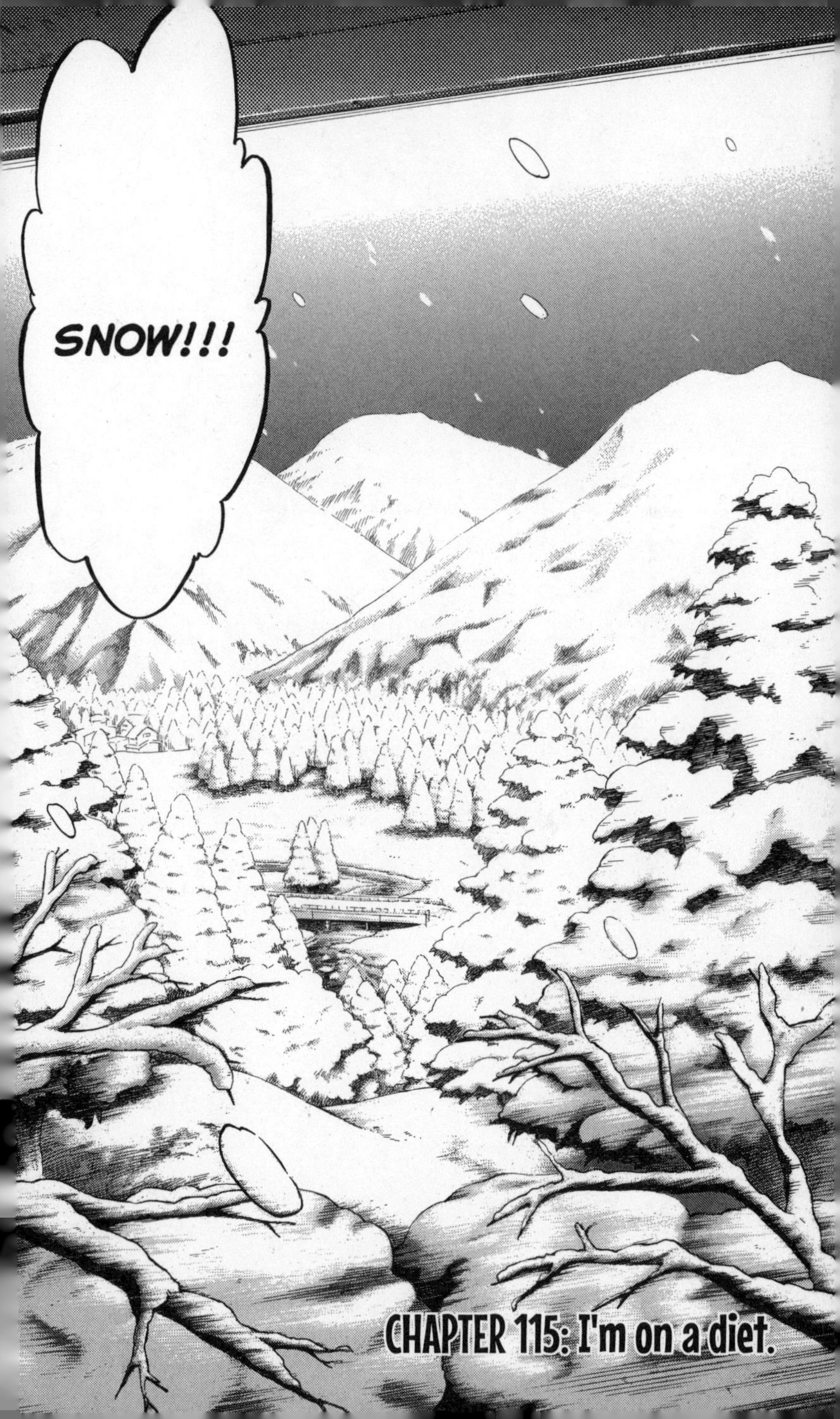
SNOW!!!

CHAPTER 115: I'm on a diet.

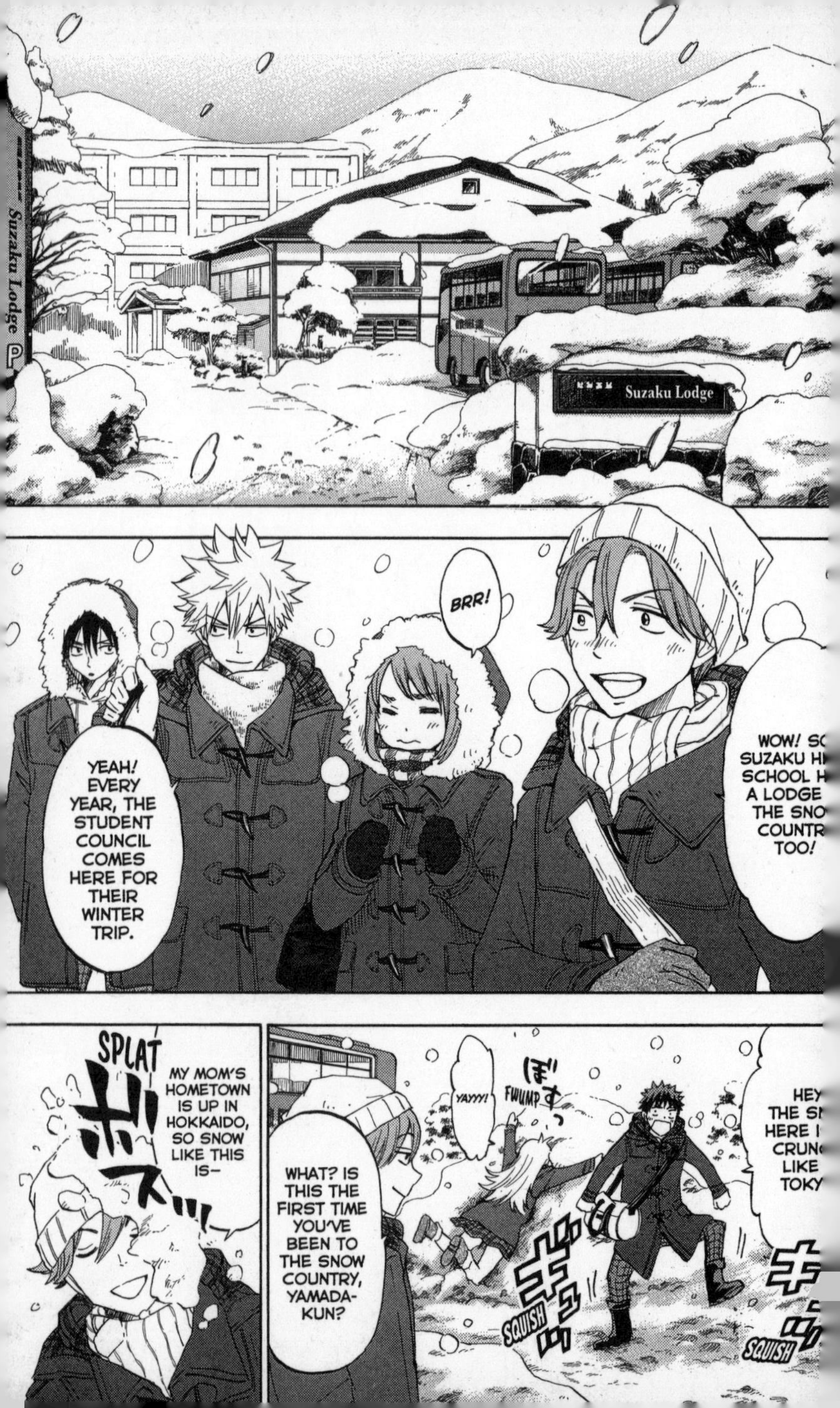

Suzaku Lodge
Suzaku Lodge
WOW! SO SUZAKU HI SCHOOL H A LODGE THE SNO COUNTR TOO!
BRR!
YEAH! EVERY YEAR, THE STUDENT COUNCIL COMES HERE FOR THEIR WINTER TRIP.
HEY THE SN HERE I CRUNC LIKE TOKY
SQUISH
YAYYY!
ぼすっ
FWUMP
SQUISH
WHAT? IS THIS THE FIRST TIME YOU'VE BEEN TO THE SNOW COUNTRY, YAMADA-KUN?
MY MOM'S HOMETOWN IS UP IN HOKKAIDO, SO SNOW LIKE THIS IS—
SPLAT

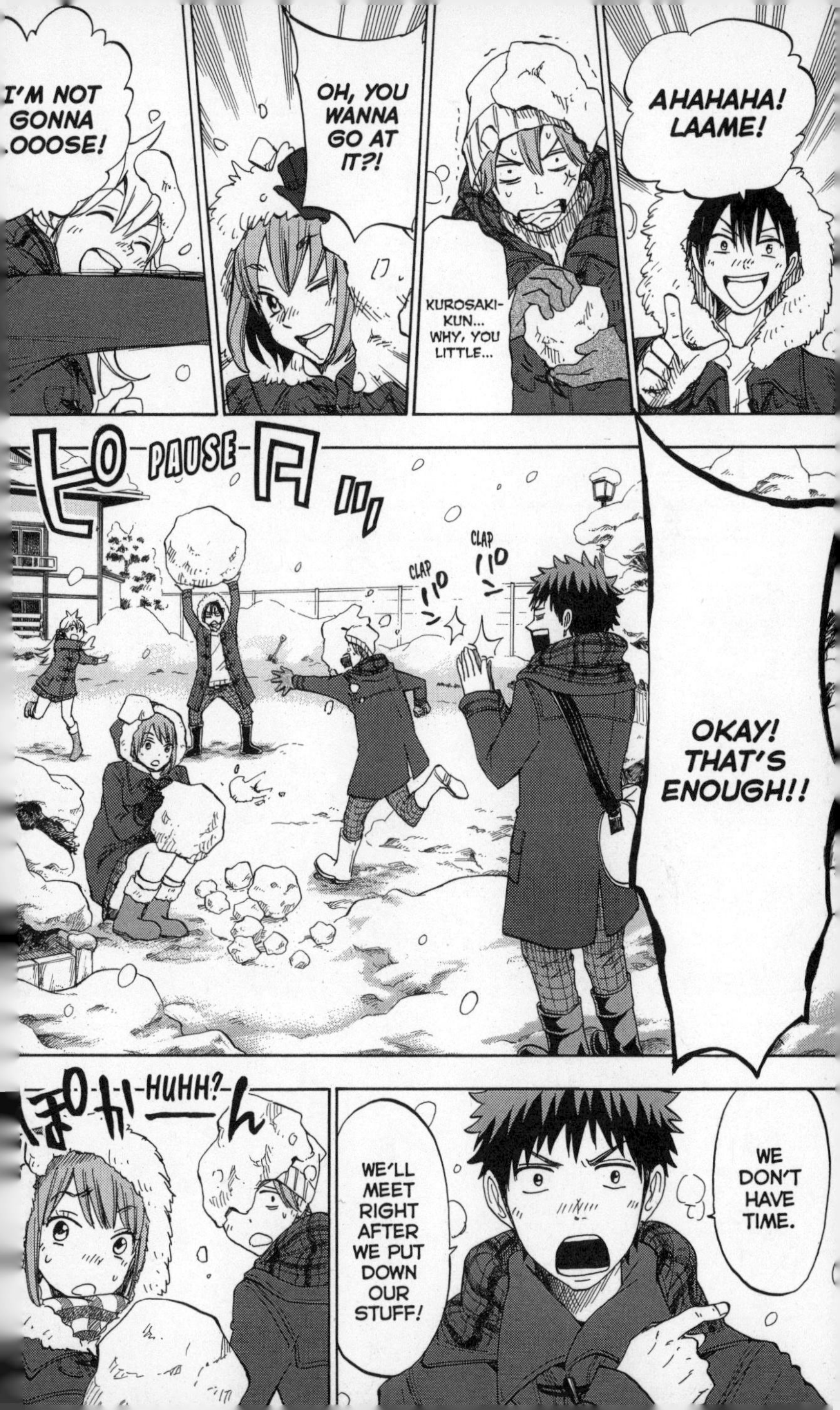
AHAHAHA! LAAME!
KUROSAKI-KUN... WHY, YOU LITTLE...
OH, YOU WANNA GO AT IT?!
I'M NOT GONNA .OOOSE!
OKAY! THAT'S ENOUGH!!
PAUSE
CLAP
CLAP
WE DON'T HAVE TIME.
WE'LL MEET RIGHT AFTER WE PUT DOWN OUR STUFF!
HUHH?

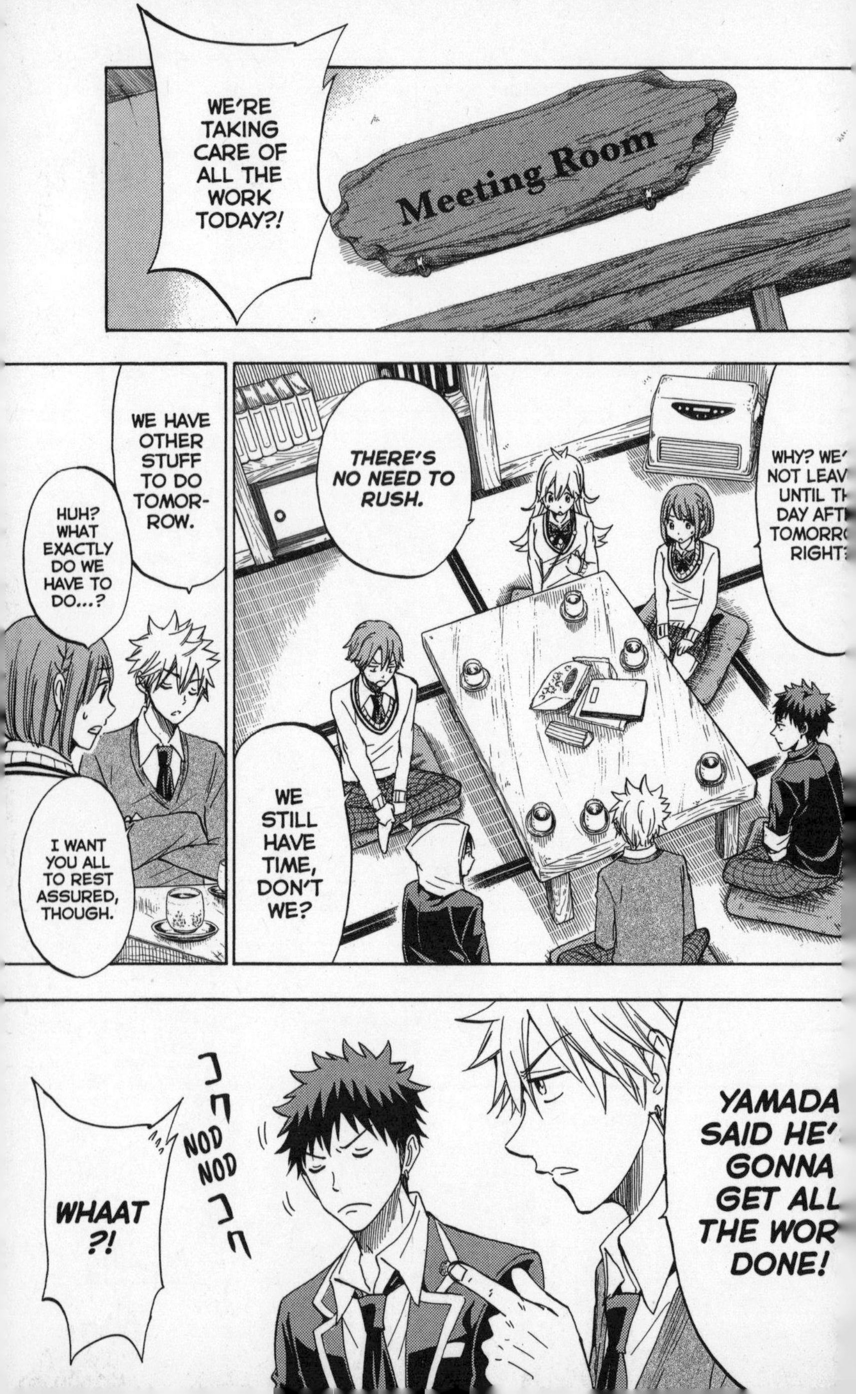
WE'RE TAKING CARE OF ALL THE WORK TODAY?!
Meeting Room
WHY? WE' NOT LEAV UNTIL TH DAY AFT TOMORR RIGHT?
THERE'S NO NEED TO RUSH.
WE STILL HAVE TIME, DON'T WE?
WE HAVE OTHER STUFF TO DO TOMOR-ROW.
HUH? WHAT EXACTLY DO WE HAVE TO DO...?
I WANT YOU ALL TO REST ASSURED, THOUGH.
YAMADA SAID HE' GONNA GET ALL THE WOR DONE!
NOD NOD
WHAAT?!

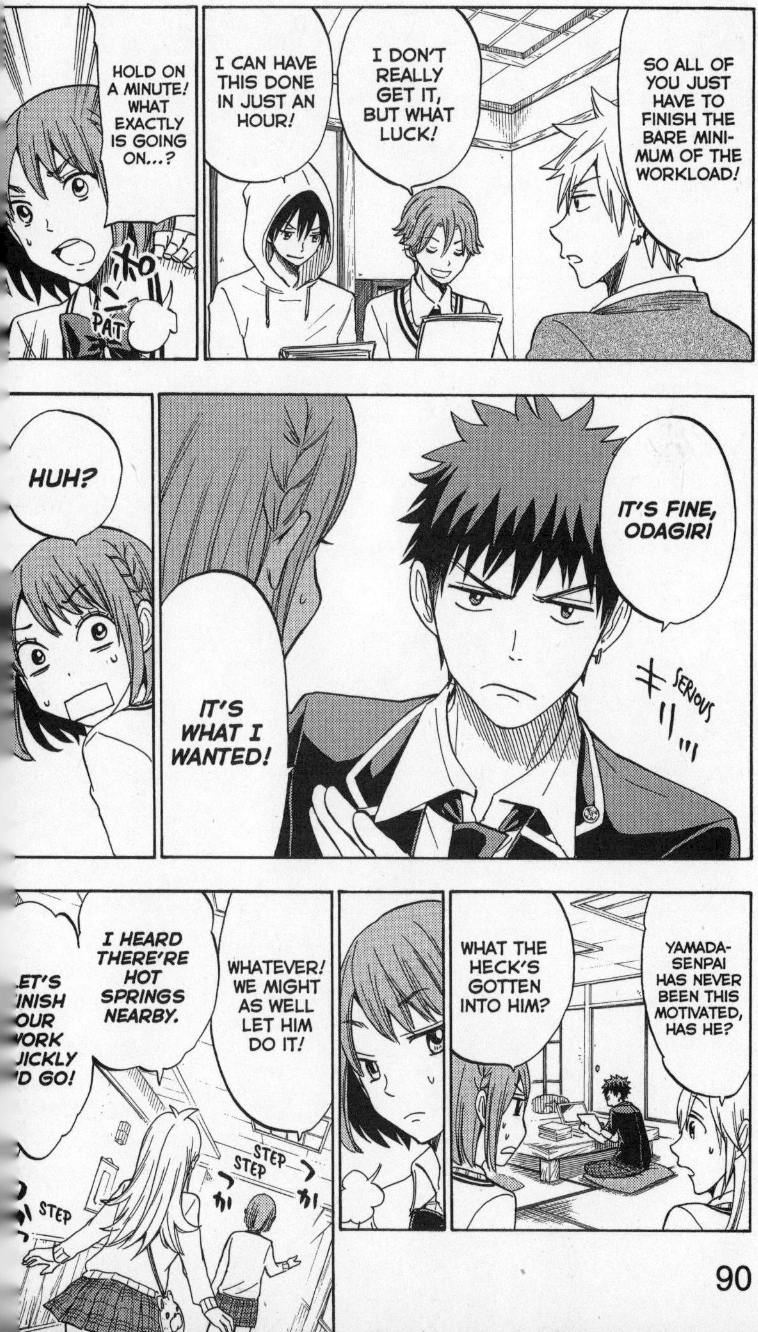
SO ALL OF YOU JUST HAVE TO FINISH THE BARE MINI-MUM OF THE WORKLOAD!
I DON'T REALLY GET IT, BUT WHAT LUCK!
I CAN HAVE THIS DONE IN JUST AN HOUR!
HOLD ON A MINUTE! WHAT EXACTLY IS GOING ON...?
PAT
IT'S FINE, ODAGIRI
IT'S WHAT I WANTED!
SERIOUS
HUH?
YAMADA-SENPAI HAS NEVER BEEN THIS MOTIVATED, HAS HE?
WHAT THE HECK'S GOTTEN INTO HIM?
WHATEVER! WE MIGHT AS WELL LET HIM DO IT!
I HEARD THERE'RE HOT SPRINGS NEARBY.
ET'S INISH OUR ORK UICKLY D GO!
STEP
STEP
STEP

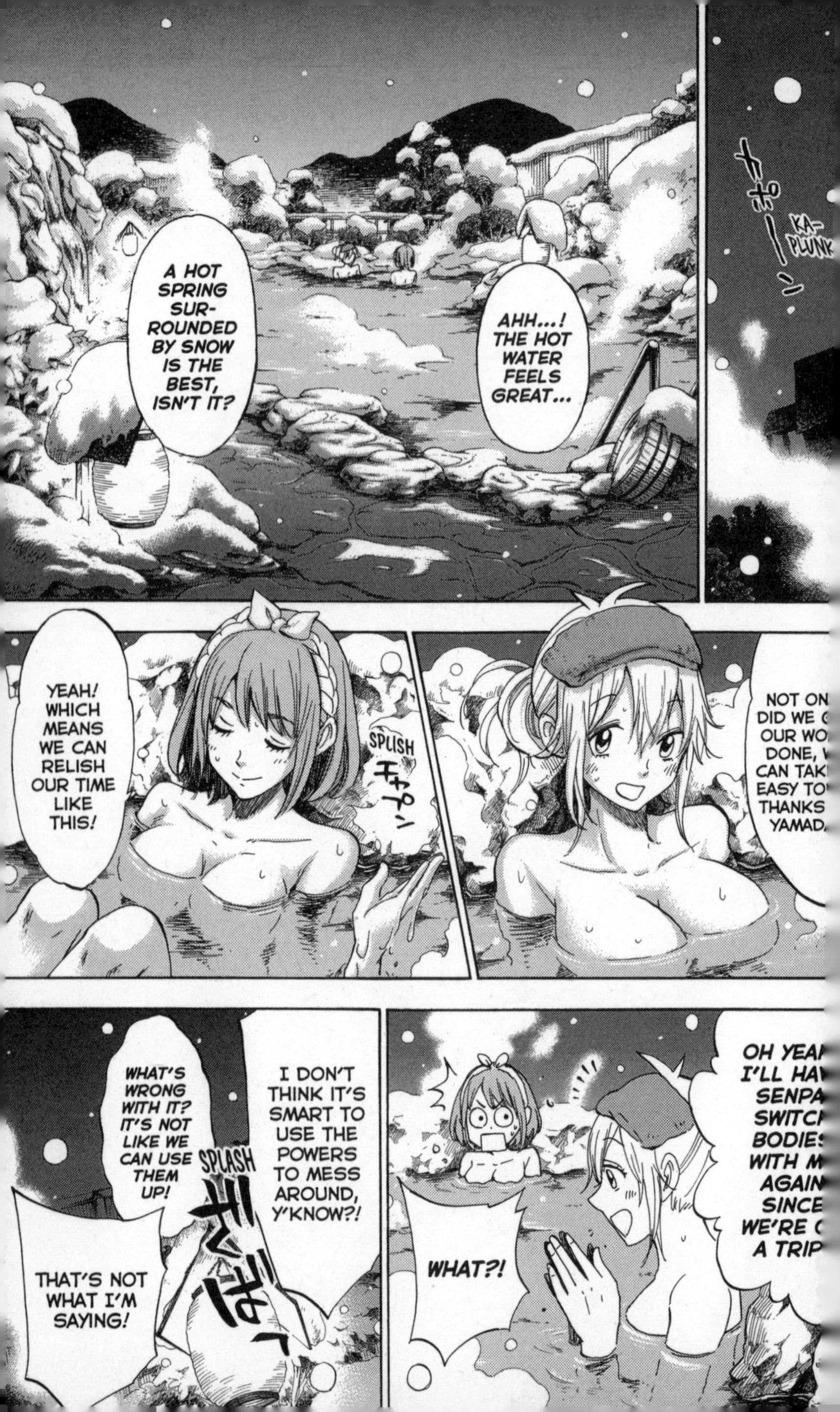
KA-PLUNK
AHH...! THE HOT WATER FEELS GREAT...
A HOT SPRING SUR-ROUNDED BY SNOW IS THE BEST, ISN'T IT?
NOT ON DID WE G OUR WO DONE, CAN TAK EASY TO THANKS YAMAD
YEAH! WHICH MEANS WE CAN RELISH OUR TIME LIKE THIS!
SPLISH
OH YEA I'LL HAV SENPA SWITCH BODIES WITH M AGAIN SINCE WE'RE A TRIP
WHAT?!
I DON'T THINK IT'S SMART TO USE THE POWERS TO MESS AROUND, Y'KNOW?!
WHAT'S WRONG WITH IT? IT'S NOT LIKE WE CAN USE THEM UP!
SPLASH
THAT'S NOT WHAT I'M SAYING!

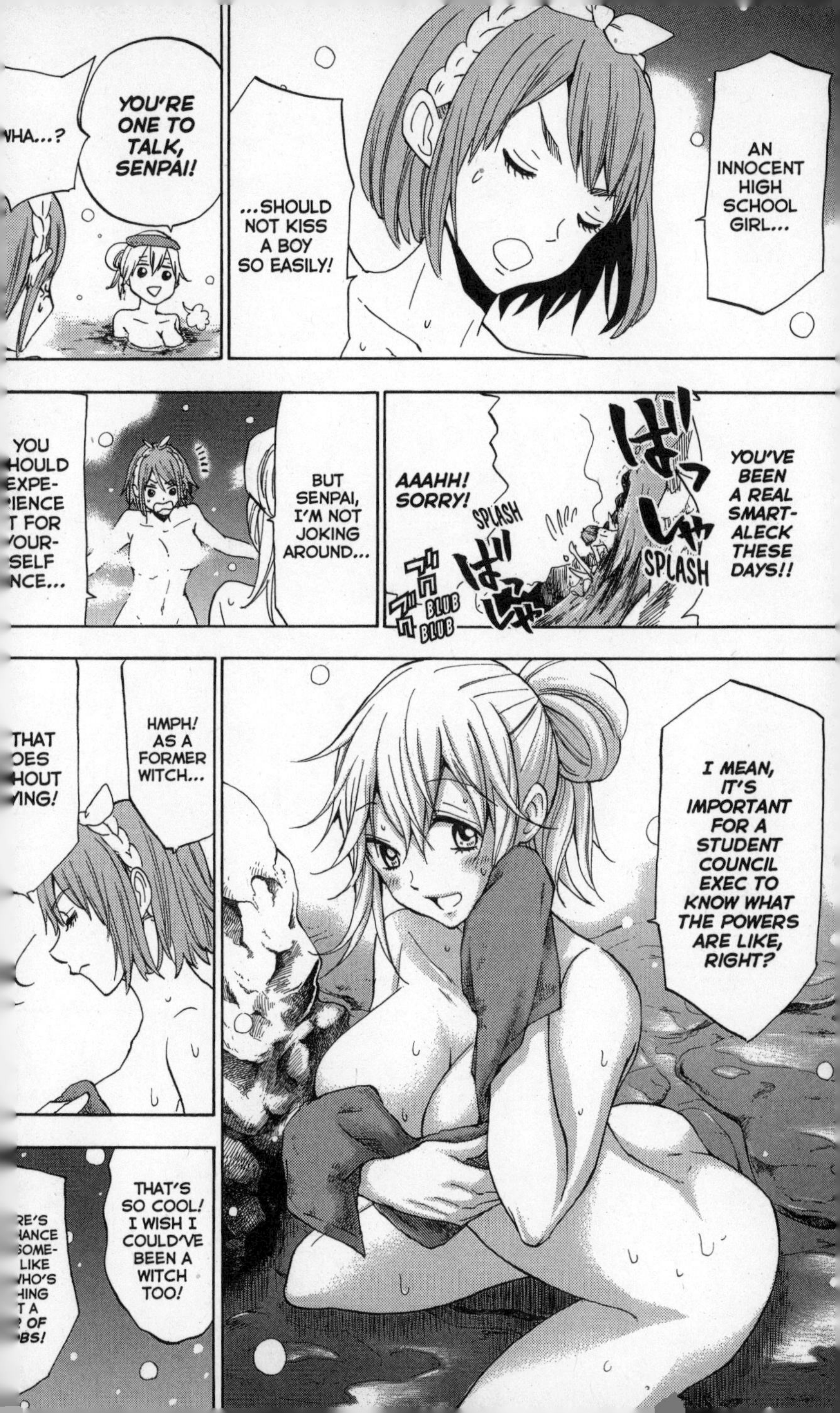

AN INNOCENT HIGH SCHOOL GIRL...
...SHOULD NOT KISS A BOY SO EASILY!
YOU'RE ONE TO TALK, SENPAI!
WHA...?
YOU'VE BEEN A REAL SMART-ALECK THESE DAYS!!
SPLASH
SPLASH
AAAHH! SORRY!
BLUB BLUB
BUT SENPAI, I'M NOT JOKING AROUND...
YOU HOULD EXPE- IENCE T FOR OUR- SELF NCE...
I MEAN, IT'S IMPORTANT FOR A STUDENT COUNCIL EXEC TO KNOW WHAT THE POWERS ARE LIKE, RIGHT?
HMPH! AS A FORMER WITCH...
THAT OES HOUT YING!
THAT'S SO COOL! I WISH I COULD'VE BEEN A WITCH TOO!
RE'S HANCE SOME- LIKE WHO'S HING T A R OF OBS!

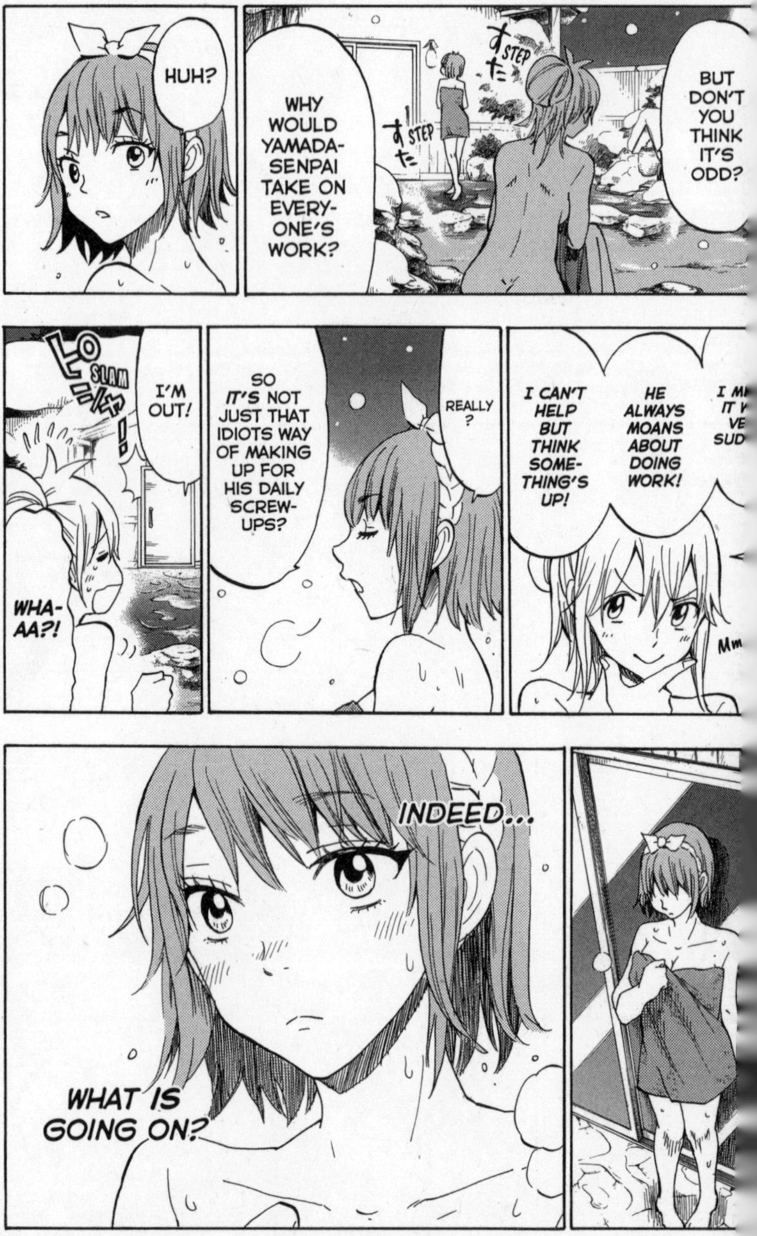

BUT DON'T YOU THINK IT'S ODD?
STEP
STEP
WHY WOULD YAMADA-SENPAI TAKE ON EVERYONE'S WORK?
HUH?
HE ALWAYS MOANS ABOUT DOING WORK!
I CAN'T HELP BUT THINK SOMETHING'S UP!
REALLY?
SO IT'S NOT JUST THAT IDIOTS WAY OF MAKING UP FOR HIS DAILY SCREW-UPS?
I'M OUT!
SLAM
WHA-AA?!
INDEED...
WHAT IS GOING ON?

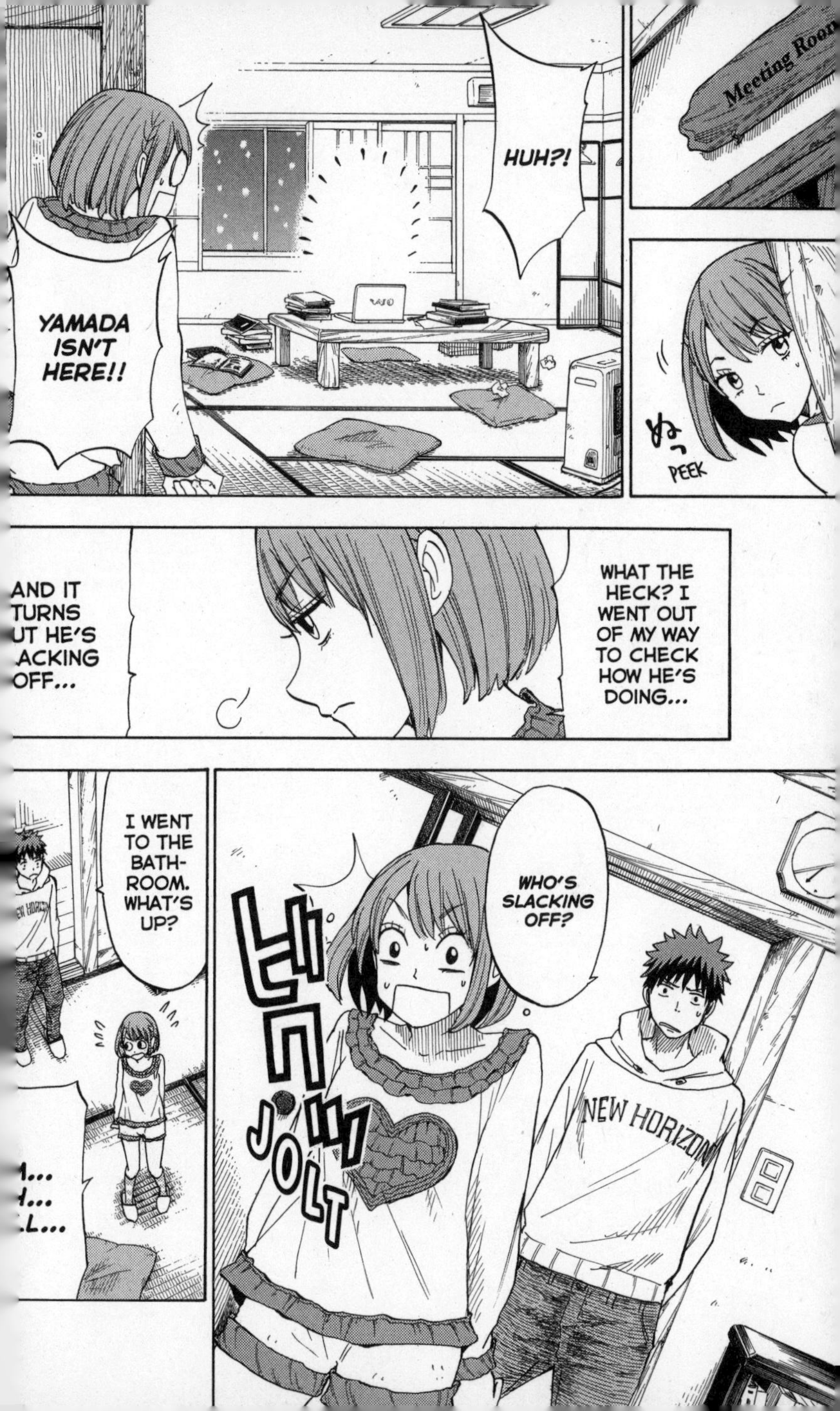
Meeting Room
ぬっ
PEEK
HUH?!
YAMADA ISN'T HERE!!
WHAT THE HECK? I WENT OUT OF MY WAY TO CHECK HOW HE'S DOING...
AND IT TURNS UT HE'S LACKING OFF...
WHO'S SLACKING OFF?
JOLT
I WENT TO THE BATH-ROOM. WHAT'S UP?
M... H... L...

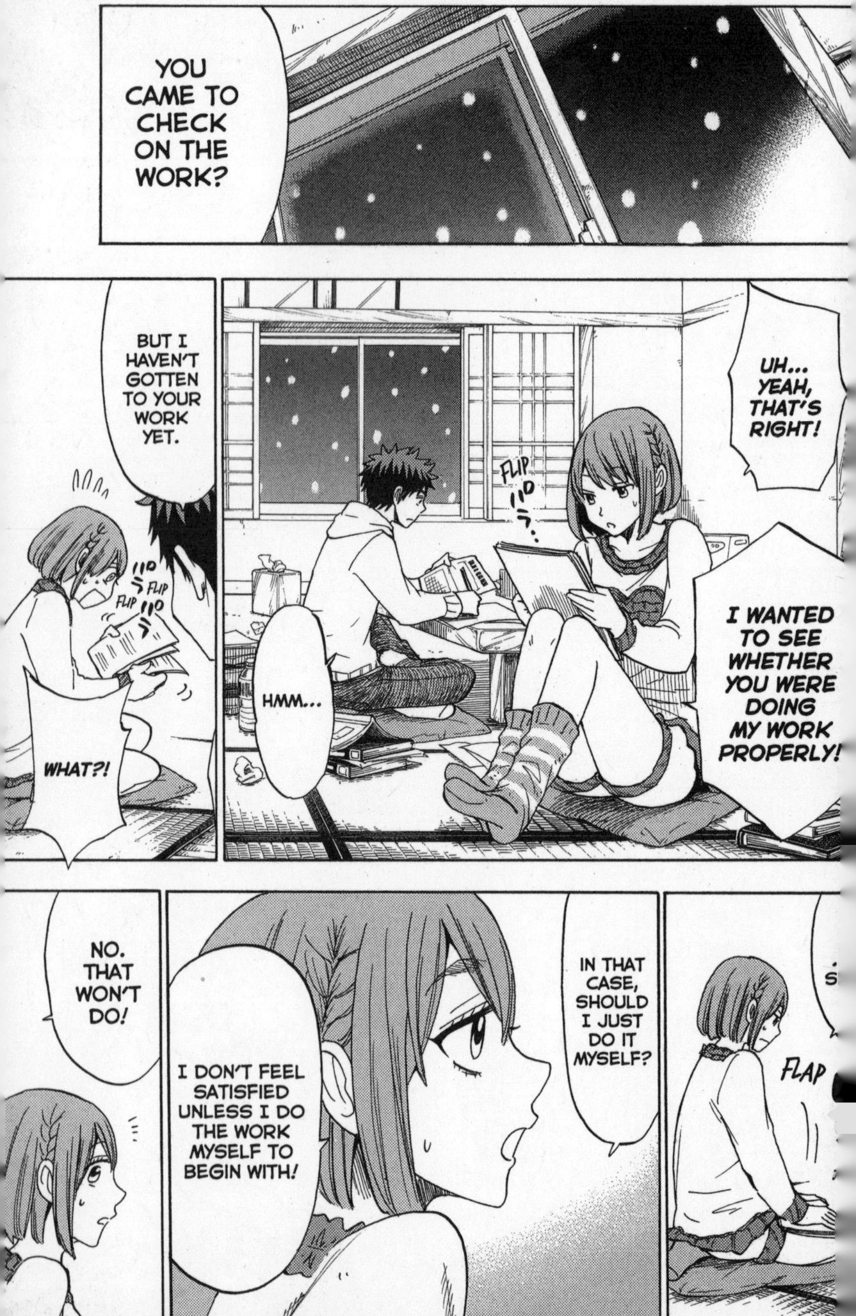
YOU CAME TO CHECK ON THE WORK?
UH... YEAH, THAT'S RIGHT!
FLIP
I WANTED TO SEE WHETHER YOU WERE DOING MY WORK PROPERLY!
HMM...
BUT I HAVEN'T GOTTEN TO YOUR WORK YET.
FLIP
FLIP
WHAT?!
FLAP
IN THAT CASE, SHOULD I JUST DO IT MYSELF?
I DON'T FEEL SATISFIED UNLESS I DO THE WORK MYSELF TO BEGIN WITH!
NO. THAT WON'T DO!

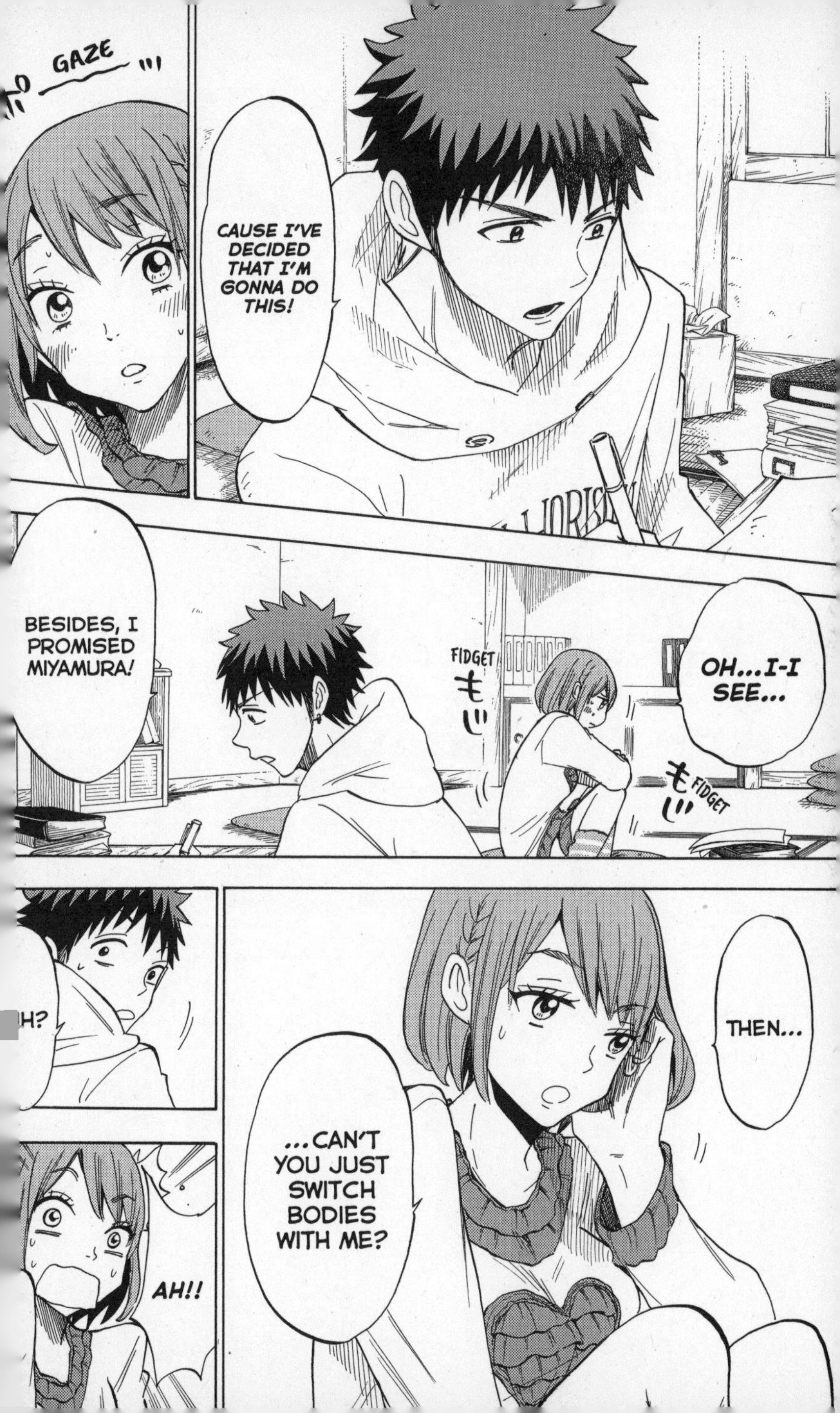
CAUSE I'VE DECIDED THAT I'M GONNA DO THIS!
GAZE
BESIDES, I PROMISED MIYAMURA!
FIDGET
もじ
FIDGET
もじ
OH...I-I SEE...
THEN...
...CAN'T YOU JUST SWITCH BODIES WITH ME?
H?
AH!!

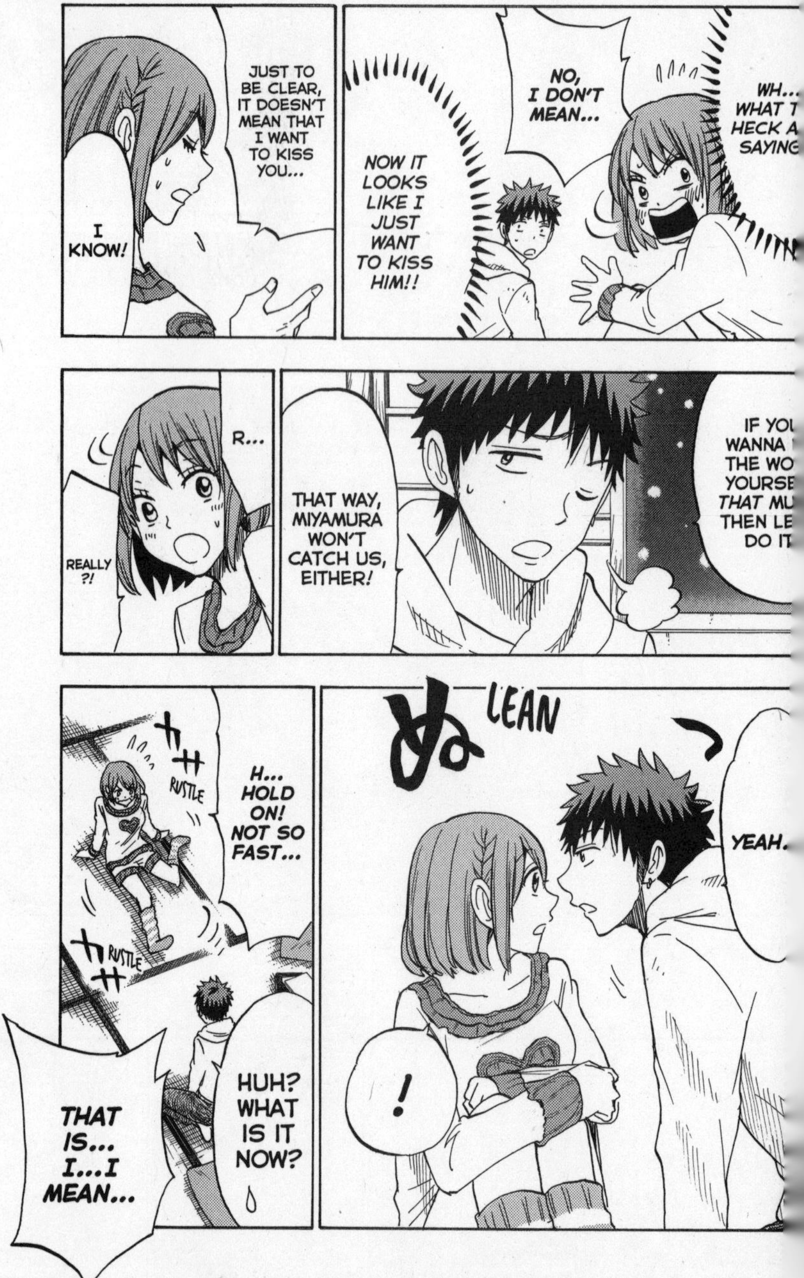
WH... WHAT T HECK A SAYING
NO, I DON'T MEAN...
NOW IT LOOKS LIKE I JUST WANT TO KISS HIM!!
JUST TO BE CLEAR, IT DOESN'T MEAN THAT I WANT TO KISS YOU...
I KNOW!
IF YOU WANNA THE WO YOURSE THAT MU THEN LE DO IT
THAT WAY, MIYAMURA WON'T CATCH US, EITHER!
R...
REALLY ?!
ぬ LEAN
YEAH.
!
RUSTLE
H... HOLD ON! NOT SO FAST...
RUSTLE
HUH? WHAT IS IT NOW?
THAT IS... I...I MEAN...

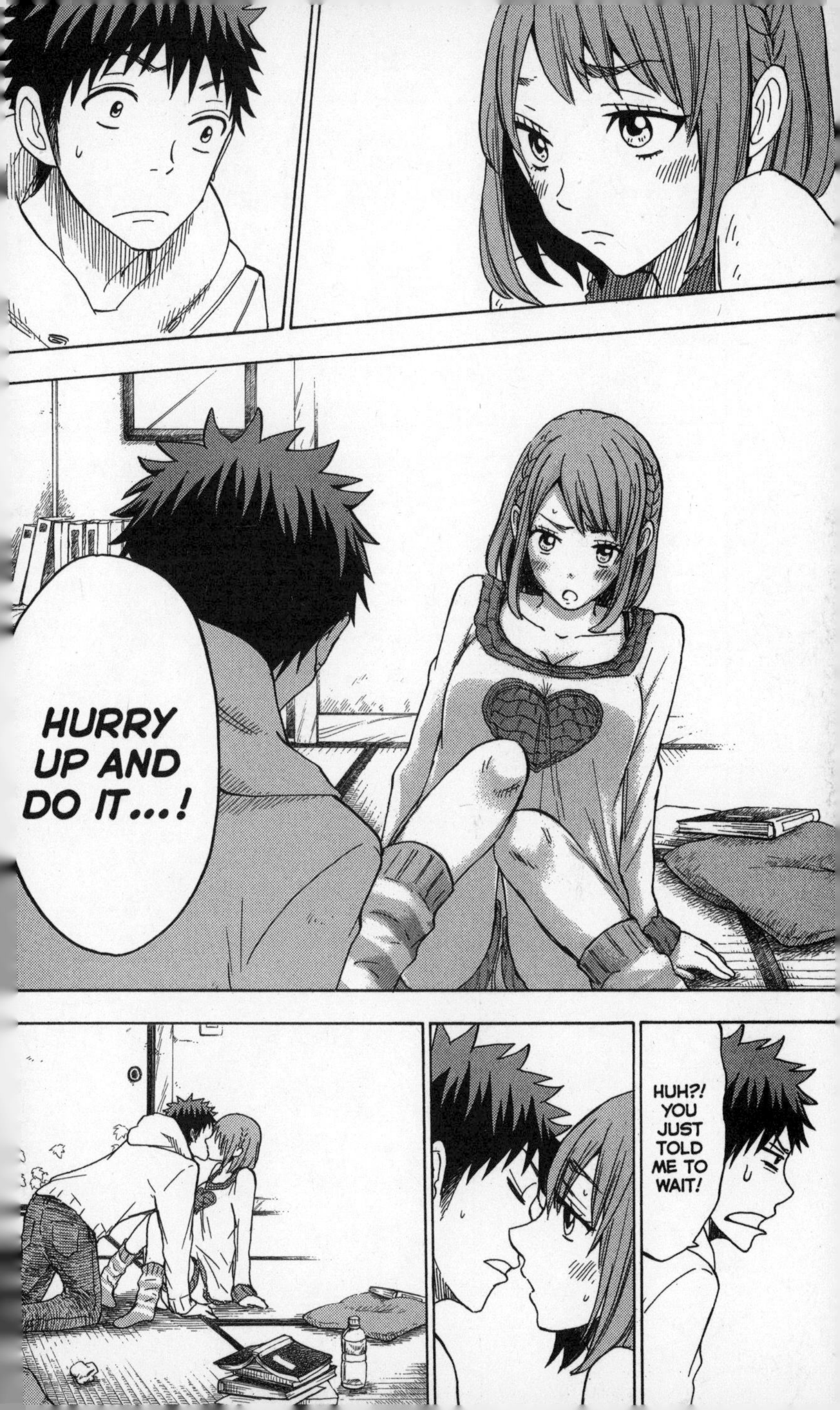
HURRY UP AND DO IT...!
HUH?! YOU JUST TOLD ME TO WAIT!

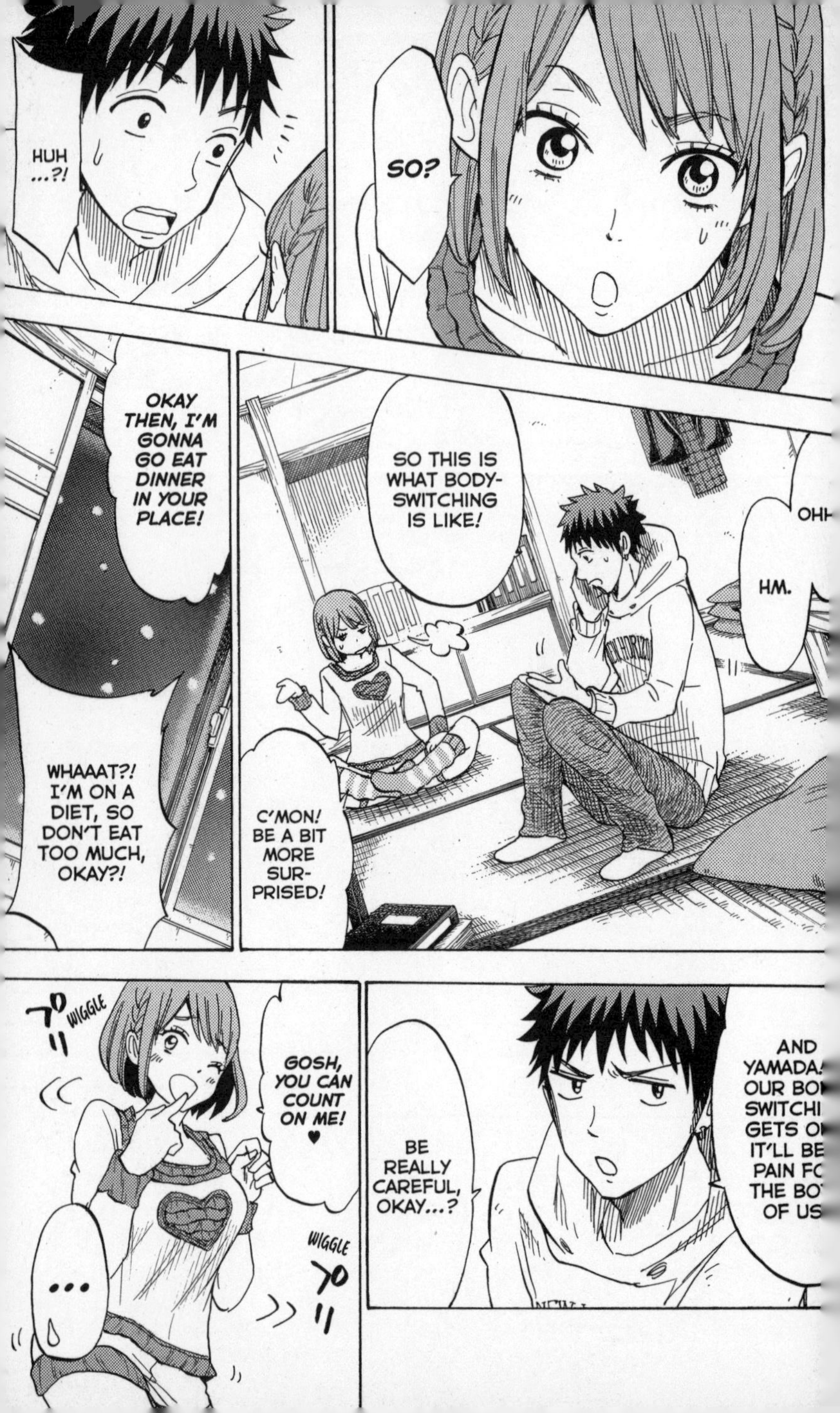
SO?
HUH ...?!
OHH
HM.
SO THIS IS WHAT BODY-SWITCHING IS LIKE!
C'MON! BE A BIT MORE SUR-PRISED!
OKAY THEN, I'M GONNA GO EAT DINNER IN YOUR PLACE!
WHAAAT?! I'M ON A DIET, SO DON'T EAT TOO MUCH, OKAY?!
AND YAMADA! OUR BO SWITCHI GETS O IT'LL BE PAIN FO THE BO OF US
BE REALLY CAREFUL, OKAY...?
GOSH, YOU CAN COUNT ON ME! ♥
WIGGLE
...
WIGGLE

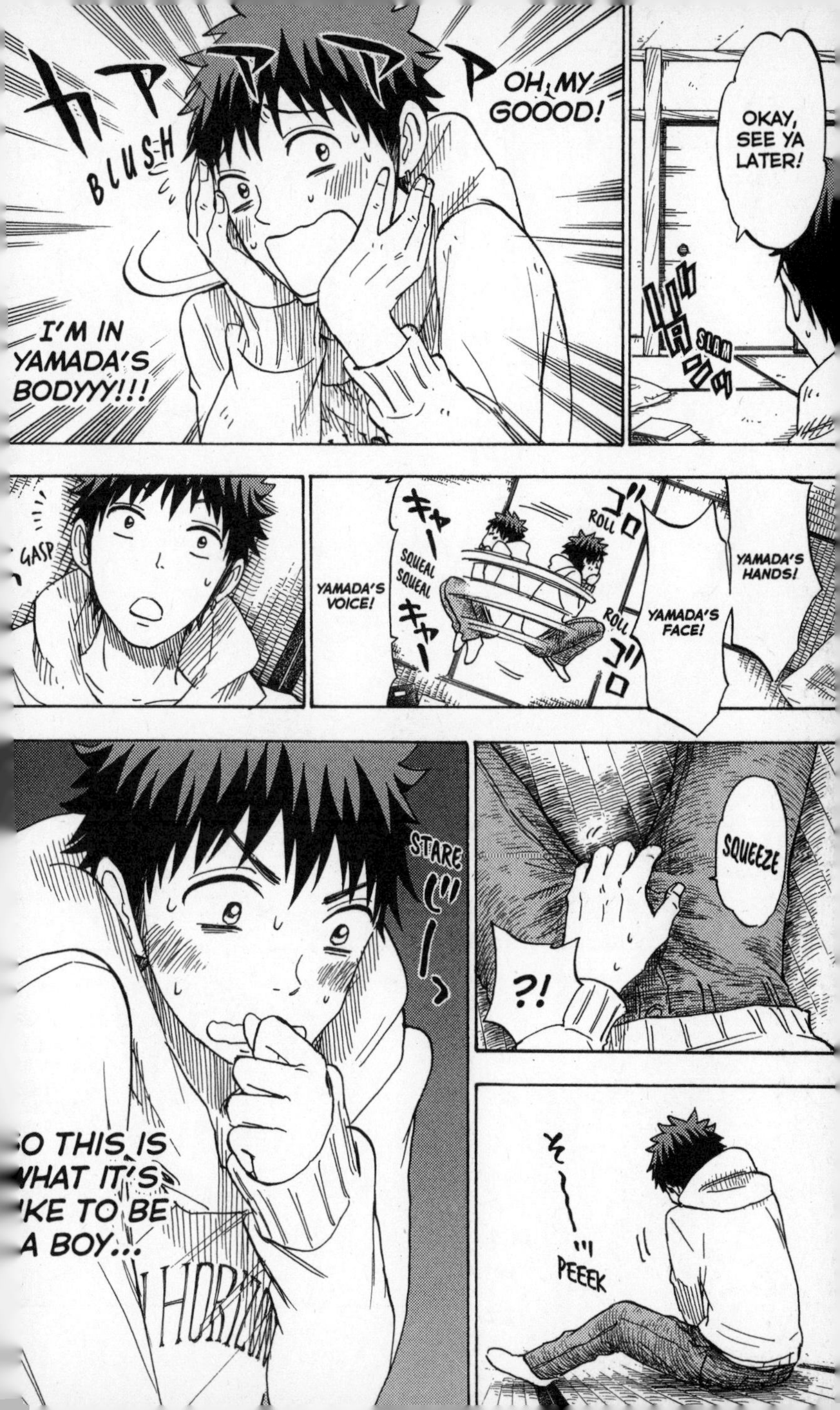

OKAY, SEE YA LATER!
SLAM
OH, MY GOOOD!
BLUSH
I'M IN YAMADA'S BODYYY!!!
YAMADA'S HANDS!
YAMADA'S FACE!
ROLL
ゴロ
SQUEAL SQUEAL
キャー
YAMADA'S VOICE!
キャー
ROLL
ゴロ
GASP
SQUEEZE
?!
そ～～
PEEEK
STARE
じー
O THIS IS
HAT IT'S
IKE TO BE
A BOY...

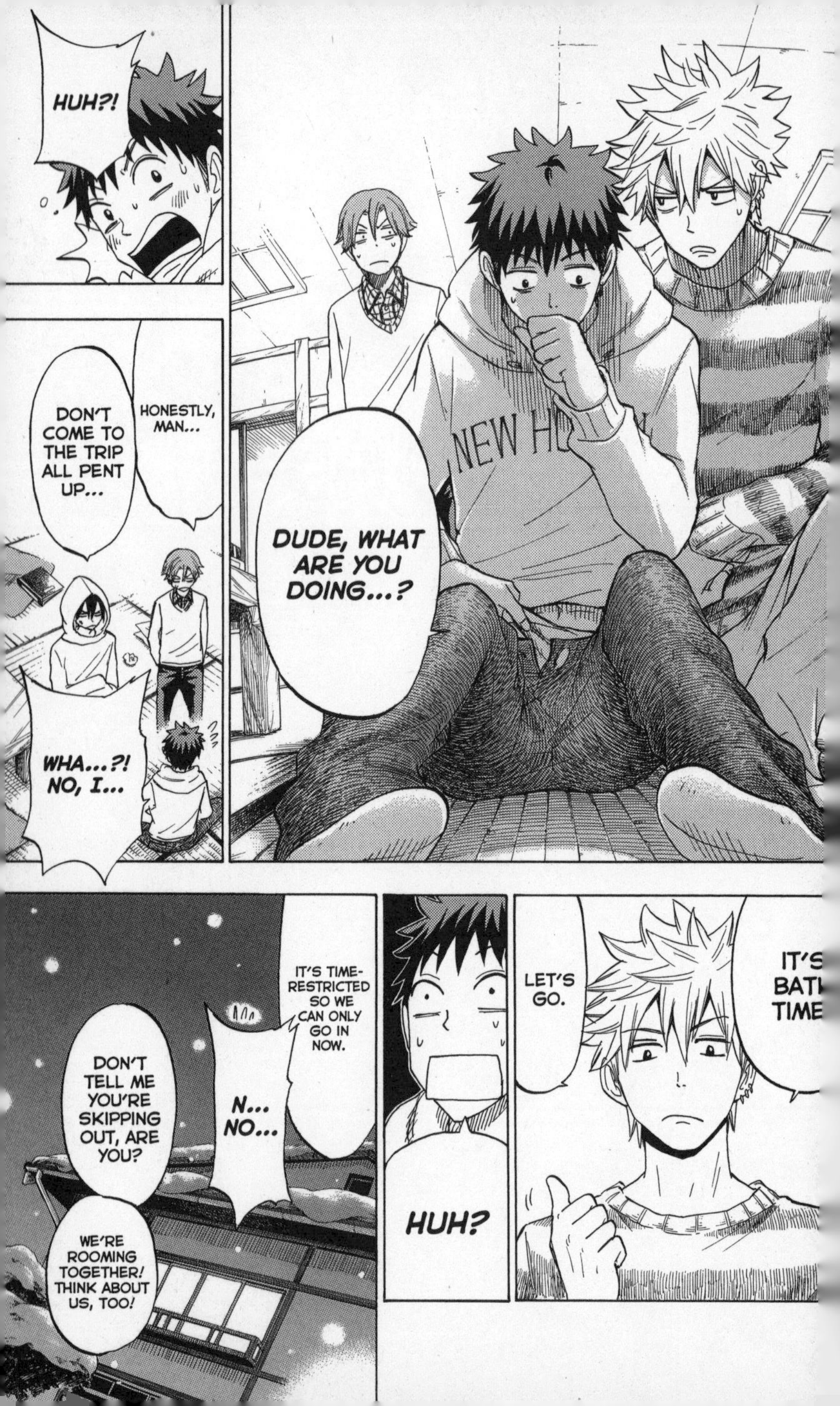
DUDE, WHAT ARE YOU DOING...?
HUH?!
HONESTLY, MAN...
DON'T COME TO THE TRIP ALL PENT UP...
WHA...?! NO, I...
IT'S BATH TIME
LET'S GO.
HUH?
IT'S TIME-RESTRICTED SO WE CAN ONLY GO IN NOW.
N... NO...
DON'T TELL ME YOU'RE SKIPPING OUT, ARE YOU?
WE'RE ROOMING TOGETHER! THINK ABOUT US, TOO!

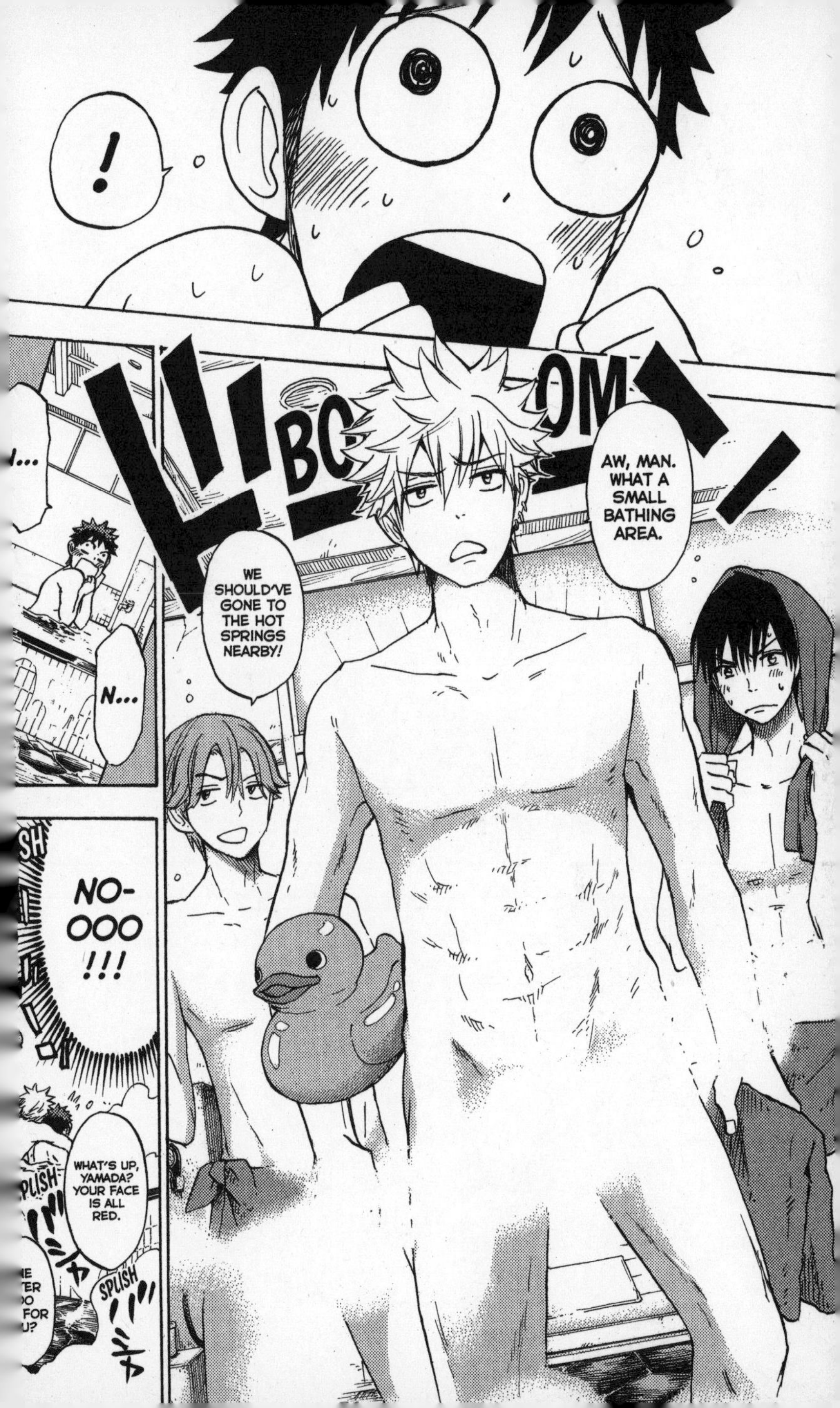
!
AW, MAN. WHAT A SMALL BATHING AREA.
WE SHOULD'VE GONE TO THE HOT SPRINGS NEARBY!
WHAT'S UP, YAMADA? YOUR FACE IS ALL RED.
N...
NO-OOO!!!
SPLISH
SPLISH

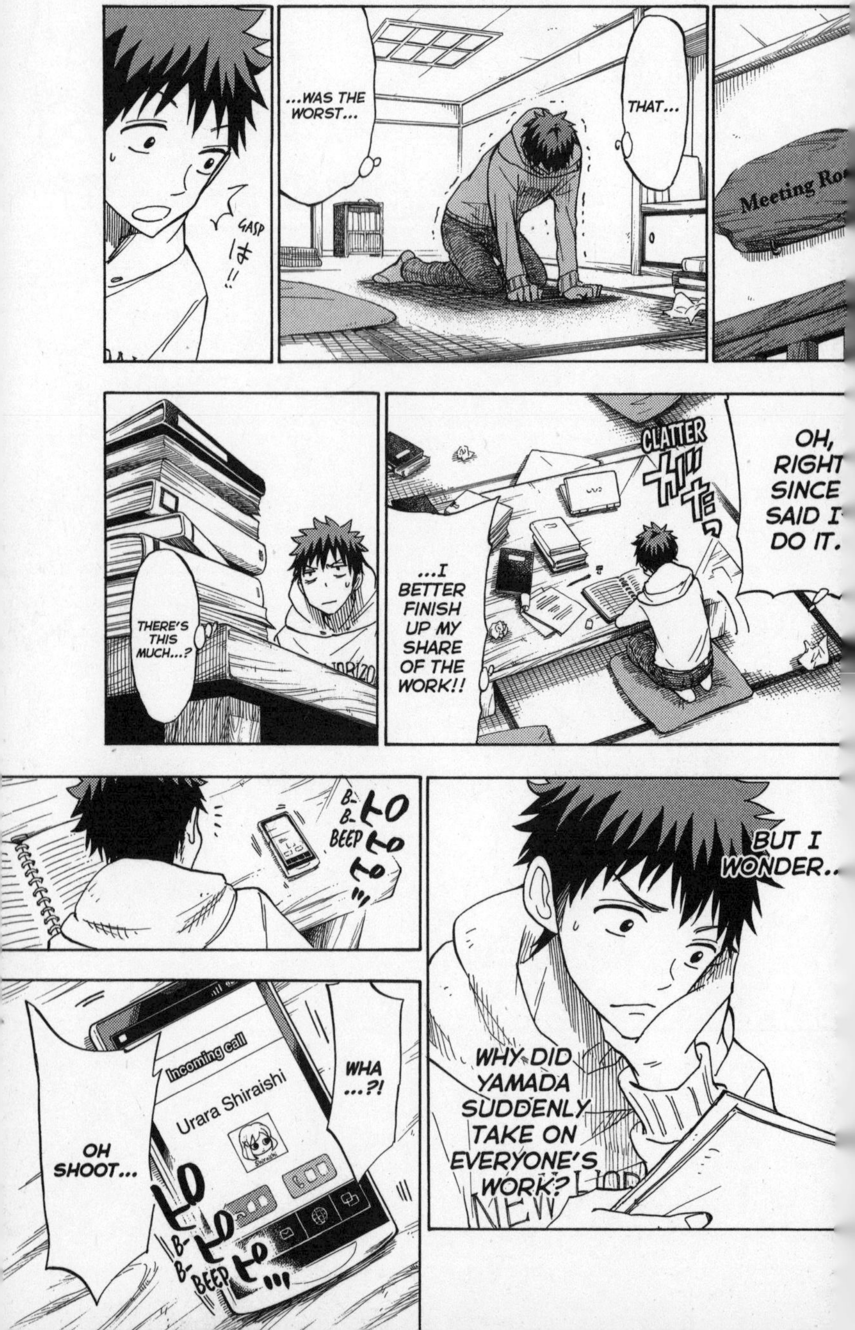
Meeting Ro
THAT...
...WAS THE WORST...
GASP
は!!
CLATTER
ガタッ
OH, RIGHT SINCE SAID I' DO IT.
...I BETTER FINISH UP MY SHARE OF THE WORK!!
THERE'S THIS MUCH...?
BUT I WONDER..
WHY DID YAMADA SUDDENLY TAKE ON EVERYONE'S WORK?
B-B-BEEP
WHA...?!
Incoming call
Urara Shiraishi
Shiraishi
OH SHOOT...
B-B-BEEP

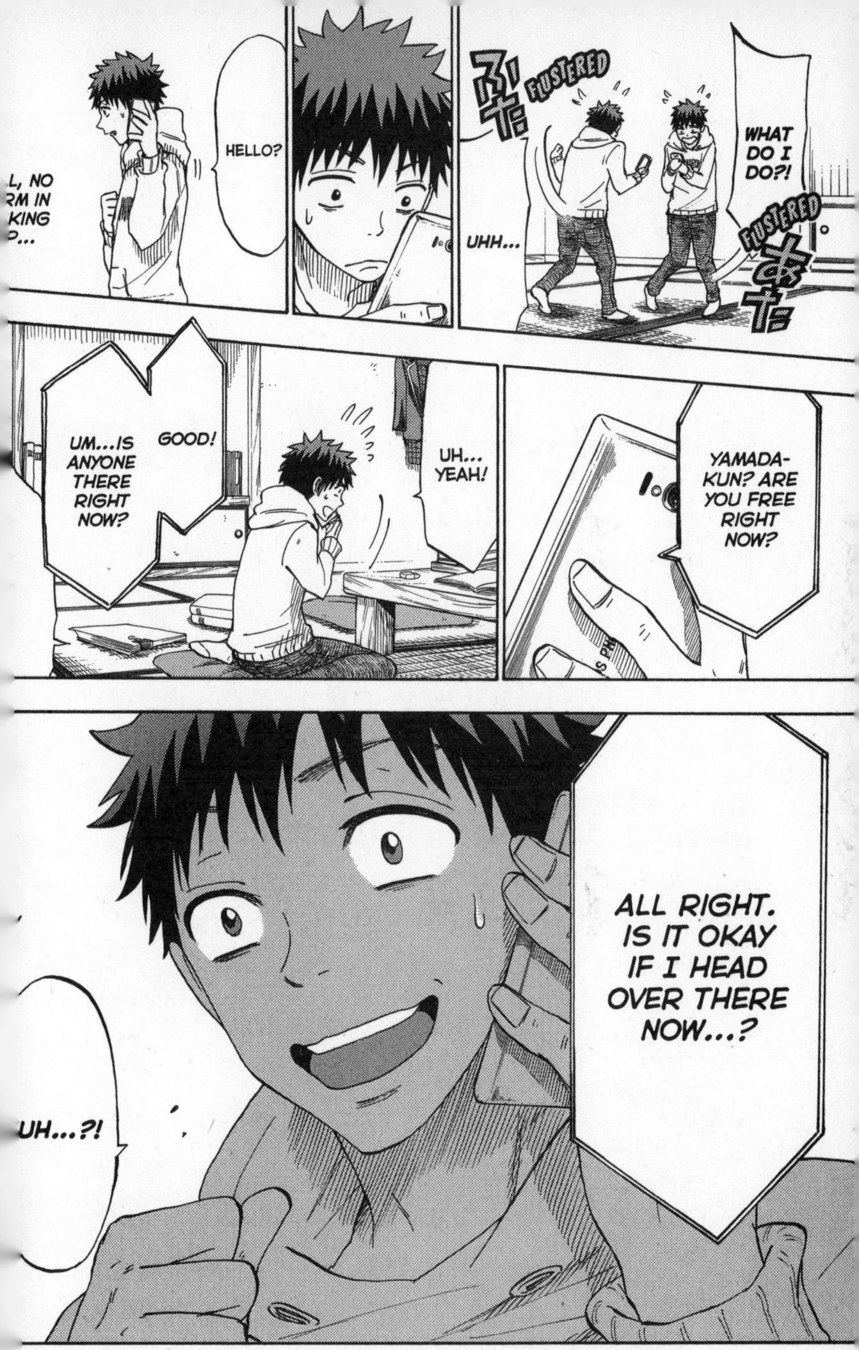

WHAT DO I DO?!
FLUSTERED
FLUSTERED
UHH...
HELLO?
L, NO RM IN KING P...
YAMADA-KUN? ARE YOU FREE RIGHT NOW?
UH... YEAH!
GOOD!
UM...IS ANYONE THERE RIGHT NOW?
ALL RIGHT. IS IT OKAY IF I HEAD OVER THERE NOW...?
UH...?!

CHAPTER 116: No one asked you!!

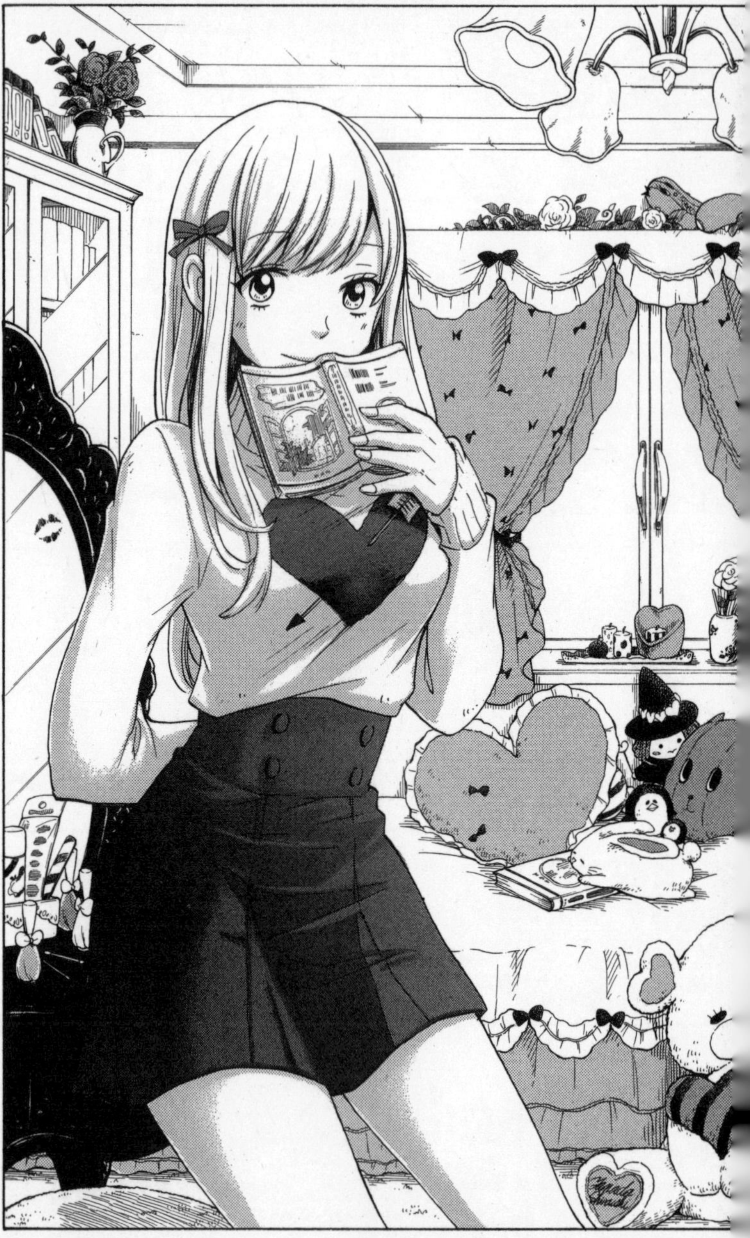

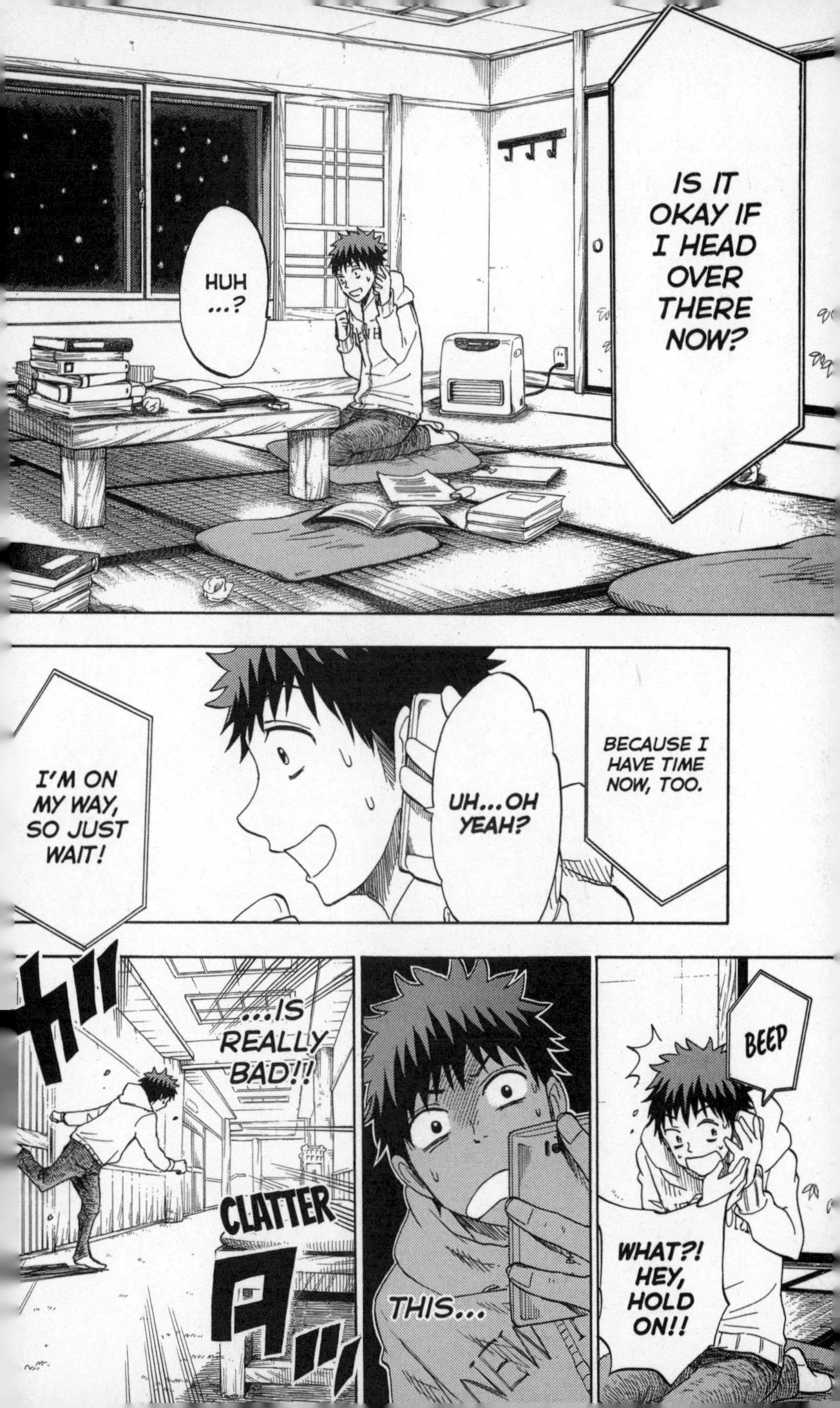
IS IT OKAY IF I HEAD OVER THERE NOW?
HUH ...?
BECAUSE I HAVE TIME NOW, TOO.
UH...OH YEAH?
I'M ON MY WAY, SO JUST WAIT!
BEEP
WHAT?! HEY, HOLD ON!!
THIS...
...IS REALLY BAD!!
CLATTER

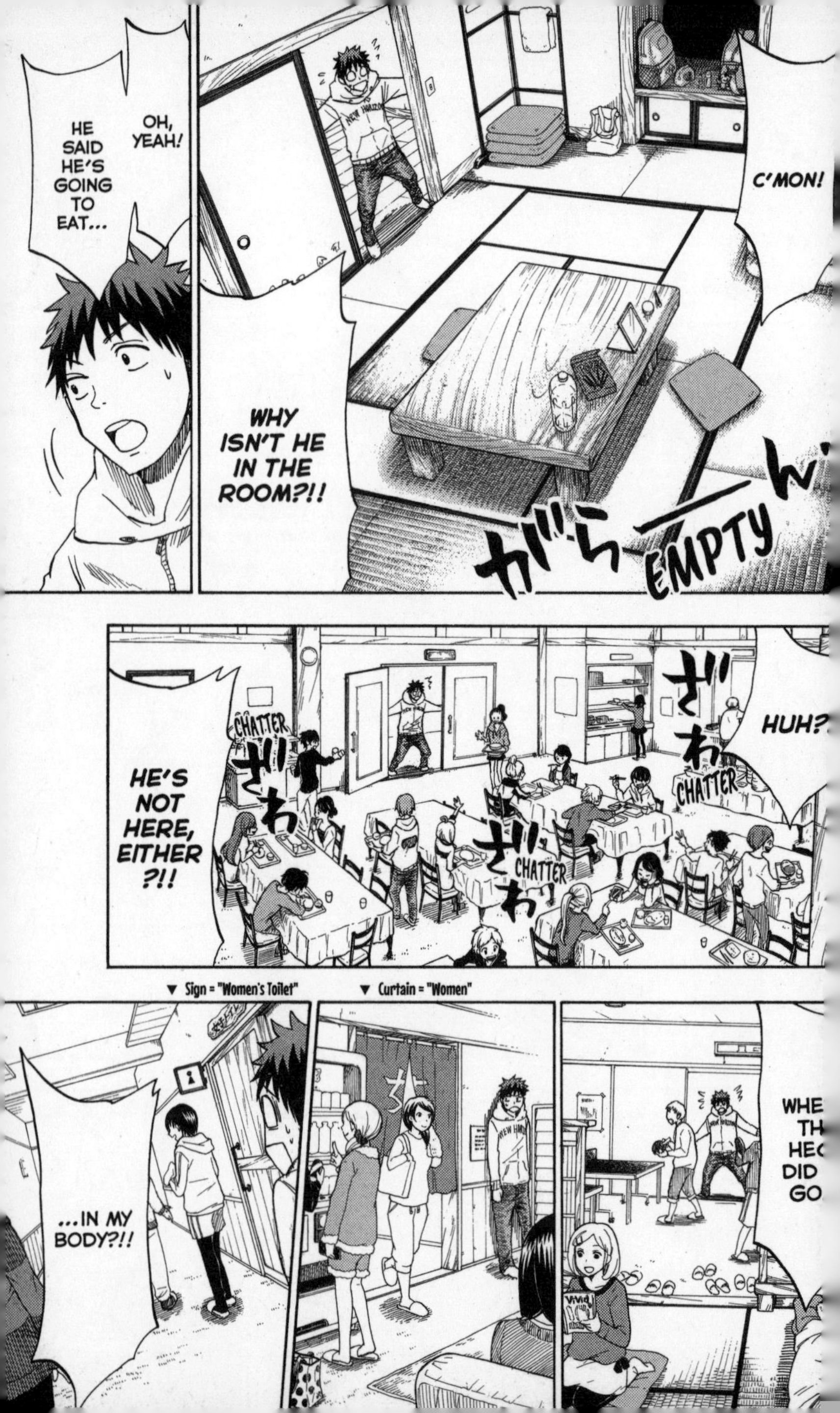
C'MON!
WHY ISN'T HE IN THE ROOM?!!
がら EMPTY
OH, YEAH!
HE SAID HE'S GOING TO EAT...
HUH?
ざわ CHATTER
ざわ CHATTER
ざわ CHATTER
HE'S NOT HERE, EITHER?!!
▼ Sign = "Women's Toilet"
▼ Curtain = "Women"
WHE TH HE DID GO
...IN MY BODY?!!

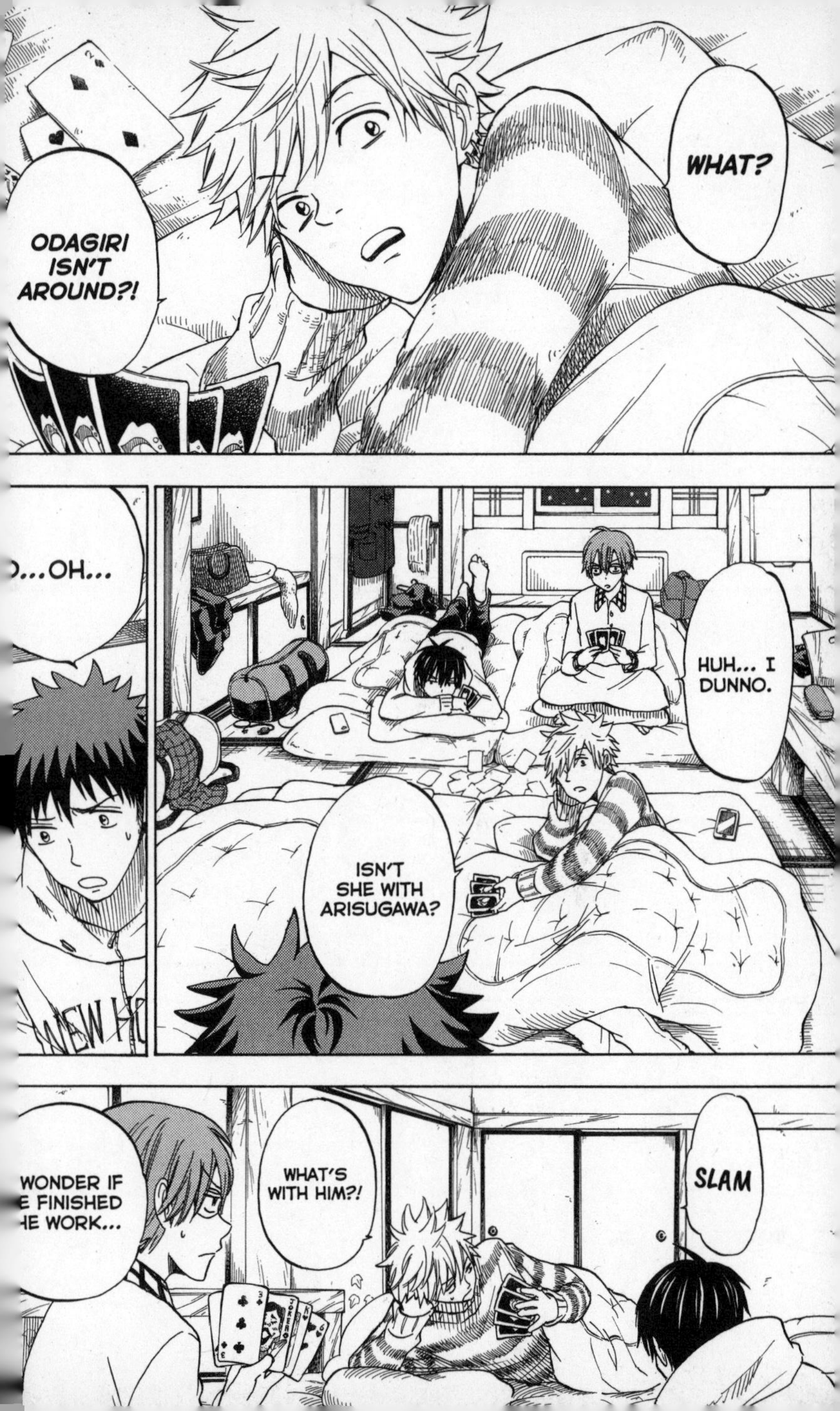
WHAT?
ODAGIRI ISN'T AROUND?!
HUH... I DUNNO.
ISN'T SHE WITH ARISUGAWA?
...OH...
SLAM
WHAT'S WITH HIM?!
WONDER IF
E FINISHED
HE WORK...

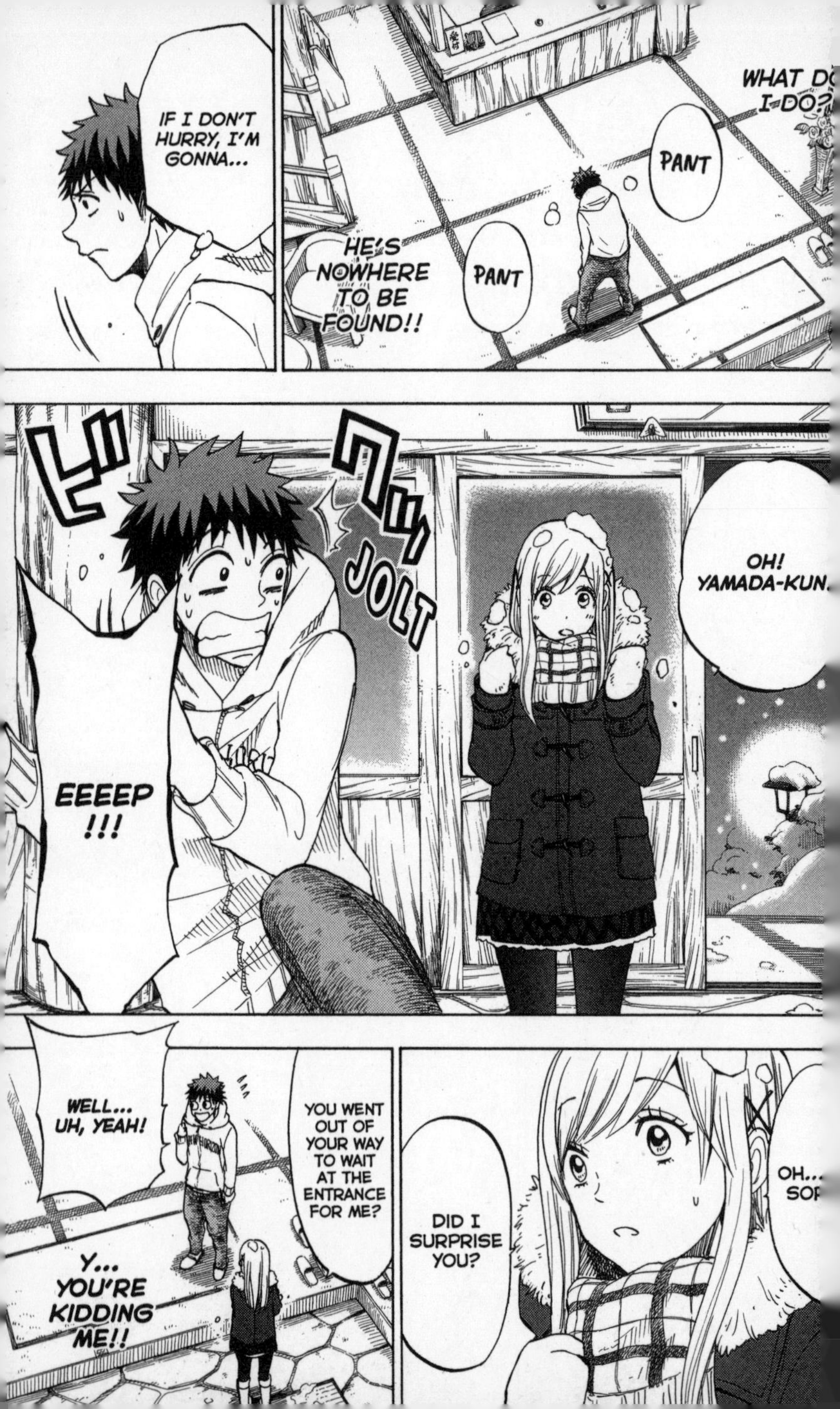
WHAT DO I DO?
PANT
PANT
HE'S NOWHERE TO BE FOUND!!
IF I DON'T HURRY, I'M GONNA...
OH! YAMADA-KUN.
JOLT
EEEEP !!!
OH... SOR
DID I SURPRISE YOU?
YOU WENT OUT OF YOUR WAY TO WAIT AT THE ENTRANCE FOR ME?
WELL... UH, YEAH!
Y... YOU'RE KIDDING ME!!

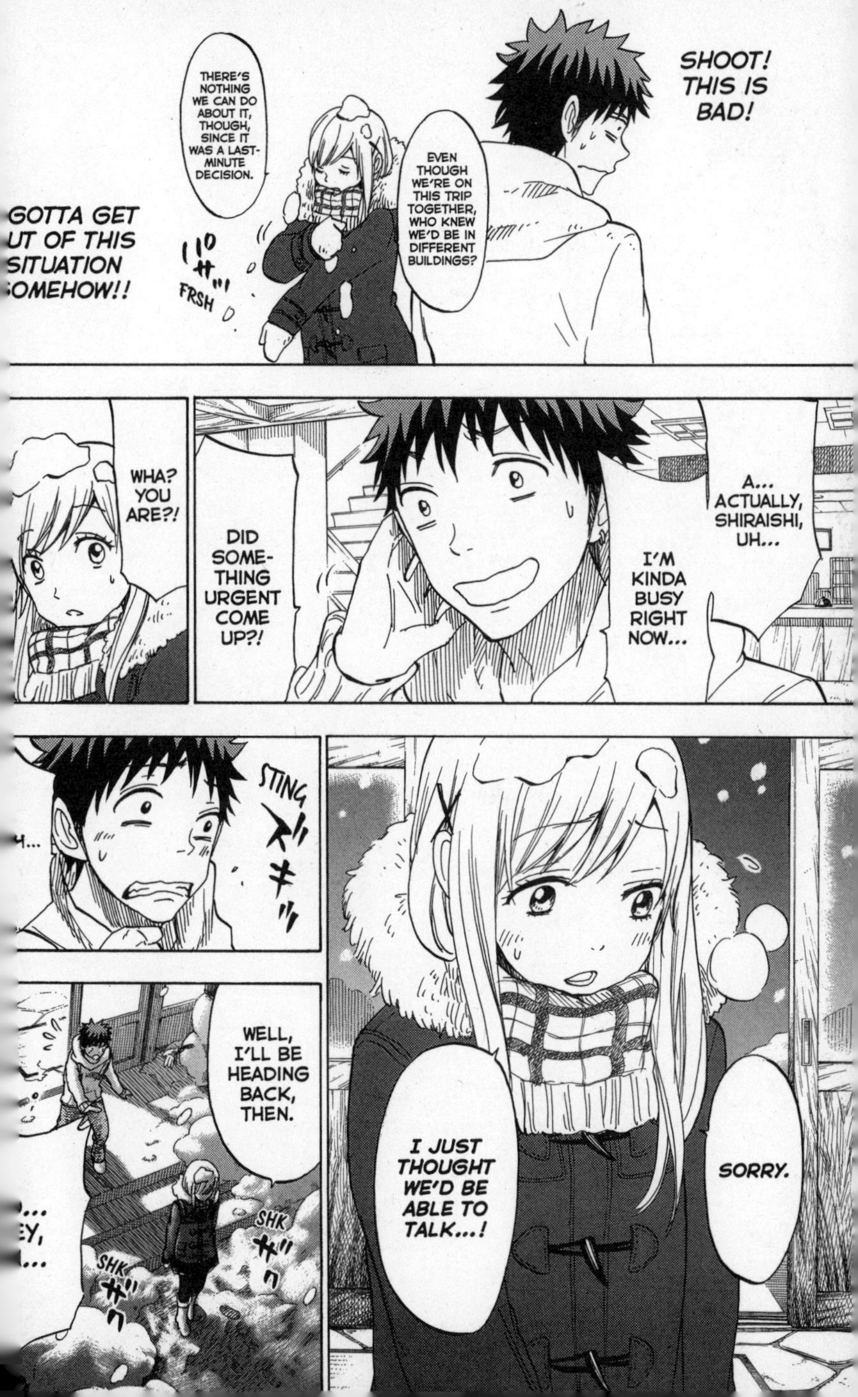
SHOOT! THIS IS BAD!
EVEN THOUGH WE'RE ON THIS TRIP TOGETHER, WHO KNEW WE'D BE IN DIFFERENT BUILDINGS?
THERE'S NOTHING WE CAN DO ABOUT IT, THOUGH, SINCE IT WAS A LAST-MINUTE DECISION.
FRSH
GOTTA GET
UT OF THIS
SITUATION
OMEHOW!!
A... ACTUALLY, SHIRAISHI, UH...
I'M KINDA BUSY RIGHT NOW...
DID SOMETHING URGENT COME UP?!
WHA? YOU ARE?!
SORRY.
I JUST THOUGHT WE'D BE ABLE TO TALK...!
STING
WELL, I'LL BE HEADING BACK, THEN.
SHK
SHK

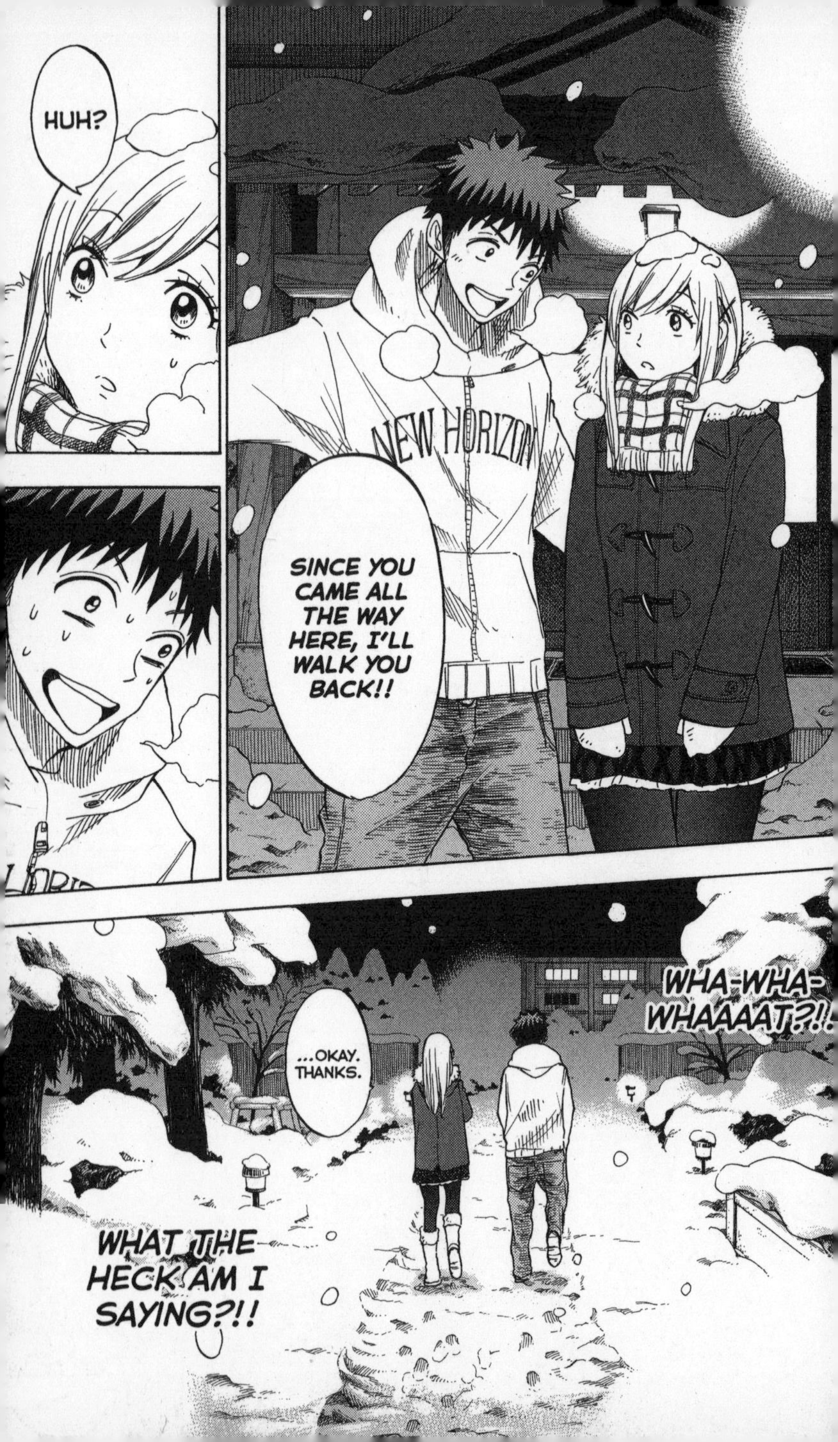
SINCE YOU CAME ALL THE WAY HERE, I'LL WALK YOU BACK!!
HUH?
WHA-WHA-WHAAAAT?!!
...OKAY. THANKS.
WHAT THE HECK AM I SAYING?!!

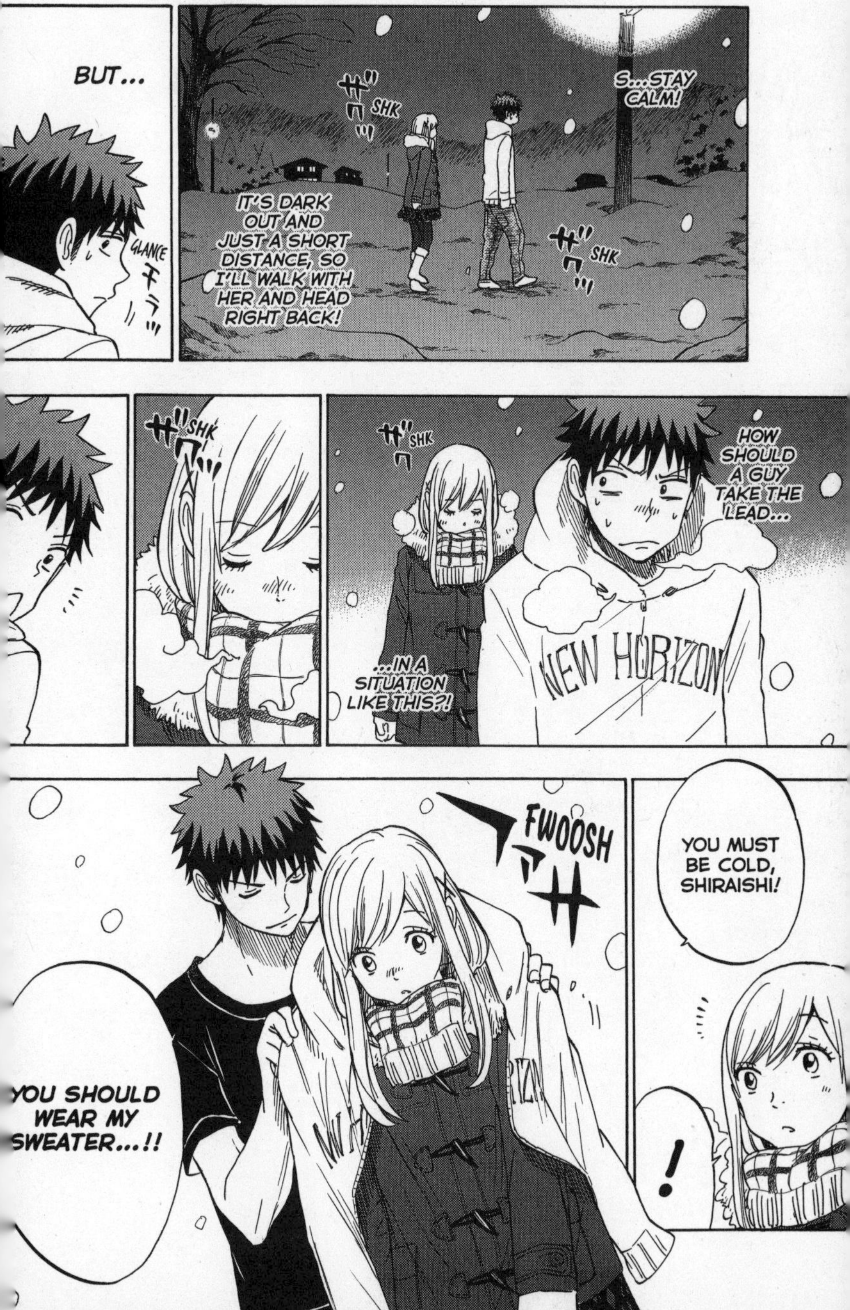
S...STAY CALM!
SHK
IT'S DARK OUT AND JUST A SHORT DISTANCE, SO I'LL WALK WITH HER AND HEAD RIGHT BACK!
SHK
BUT...
GLANCE
HOW SHOULD A GUY TAKE THE LEAD...
SHK
NEW HORIZON
...IN A SITUATION LIKE THIS?!
SHK
YOU MUST BE COLD, SHIRAISHI!
!
FWOOSH
YOU SHOULD WEAR MY SWEATER...!!

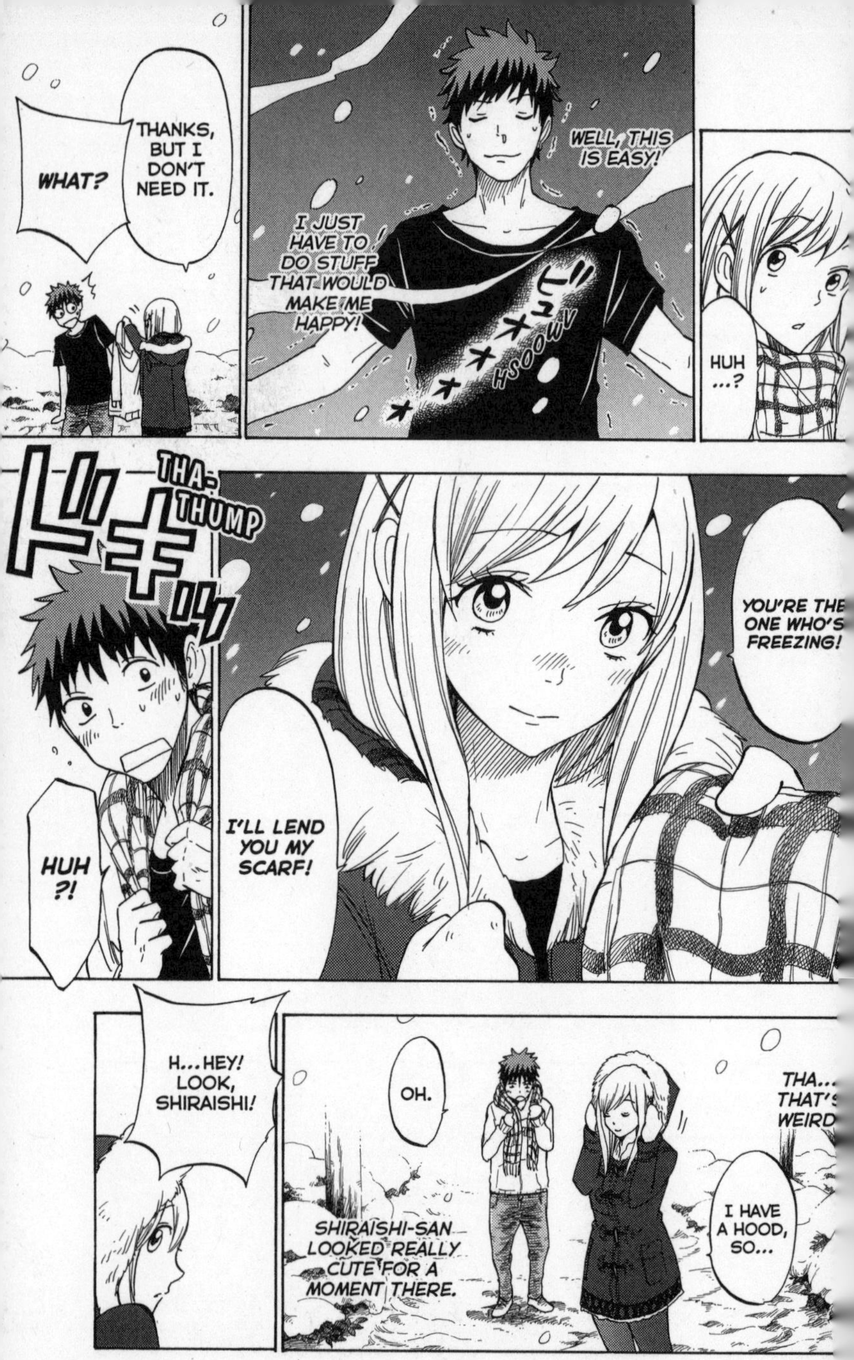
HUH ...?
WELL, THIS IS EASY!
I JUST HAVE TO DO STUFF THAT WOULD MAKE ME HAPPY!
ビュオオオオ
VWOOSH
THANKS, BUT I DON'T NEED IT.
WHAT?
YOU'RE THE ONE WHO'S FREEZING!
I'LL LEND YOU MY SCARF!
ドキッ
THA-THUMP
HUH ?!
THA... THAT'S WEIRD
I HAVE A HOOD, SO...
OH.
SHIRAISHI-SAN LOOKED REALLY CUTE FOR A MOMENT THERE.
H...HEY! LOOK, SHIRAISHI!

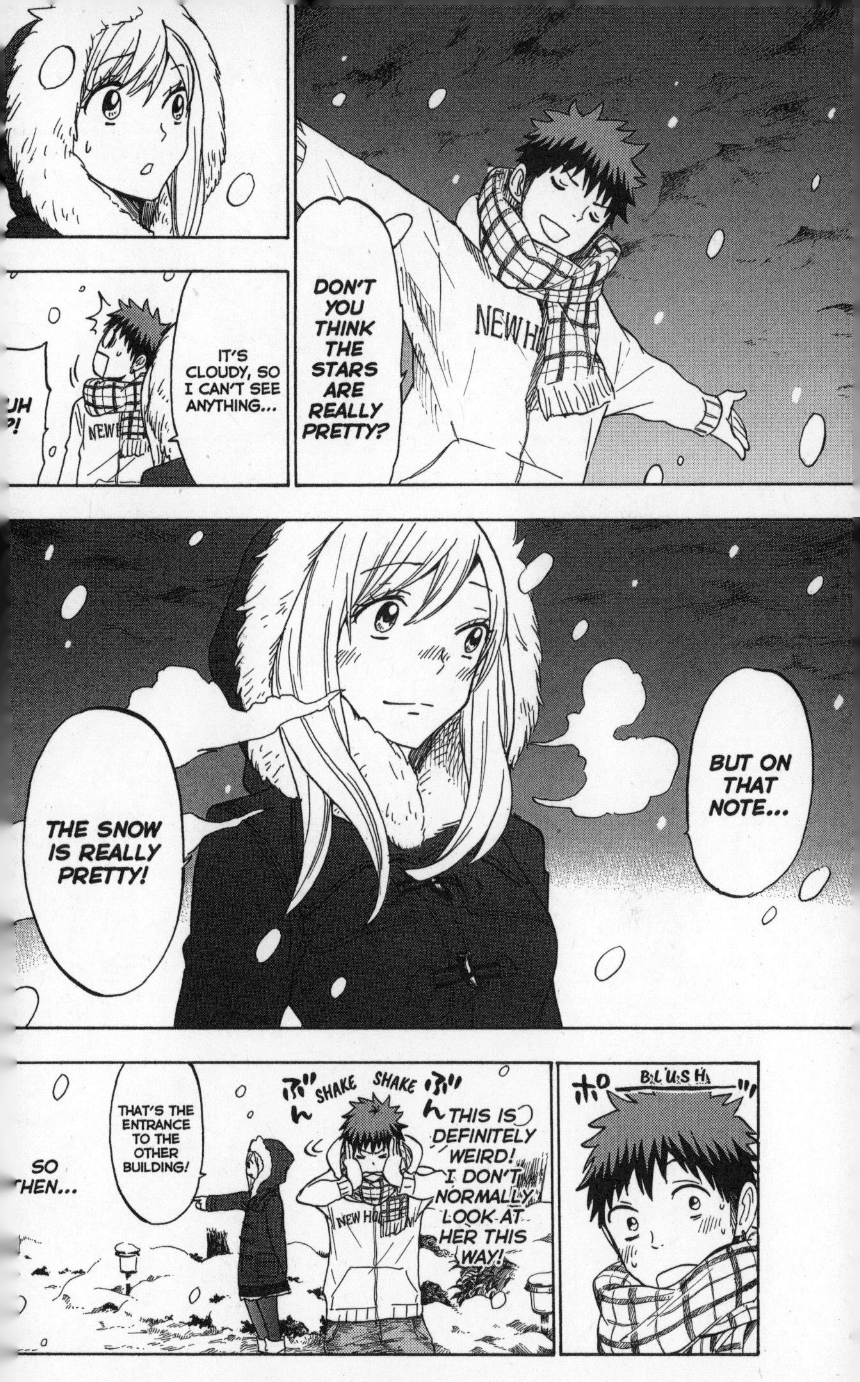

DON'T YOU THINK THE STARS ARE REALLY PRETTY?
IT'S CLOUDY, SO I CAN'T SEE ANYTHING...
BUT ON THAT NOTE...
THE SNOW IS REALLY PRETTY!
ポ
BLUSH
ぶん
SHAKE
SHAKE
ぶん
THIS IS DEFINITELY WEIRD! I DON'T NORMALLY LOOK AT HER THIS WAY!
THAT'S THE ENTRANCE TO THE OTHER BUILDING!
SO THEN...

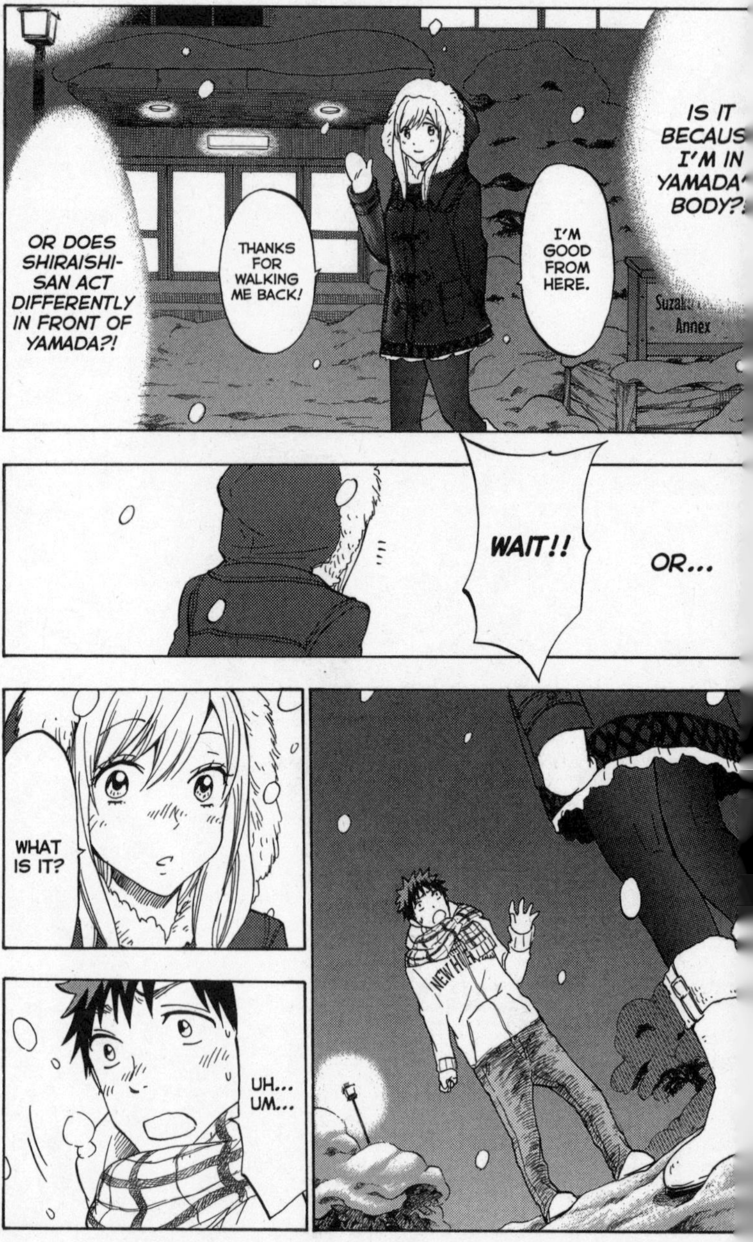
IS IT BECAUS I'M IN YAMADA' BODY?!
I'M GOOD FROM HERE.
THANKS FOR WALKING ME BACK!
Annex
OR DOES SHIRAISHI-SAN ACT DIFFERENTLY IN FRONT OF YAMADA?!
OR...
WAIT!!
...
WHAT IS IT?
UH... UM...

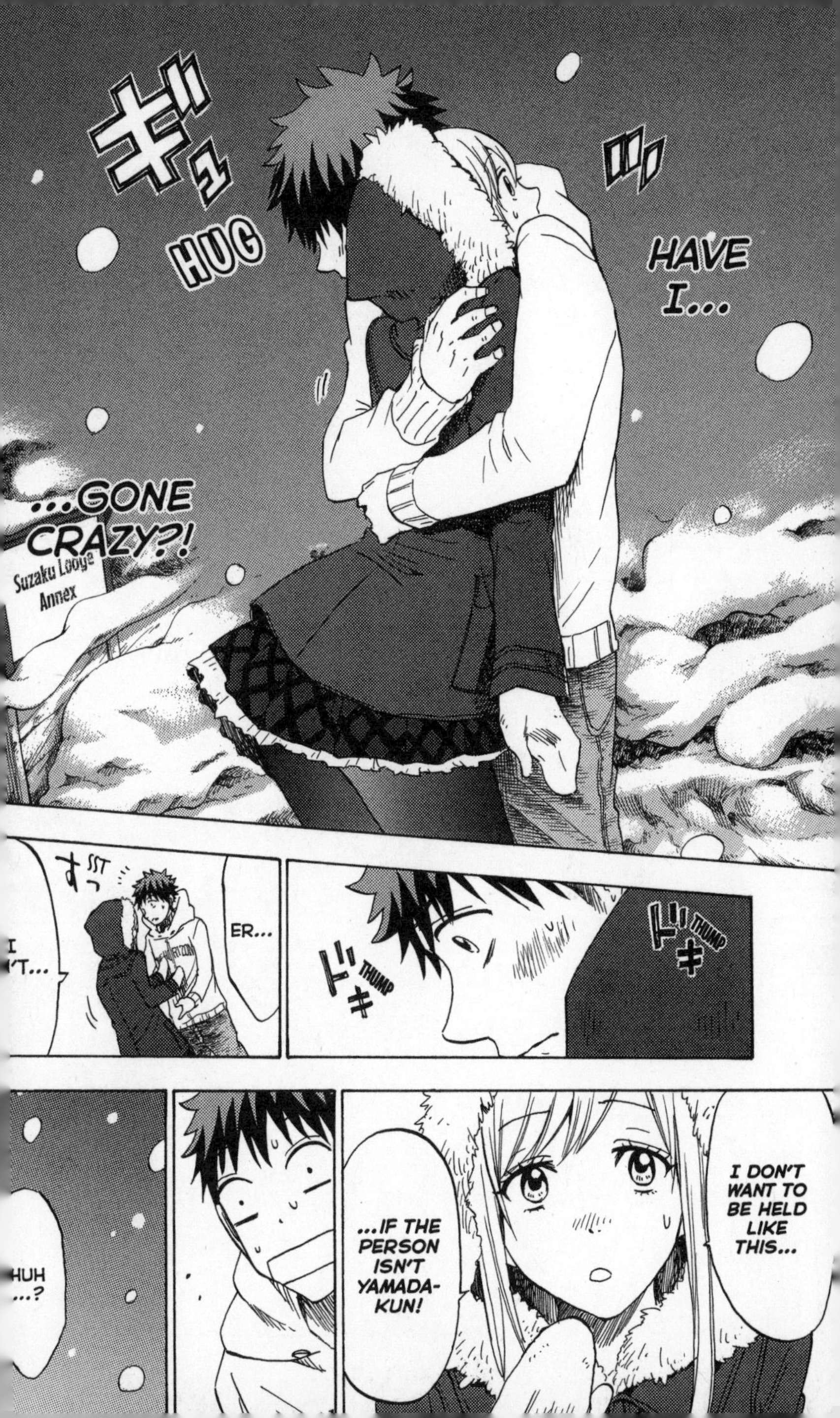
ギュ
HUG
HAVE I...
...GONE CRAZY?!
Suzaku
Annex
ドキ THUMP
ドキ THUMP
ER...
すッ SST
HUH ...?
I DON'T WANT TO BE HELD LIKE THIS...
...IF THE PERSON ISN'T YAMADA-KUN!

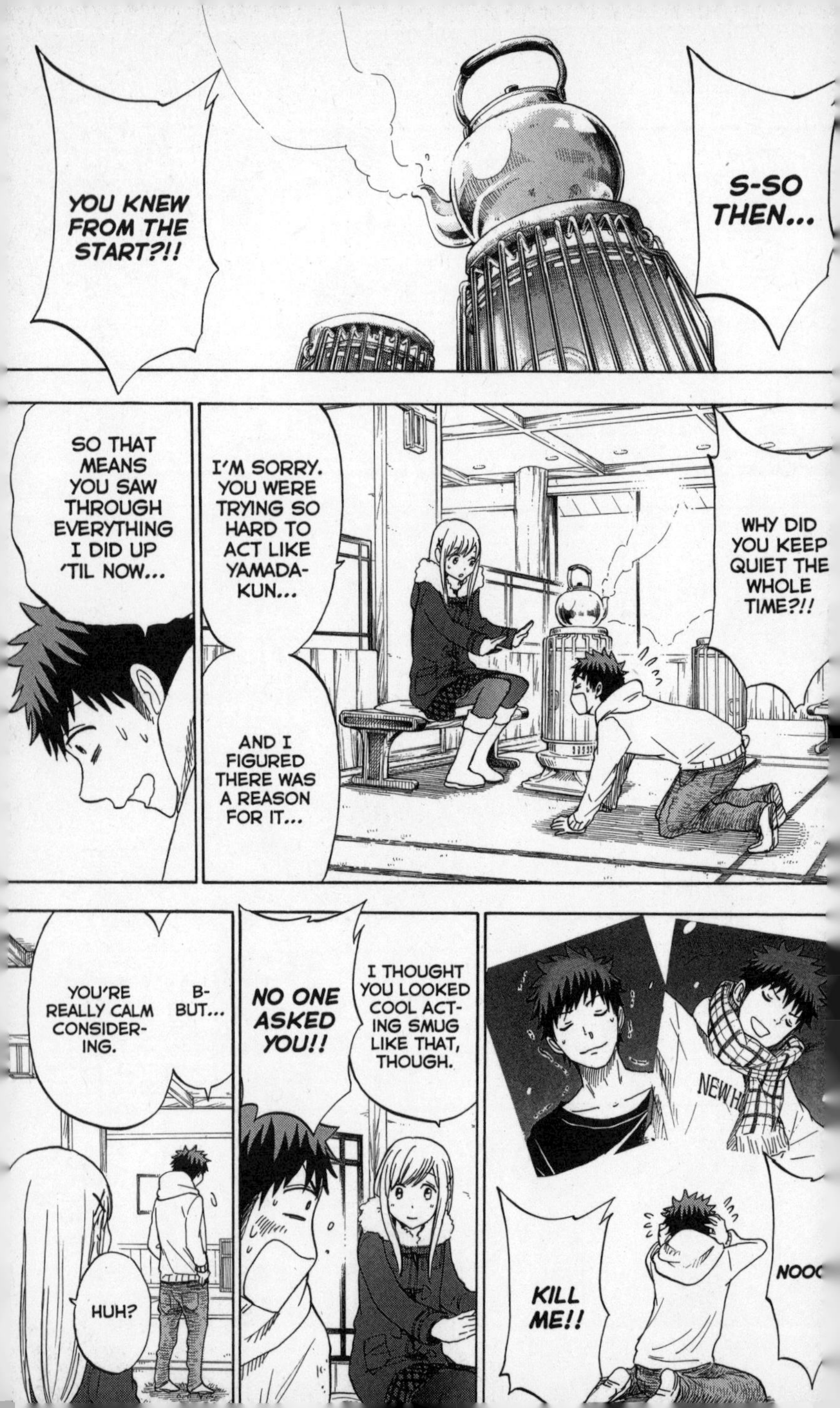
S-SO THEN...
YOU KNEW FROM THE START?!!
WHY DID YOU KEEP QUIET THE WHOLE TIME?!!
I'M SORRY. YOU WERE TRYING SO HARD TO ACT LIKE YAMADA-KUN...
AND I FIGURED THERE WAS A REASON FOR IT...
SO THAT MEANS YOU SAW THROUGH EVERYTHING I DID UP 'TIL NOW...
NOO
KILL ME!!
I THOUGHT YOU LOOKED COOL ACT-ING SMUG LIKE THAT, THOUGH.
NO ONE ASKED YOU!!
B-BUT...
YOU'RE REALLY CALM CONSIDER-ING.
HUH?
NEW H

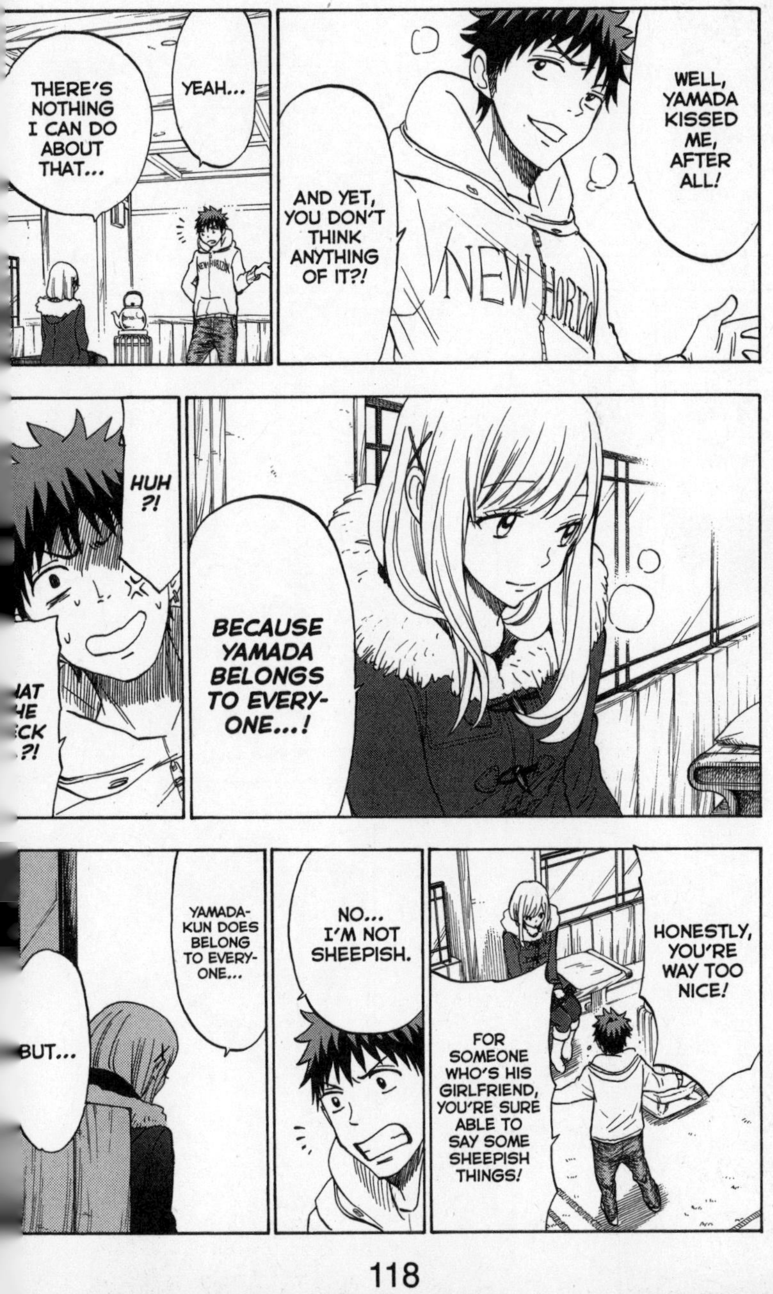
WELL, YAMADA KISSED ME, AFTER ALL!
AND YET, YOU DON'T THINK ANYTHING OF IT?!
YEAH...
THERE'S NOTHING I CAN DO ABOUT THAT...
BECAUSE YAMADA BELONGS TO EVERY-ONE...!
HUH?!
HONESTLY, YOU'RE WAY TOO NICE!
FOR SOMEONE WHO'S HIS GIRLFRIEND, YOU'RE SURE ABLE TO SAY SOME SHEEPISH THINGS!
NO... I'M NOT SHEEPISH.
YAMADA-KUN DOES BELONG TO EVERY-ONE...
BUT...

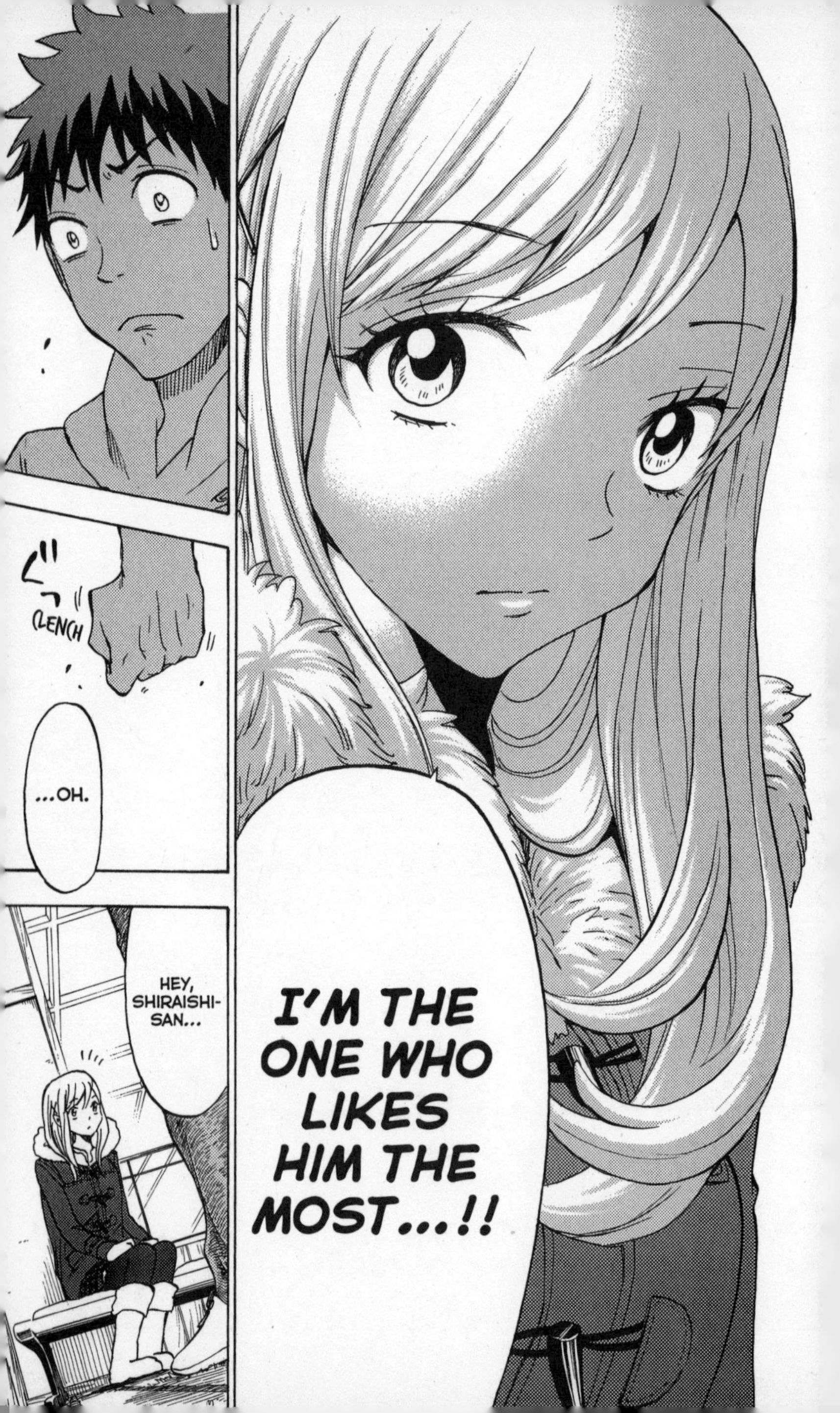
I'M THE ONE WHO LIKES HIM THE MOST...!!
ぐっ
CLENCH
...OH.
HEY, SHIRAISHI-SAN...

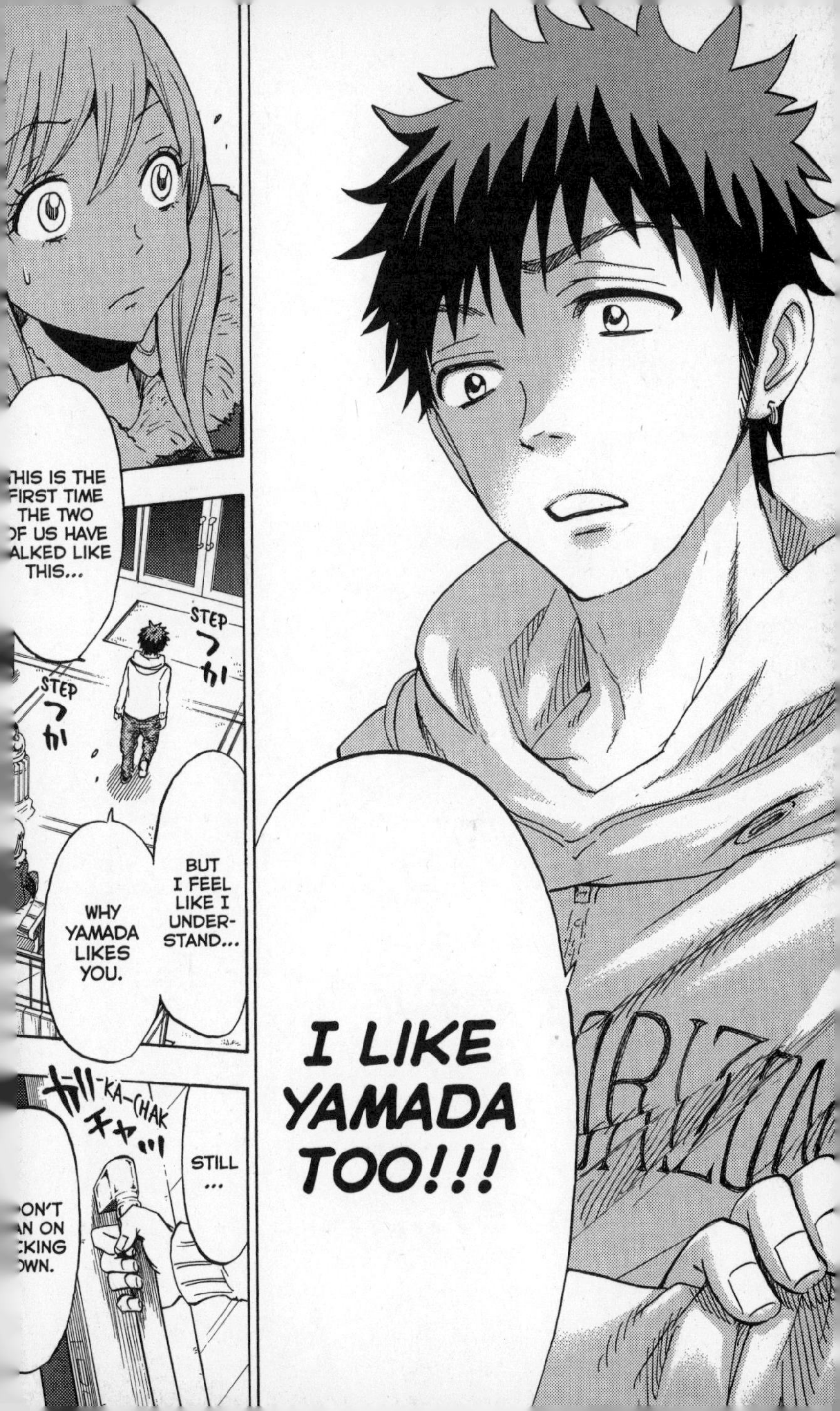

I LIKE YAMADA TOO!!!
THIS IS THE FIRST TIME THE TWO OF US HAVE ALKED LIKE THIS...
STEP つか
STEP つか
BUT I FEEL LIKE I UNDER-STAND...
WHY YAMADA LIKES YOU.
ガリ KA-CHAK チャッ
STILL ...
ON'T AN ON CKING WN.

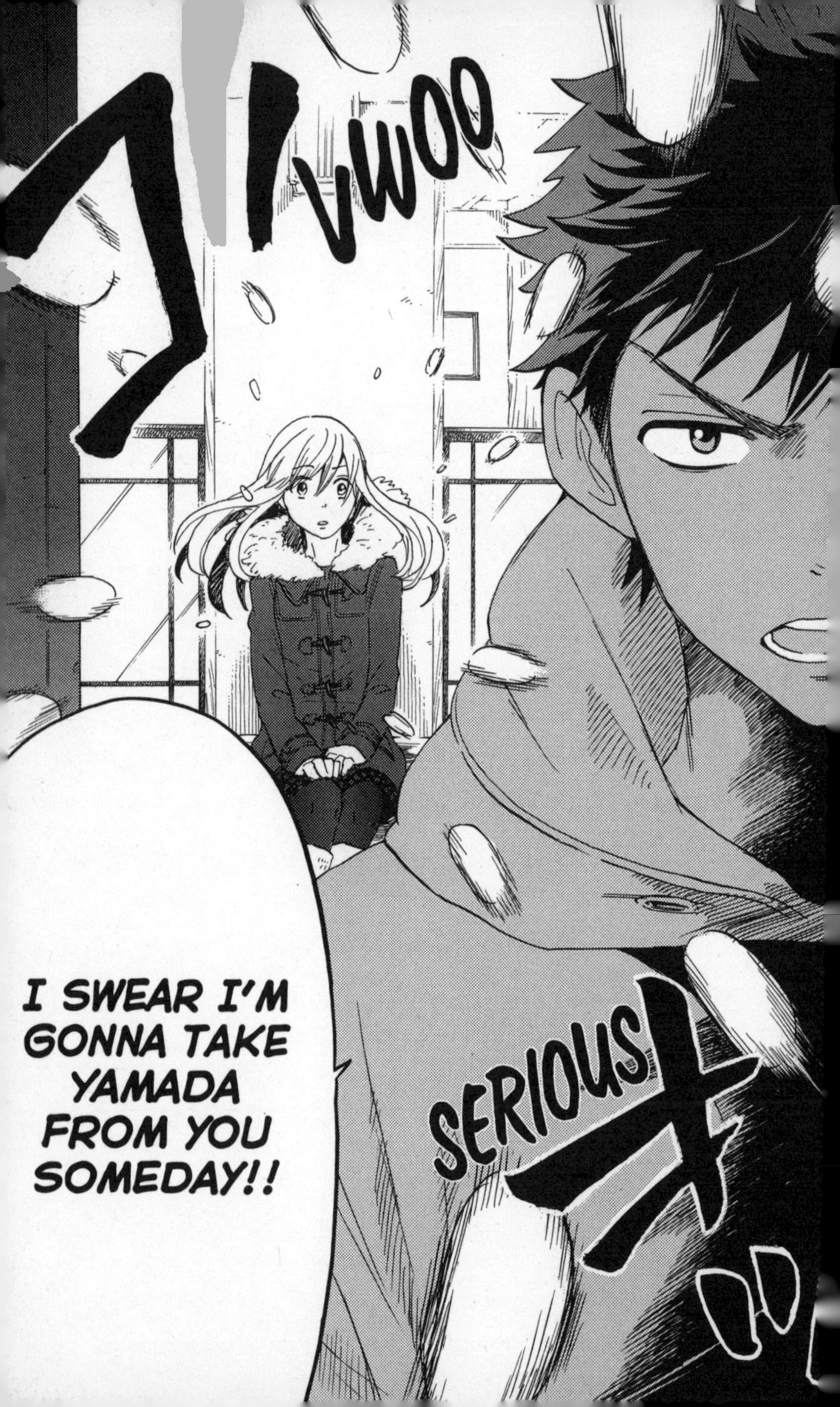
VWOO
SERIOUS
I SWEAR I'M GONNA TAKE YAMADA FROM YOU SOMEDAY!!

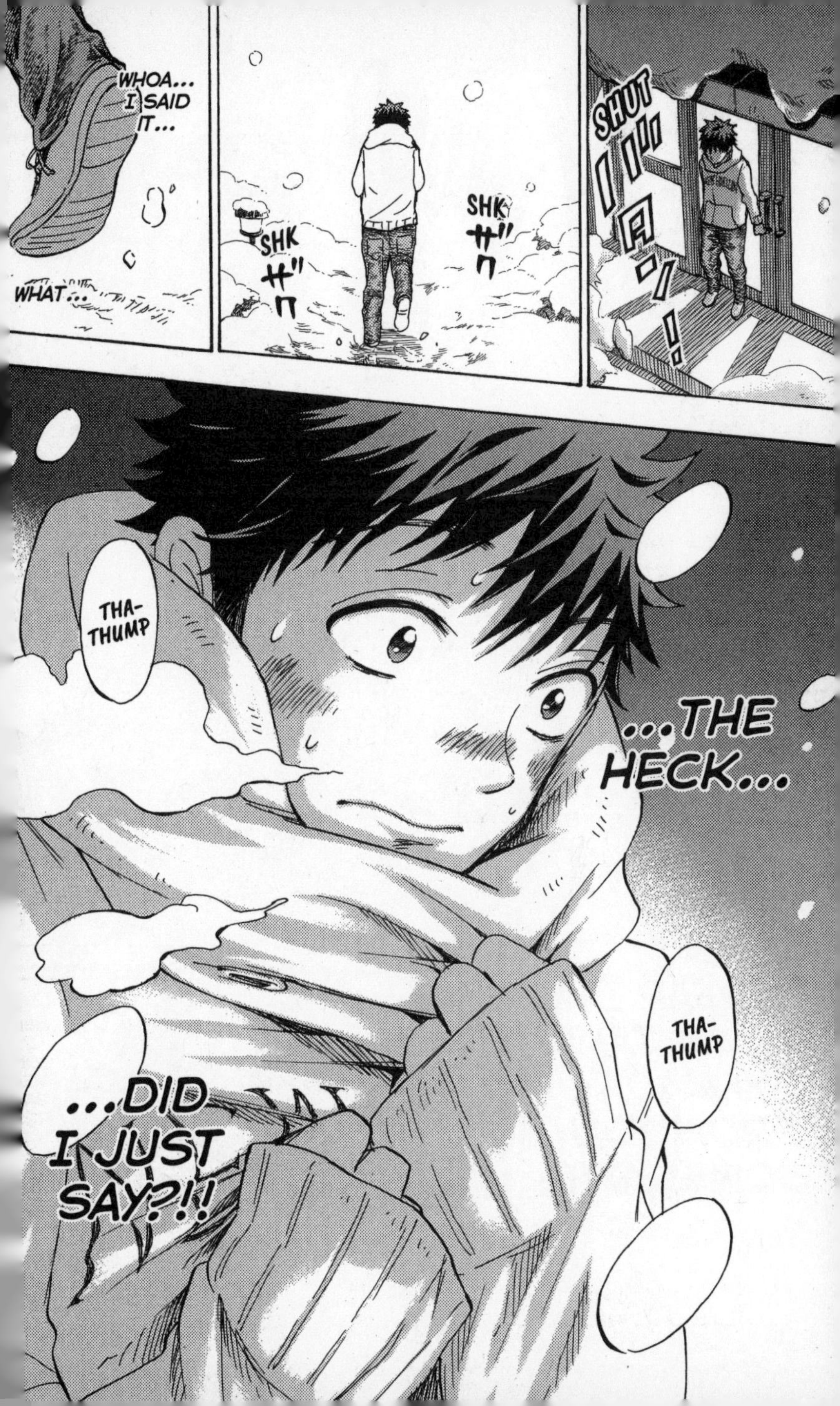
SHUT
SHK
ザッ
SHK
ザッ
WHOA... I SAID IT...
WHAT...
THA-THUMP
...THE HECK...
THA-THUMP
...DID I JUST SAY?!!

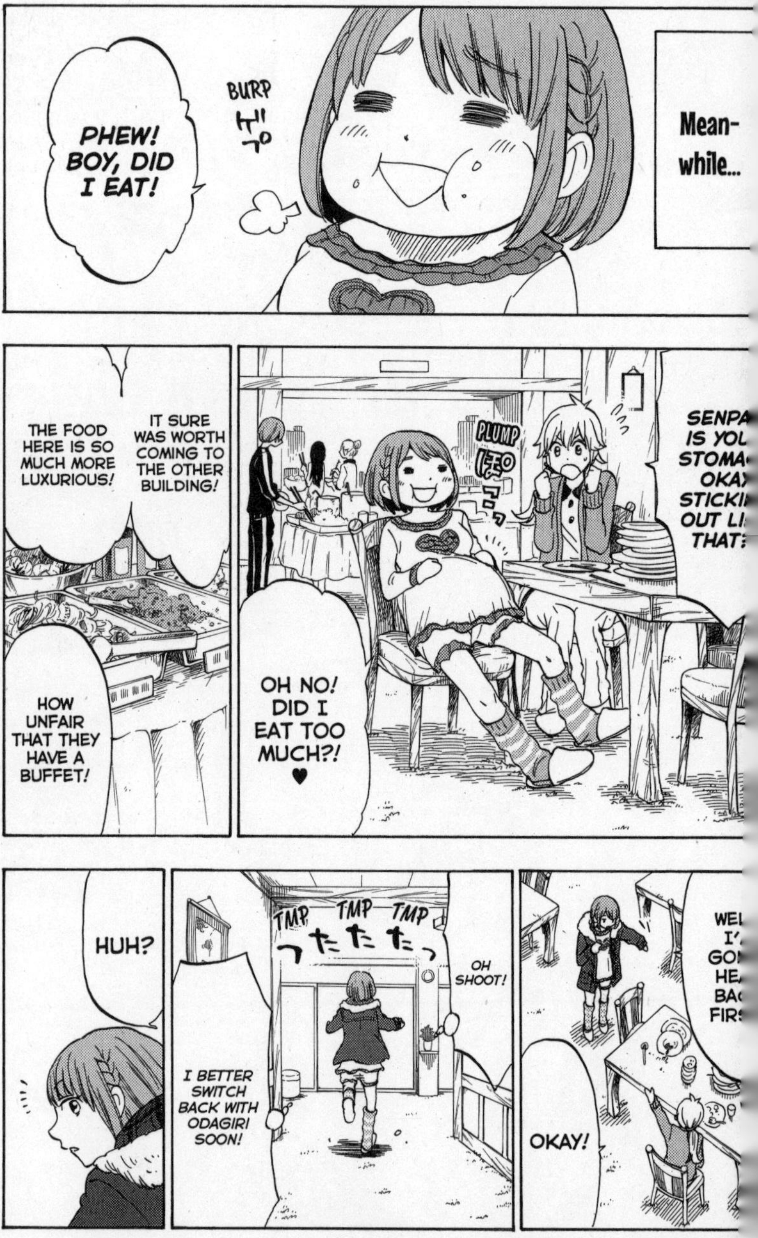

Mean-while...
BURP
ゲプ
PHEW! BOY, DID I EAT!
SENPA IS YOU STOMA OKAY STICKI OUT LI THAT?
PLUMP
OH NO! DID I EAT TOO MUCH?! ♥
IT SURE WAS WORTH COMING TO THE OTHER BUILDING!
THE FOOD HERE IS SO MUCH MORE LUXURIOUS!
HOW UNFAIR THAT THEY HAVE A BUFFET!
WEL I' GO HE BAC FIRS
OKAY!
TMP TMP TMP
つたたたっ
OH SHOOT!
I BETTER SWITCH BACK WITH ODAGIRI SOON!
HUH?

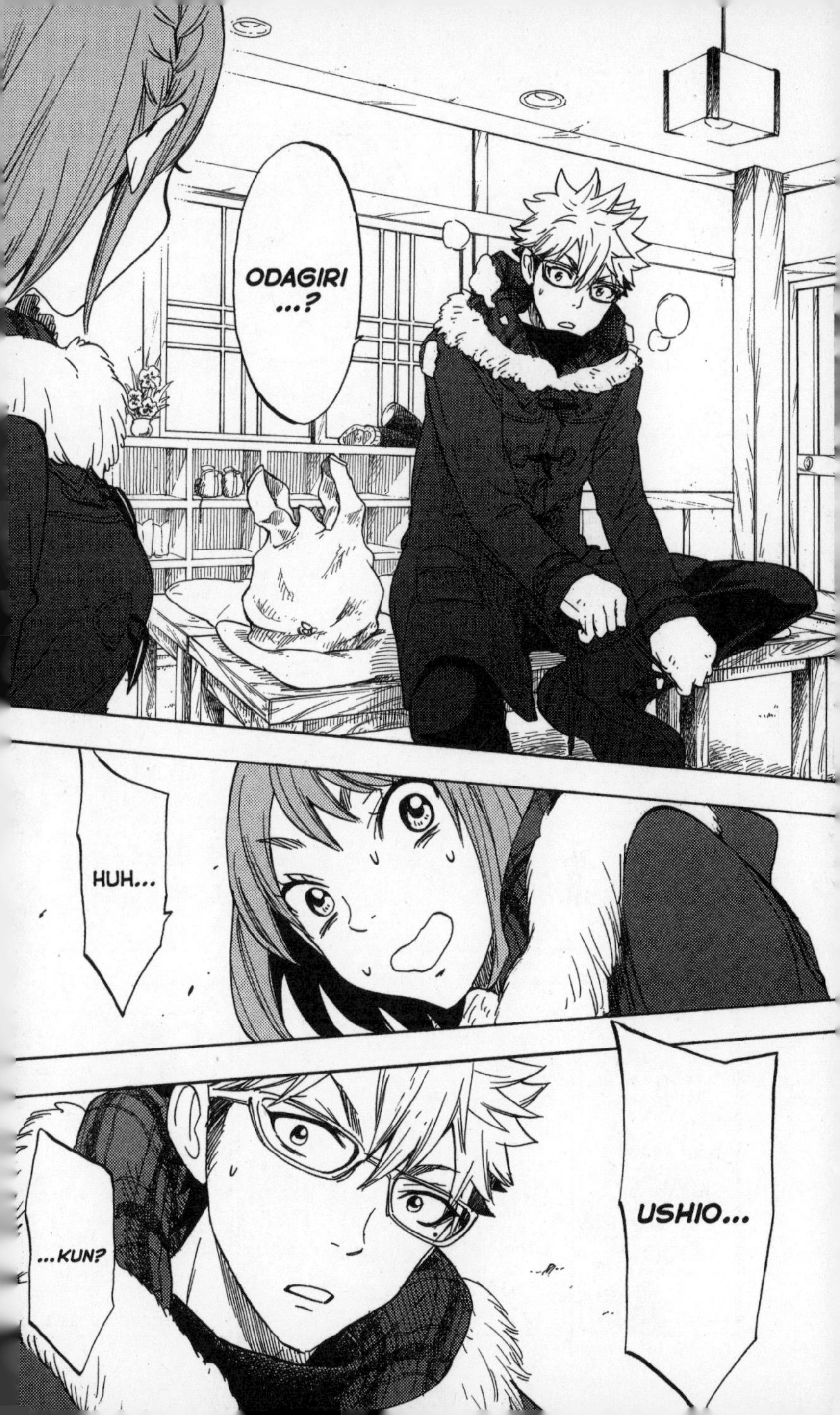
ODAGIRI ...?
HUH...
USHIO...
...KUN?

CHAPTER 117: Gotta get back!

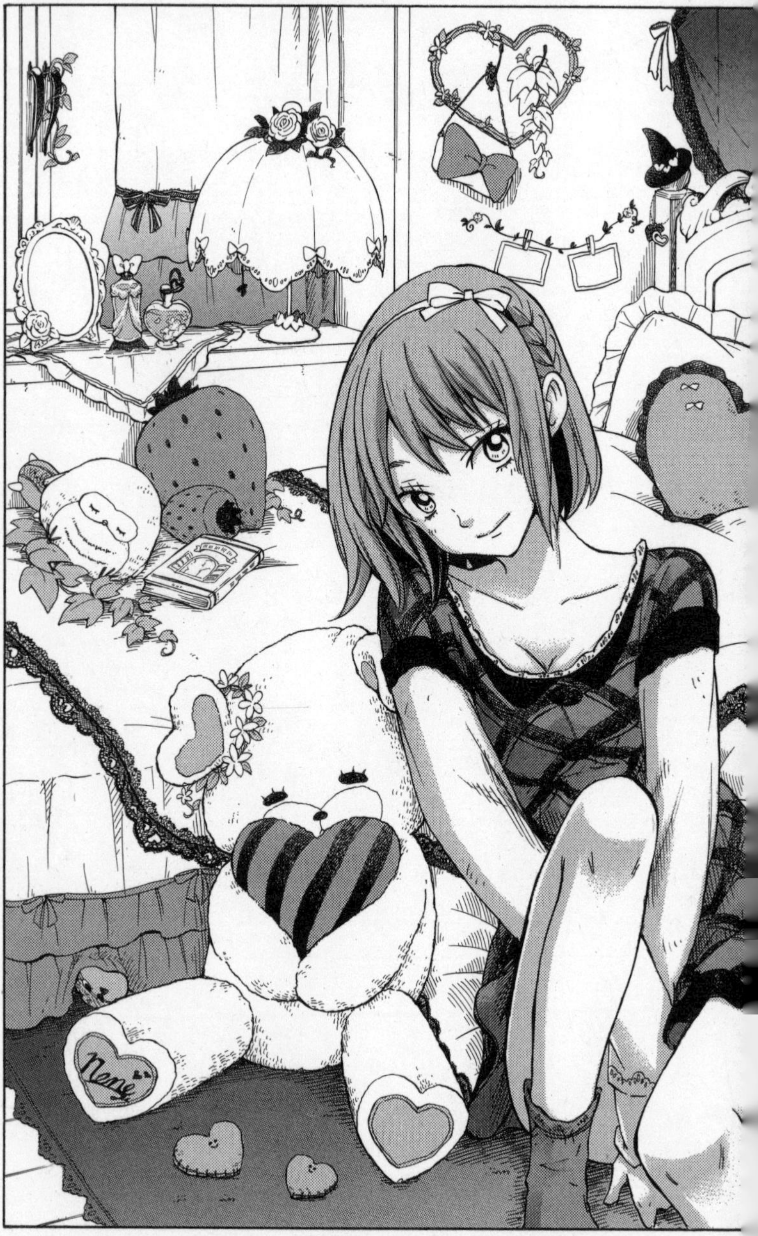
Nene

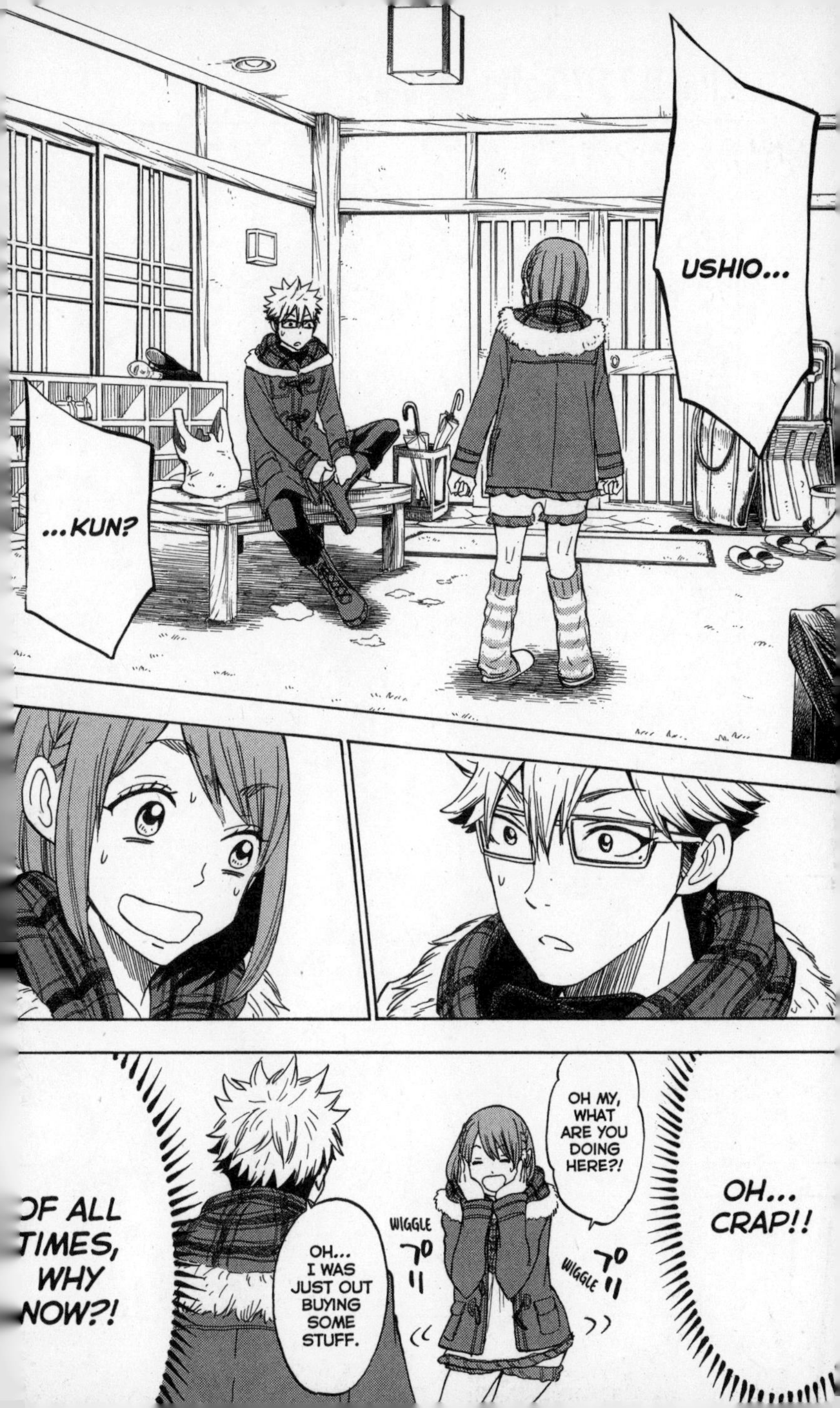
USHIO...
...KUN?
OH... CRAP!!
OH MY, WHAT ARE YOU DOING HERE?!
WIGGLE
WIGGLE
OH... I WAS JUST OUT BUYING SOME STUFF.
OF ALL TIMES, WHY NOW?!

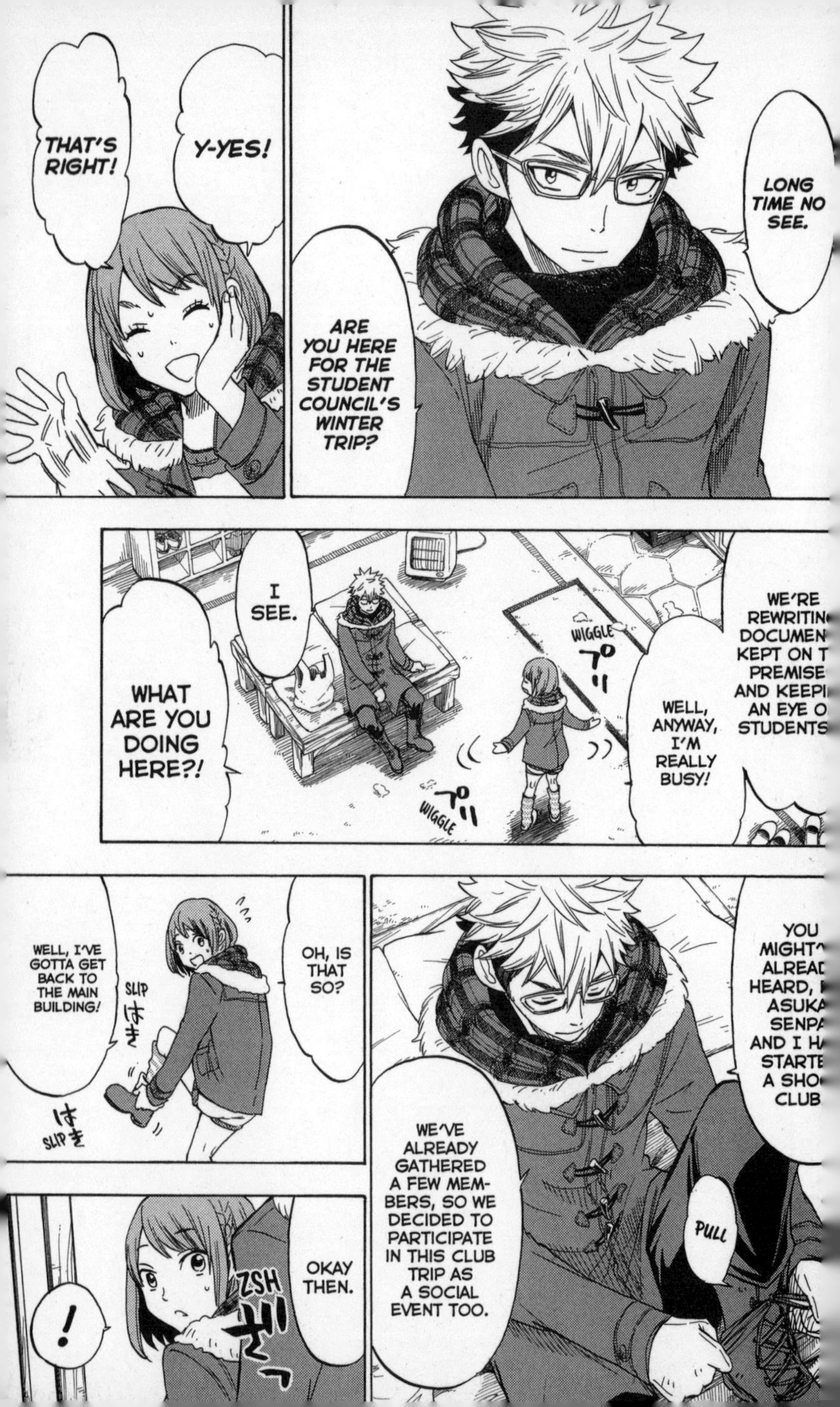
LONG TIME NO SEE.
ARE YOU HERE FOR THE STUDENT COUNCIL'S WINTER TRIP?
Y-YES!
THAT'S RIGHT!
WE'RE REWRITIN DOCUMEN KEPT ON T PREMISE AND KEEPI AN EYE O STUDENTS
WELL, ANYWAY, I'M REALLY BUSY!
WIGGLE
WIGGLE
I SEE.
WHAT ARE YOU DOING HERE?!
YOU MIGHT ALREAD HEARD, ASUKA SENPA AND I HA STARTE A SHO CLUB
WE'VE ALREADY GATHERED A FEW MEM-BERS, SO WE DECIDED TO PARTICIPATE IN THIS CLUB TRIP AS A SOCIAL EVENT TOO.
PULL
OH, IS THAT SO?
WELL, I'VE GOTTA GET BACK TO THE MAIN BUILDING!
SLIP
SLIP
OKAY THEN.
ZSH
!

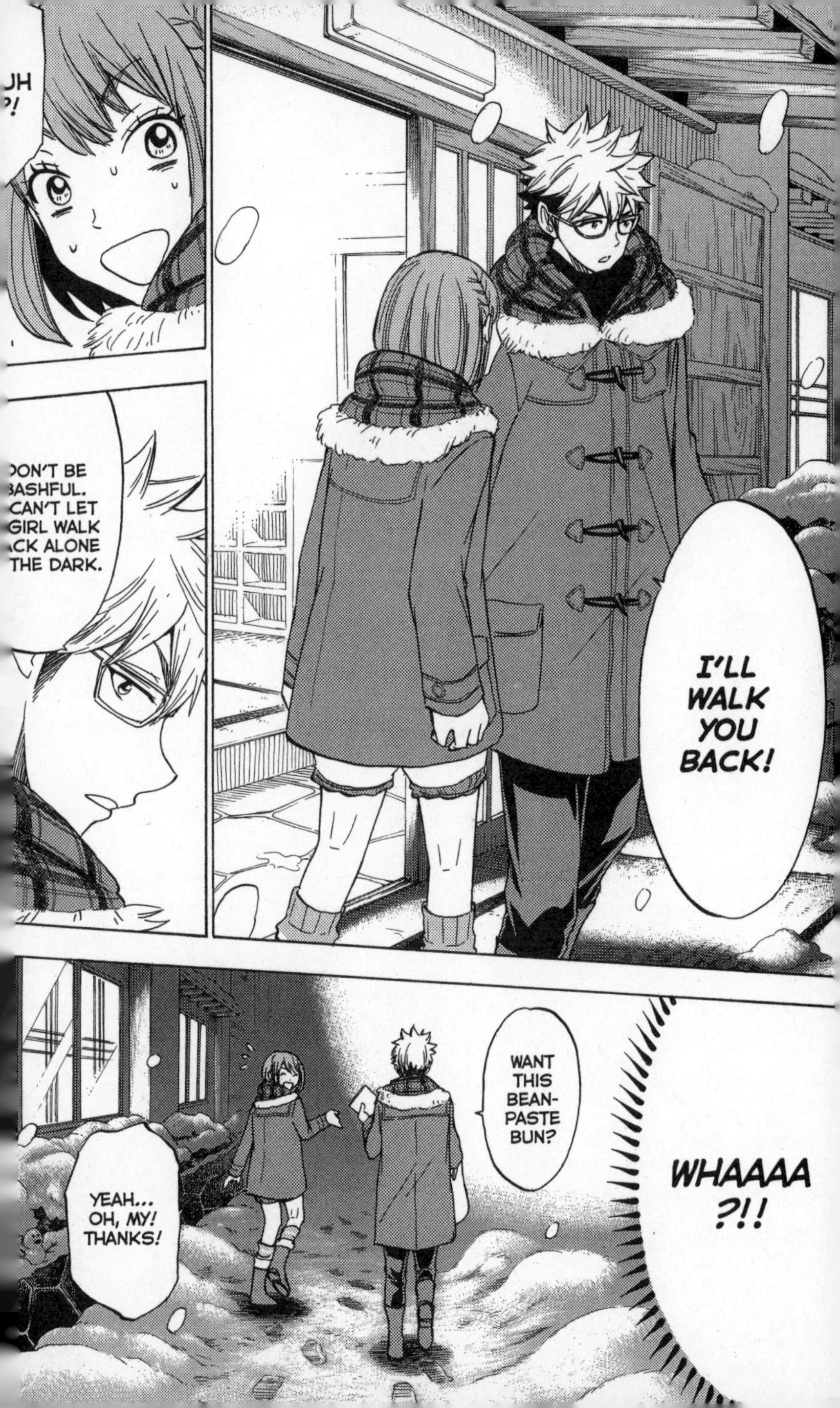
I'LL WALK YOU BACK!
UH ?!
DON'T BE BASHFUL. CAN'T LET GIRL WALK ACK ALONE THE DARK.
WHAAAA ?!!
WANT THIS BEAN-PASTE BUN?
YEAH... OH, MY! THANKS!

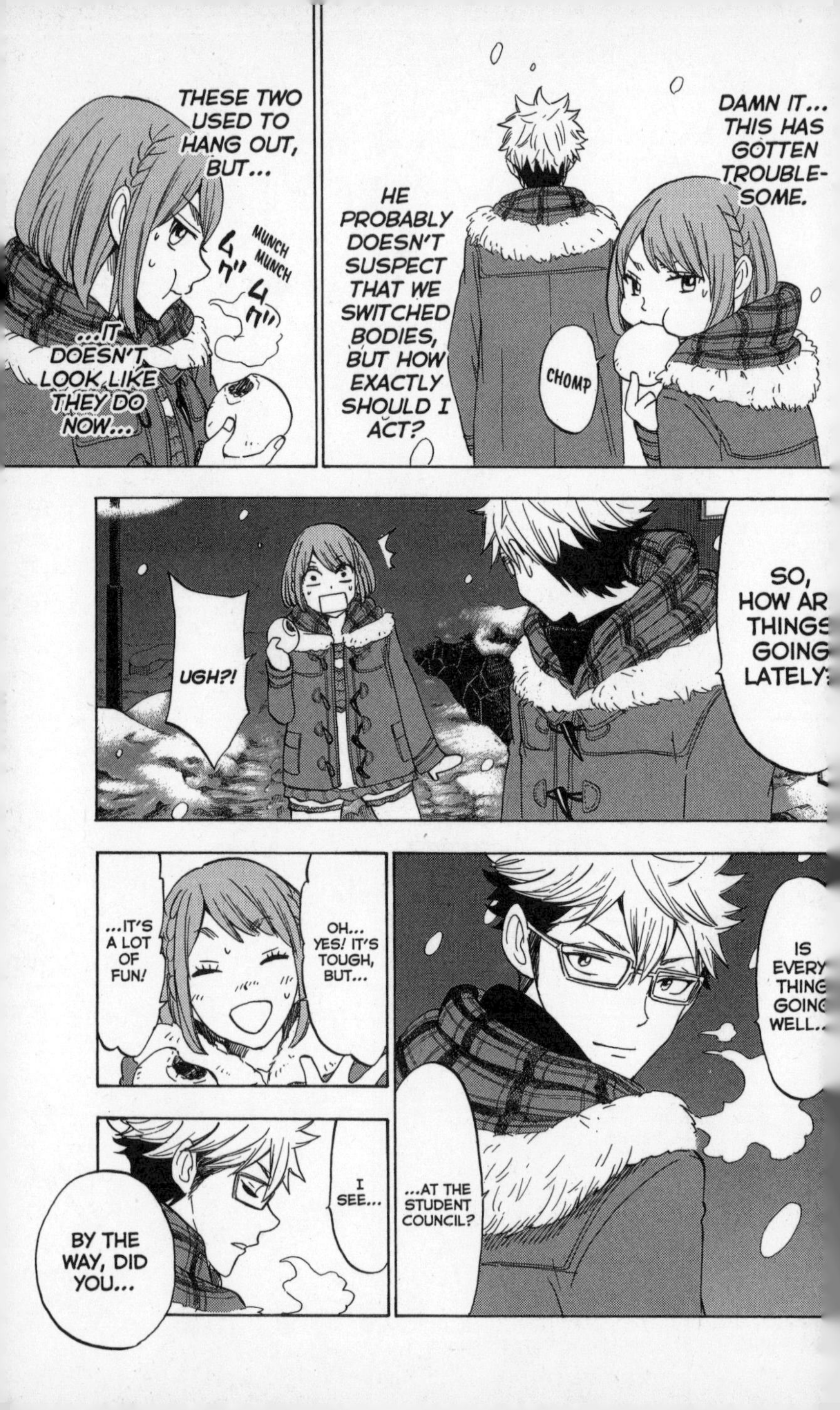
DAMN IT... THIS HAS GOTTEN TROUBLE-SOME.
HE PROBABLY DOESN'T SUSPECT THAT WE SWITCHED BODIES, BUT HOW EXACTLY SHOULD I ACT?
CHOMP
THESE TWO USED TO HANG OUT, BUT...
MUNCH MUNCH
ムグ ムグ
...IT DOESN'T LOOK LIKE THEY DO NOW...
SO, HOW AR THINGS GOING LATELY
UGH?!
IS EVERY THING GOING WELL..
...AT THE STUDENT COUNCIL?
OH... YES! IT'S TOUGH, BUT...
...IT'S A LOT OF FUN!
I SEE...
BY THE WAY, DID YOU...

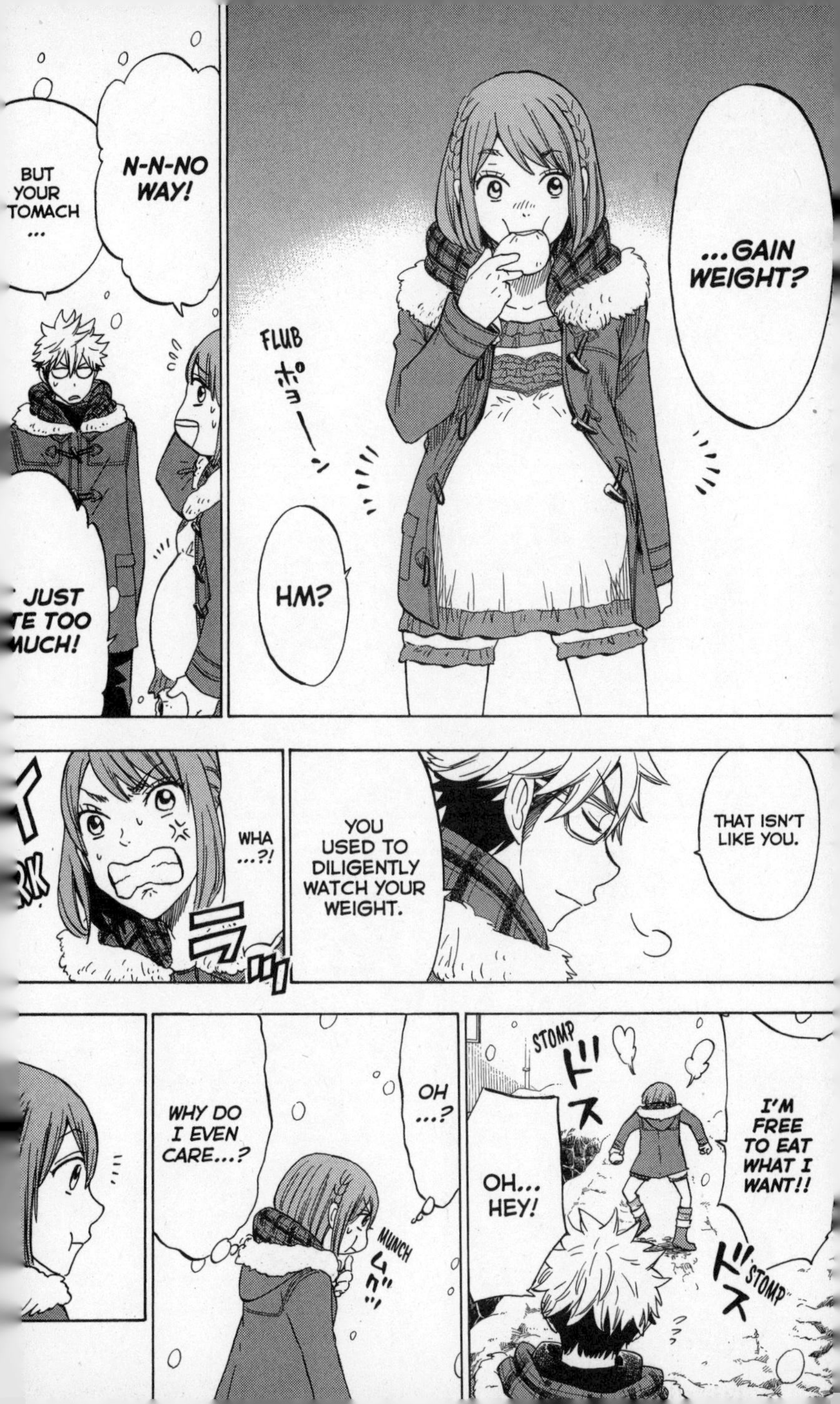
...GAIN WEIGHT?
FLUB
ポヨーン
HM?
N-N-NO WAY!
BUT YOUR TOMACH ...
JUST TE TOO MUCH!
THAT ISN'T LIKE YOU.
YOU USED TO DILIGENTLY WATCH YOUR WEIGHT.
WHA ...?!
I'M FREE TO EAT WHAT I WANT!!
STOMP
ドス
STOMP
ドス
OH... HEY!
OH ...?
WHY DO I EVEN CARE...?
MUNCH
ムグ

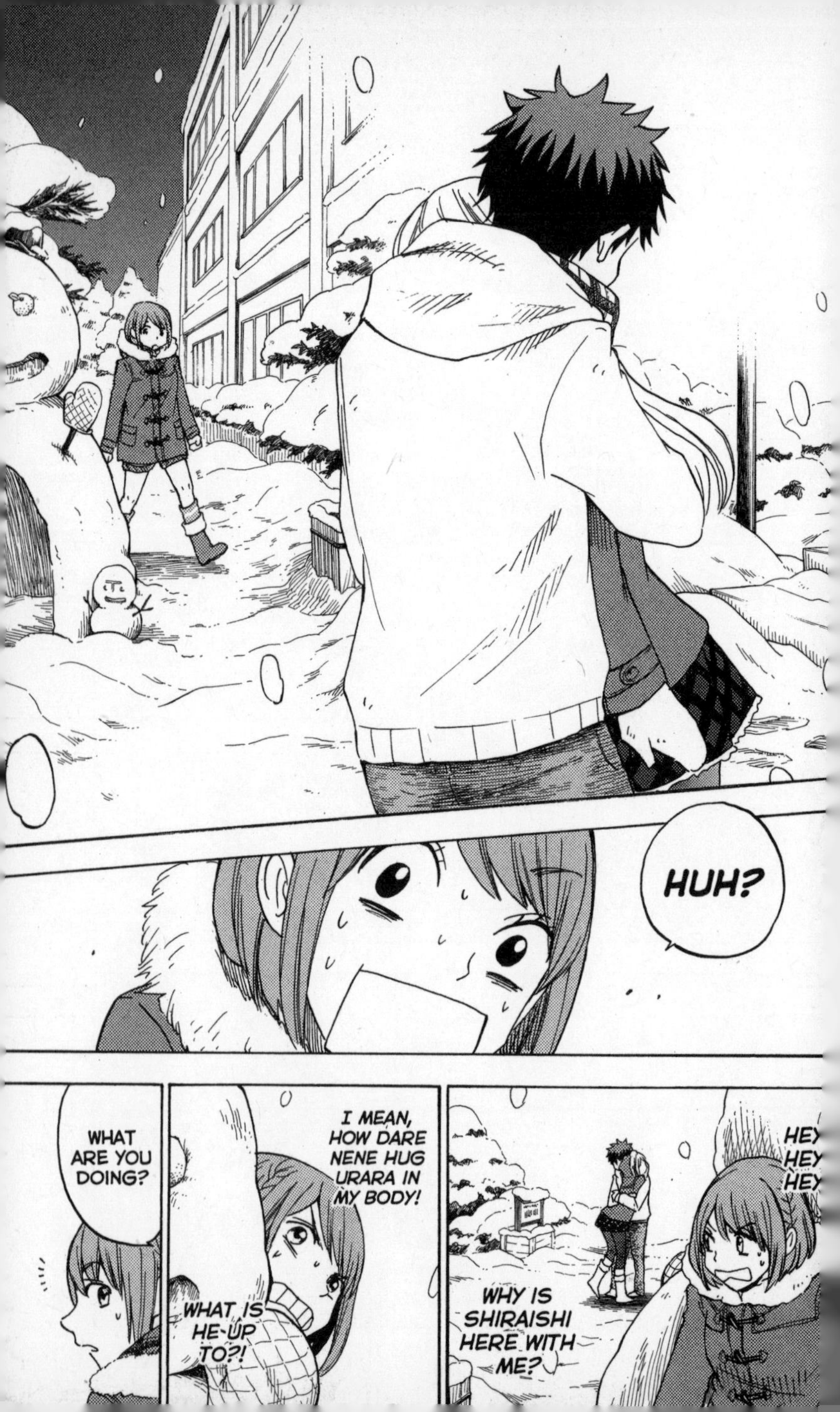
HUH?
HEY HEY HEY
WHY IS SHIRAISHI HERE WITH ME?
I MEAN, HOW DARE NENE HUG URARA IN MY BODY!
WHAT IS HE UP TO?!
WHAT ARE YOU DOING?

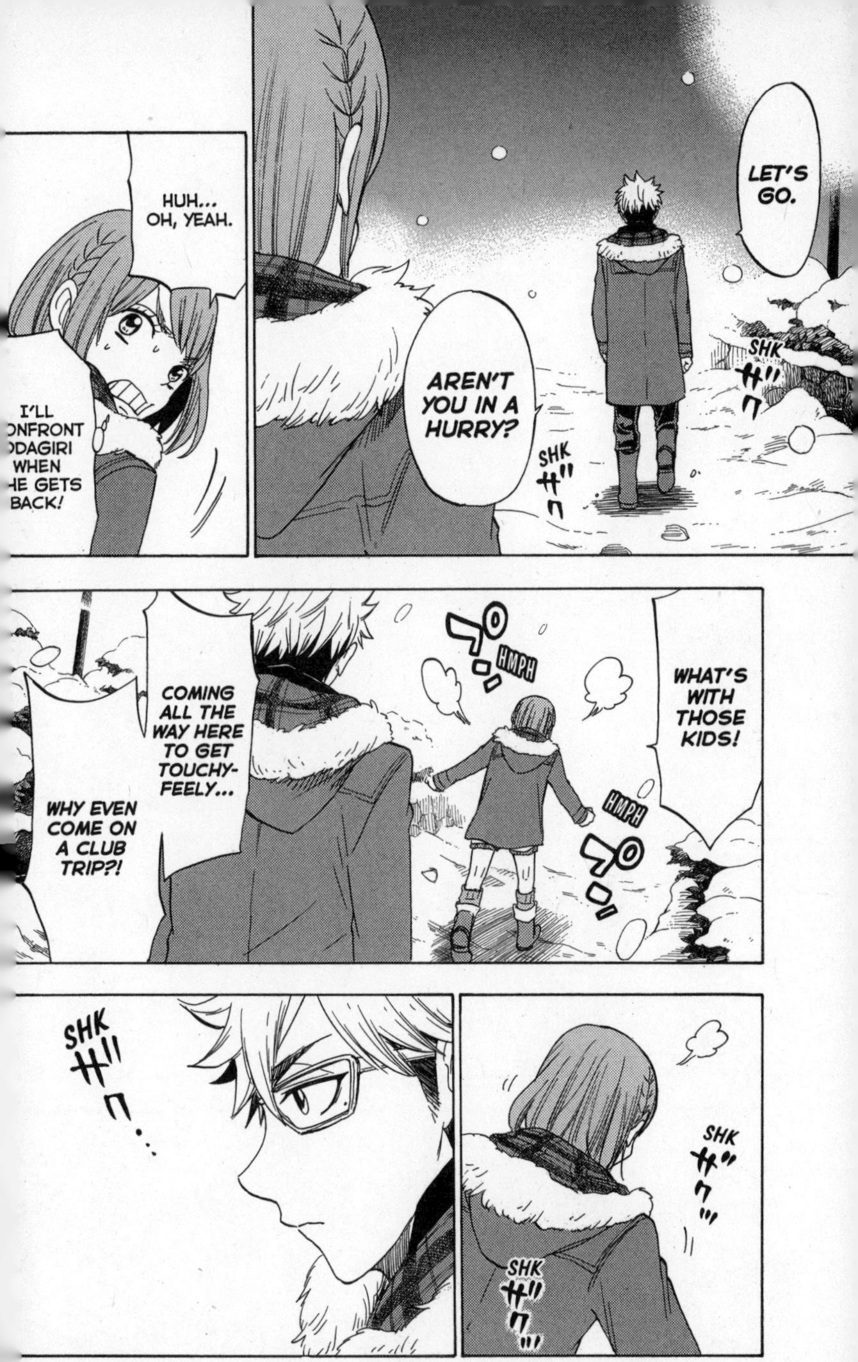
LET'S GO.
AREN'T YOU IN A HURRY?
SHK
SHK
HUH... OH, YEAH.
I'LL ONFRONT ODAGIRI WHEN HE GETS BACK!
WHAT'S WITH THOSE KIDS!
HMPH
HMPH
COMING ALL THE WAY HERE TO GET TOUCHY-FEELY...
WHY EVEN COME ON A CLUB TRIP?!
SHK
SHK
SHK...

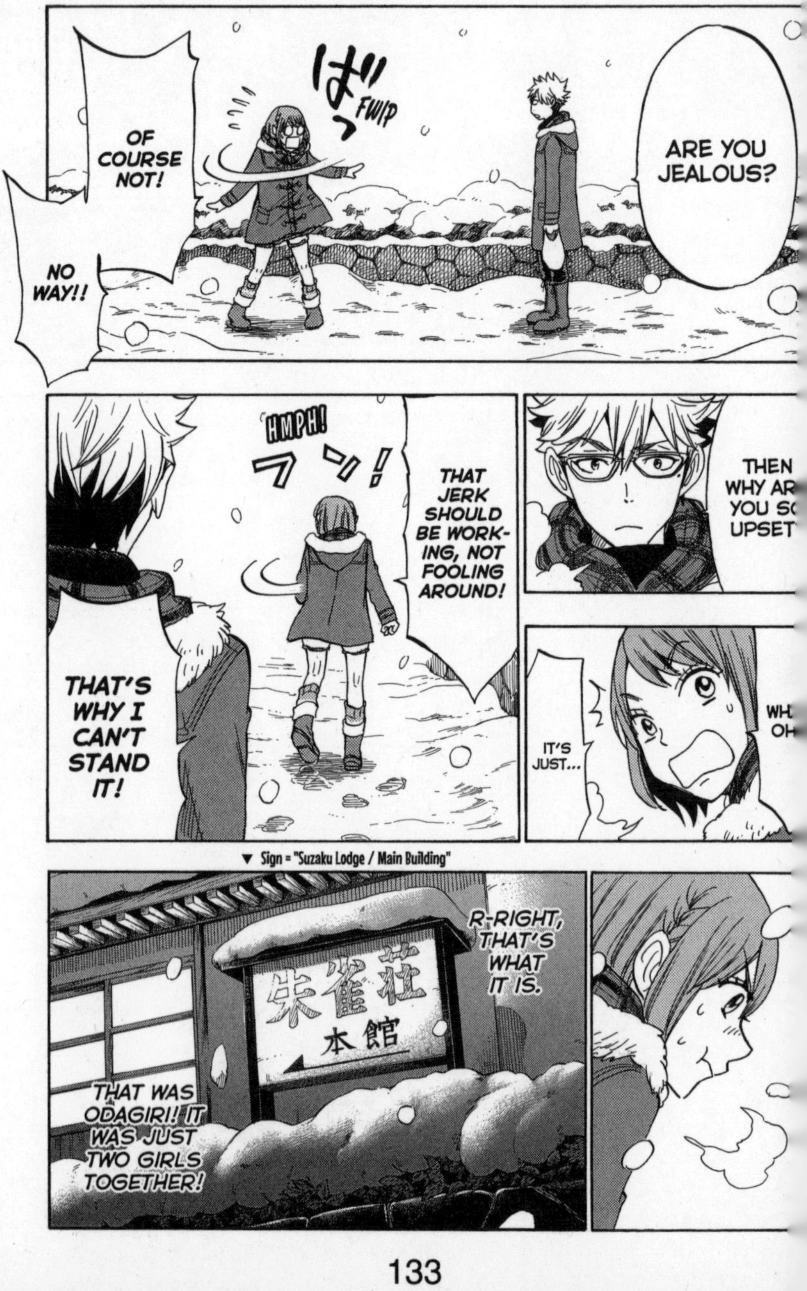
ARE YOU JEALOUS?
ばっ FWIP
OF COURSE NOT!
NO WAY!!
THEN WHY AR YOU S UPSET
WH OH
IT'S JUST...
HMPH! フンッ!
THAT JERK SHOULD BE WORK-ING, NOT FOOLING AROUND!
THAT'S WHY I CAN'T STAND IT!
朱雀荘 本館
R-RIGHT, THAT'S WHAT IT IS.
THAT WAS ODAGIRI! IT WAS JUST TWO GIRLS TOGETHER!

▼ Sign = "Suzaku Lodge / Main Building"

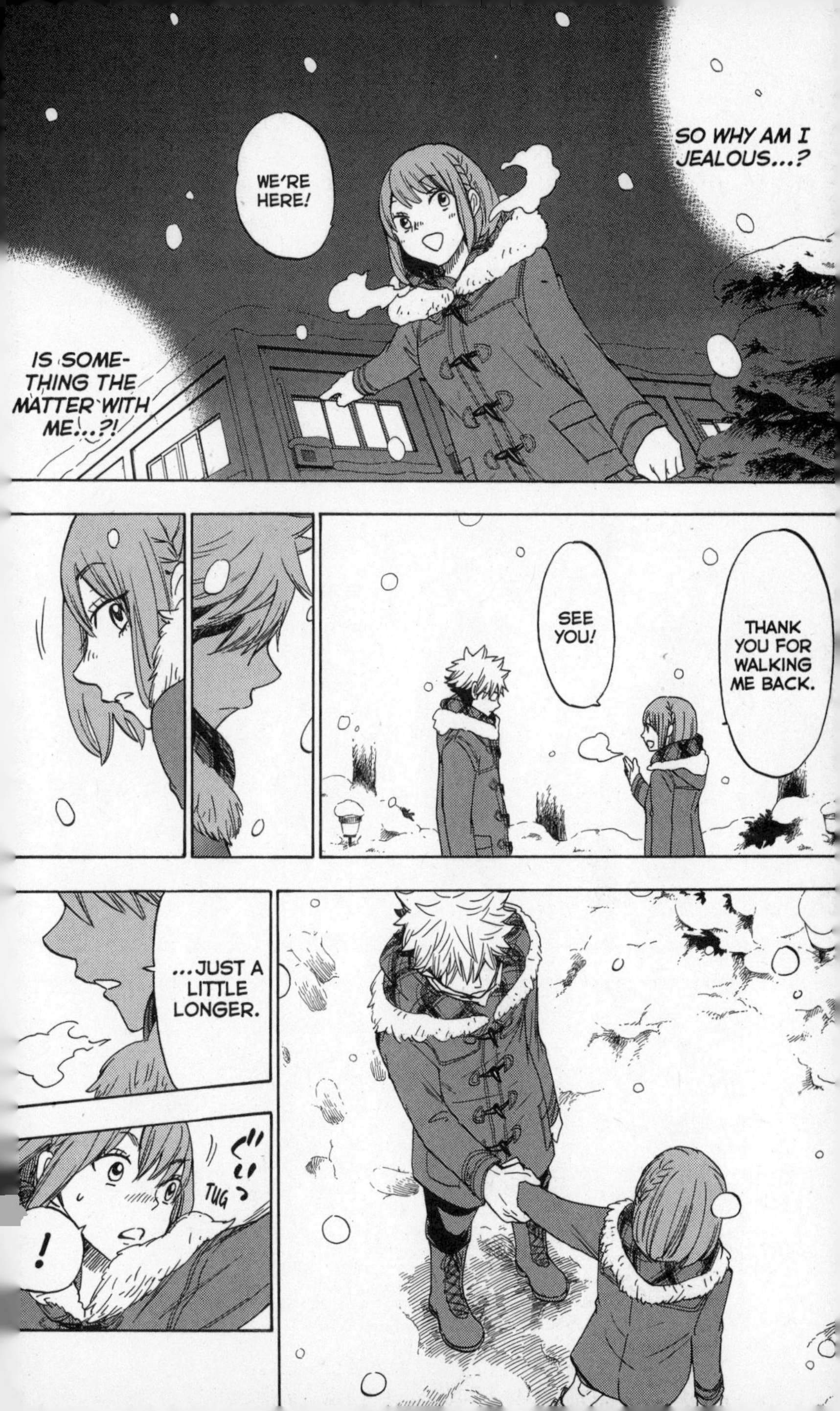
SO WHY AM I JEALOUS...?
WE'RE HERE!
IS SOME-THING THE MATTER WITH ME...?!
THANK YOU FOR WALKING ME BACK.
SEE YOU!
...JUST A LITTLE LONGER.
TUG
!

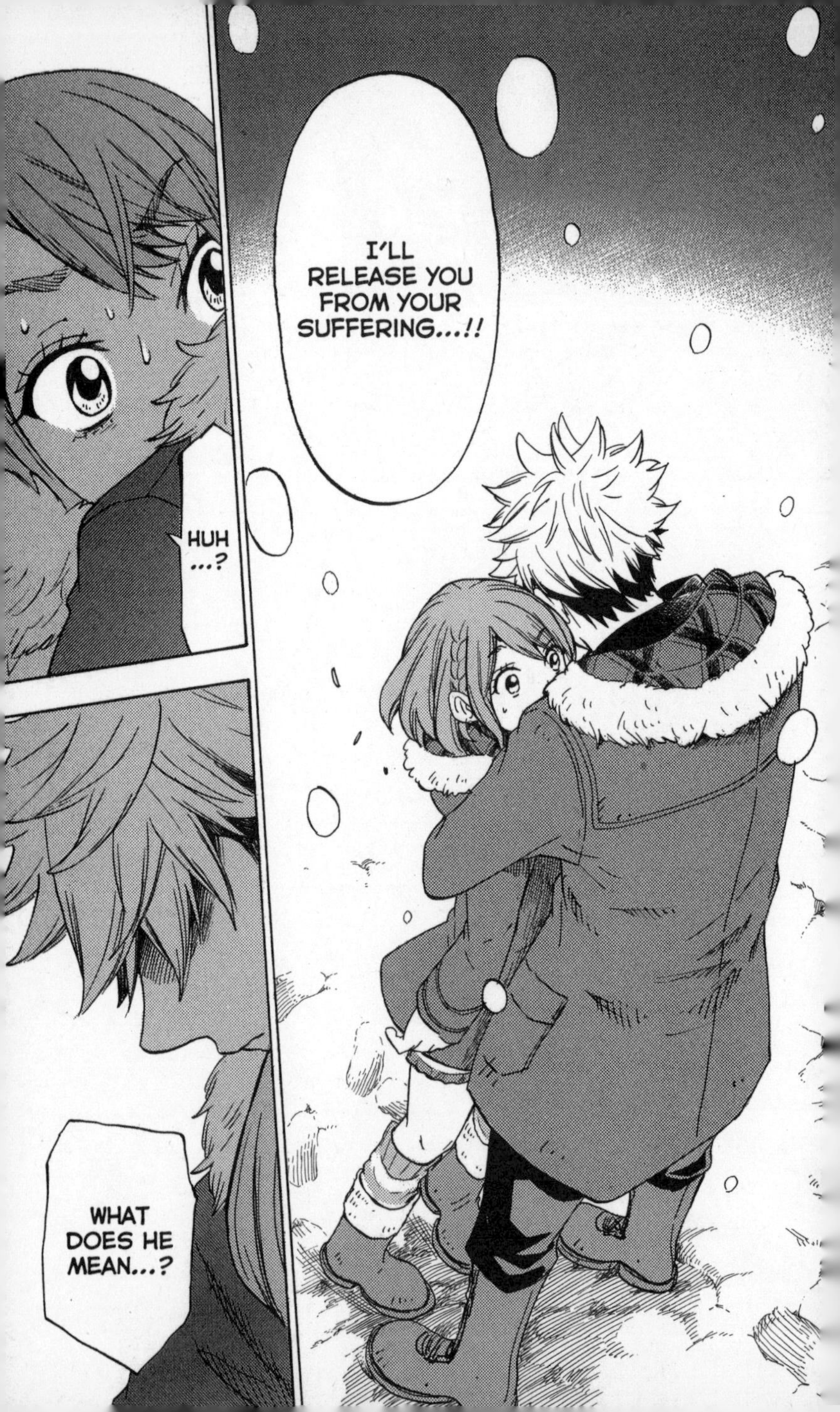
I'LL RELEASE YOU FROM YOUR SUFFERING...!!
HUH ...?
WHAT DOES HE MEAN...?

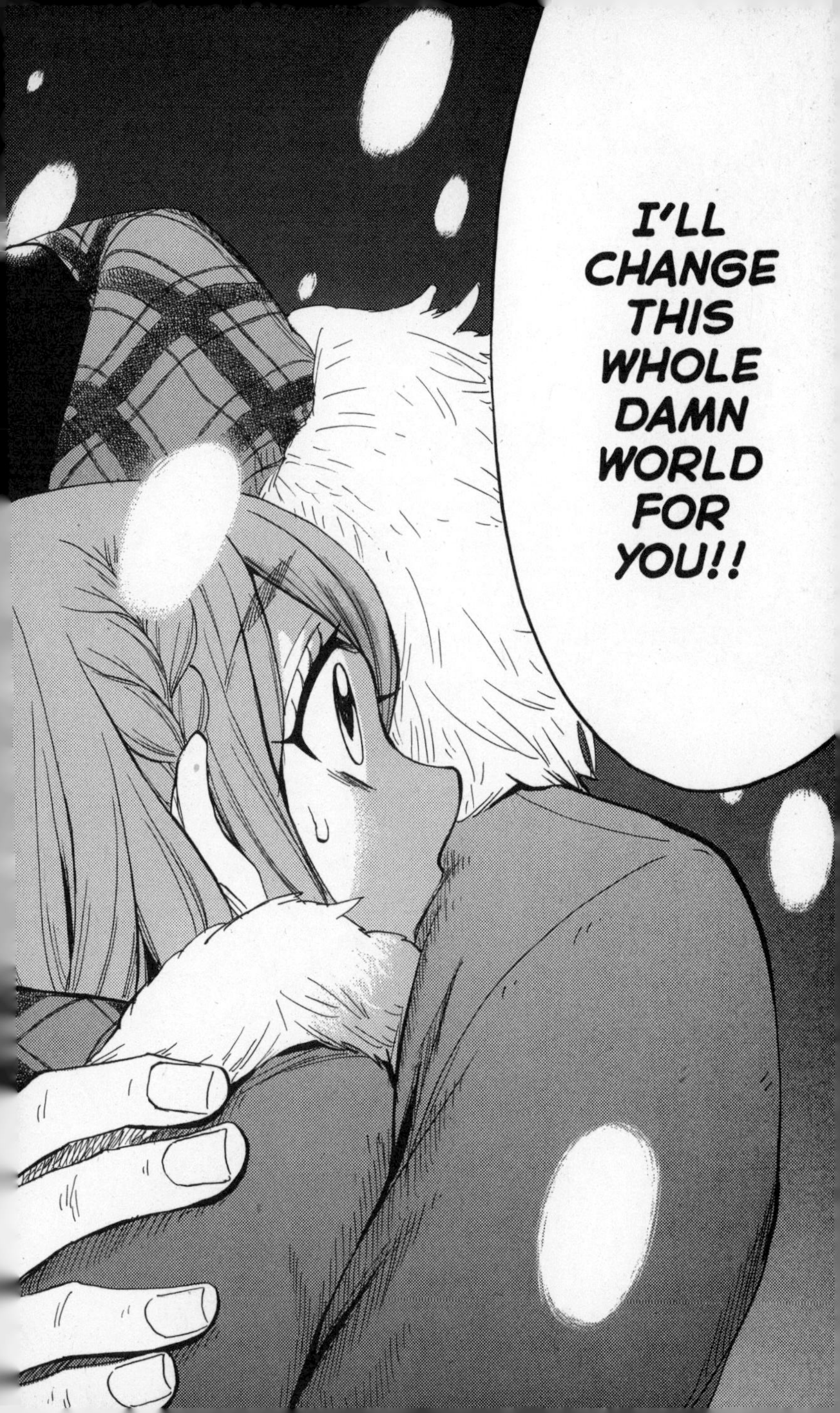
I'LL CHANGE THIS WHOLE DAMN WORLD FOR YOU!!

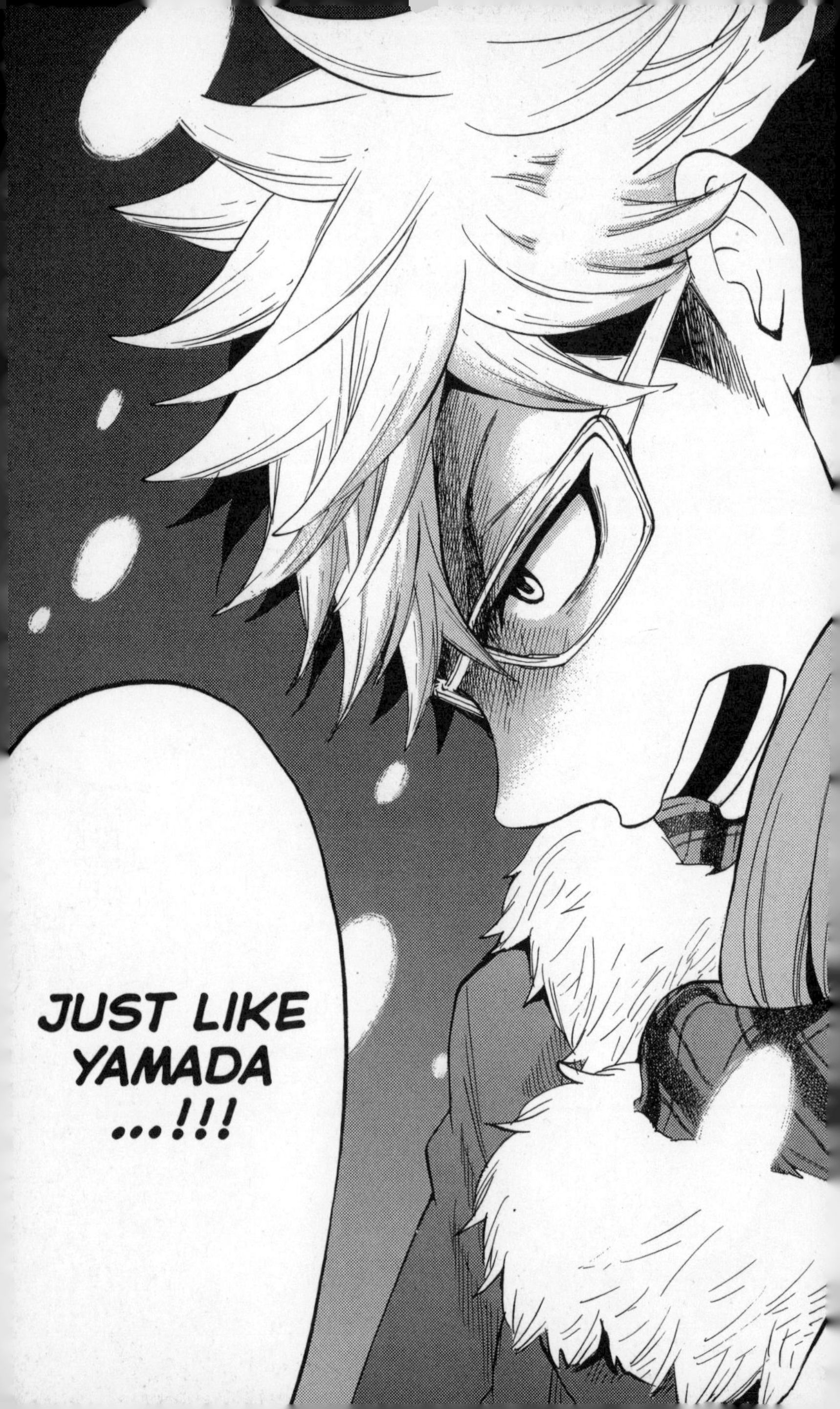
JUST LIKE YAMADA ...!!!

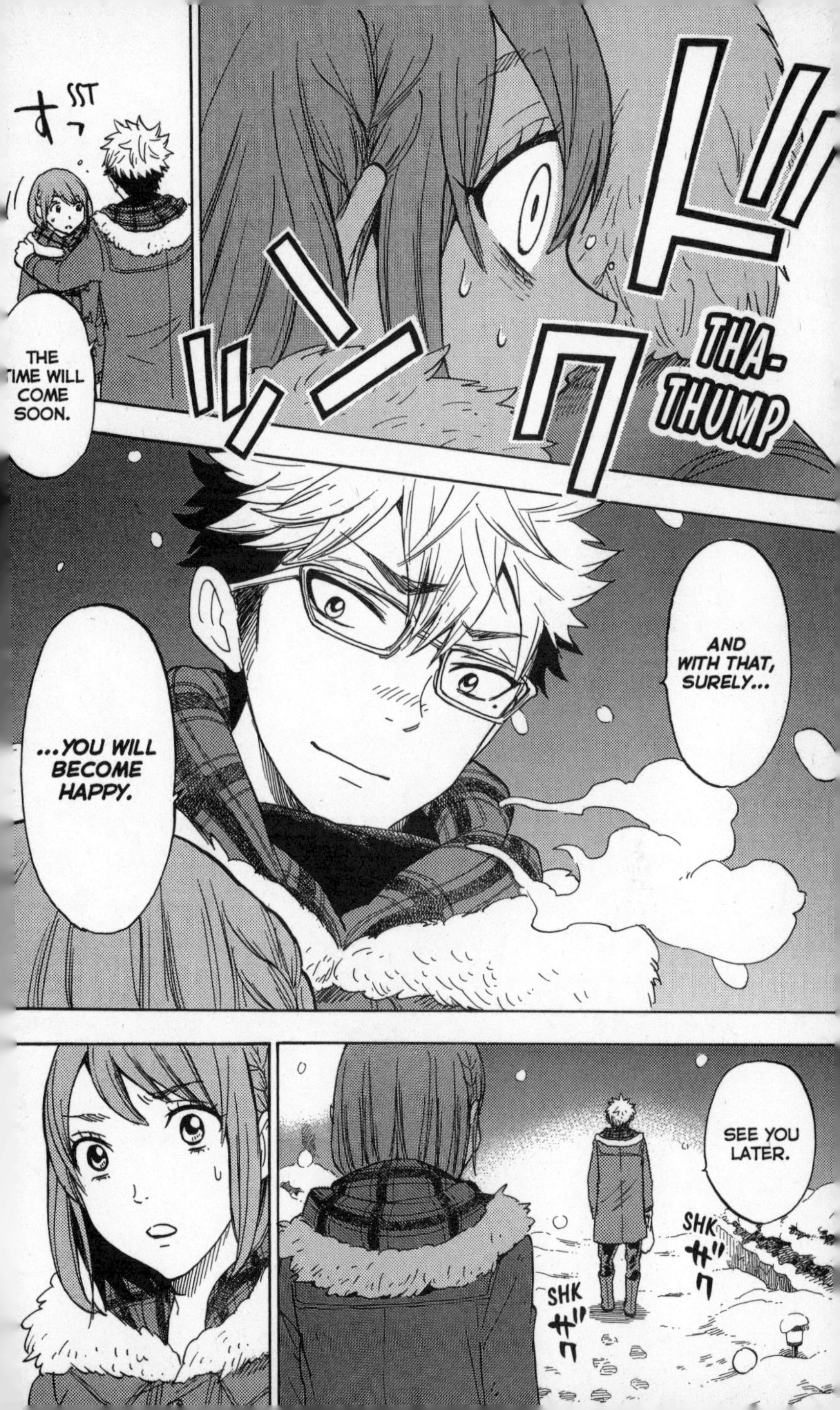
ドクン
THA-THUMP
すっ
SST
THE TIME WILL COME SOON.
AND WITH THAT, SURELY...
...YOU WILL BECOME HAPPY.
SEE YOU LATER.
SHK
ザク
SHK
ザク

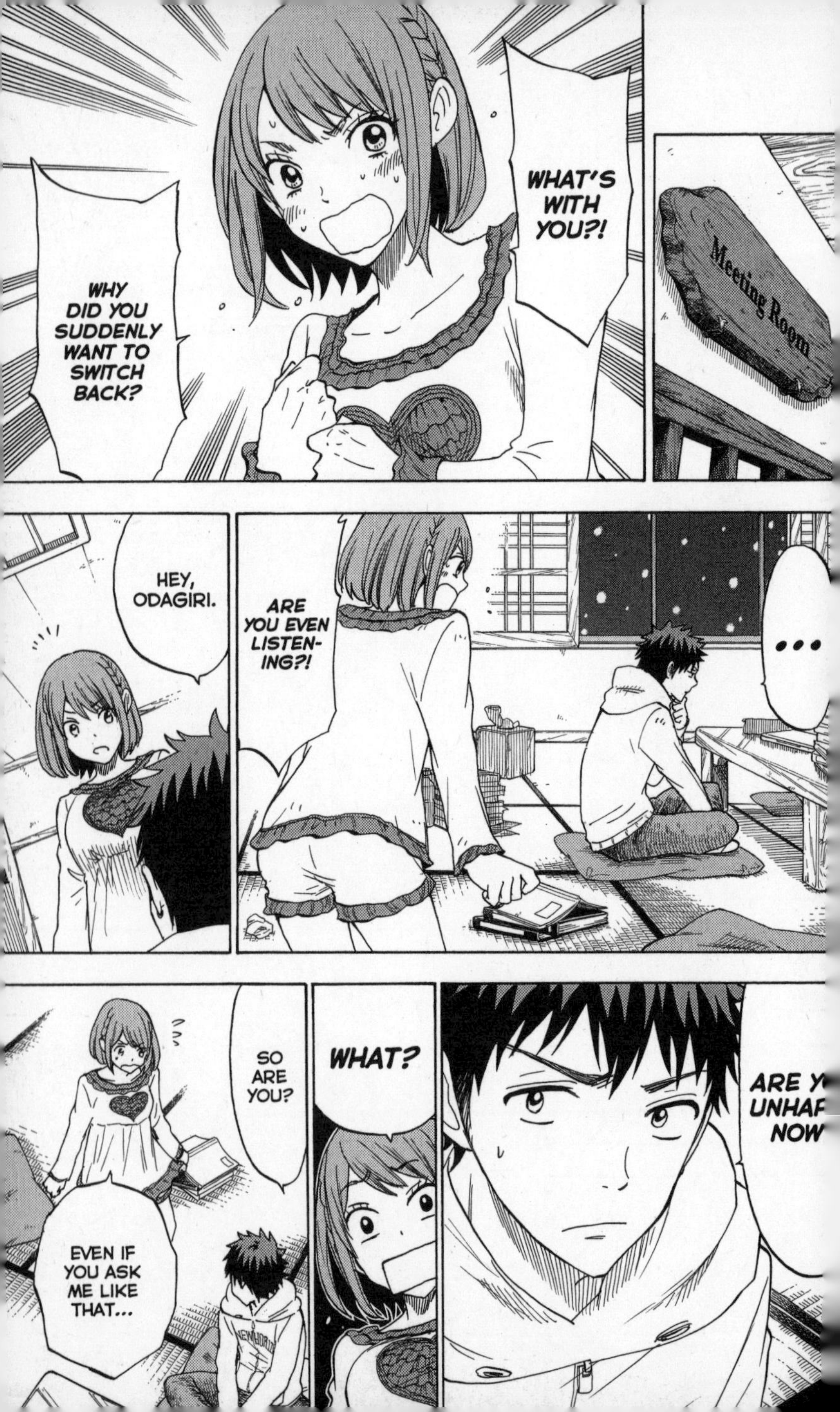
Meeting Room
WHAT'S WITH YOU?!
WHY DID YOU SUDDENLY WANT TO SWITCH BACK?
...
ARE YOU EVEN LISTEN-ING?!
HEY, ODAGIRI.
ARE Y
UNHAP
NOW
WHAT?
SO ARE YOU?
EVEN IF YOU ASK ME LIKE THAT...

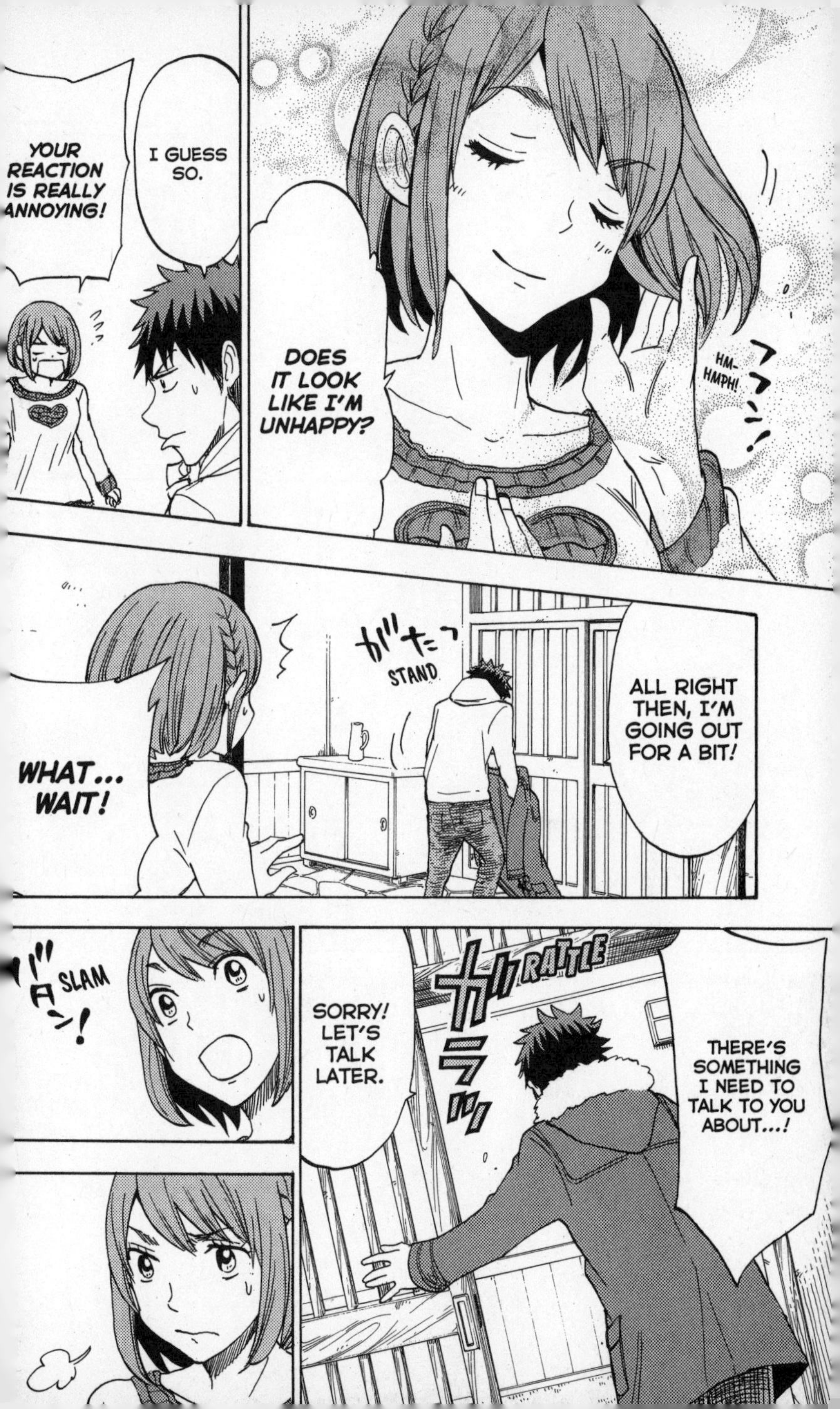

HM-HMPH!
DOES IT LOOK LIKE I'M UNHAPPY?
I GUESS SO.
YOUR REACTION IS REALLY ANNOYING!
ALL RIGHT THEN, I'M GOING OUT FOR A BIT!
STAND
WHAT... WAIT!
THERE'S SOMETHING I NEED TO TALK TO YOU ABOUT...!
RATTLE
SORRY! LET'S TALK LATER.
SLAM

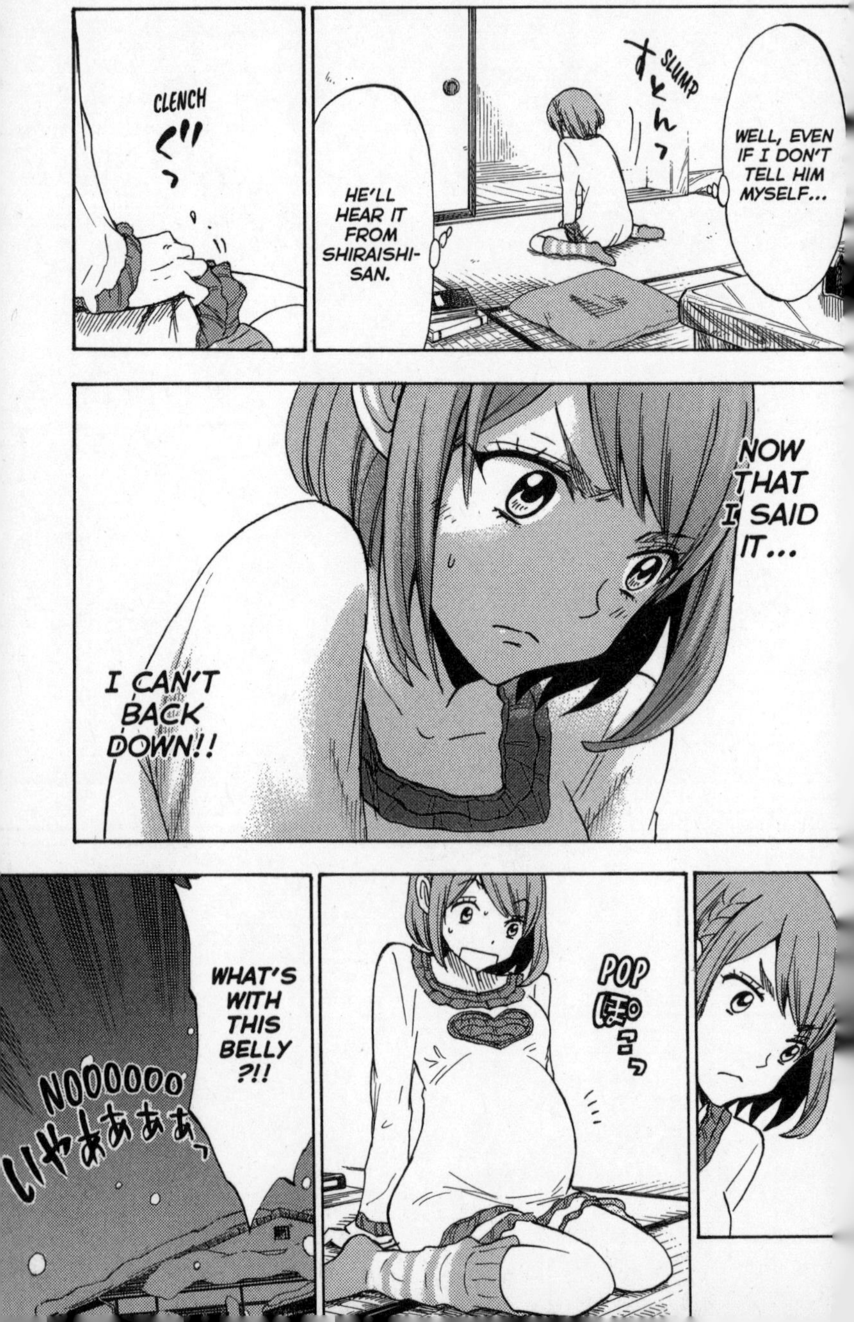
WELL, EVEN IF I DON'T TELL HIM MYSELF...
SLUMP
すとんっ
HE'LL HEAR IT FROM SHIRAISHI-SAN.
CLENCH
ぐっ
NOW THAT I SAID IT...
I CAN'T BACK DOWN!!
POP
ぽこっ
WHAT'S WITH THIS BELLY?!!
NOOOOOO
いやああああっ

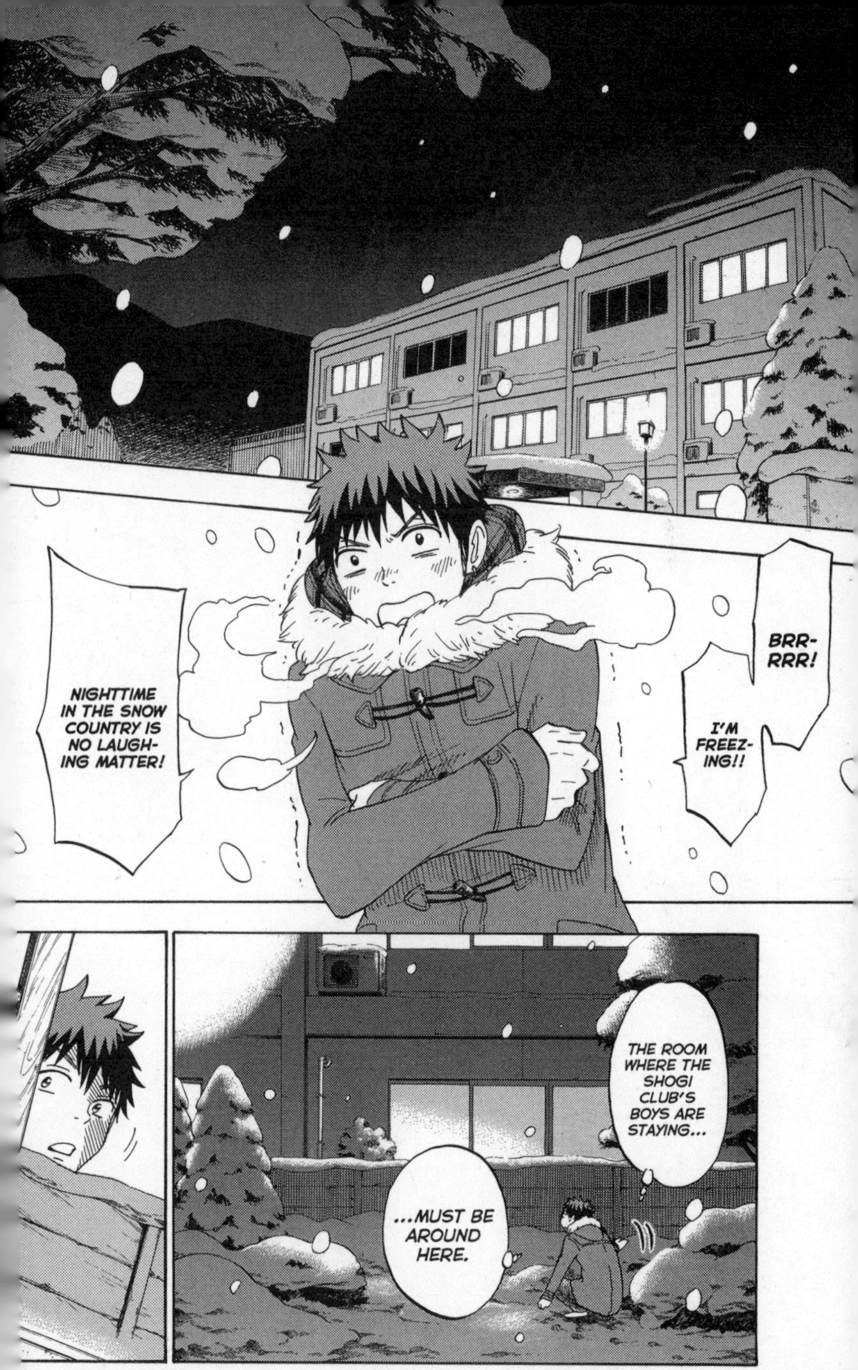
BRR-RRR!
I'M FREEZ-ING!!
NIGHTTIME IN THE SNOW COUNTRY IS NO LAUGHING MATTER!
THE ROOM WHERE THE SHOGI CLUB'S BOYS ARE STAYING...
...MUST BE AROUND HERE.

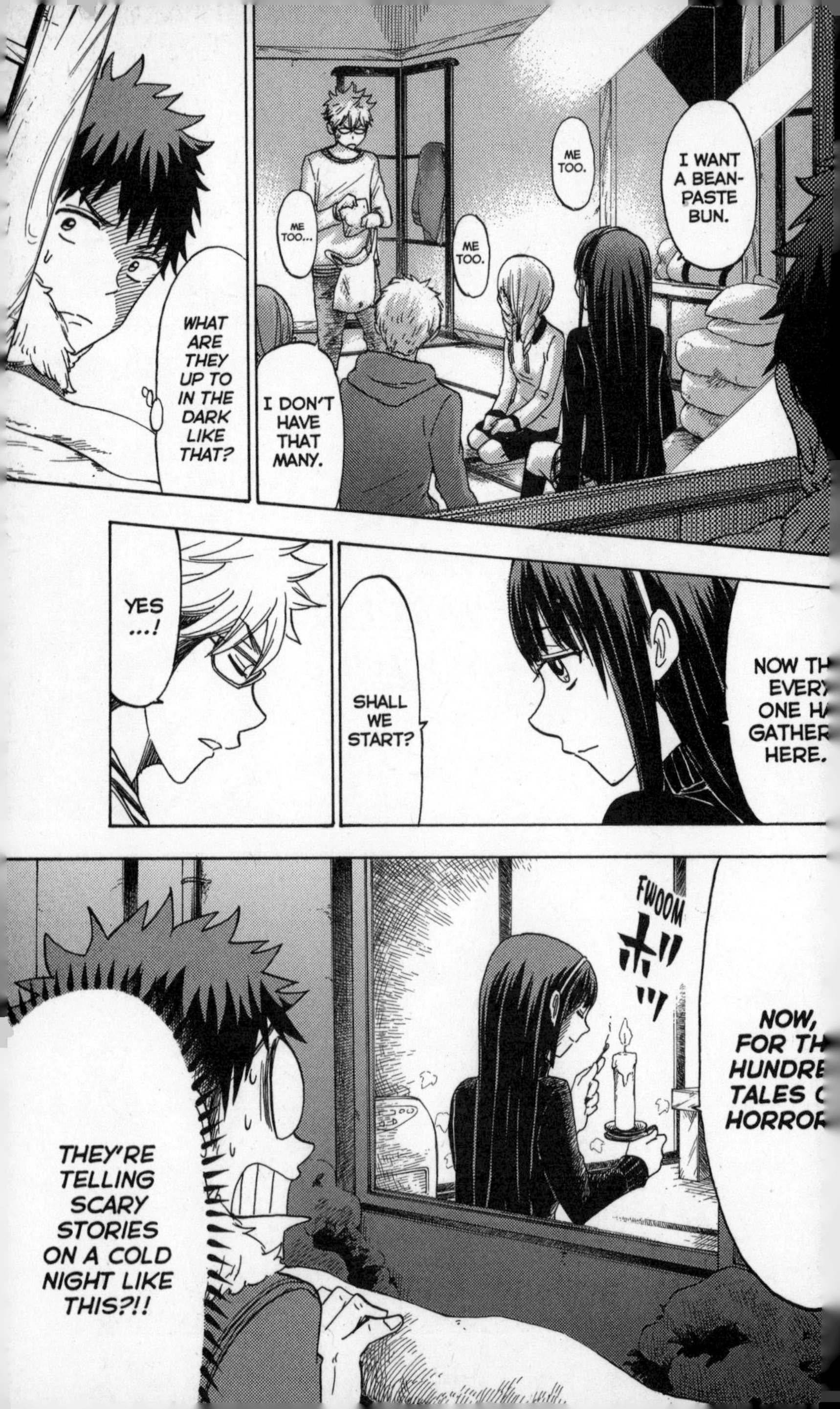
I WANT A BEAN-PASTE BUN.
ME TOO.
ME TOO.
ME TOO...
I DON'T HAVE THAT MANY.
WHAT ARE THEY UP TO IN THE DARK LIKE THAT?
NOW TH EVERY ONE HA GATHER HERE.
SHALL WE START?
YES ...!
FWOOM
NOW, FOR TH HUNDRE TALES O HORROR
THEY'RE TELLING SCARY STORIES ON A COLD NIGHT LIKE THIS?!!

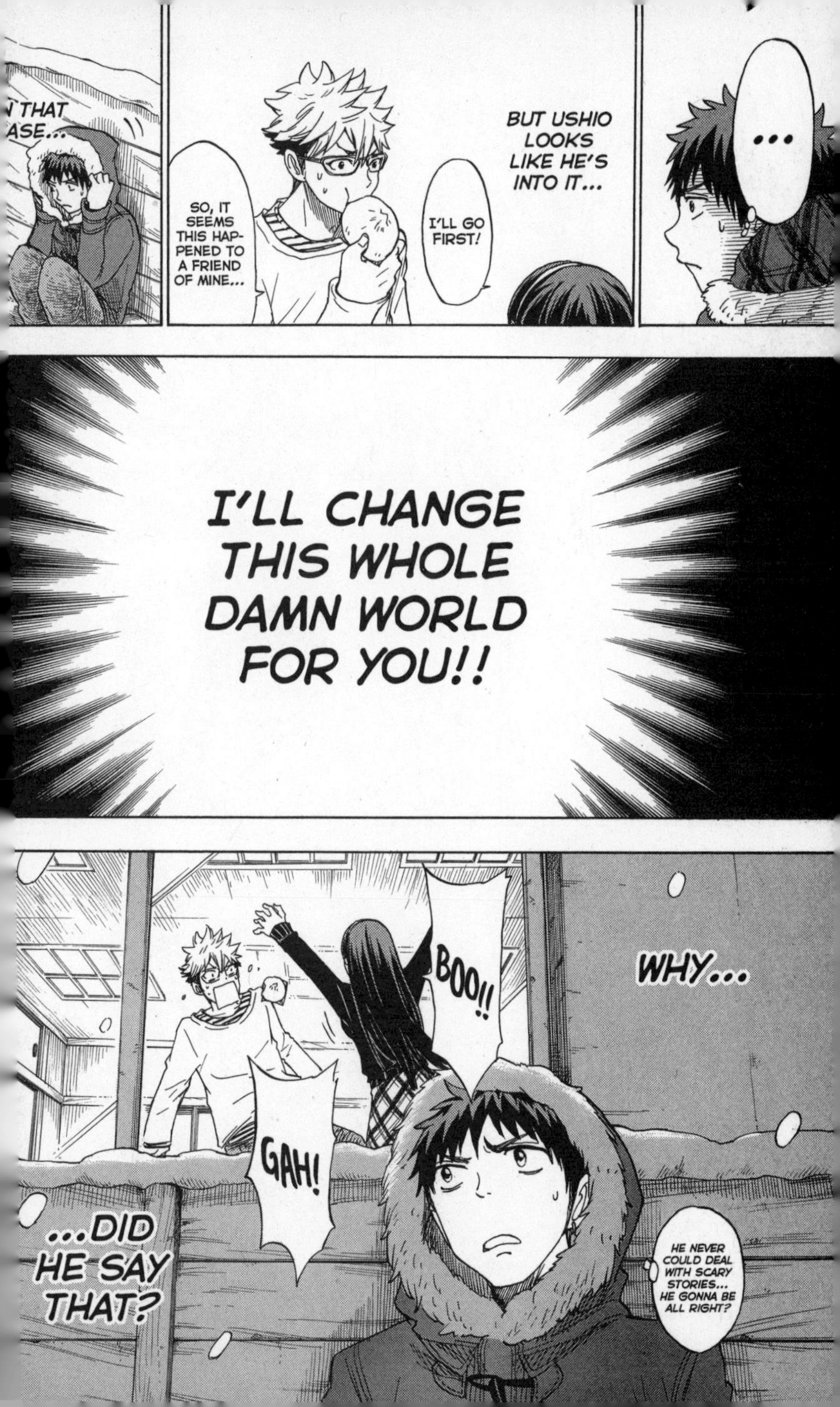
...
BUT USHIO LOOKS LIKE HE'S INTO IT...
I'LL GO FIRST!
SO, IT SEEMS THIS HAPPENED TO A FRIEND OF MINE...
N THAT ASE...
I'LL CHANGE THIS WHOLE DAMN WORLD FOR YOU!!
WHY...
BOO!!
GAH!
HE NEVER COULD DEAL WITH SCARY STORIES... HE GONNA BE ALL RIGHT?
...DID HE SAY THAT?

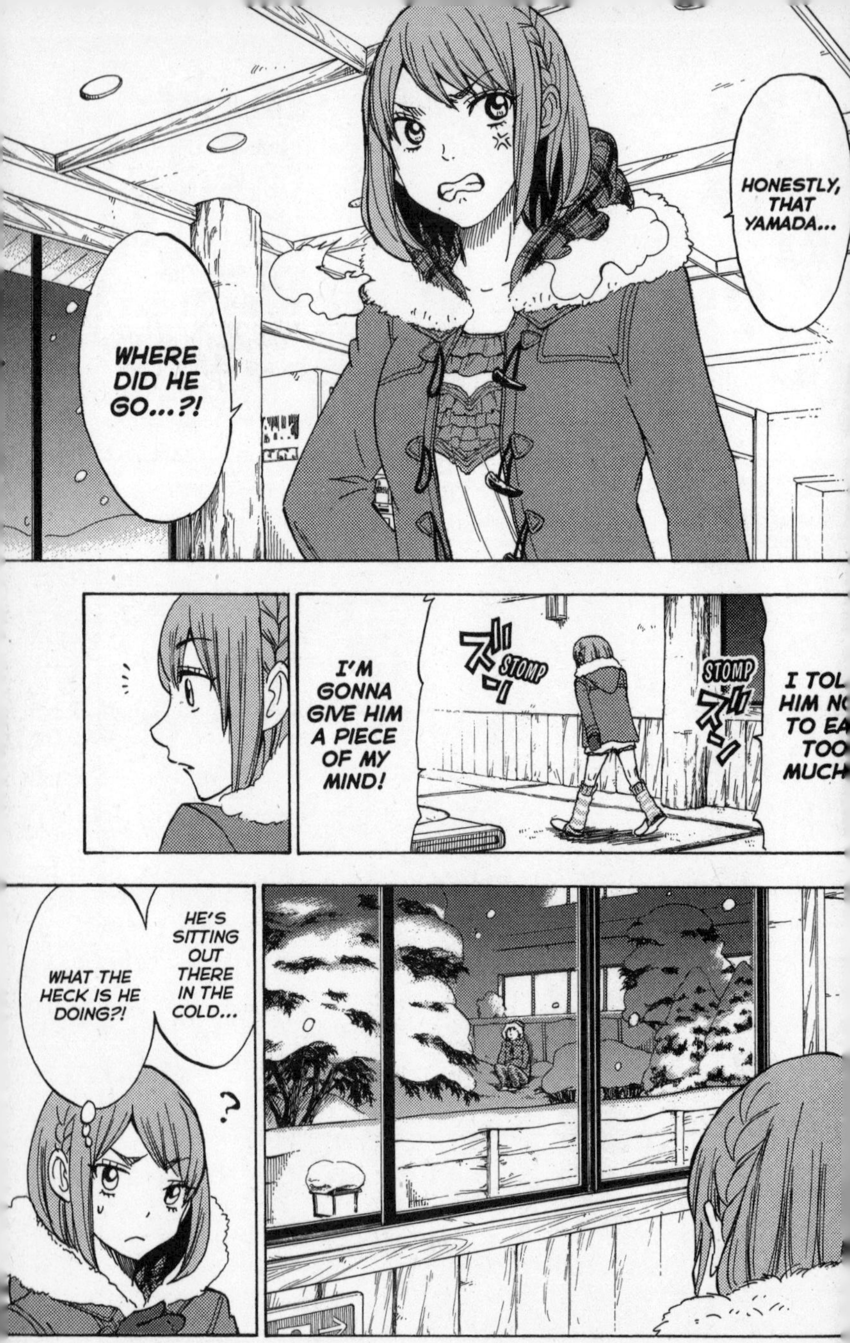
HONESTLY, THAT YAMADA...
WHERE DID HE GO...?!
I TOL HIM N TO EA TOO MUCH
STOMP
STOMP
I'M GONNA GIVE HIM A PIECE OF MY MIND!
HE'S SITTING OUT THERE IN THE COLD...
WHAT THE HECK IS HE DOING?!
?

CHAPTER 118: You sawww!

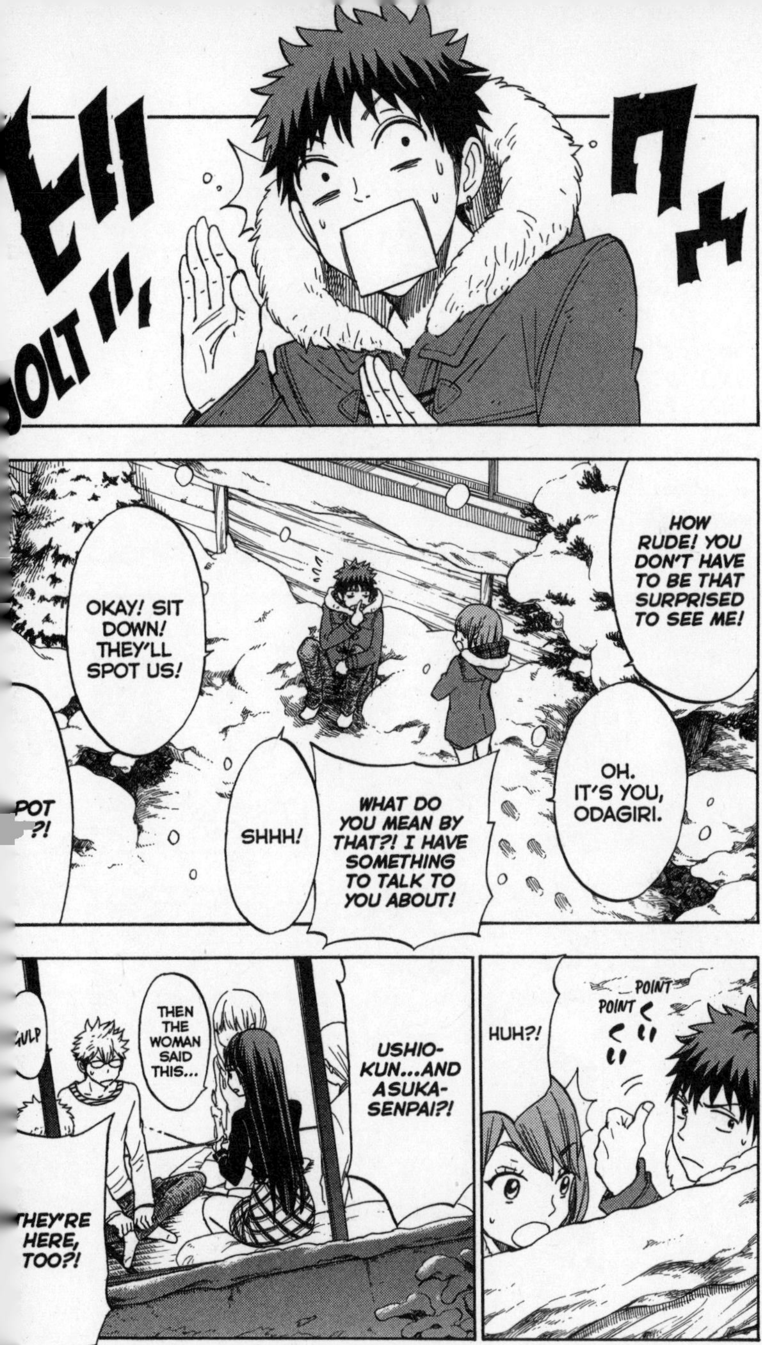
JOLT!!
HOW RUDE! YOU DON'T HAVE TO BE THAT SURPRISED TO SEE ME!
OH. IT'S YOU, ODAGIRI.
WHAT DO YOU MEAN BY THAT?! I HAVE SOMETHING TO TALK TO YOU ABOUT!
SHHH!
OKAY! SIT DOWN! THEY'LL SPOT US!
POINT
POINT
HUH?!
USHIO-KUN...AND ASUKA-SENPAI?!
THEN THE WOMAN SAID THIS...
THEY'RE HERE, TOO?!

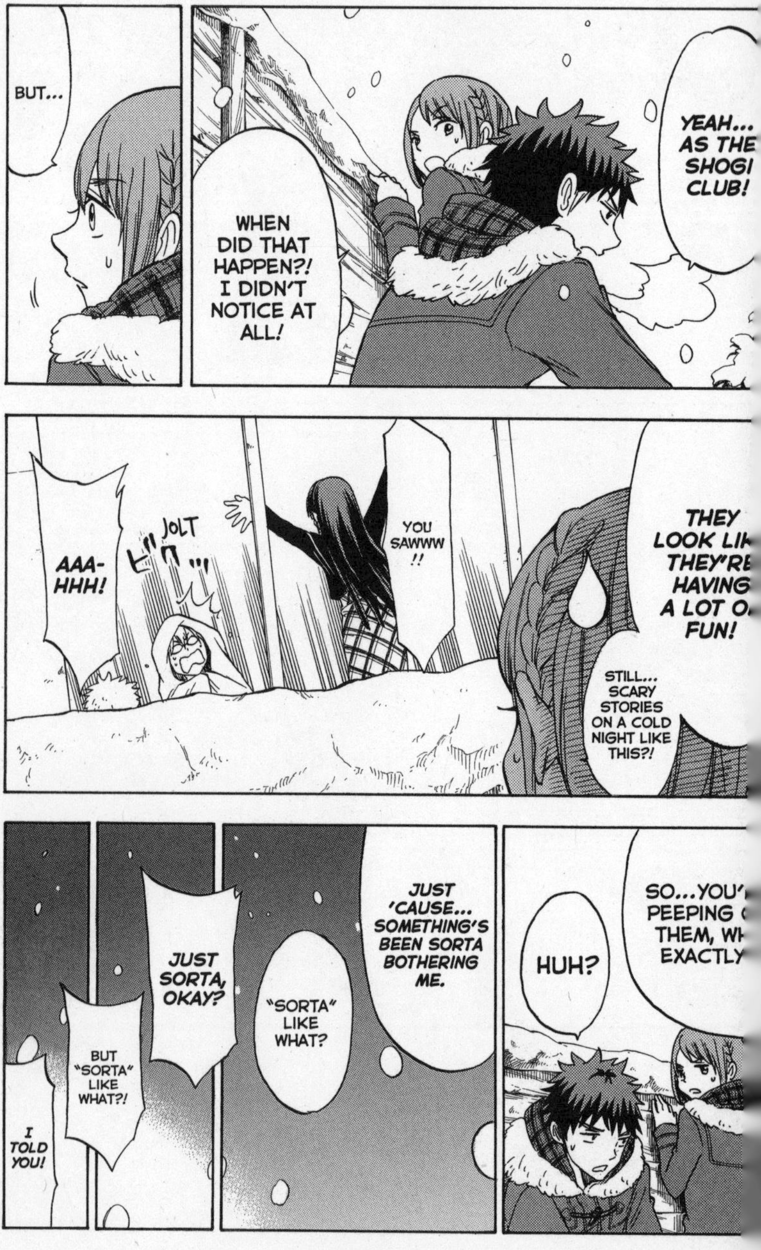
YEAH... AS THE SHOGI CLUB!
WHEN DID THAT HAPPEN?! I DIDN'T NOTICE AT ALL!
BUT...
THEY LOOK LIK THEY'RE HAVING A LOT O FUN!
STILL... SCARY STORIES ON A COLD NIGHT LIKE THIS?!
YOU SAWWW!!
JOLT
AAA-HHH!
SO...YOU' PEEPING THEM, WH EXACTLY
HUH?
JUST 'CAUSE... SOMETHING'S BEEN SORTA BOTHERING ME.
"SORTA" LIKE WHAT?
JUST SORTA, OKAY?
BUT "SORTA" LIKE WHAT?!
I TOLD YOU!

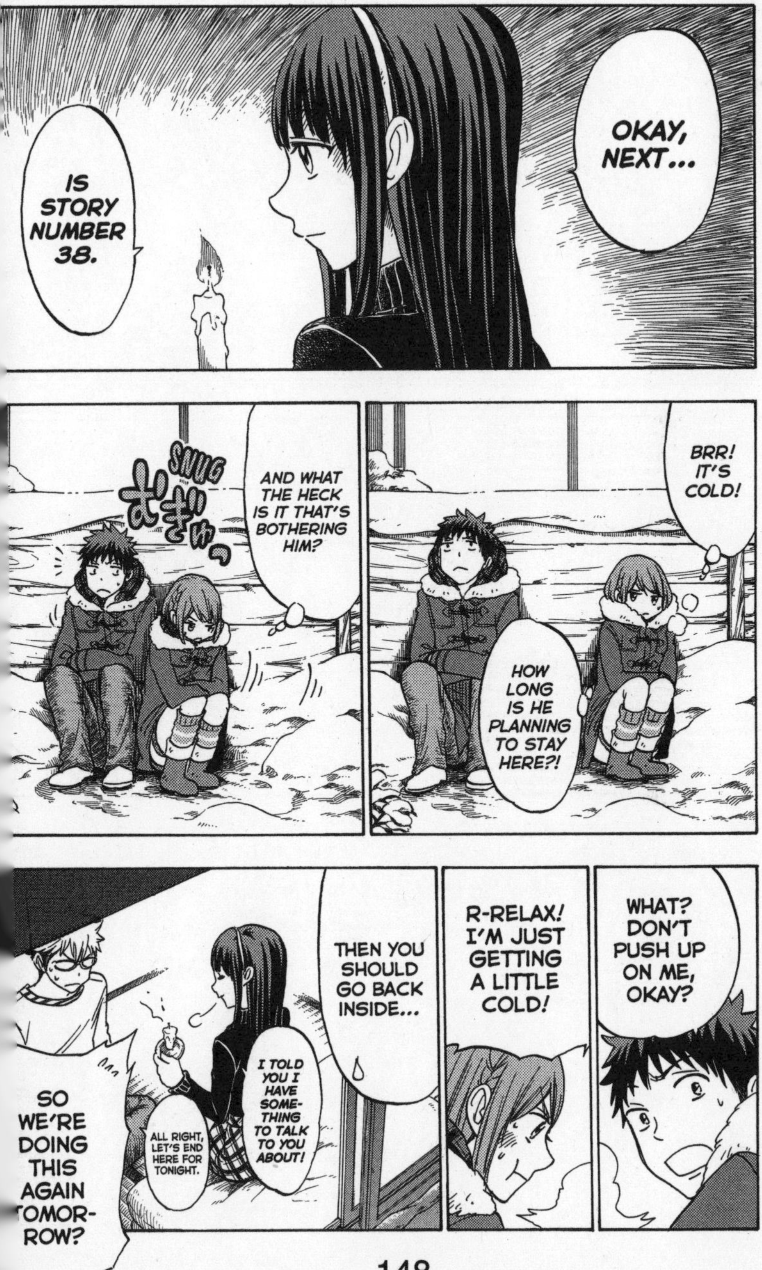
OKAY, NEXT...
IS STORY NUMBER 38.
BRR! IT'S COLD!
HOW LONG IS HE PLANNING TO STAY HERE?!
AND WHAT THE HECK IS IT THAT'S BOTHERING HIM?
SNUG
WHAT? DON'T PUSH UP ON ME, OKAY?
R-RELAX! I'M JUST GETTING A LITTLE COLD!
THEN YOU SHOULD GO BACK INSIDE...
I TOLD YOU I HAVE SOME-THING TO TALK TO YOU ABOUT!
ALL RIGHT, LET'S END HERE FOR TONIGHT.
SO WE'RE DOING THIS AGAIN TOMOR-ROW?

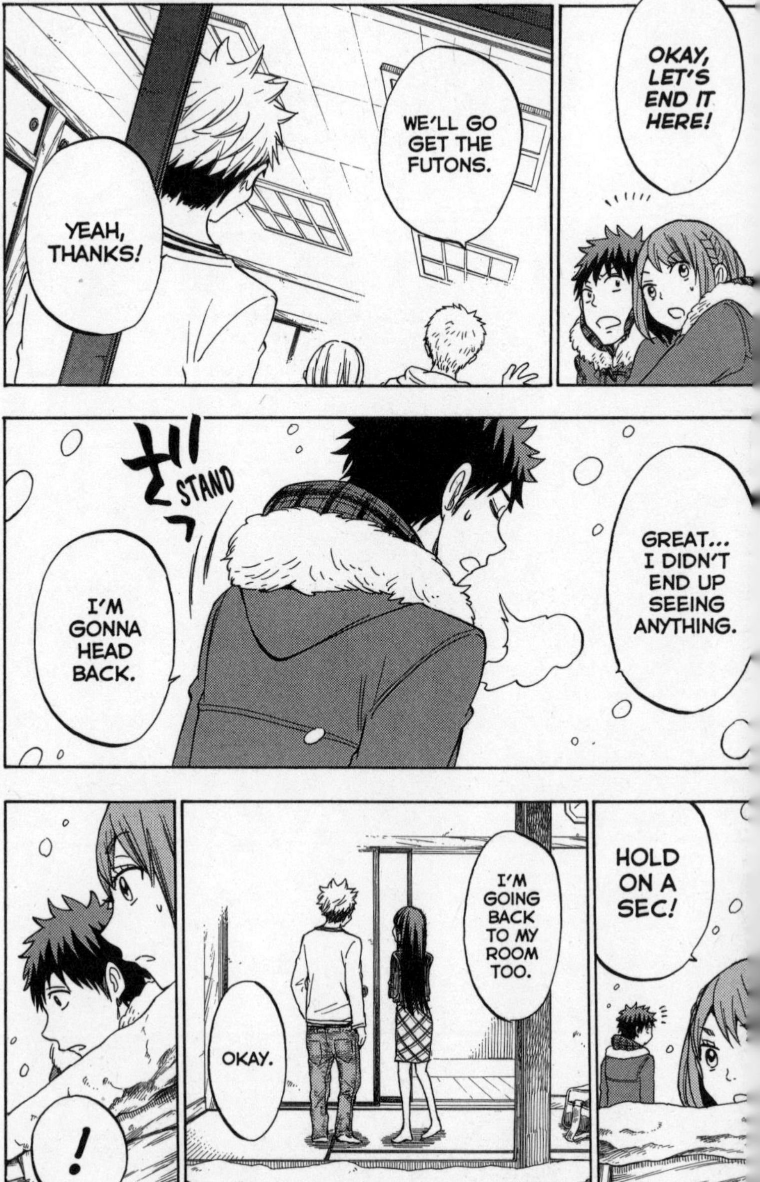
OKAY, LET'S END IT HERE!
WE'LL GO GET THE FUTONS.
YEAH, THANKS!
GREAT... I DIDN'T END UP SEEING ANYTHING.
STAND
I'M GONNA HEAD BACK.
HOLD ON A SEC!
I'M GOING BACK TO MY ROOM TOO.
OKAY.
!

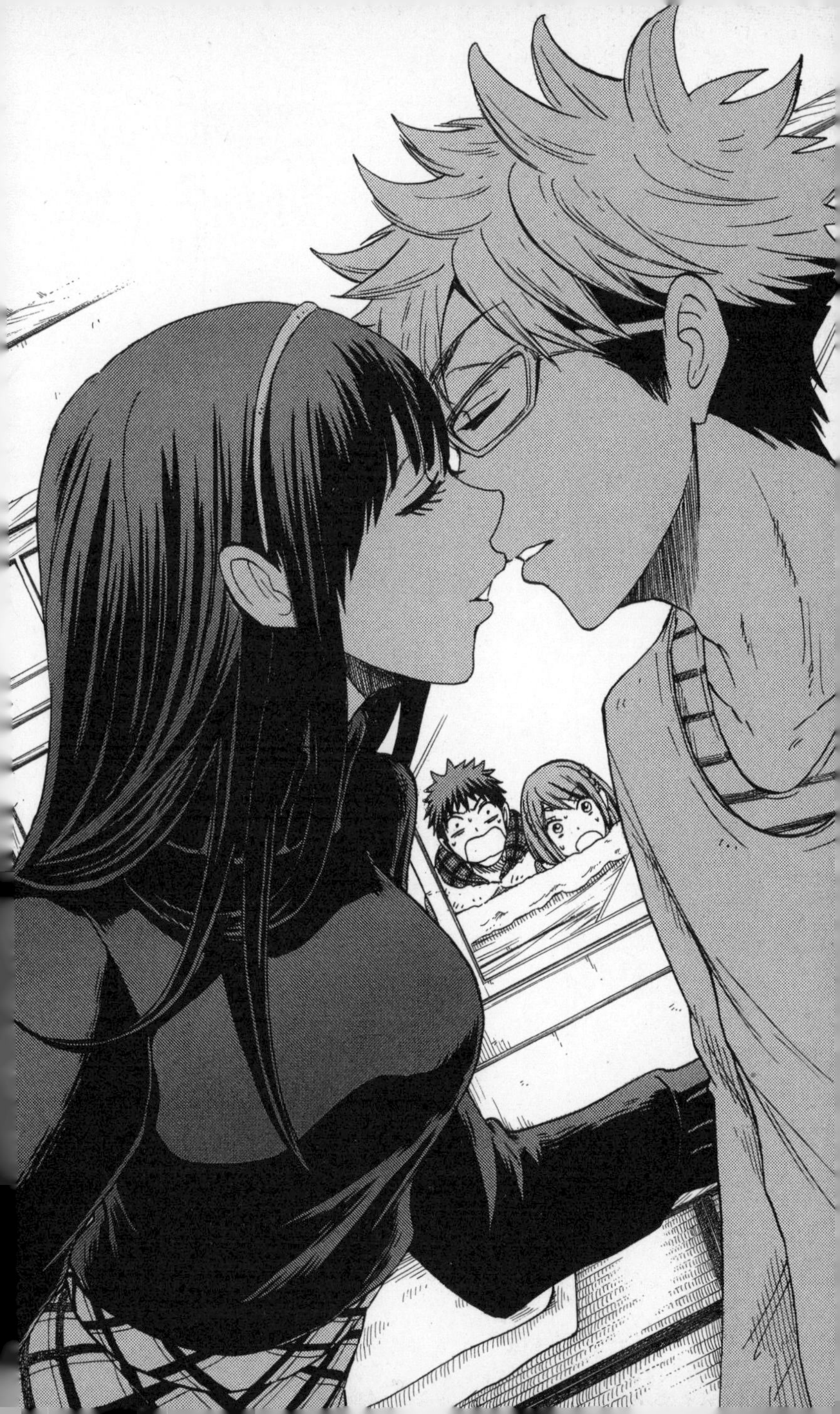

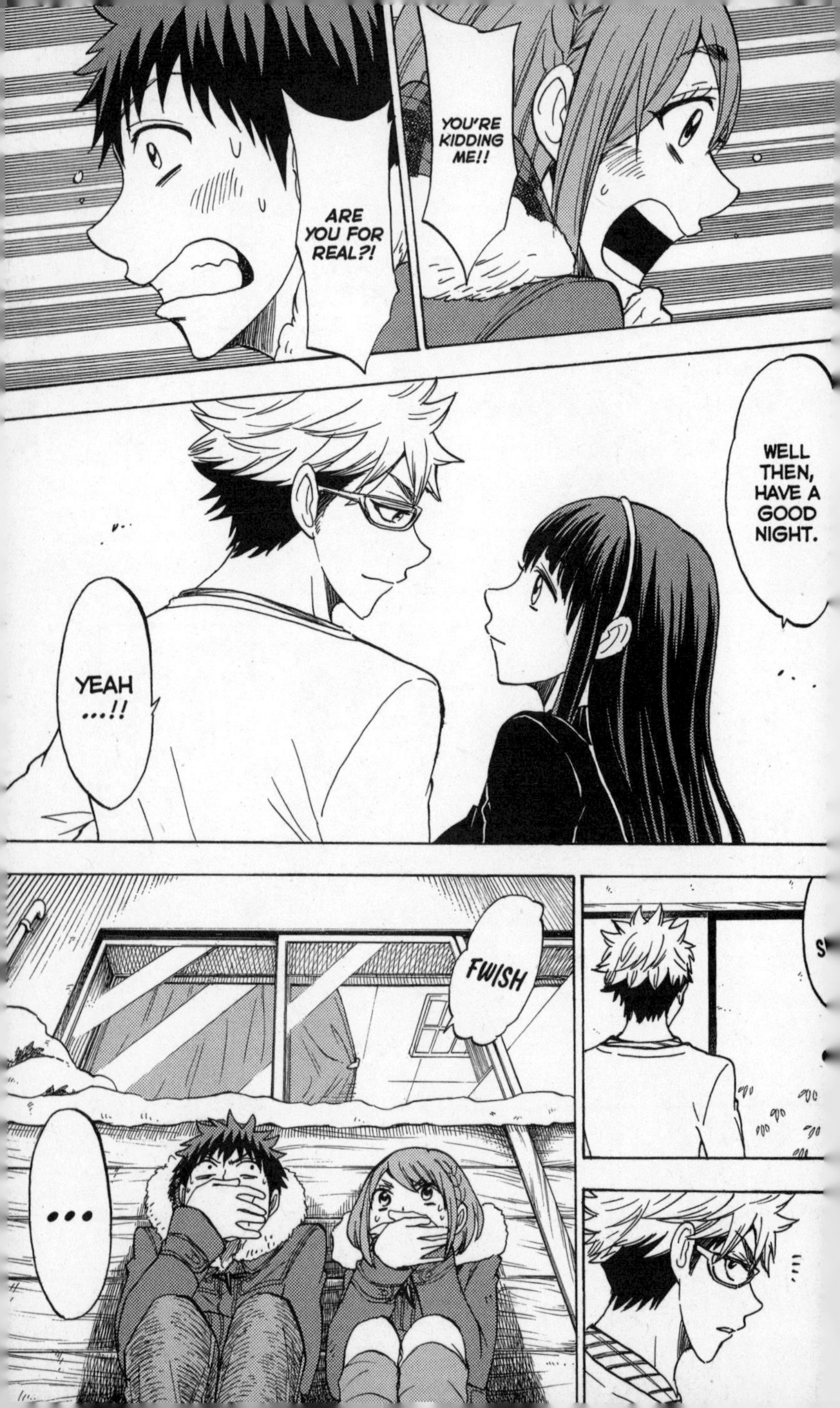
YOU'RE KIDDING ME!!
ARE YOU FOR REAL?!
WELL THEN, HAVE A GOOD NIGHT.
YEAH ...!!
FWISH
...

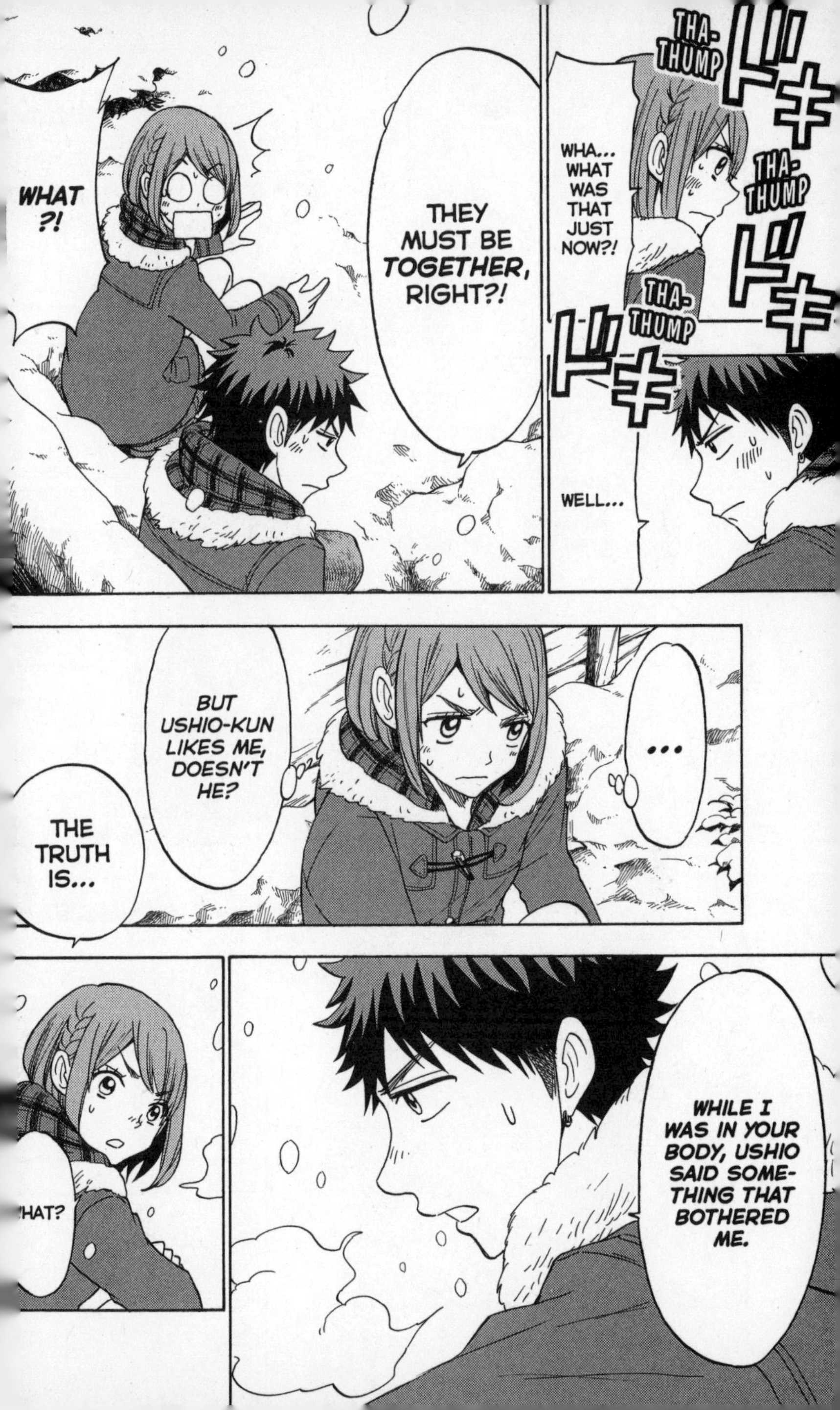
THA-THUMP
ドキ
THA-THUMP
ドキ
THA-THUMP
ドキ
WHA... WHAT WAS THAT JUST NOW?!
WELL...
THEY MUST BE TOGETHER, RIGHT?!
WHAT ?!
...
BUT USHIO-KUN LIKES ME, DOESN'T HE?
THE TRUTH IS...
WHILE I WAS IN YOUR BODY, USHIO SAID SOME-THING THAT BOTHERED ME.
HAT?

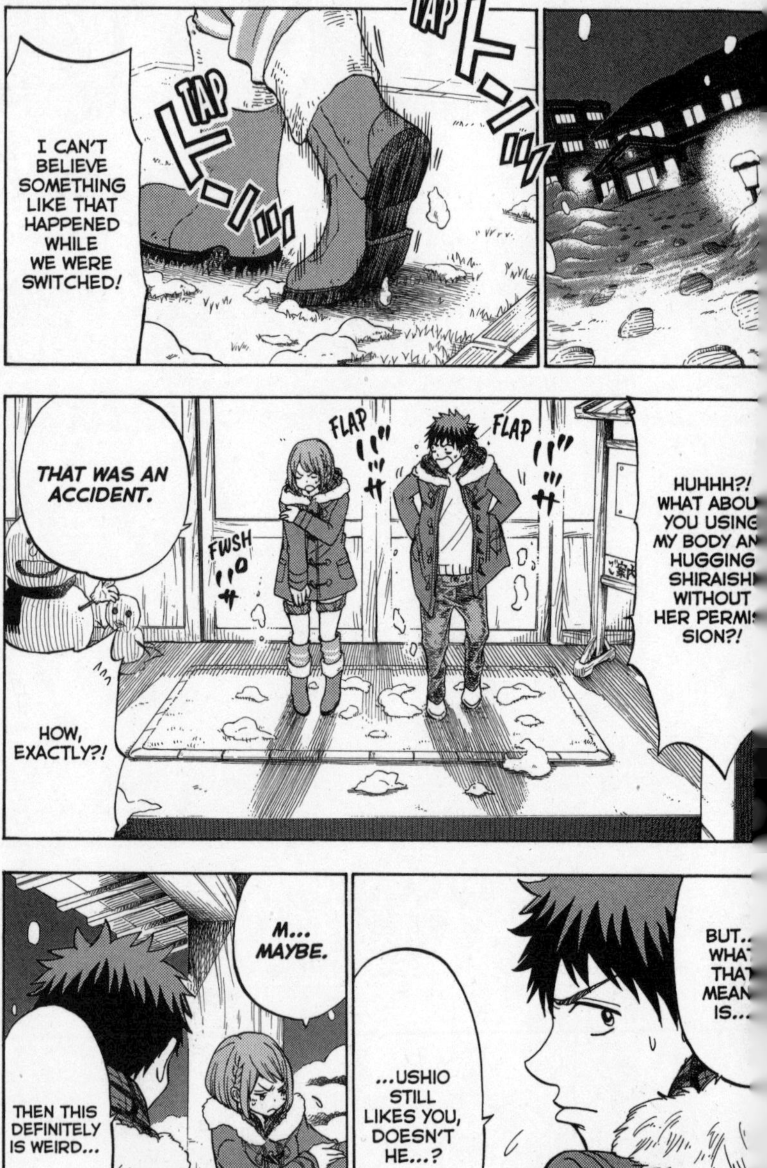
TAP
TAP
I CAN'T BELIEVE SOMETHING LIKE THAT HAPPENED WHILE WE WERE SWITCHED!
HUHHH?! WHAT ABOU YOU USING MY BODY AN HUGGING SHIRAISH WITHOUT HER PERMIS SION?!
FLAP
FLAP
FWSH
THAT WAS AN ACCIDENT.
HOW, EXACTLY?!
BUT... WHAT THAT MEAN IS...
...USHIO STILL LIKES YOU, DOESN'T HE...?
M... MAYBE.
THEN THIS DEFINITELY IS WEIRD...

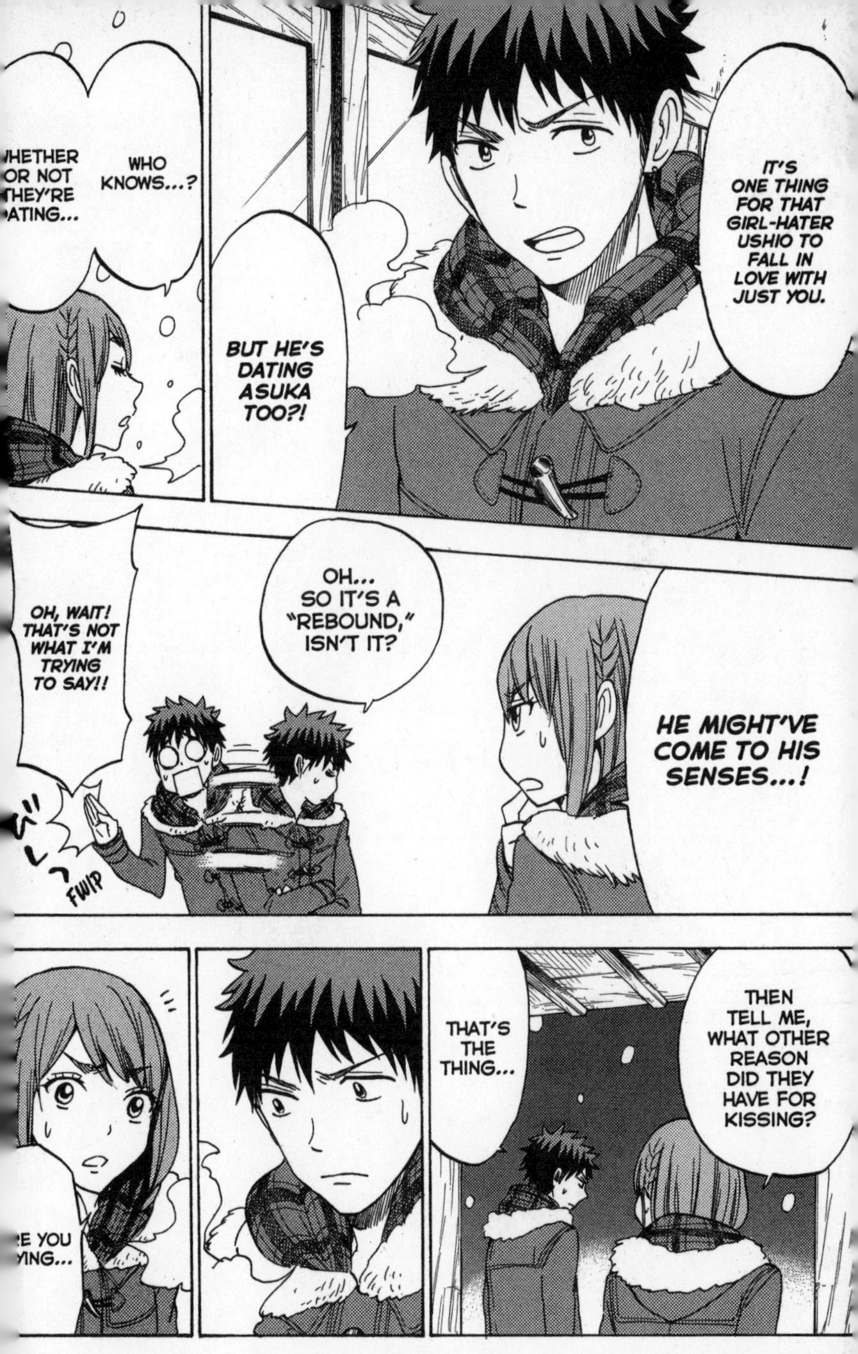
IT'S ONE THING FOR THAT GIRL-HATER USHIO TO FALL IN LOVE WITH JUST YOU.
BUT HE'S DATING ASUKA TOO?!
WHO KNOWS...?
HETHER OR NOT HEY'RE ATING...
HE MIGHT'VE COME TO HIS SENSES...!
OH... SO IT'S A "REBOUND," ISN'T IT?
OH, WAIT! THAT'S NOT WHAT I'M TRYING TO SAY!!
FWIP
THEN TELL ME, WHAT OTHER REASON DID THEY HAVE FOR KISSING?
THAT'S THE THING...
E YOU YING...

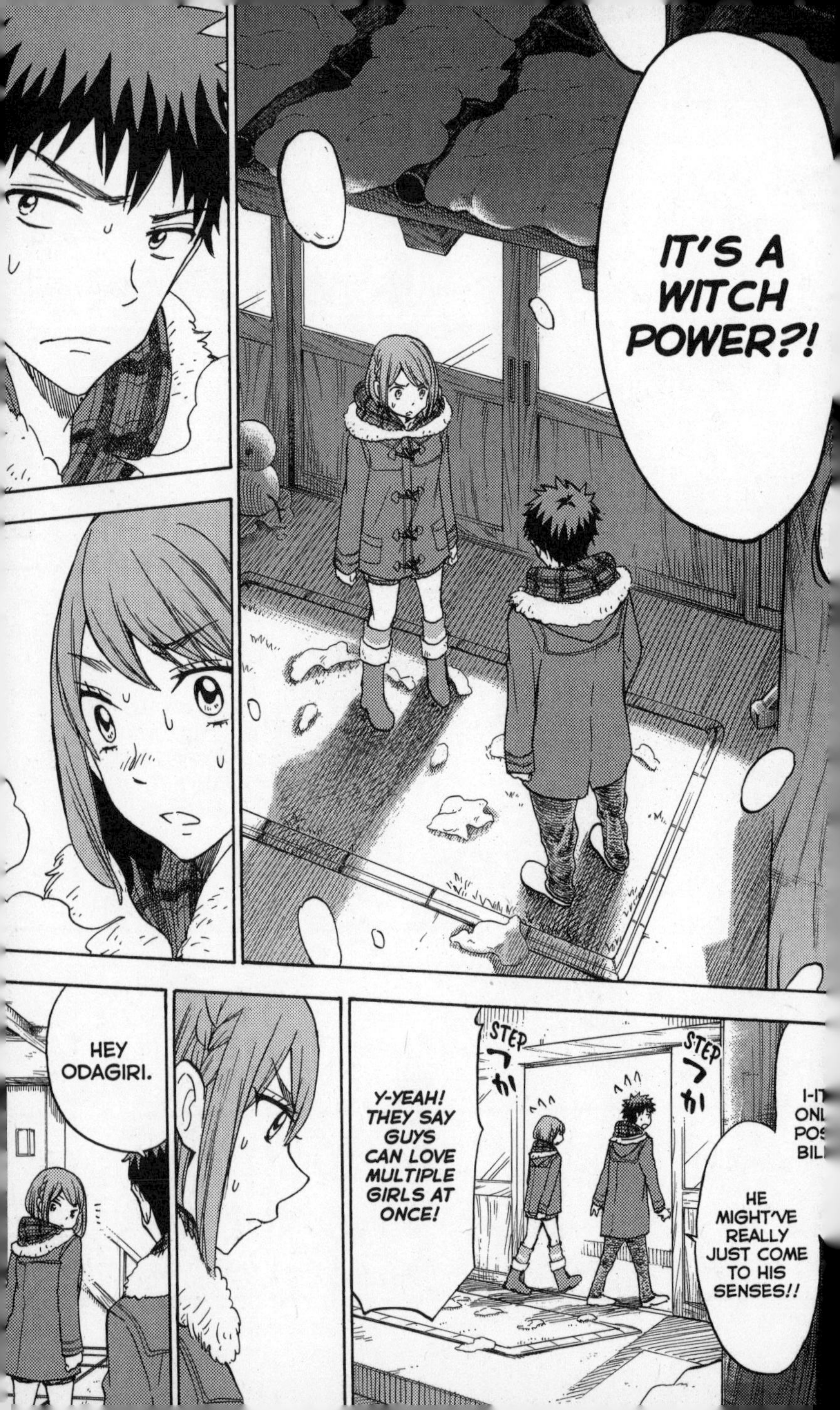

IT'S A WITCH POWER?!
I-IT ONL POS BIL
HE MIGHT'VE REALLY JUST COME TO HIS SENSES!!
STEP つか
STEP つか
Y-YEAH! THEY SAY GUYS CAN LOVE MULTIPLE GIRLS AT ONCE!
HEY ODAGIRI.

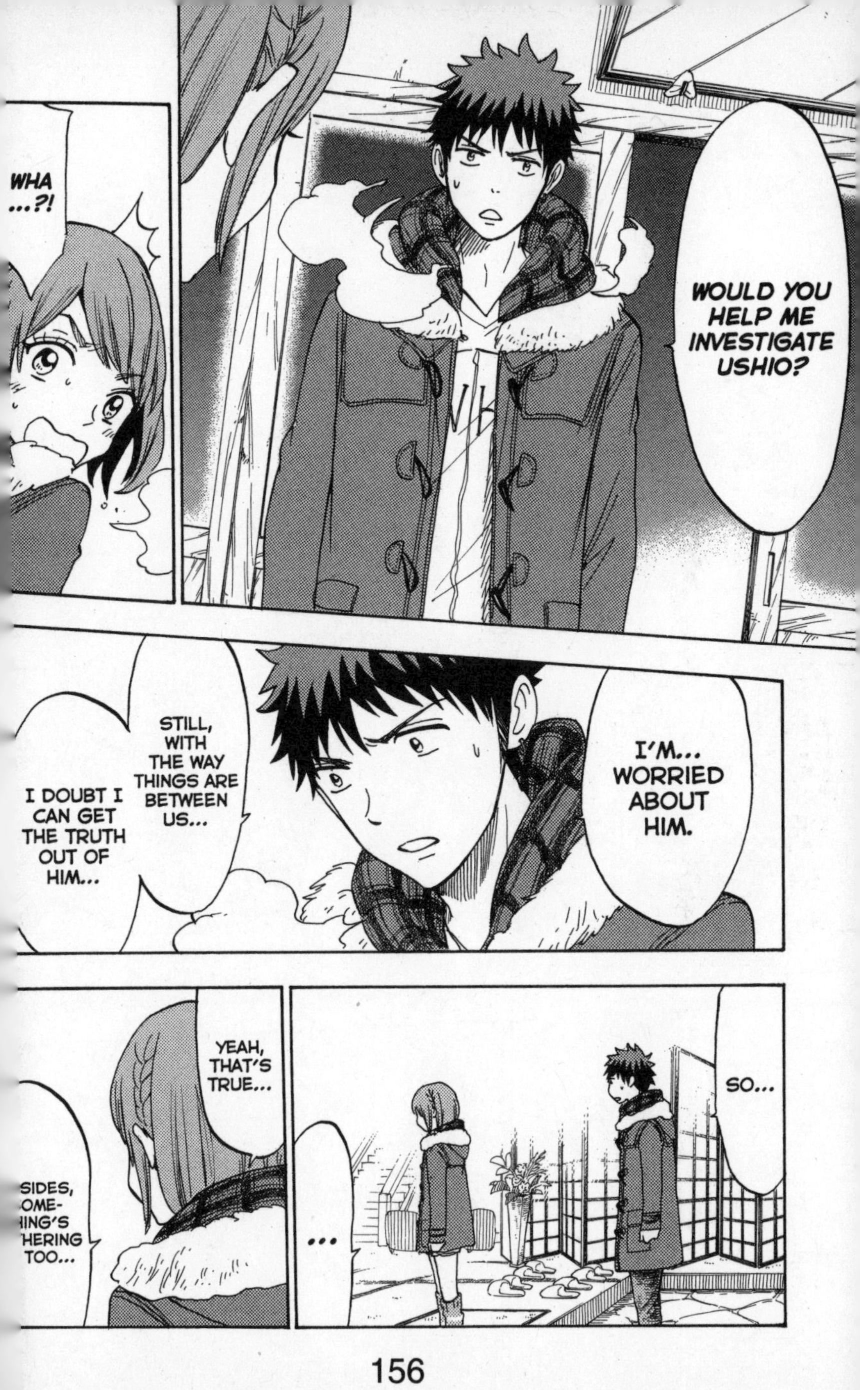
WOULD YOU HELP ME INVESTIGATE USHIO?
WHA ...?!
I'M... WORRIED ABOUT HIM.
STILL, WITH THE WAY THINGS ARE BETWEEN US...
I DOUBT I CAN GET THE TRUTH OUT OF HIM...
SO...
...
YEAH, THAT'S TRUE...
SIDES, OME- HING'S HERING TOO...

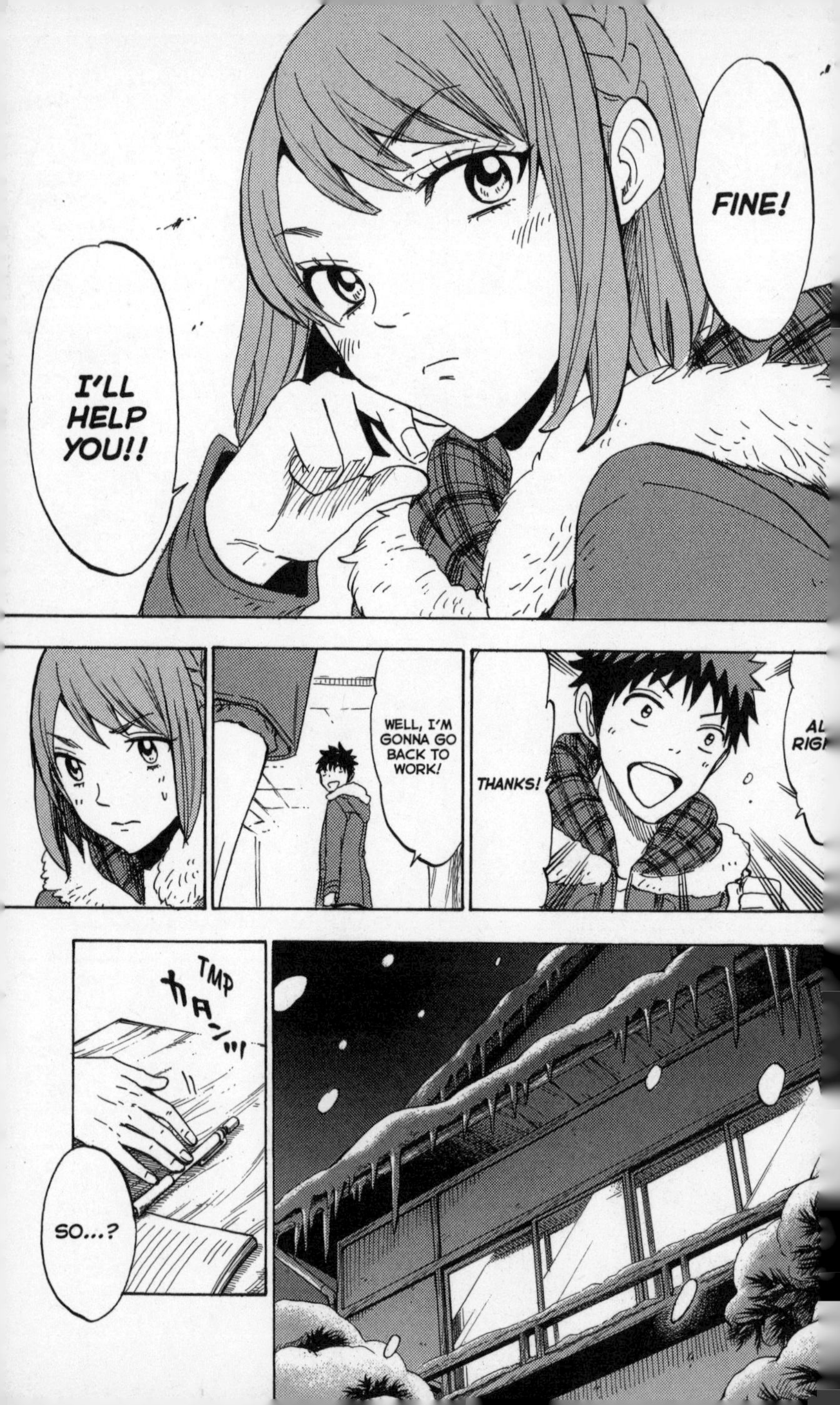
FINE!
I'LL HELP YOU!!
THANKS!
WELL, I'M GONNA GO BACK TO WORK!
TMP
SO...?

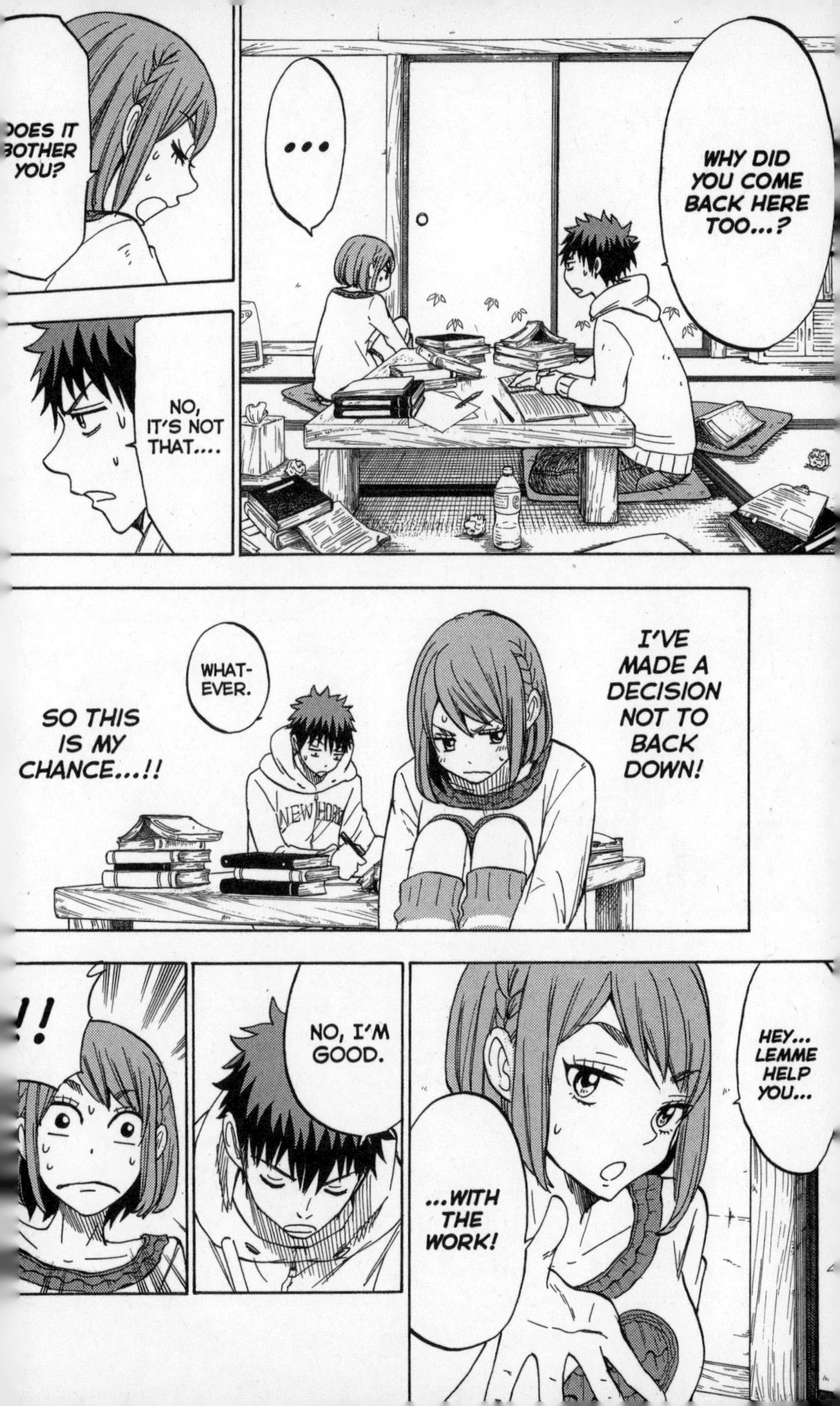

WHY DID YOU COME BACK HERE TOO...?
...
DOES IT BOTHER YOU?
NO, IT'S NOT THAT....
I'VE MADE A DECISION NOT TO BACK DOWN!
WHAT-EVER.
SO THIS IS MY CHANCE...!!
HEY... LEMME HELP YOU...
...WITH THE WORK!
NO, I'M GOOD.
!!

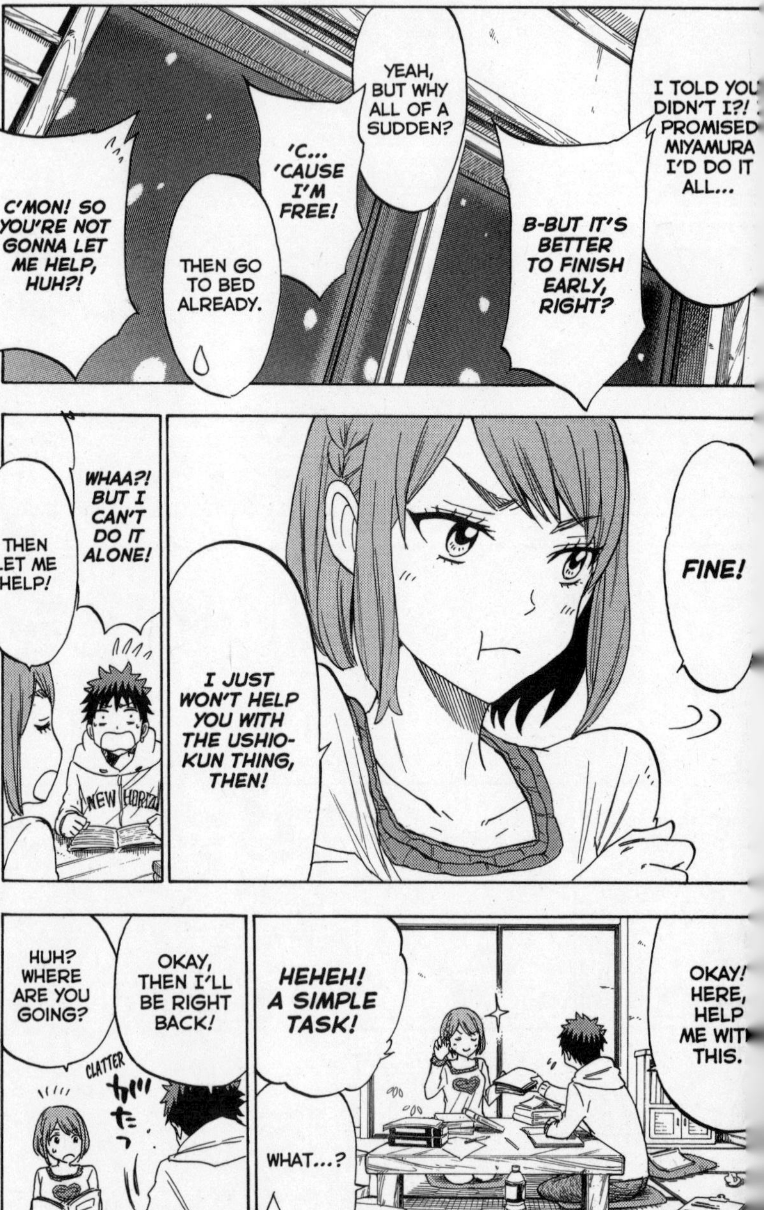
I TOLD YOU DIDN'T I?! PROMISED MIYAMURA I'D DO IT ALL...
B-BUT IT'S BETTER TO FINISH EARLY, RIGHT?
YEAH, BUT WHY ALL OF A SUDDEN?
'C... 'CAUSE I'M FREE!
THEN GO TO BED ALREADY.
C'MON! SO YOU'RE NOT GONNA LET ME HELP, HUH?!
FINE!
I JUST WON'T HELP YOU WITH THE USHIO-KUN THING, THEN!
WHAA?! BUT I CAN'T DO IT ALONE!
THEN LET ME HELP!
OKAY! HERE, HELP ME WIT THIS.
HEHEH! A SIMPLE TASK!
WHAT...?
OKAY, THEN I'LL BE RIGHT BACK!
HUH? WHERE ARE YOU GOING?
CLATTER

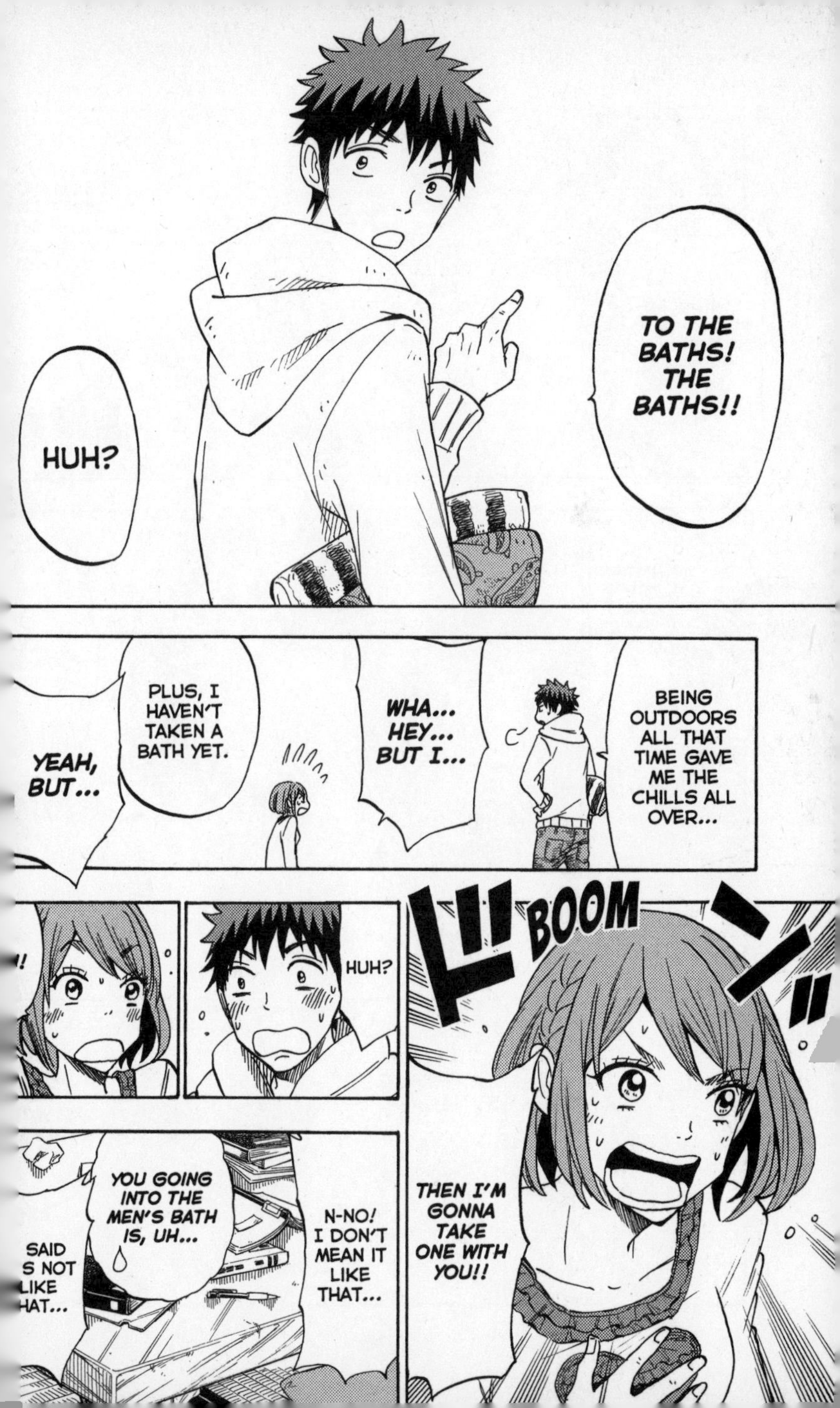
TO THE BATHS! THE BATHS!!
HUH?
BEING OUTDOORS ALL THAT TIME GAVE ME THE CHILLS ALL OVER...
WHA... HEY... BUT I...
PLUS, I HAVEN'T TAKEN A BATH YET.
YEAH, BUT...
BOOM
THEN I'M GONNA TAKE ONE WITH YOU!!
HUH?
N-NO! I DON'T MEAN IT LIKE THAT...
YOU GOING INTO THE MEN'S BATH IS, UH...
SAID
S NOT
LIKE
HAT...

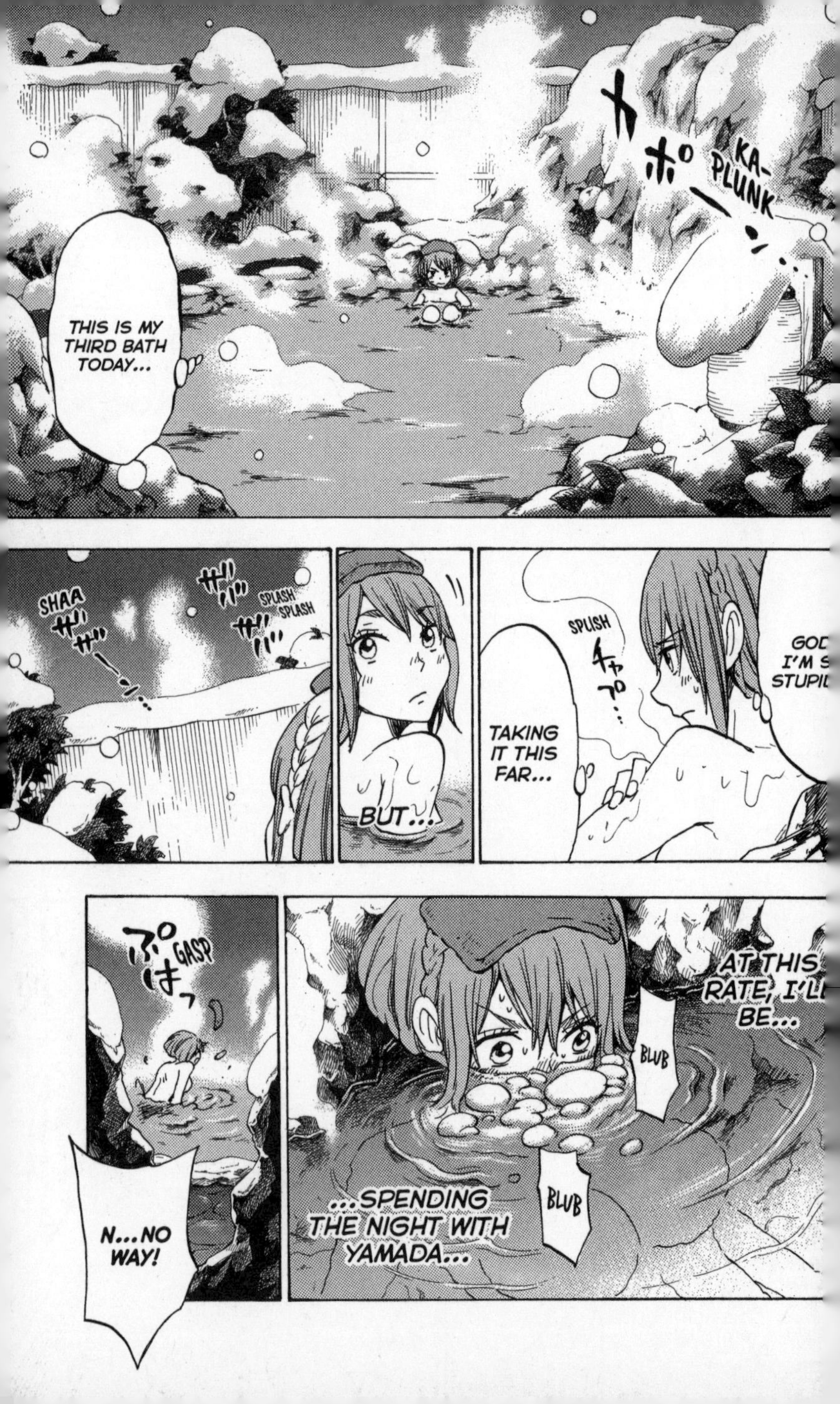

カポーン
KA-PLUNK
THIS IS MY THIRD BATH TODAY...
GOD I'M S STUPI
SPLISH
チャプ...
TAKING IT THIS FAR...
BUT...
ザバ ザバ
SPLASH SPLASH
SHAA
ザザーッ
AT THIS RATE, I'L BE...
BLUB
BLUB
...SPENDING THE NIGHT WITH YAMADA...
ぷはっ
GASP
N...NO WAY!

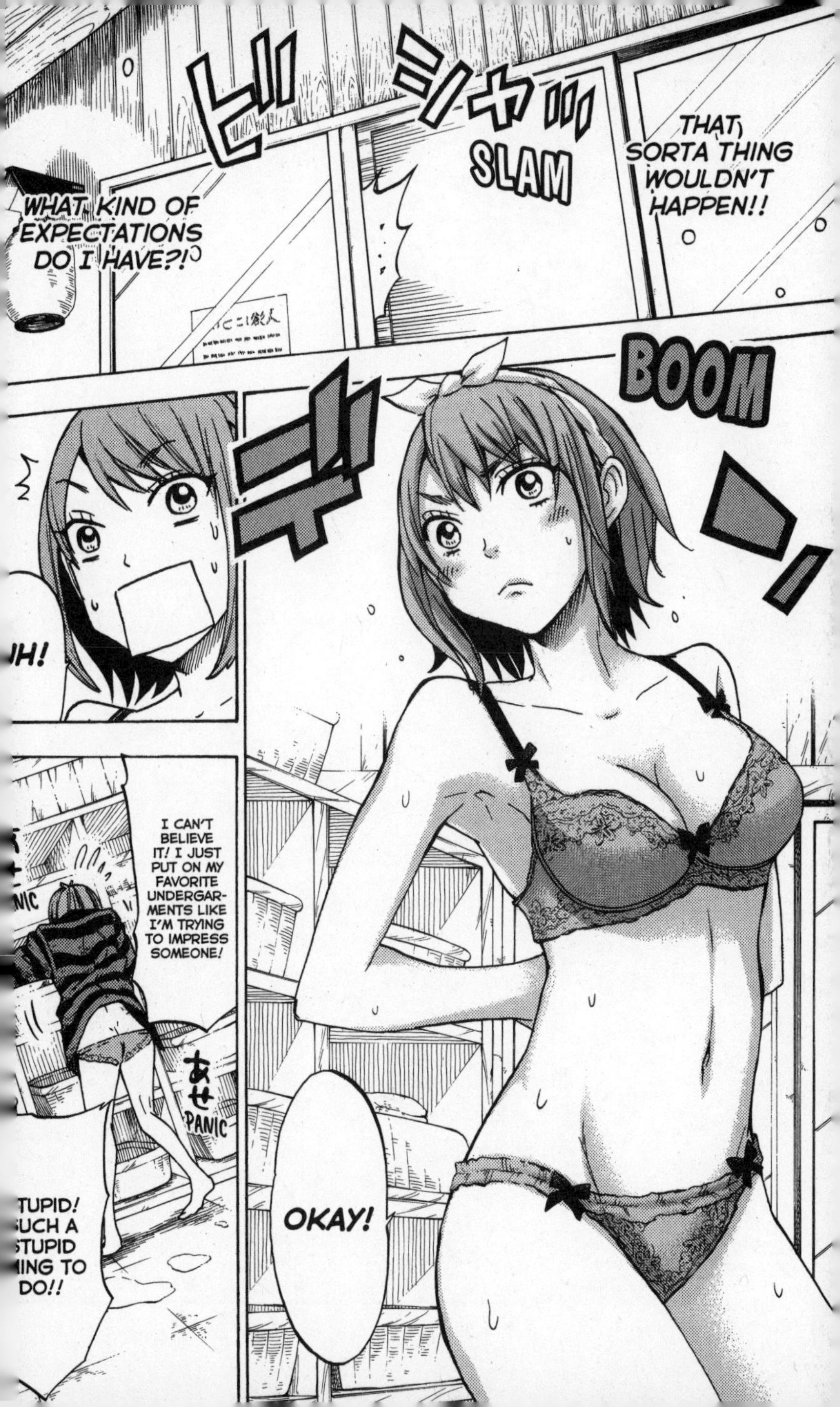
THAT SORTA THING WOULDN'T HAPPEN!!
SLAM
WHAT KIND OF EXPECTATIONS DO I HAVE?!
BOOM
OKAY!
I CAN'T BELIEVE IT! I JUST PUT ON MY FAVORITE UNDERGARMENTS LIKE I'M TRYING TO IMPRESS SOMEONE!
あせ
PANIC

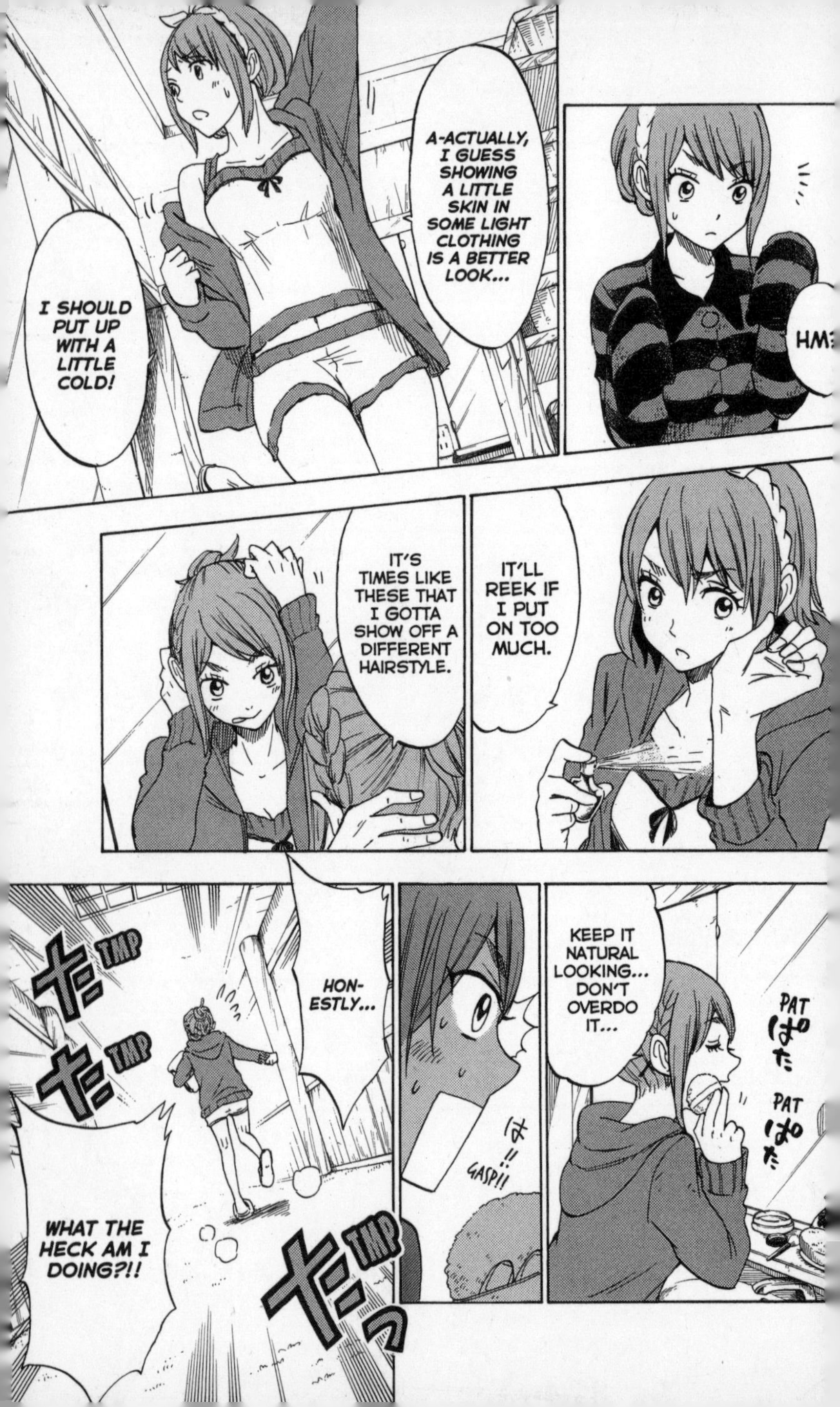
HM?
A-ACTUALLY, I GUESS SHOWING A LITTLE SKIN IN SOME LIGHT CLOTHING IS A BETTER LOOK...
I SHOULD PUT UP WITH A LITTLE COLD!
IT'LL REEK IF I PUT ON TOO MUCH.
IT'S TIMES LIKE THESE THAT I GOTTA SHOW OFF A DIFFERENT HAIRSTYLE.
KEEP IT NATURAL LOOKING... DON'T OVERDO IT...
PAT ぱた
PAT ぱた
は!! GASP!!
HON-ESTLY...
TMP
TMP
TMP
WHAT THE HECK AM I DOING?!!

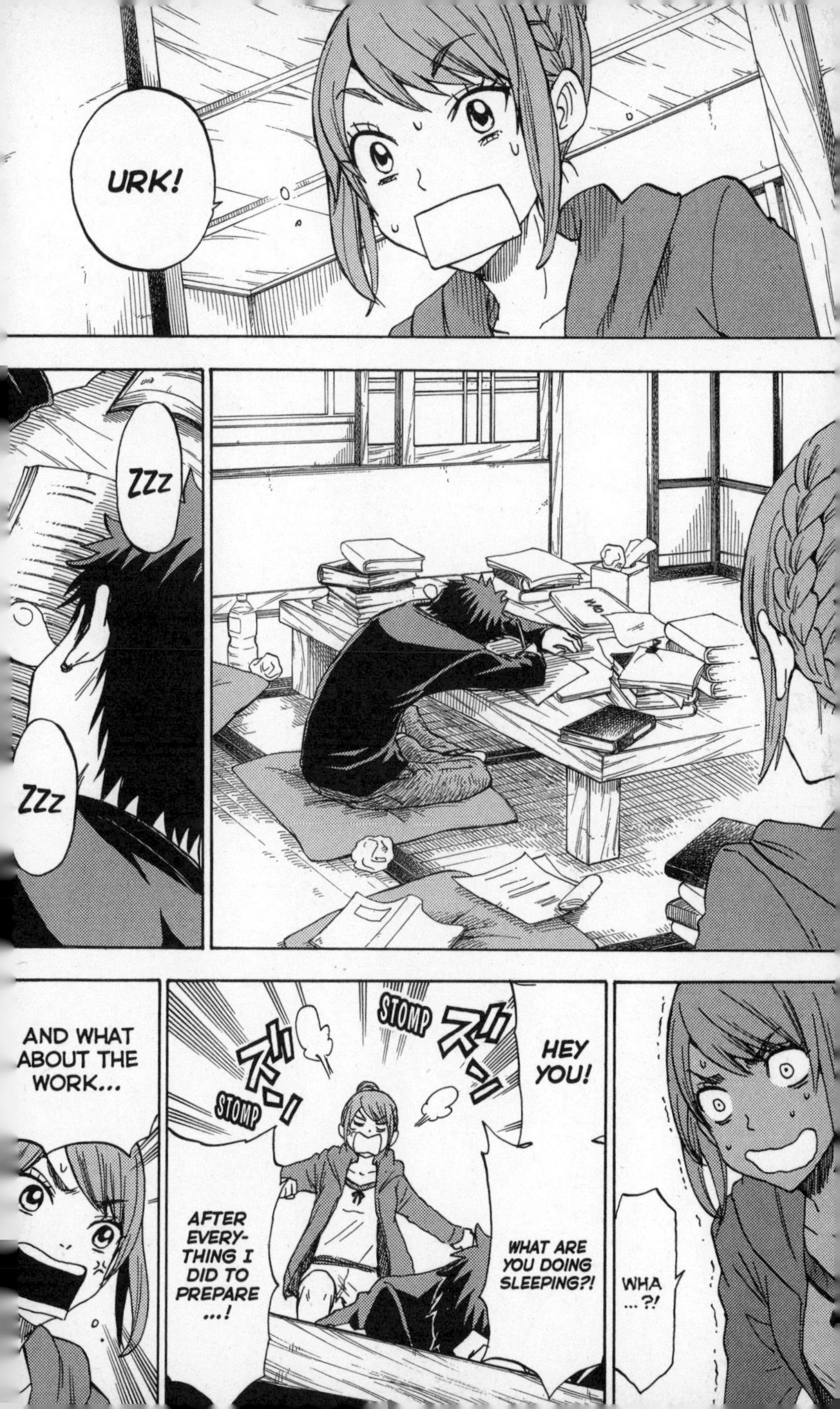
URK!
ZZZ
ZZZ
WHA ...?!
HEY YOU!
STOMP
STOMP
WHAT ARE YOU DOING SLEEPING?!
AFTER EVERY-THING I DID TO PREPARE ...!
AND WHAT ABOUT THE WORK...

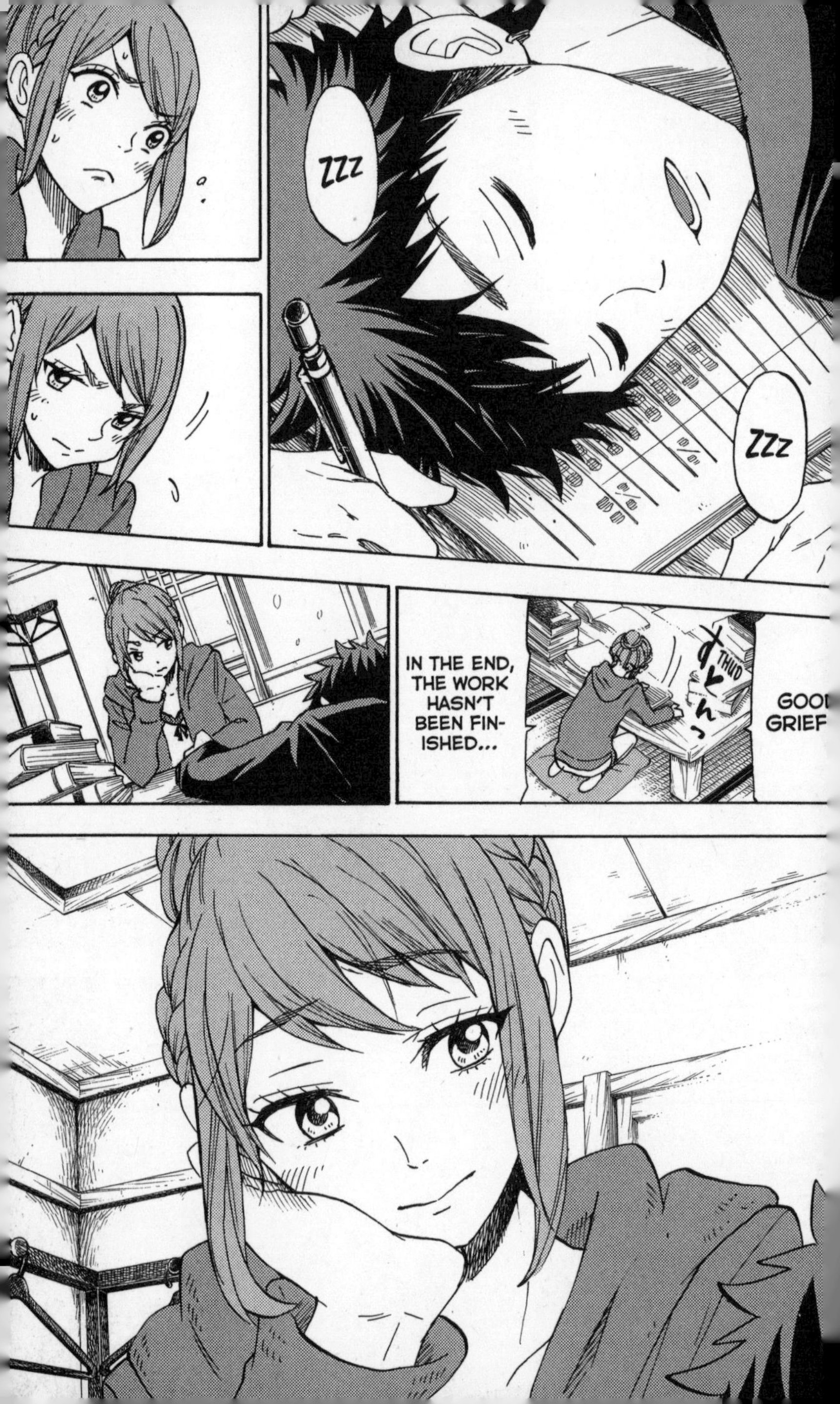
ZZZ
ZZZ
GOOD GRIEF
THUD
IN THE END, THE WORK HASN'T BEEN FIN-ISHED...

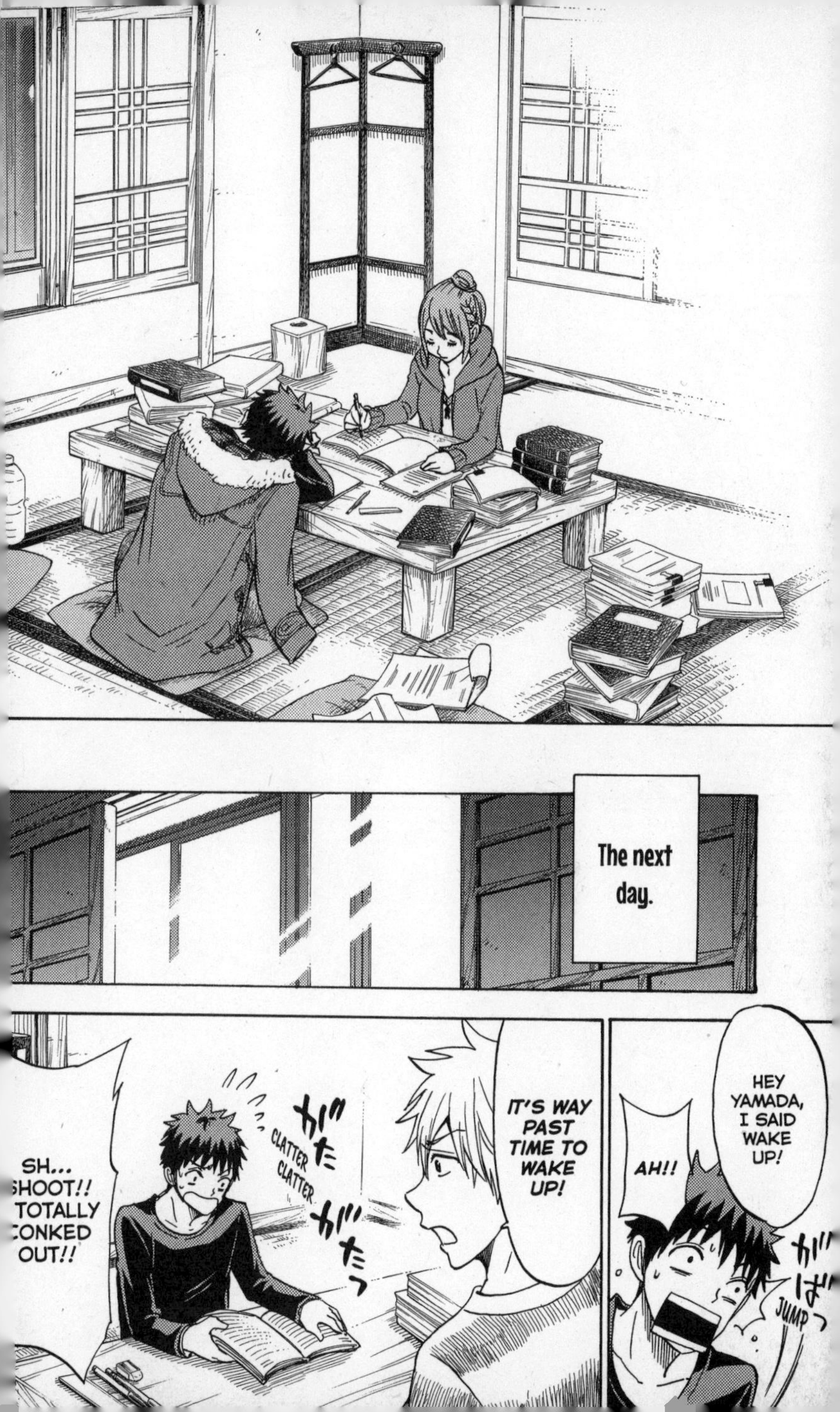
The next day.
HEY YAMADA, I SAID WAKE UP!
AH!!
がばっ
JUMP
IT'S WAY PAST TIME TO WAKE UP!
がたがたっ
CLATTER CLATTER
SH... SHOOT!! TOTALLY CONKED OUT!!

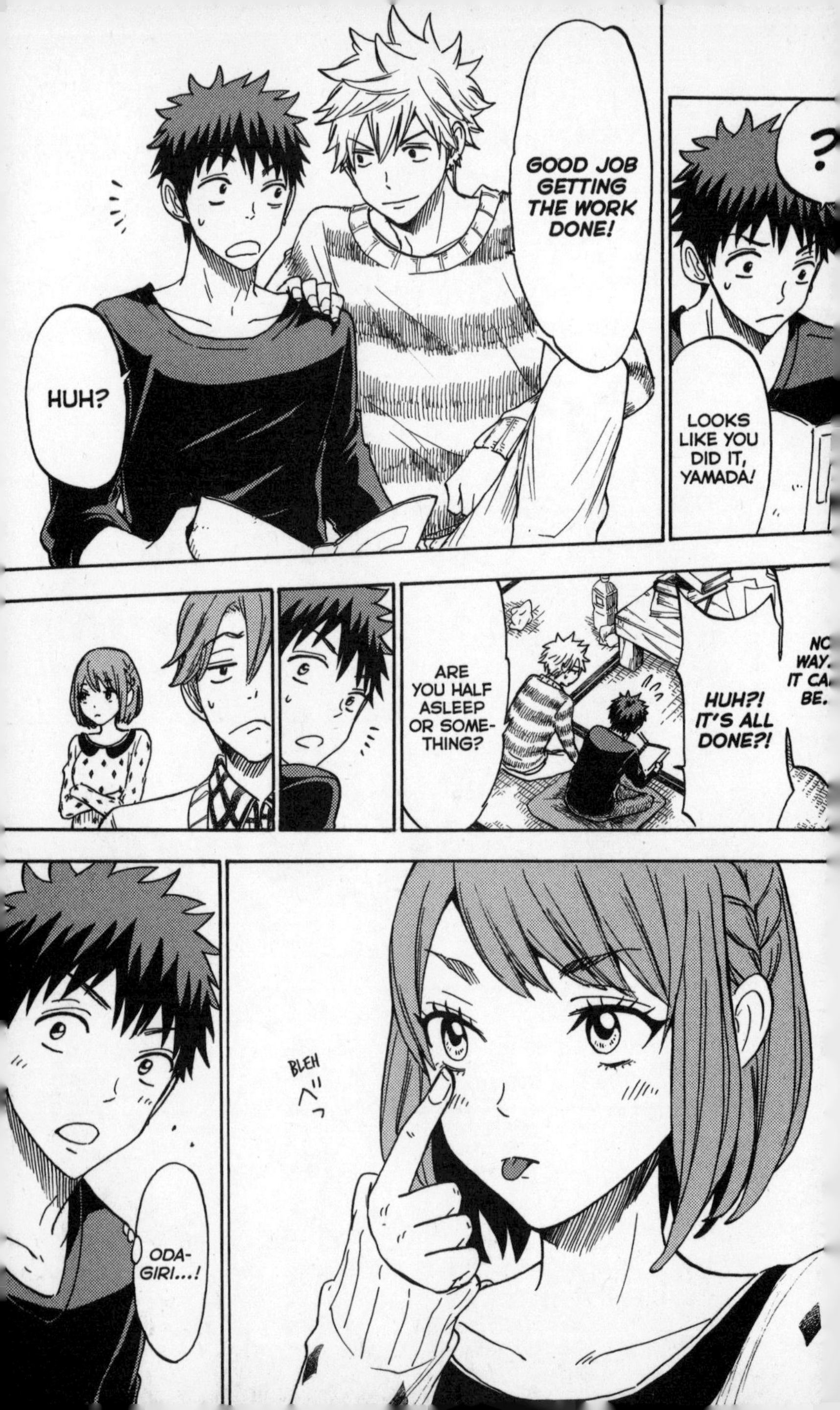
?
LOOKS LIKE YOU DID IT, YAMADA!
GOOD JOB GETTING THE WORK DONE!
HUH?
NO WAY. IT CA BE.
HUH?! IT'S ALL DONE?!
ARE YOU HALF ASLEEP OR SOME-THING?
BLEH
ODA-GIRI...!

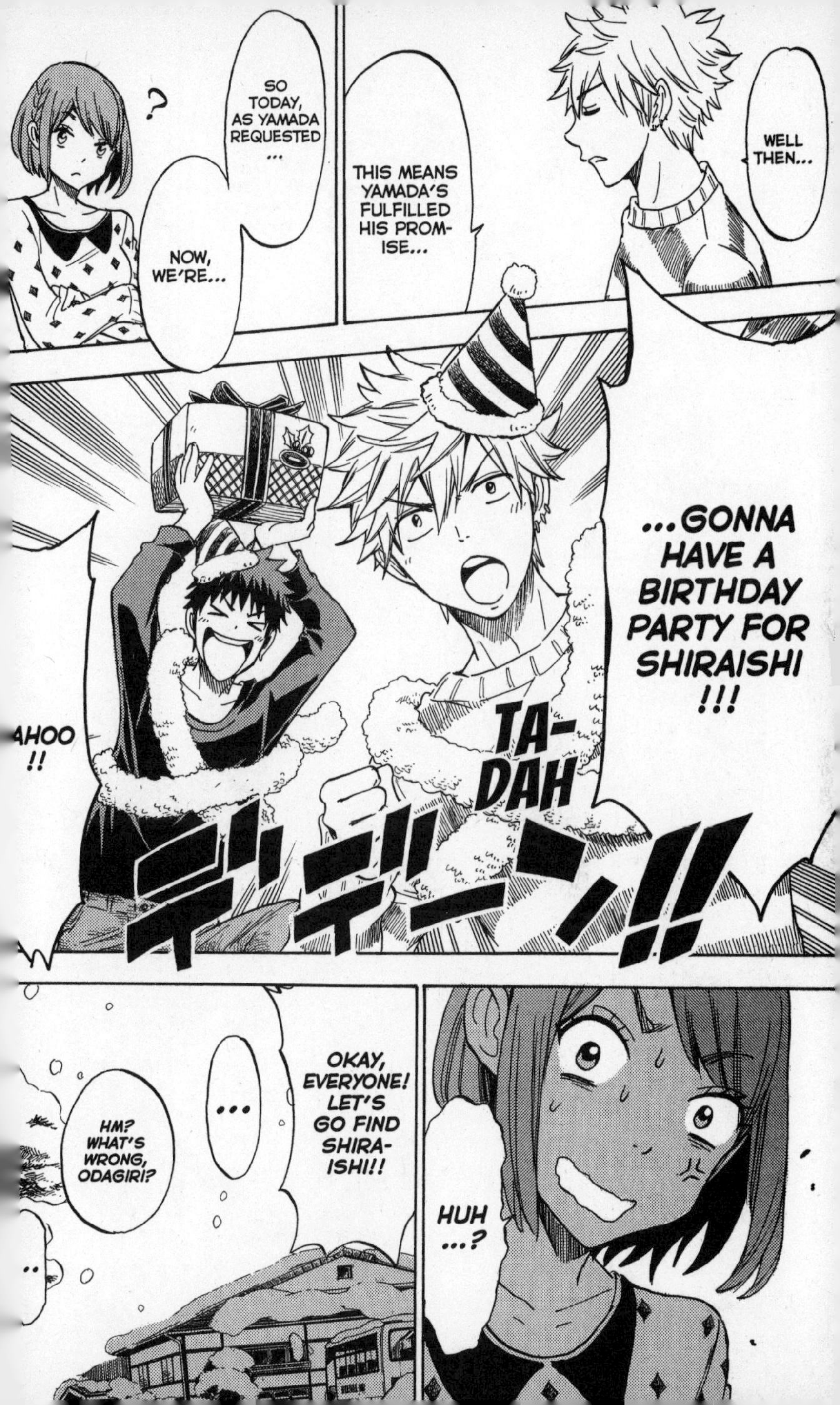
WELL THEN...
THIS MEANS YAMADA'S FULFILLED HIS PROMISE...
SO TODAY, AS YAMADA REQUESTED...
NOW, WE'RE...
?
...GONNA HAVE A BIRTHDAY PARTY FOR SHIRAISHI!!!
TA-DAH
AHOO!!
HUH...?
OKAY, EVERYONE! LET'S GO FIND SHIRAISHI!!
...
HM? WHAT'S WRONG, ODAGIRI?

CHAPTER 119: Do your hair up like me!!

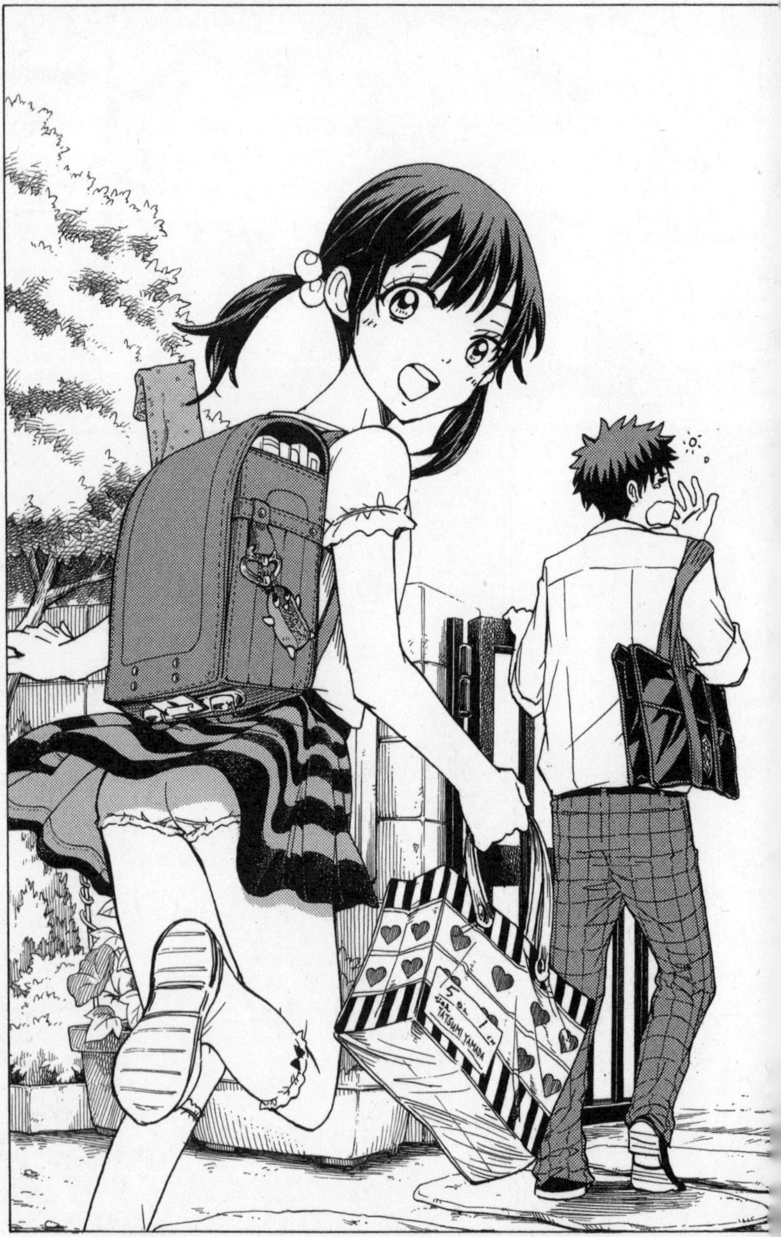
TATSUMI YAMADA

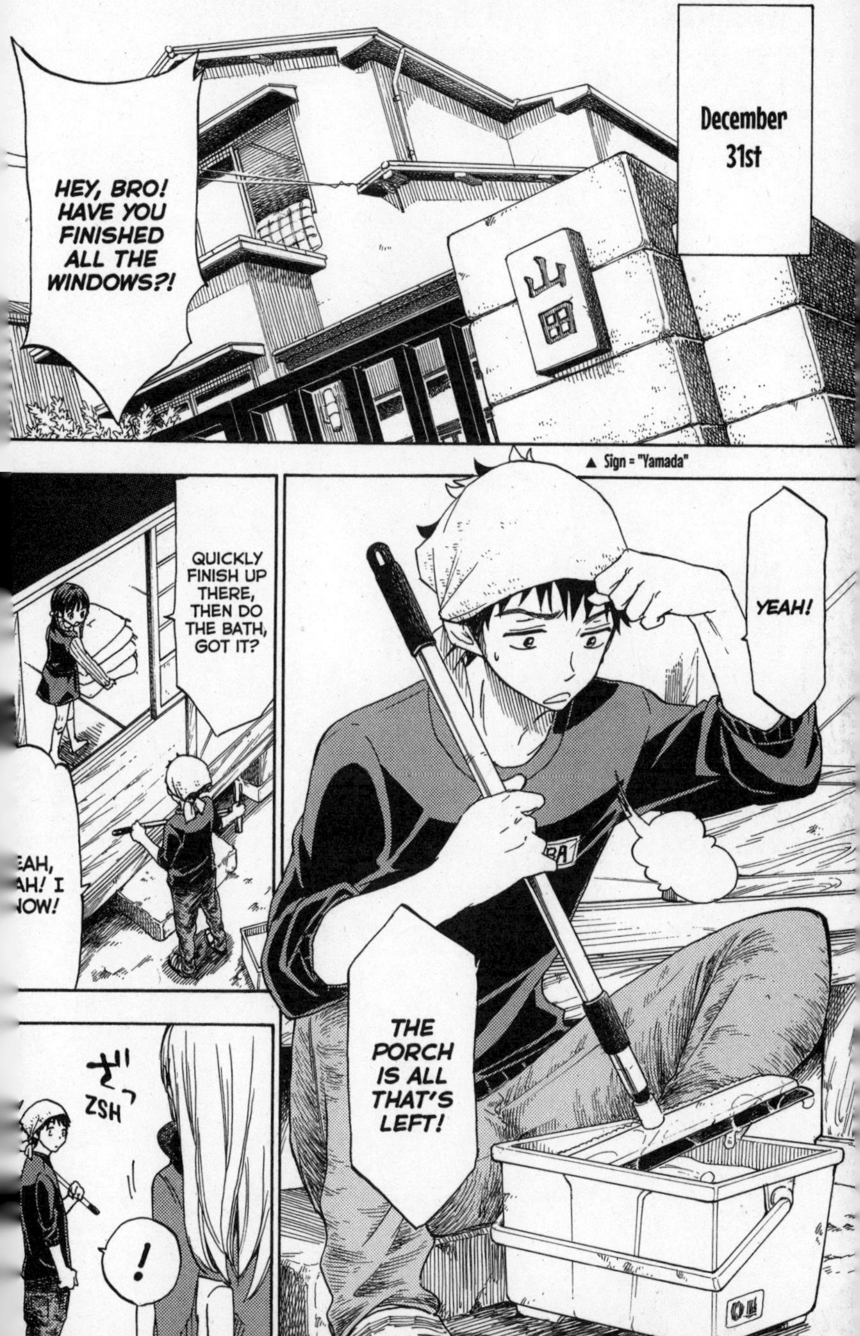
December 31st
HEY, BRO! HAVE YOU FINISHED ALL THE WINDOWS?!
山田
▲ Sign = "Yamada"
YEAH!
THE PORCH IS ALL THAT'S LEFT!
QUICKLY FINISH UP THERE, THEN DO THE BATH, GOT IT?
EAH, AH! I NOW!
ZSH
!

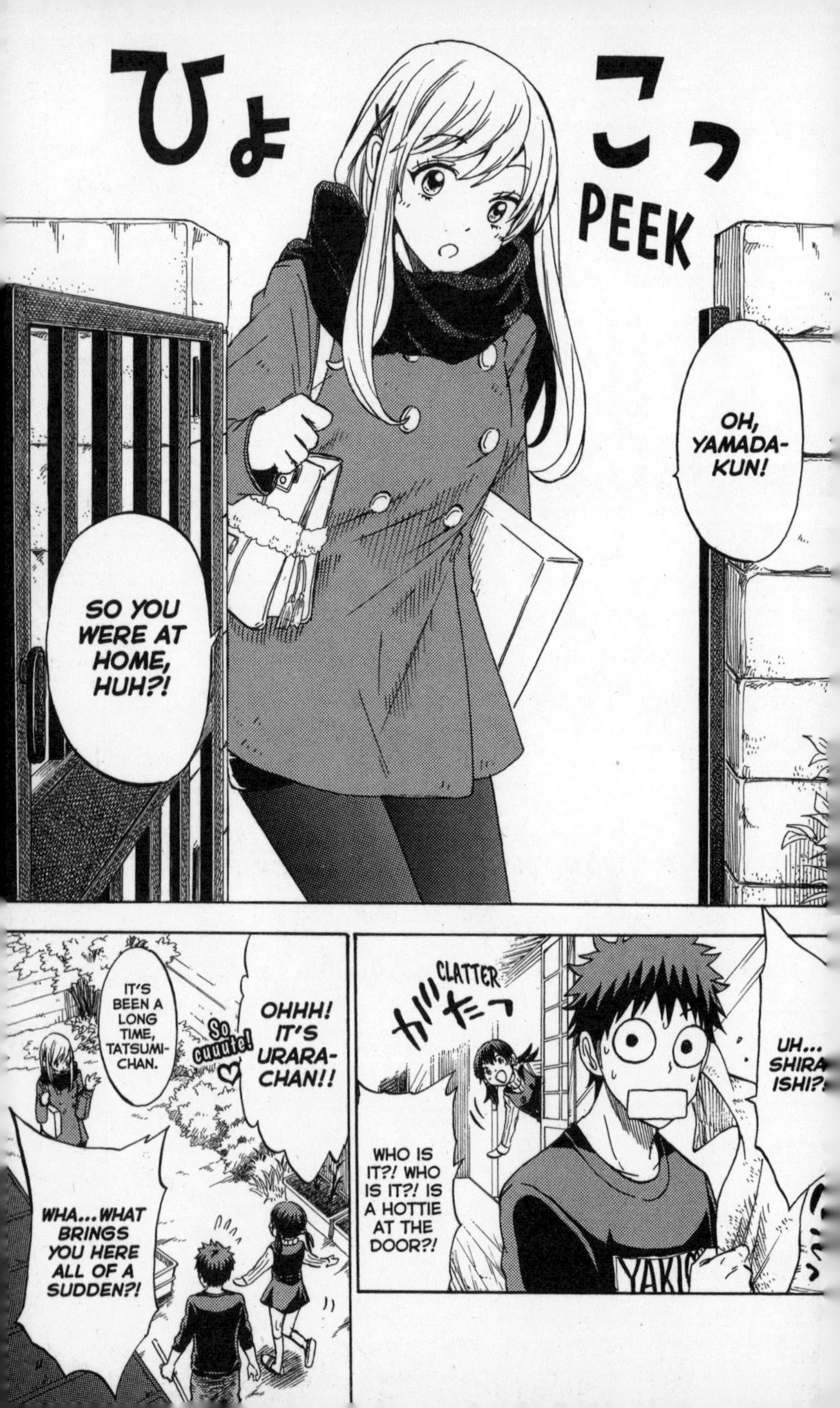

ひょこっ
PEEK
OH, YAMADA-KUN!
SO YOU WERE AT HOME, HUH?!
UH... SHIRAISHI?!
ガタッ
CLATTER
WHO IS IT?! WHO IS IT?! IS A HOTTIE AT THE DOOR?!
YAKI
OHHH! IT'S URARA-CHAN!!
So cuuute!
IT'S BEEN A LONG TIME, TATSUMI-CHAN.
WHA...WHAT BRINGS YOU HERE ALL OF A SUDDEN?!

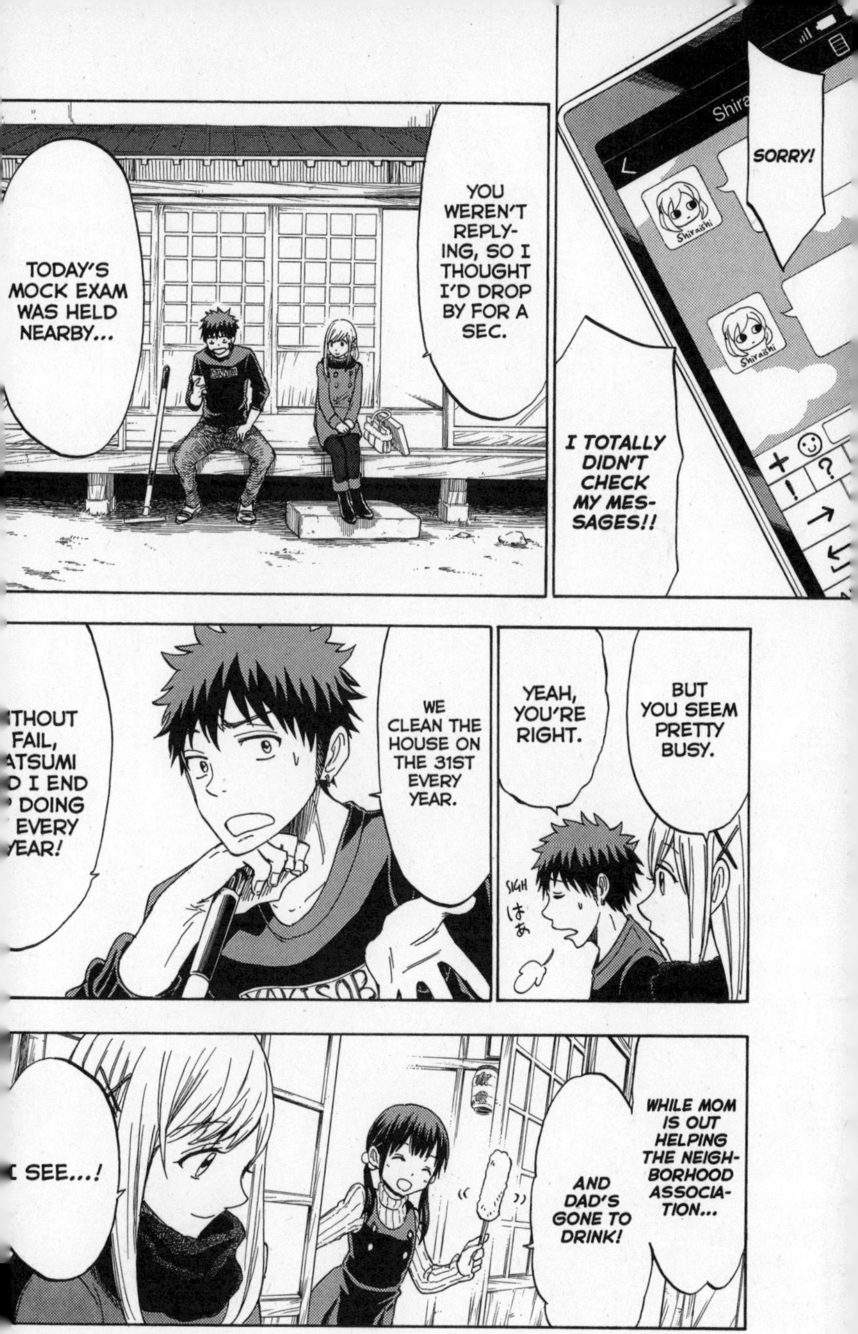
SORRY!
I TOTALLY DIDN'T CHECK MY MES-SAGES!!
YOU WEREN'T REPLY-ING, SO I THOUGHT I'D DROP BY FOR A SEC.
TODAY'S MOCK EXAM WAS HELD NEARBY...
BUT YOU SEEM PRETTY BUSY.
YEAH, YOU'RE RIGHT.
SIGH
はあ
WE CLEAN THE HOUSE ON THE 31ST EVERY YEAR.
THOUT FAIL, ATSUMI D I END DOING EVERY YEAR!
WHILE MOM IS OUT HELPING THE NEIGH-BORHOOD ASSOCIA-TION...
AND DAD'S GONE TO DRINK!
SEE...!

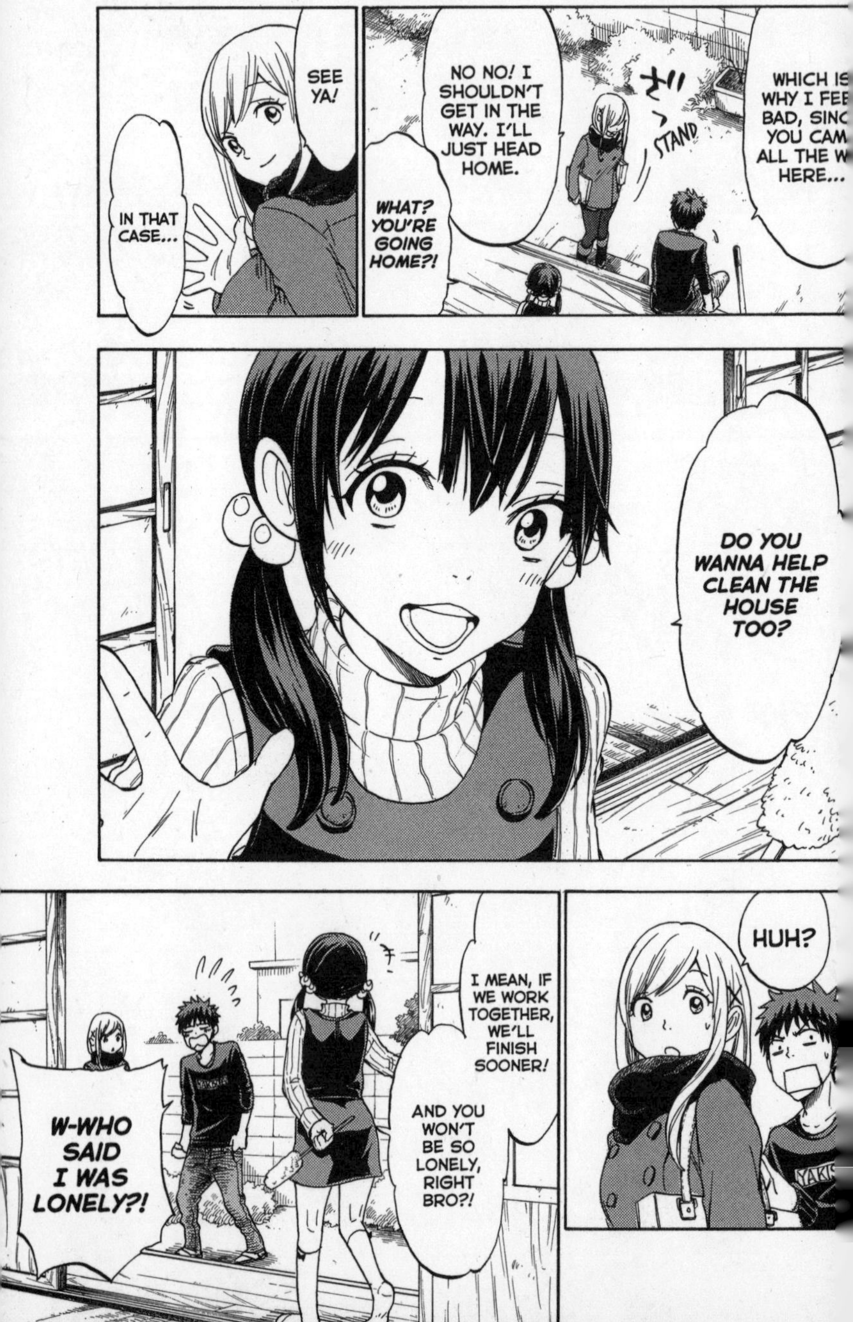
WHICH IS WHY I FEE BAD, SINC YOU CAM ALL THE W HERE...
ざ
STAND
NO NO! I SHOULDN'T GET IN THE WAY. I'LL JUST HEAD HOME.
WHAT? YOU'RE GOING HOME?!
SEE YA!
IN THAT CASE...
DO YOU WANNA HELP CLEAN THE HOUSE TOO?
HUH?
I MEAN, IF WE WORK TOGETHER, WE'LL FINISH SOONER!
AND YOU WON'T BE SO LONELY, RIGHT BRO?!
W-WHO SAID I WAS LONELY?!

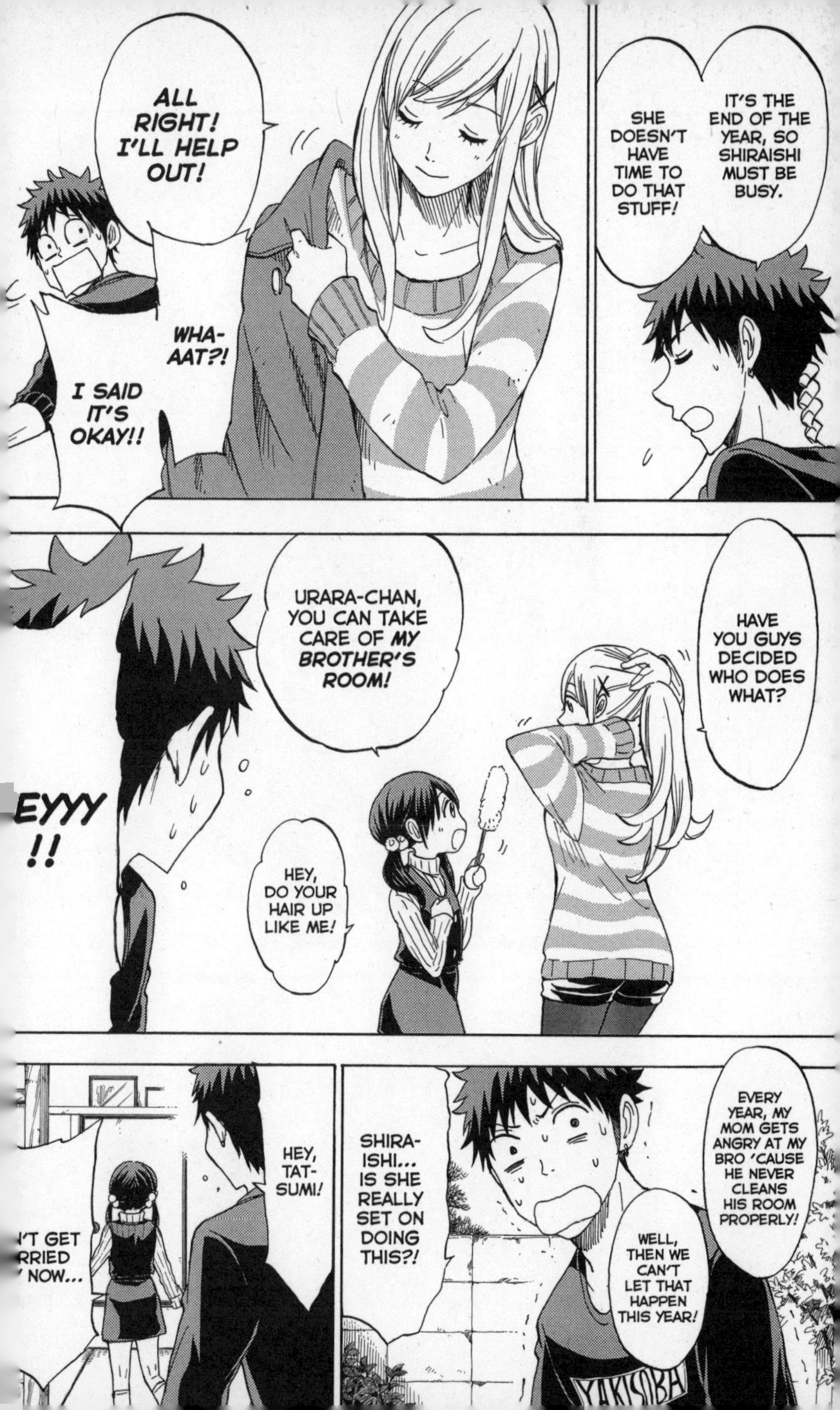
IT'S THE END OF THE YEAR, SO SHIRAISHI MUST BE BUSY.
SHE DOESN'T HAVE TIME TO DO THAT STUFF!
ALL RIGHT! I'LL HELP OUT!
WHA-AAT?!
I SAID IT'S OKAY!!
HAVE YOU GUYS DECIDED WHO DOES WHAT?
URARA-CHAN, YOU CAN TAKE CARE OF MY BROTHER'S ROOM!
HEY, DO YOUR HAIR UP LIKE ME!
EYYY !!
EVERY YEAR, MY MOM GETS ANGRY AT MY BRO 'CAUSE HE NEVER CLEANS HIS ROOM PROPERLY!
WELL, THEN WE CAN'T LET THAT HAPPEN THIS YEAR!
YAKISOBA
SHIRA-ISHI... IS SHE REALLY SET ON DOING THIS?!
HEY, TAT-SUMI!

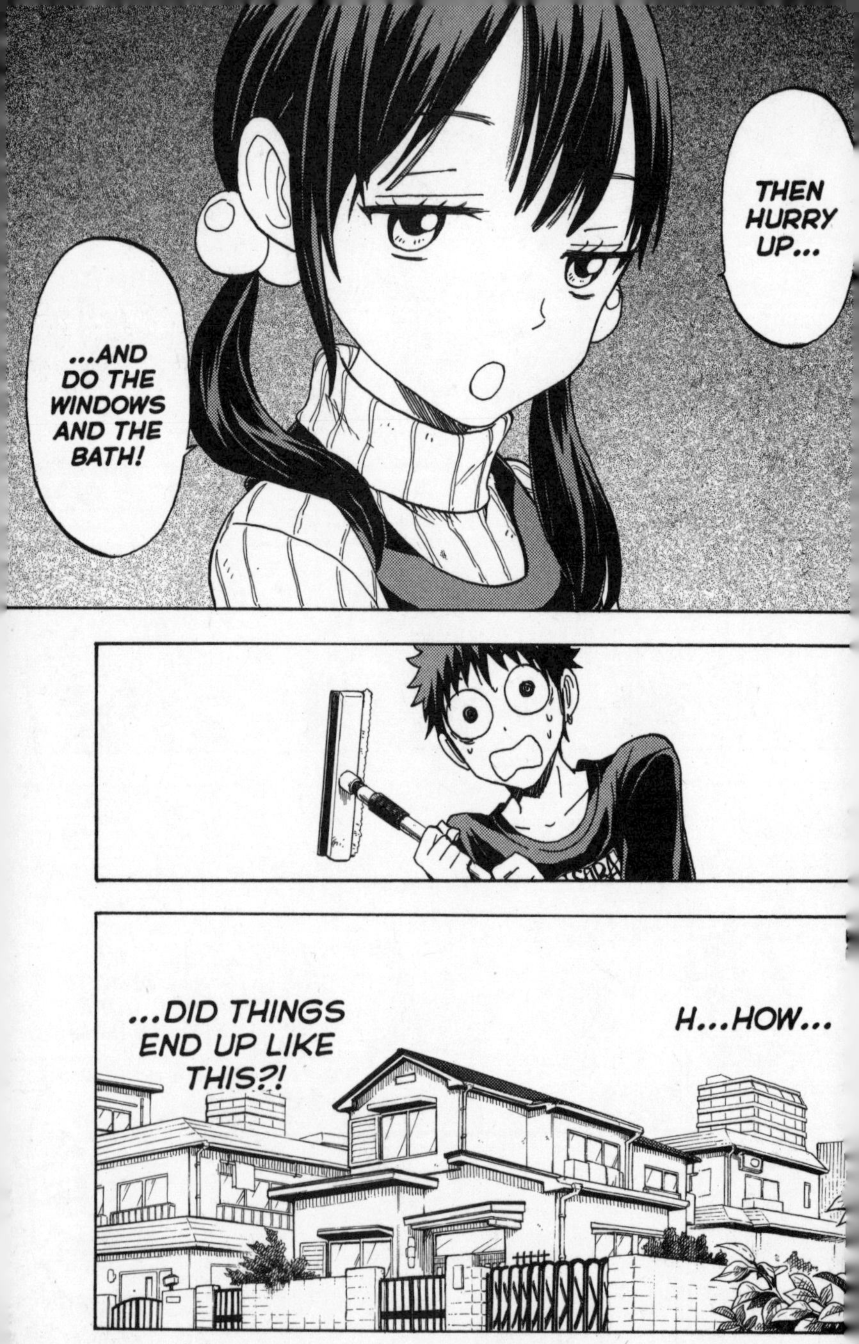
THEN HURRY UP...
...AND DO THE WINDOWS AND THE BATH!
H...HOW...
...DID THINGS END UP LIKE THIS?!

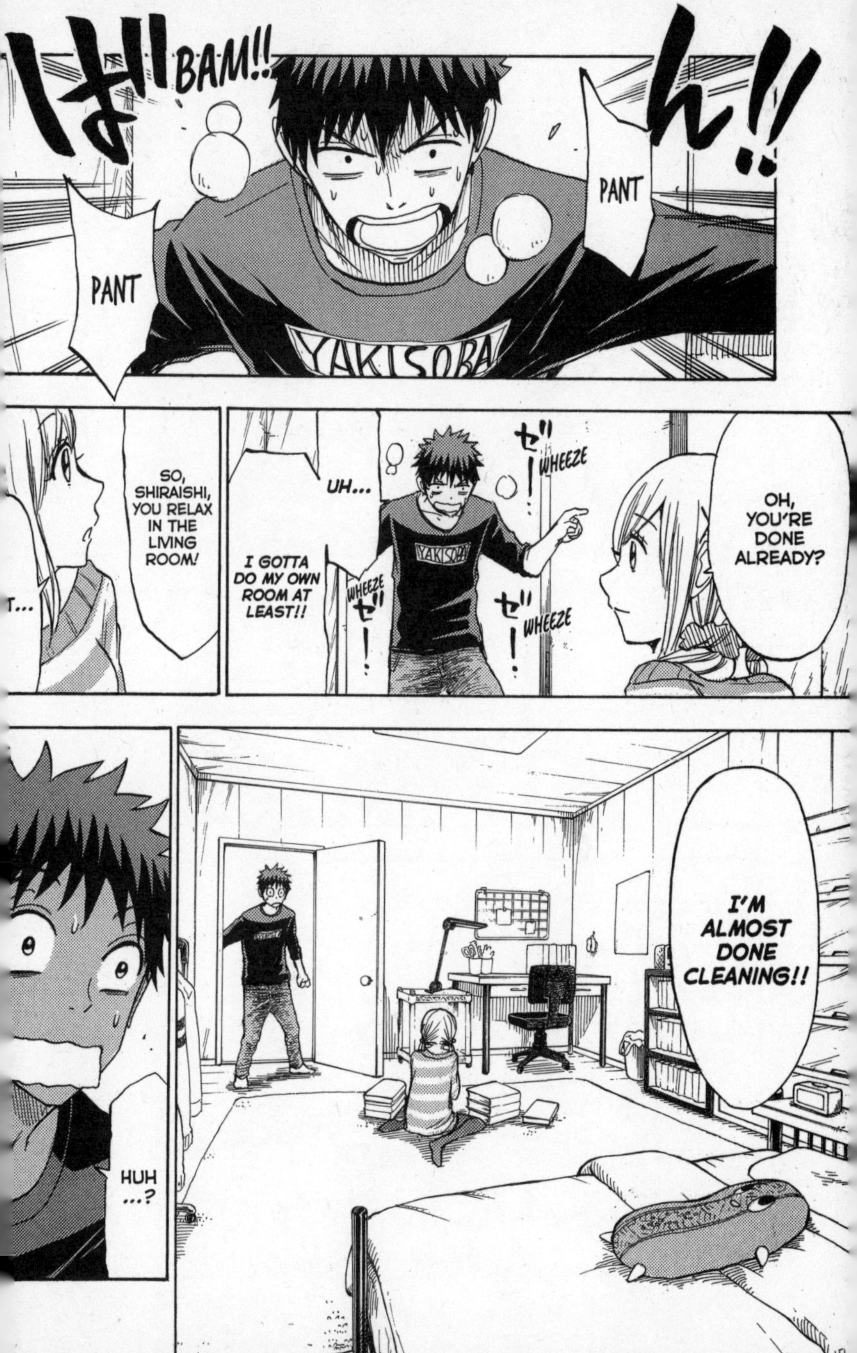
ば
BAM!!
ん!!
PANT
PANT
OH, YOU'RE DONE ALREADY?
ゼー WHEEZE
ゼー WHEEZE
UH...
I GOTTA DO MY OWN ROOM AT LEAST!!
ゼー WHEEZE
SO, SHIRAISHI, YOU RELAX IN THE LIVING ROOM!
T...
I'M ALMOST DONE CLEANING!!
HUH ...?

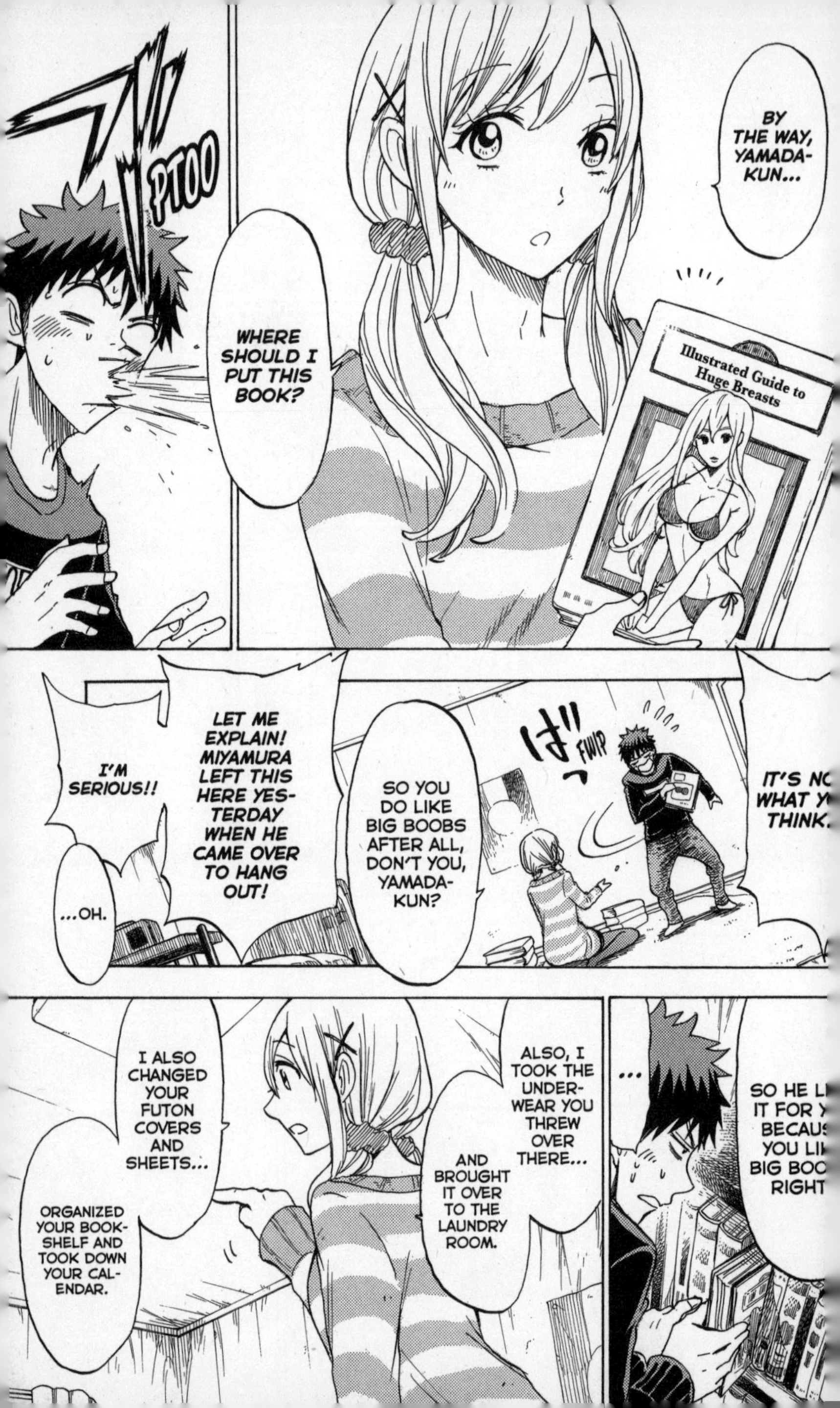

BY THE WAY, YAMADA-KUN...
Illustrated Guide to Huge Breasts
WHERE SHOULD I PUT THIS BOOK?
PTOO
IT'S NC WHAT Y THINK.
FWIP
SO YOU DO LIKE BIG BOOBS AFTER ALL, DON'T YOU, YAMADA-KUN?
LET ME EXPLAIN! MIYAMURA LEFT THIS HERE YES-TERDAY WHEN HE CAME OVER TO HANG OUT!
I'M SERIOUS!!
...OH.
SO HE L IT FOR Y BECAUS YOU LI BIG BOO RIGHT
...
ALSO, I TOOK THE UNDER-WEAR YOU THREW OVER THERE...
AND BROUGHT IT OVER TO THE LAUNDRY ROOM.
I ALSO CHANGED YOUR FUTON COVERS AND SHEETS...
ORGANIZED YOUR BOOK-SHELF AND TOOK DOWN YOUR CAL-ENDAR.

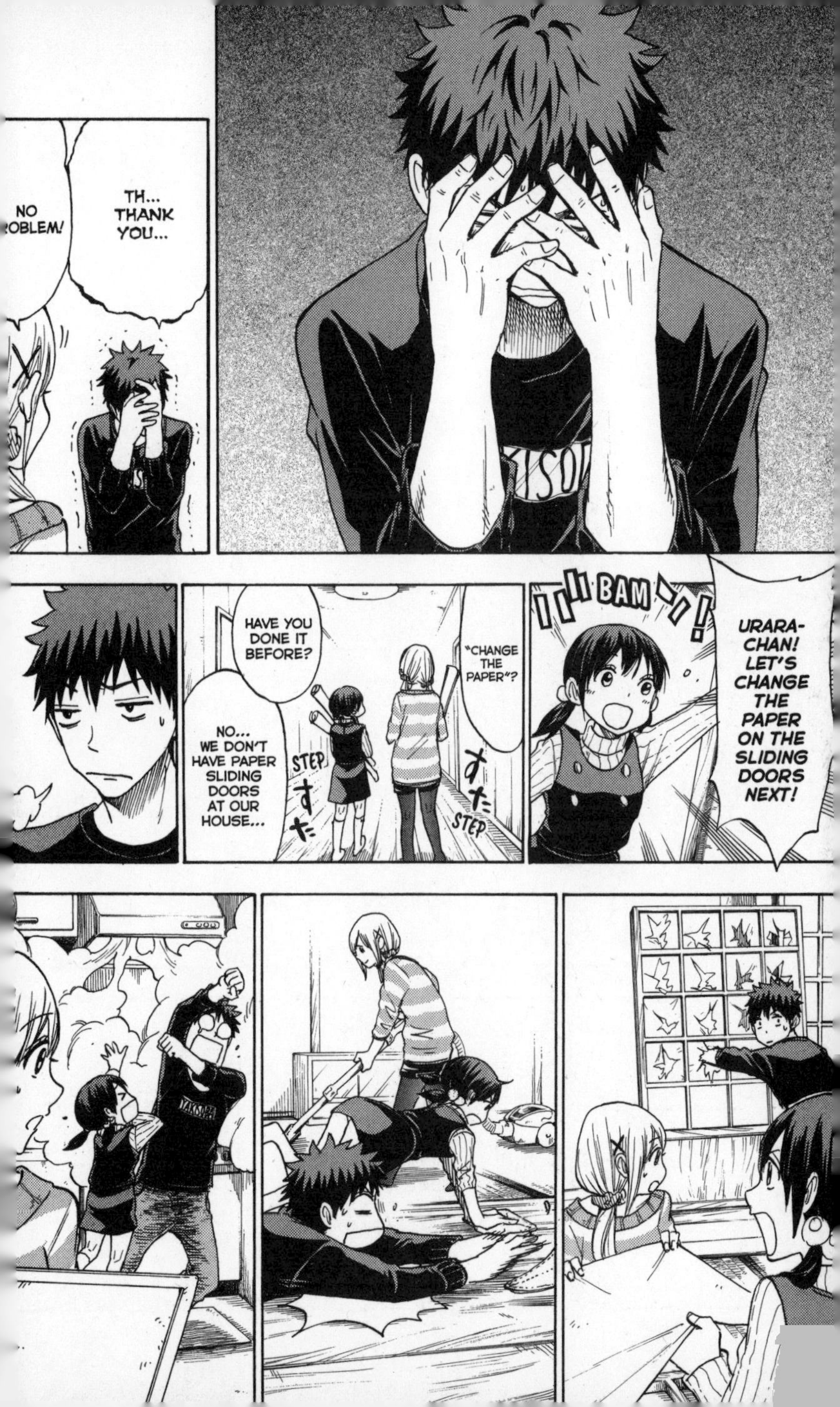
TH... THANK YOU...
NO ROBLEM!
BAM
URARA-CHAN! LET'S CHANGE THE PAPER ON THE SLIDING DOORS NEXT!
"CHANGE THE PAPER"?
すた STEP
HAVE YOU DONE IT BEFORE?
NO... WE DON'T HAVE PAPER SLIDING DOORS AT OUR HOUSE...
STEP すた

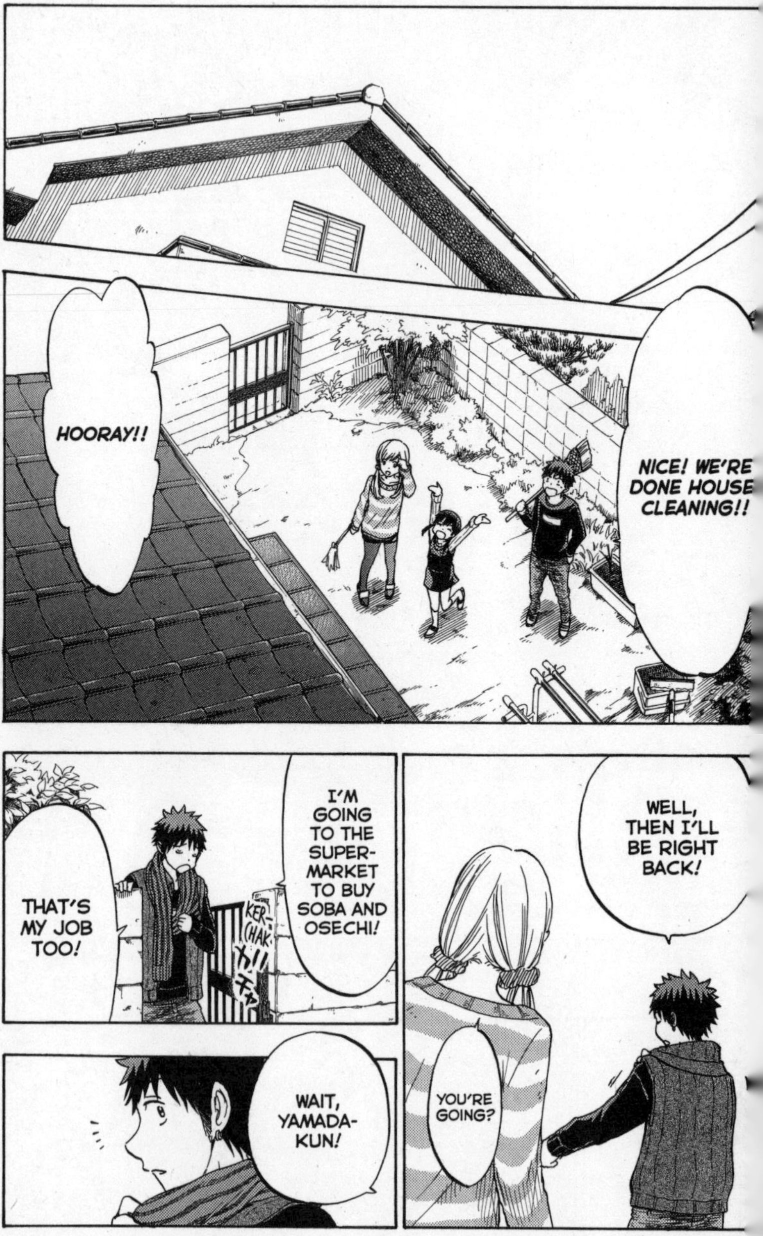
NICE! WE'RE DONE HOUSE CLEANING!!
HOORAY!!
WELL, THEN I'LL BE RIGHT BACK!
YOU'RE GOING?
I'M GOING TO THE SUPER-MARKET TO BUY SOBA AND OSECHI!
KER-CHAK
THAT'S MY JOB TOO!
WAIT, YAMADA-KUN!

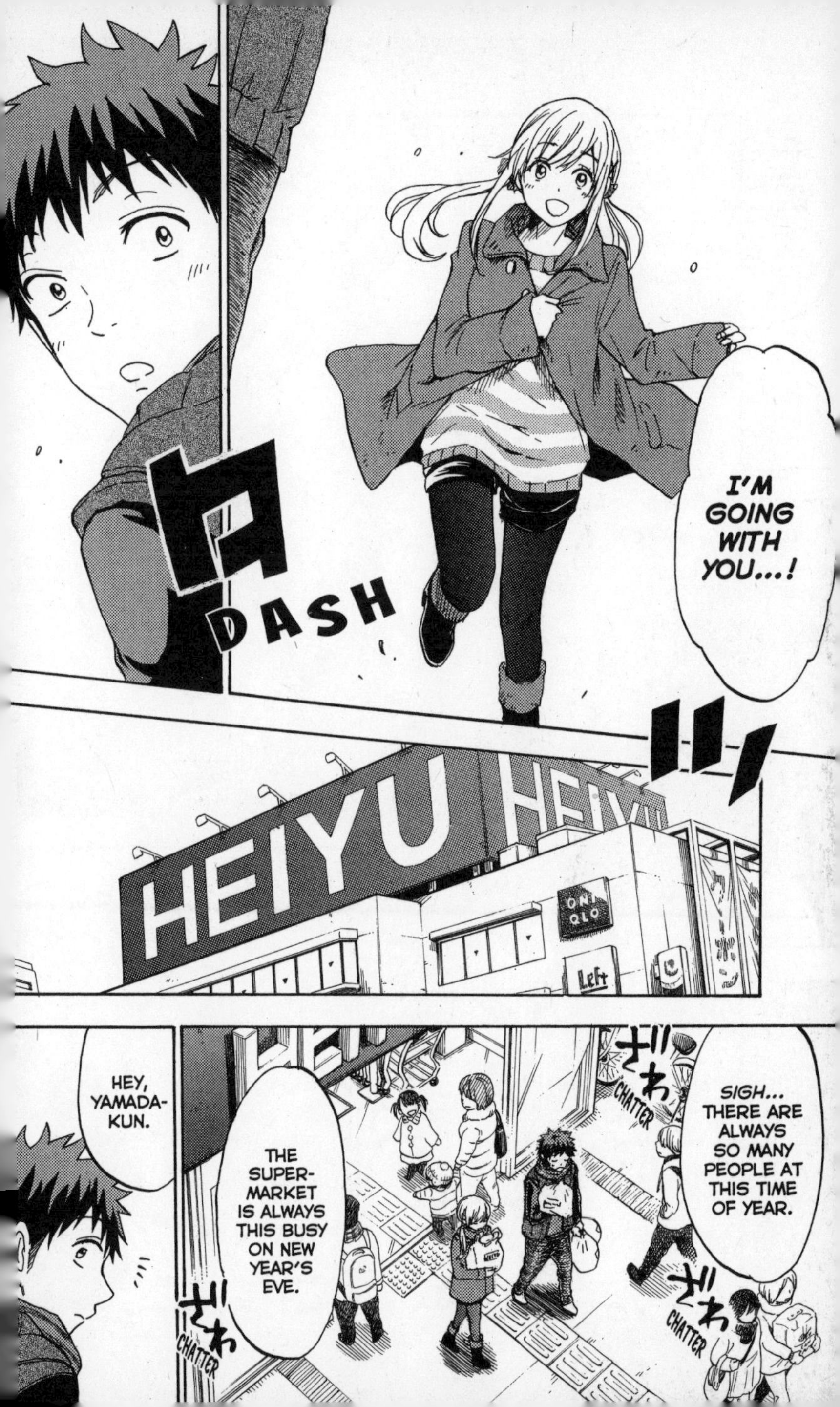
I'M GOING WITH YOU...!
DASH
HEIYU
SIGH... THERE ARE ALWAYS SO MANY PEOPLE AT THIS TIME OF YEAR.
CHATTER
CHATTER
THE SUPER-MARKET IS ALWAYS THIS BUSY ON NEW YEAR'S EVE.
CHATTER
HEY, YAMADA-KUN.

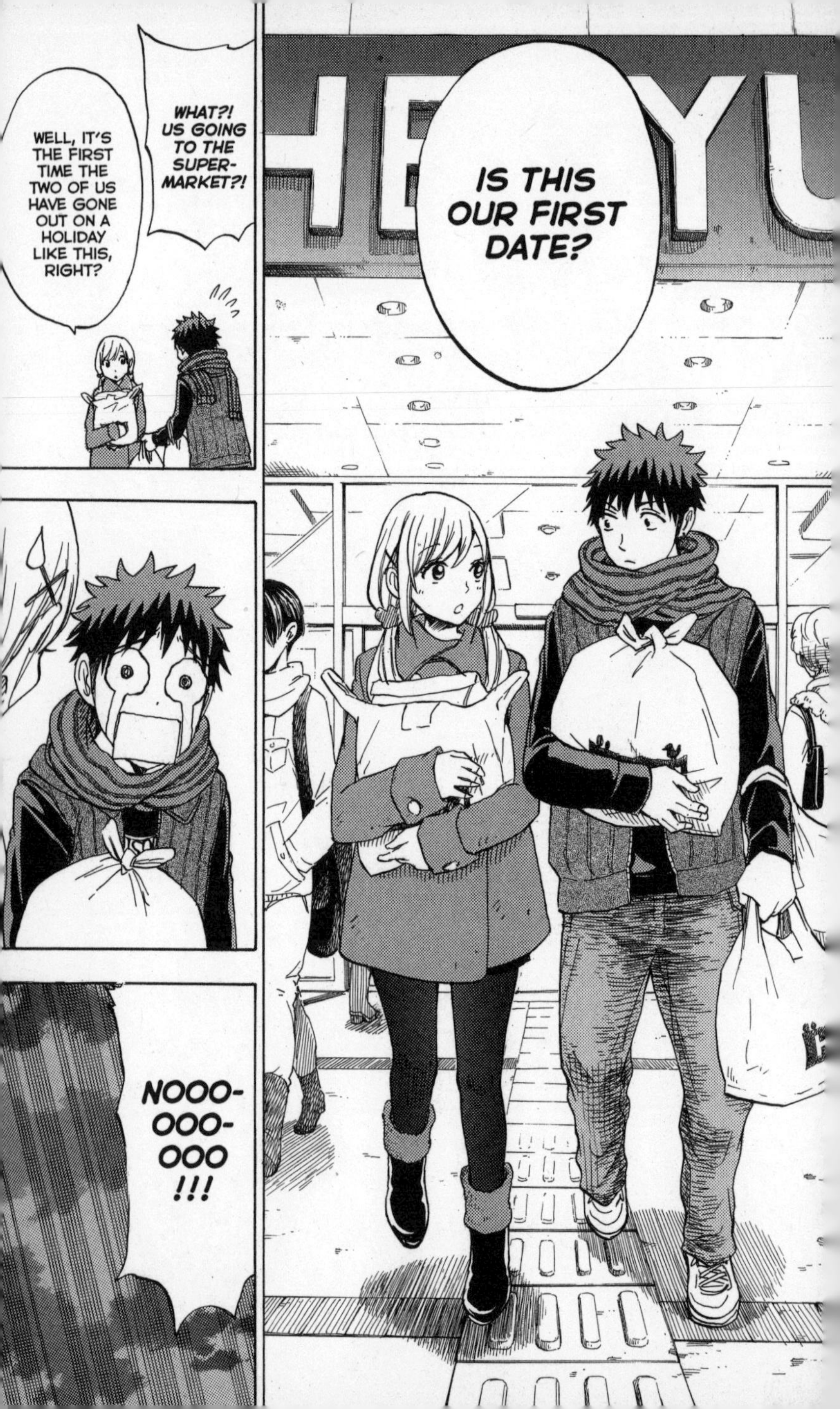
IS THIS OUR FIRST DATE?
WHAT?! US GOING TO THE SUPER-MARKET?!
WELL, IT'S THE FIRST TIME THE TWO OF US HAVE GONE OUT ON A HOLIDAY LIKE THIS, RIGHT?
NOOO-OOO-OOO !!!

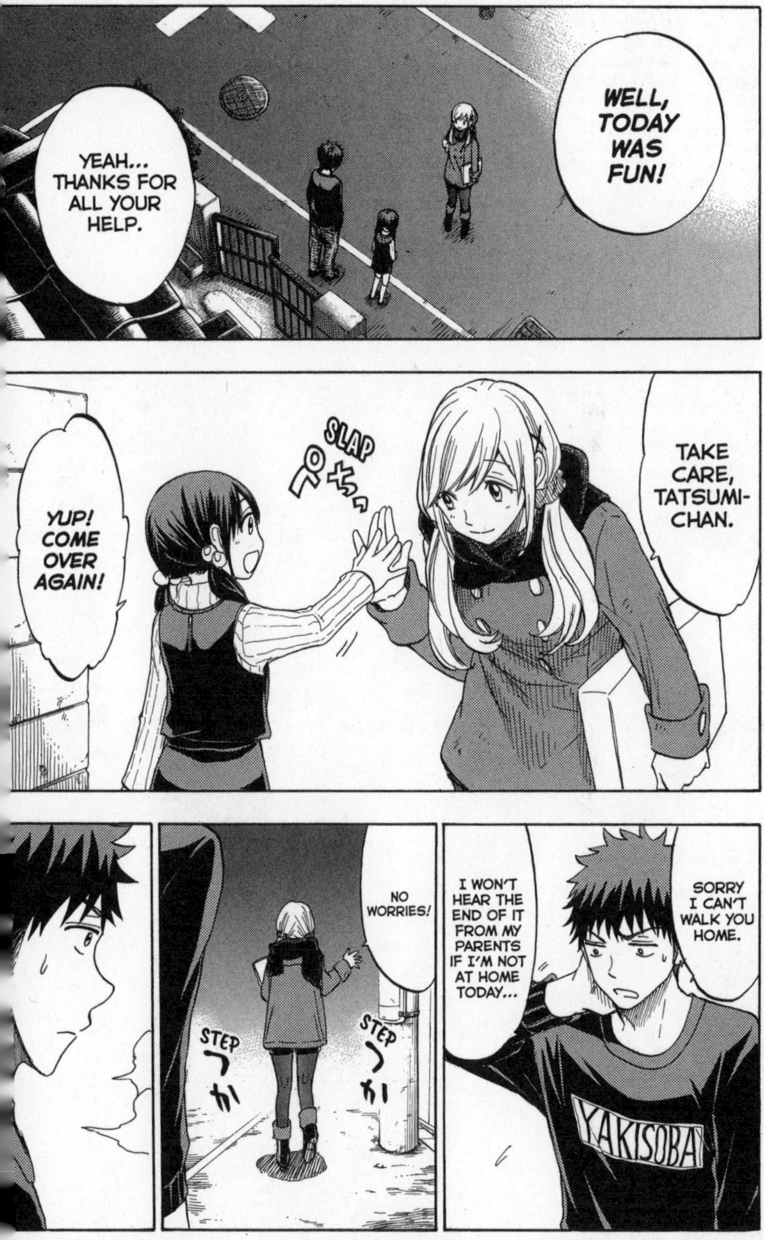
WELL, TODAY WAS FUN!
YEAH... THANKS FOR ALL YOUR HELP.
TAKE CARE, TATSUMI-CHAN.
SLAP
YUP! COME OVER AGAIN!
SORRY I CAN'T WALK YOU HOME.
YAKISOBA
I WON'T HEAR THE END OF IT FROM MY PARENTS IF I'M NOT AT HOME TODAY...
NO WORRIES!
STEP
STEP

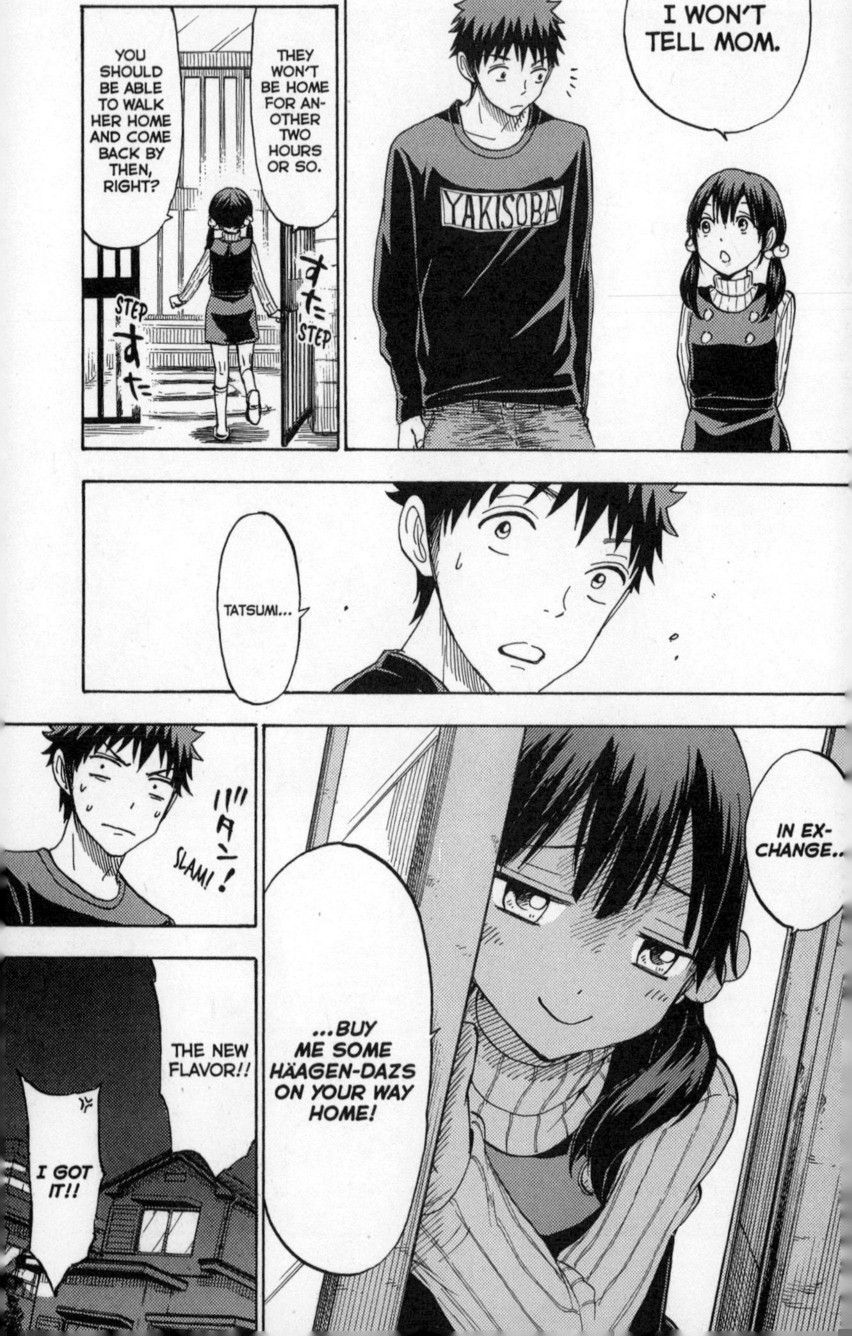
I WON'T TELL MOM.
THEY WON'T BE HOME FOR AN-OTHER TWO HOURS OR SO.
YOU SHOULD BE ABLE TO WALK HER HOME AND COME BACK BY THEN, RIGHT?
すた STEP
STEP すた
TATSUMI...
IN EX-CHANGE..
...BUY ME SOME HÄAGEN-DAZS ON YOUR WAY HOME!
バタン!
SLAM!
THE NEW FLAVOR!!
I GOT IT!!

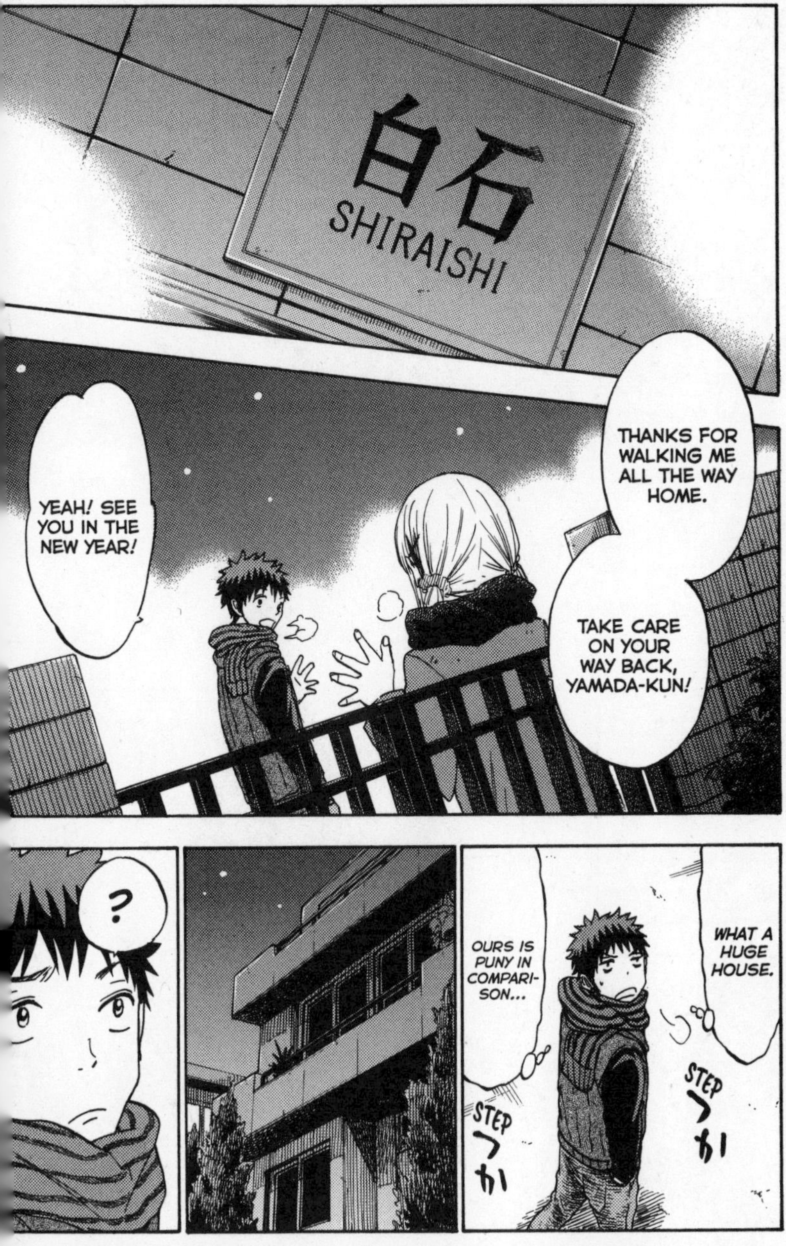
白石
SHIRAISHI
THANKS FOR WALKING ME ALL THE WAY HOME.
TAKE CARE ON YOUR WAY BACK, YAMADA-KUN!
YEAH! SEE YOU IN THE NEW YEAR!
WHAT A HUGE HOUSE.
STEP
つか
OURS IS PUNY IN COMPARI-SON...
STEP
つか
?

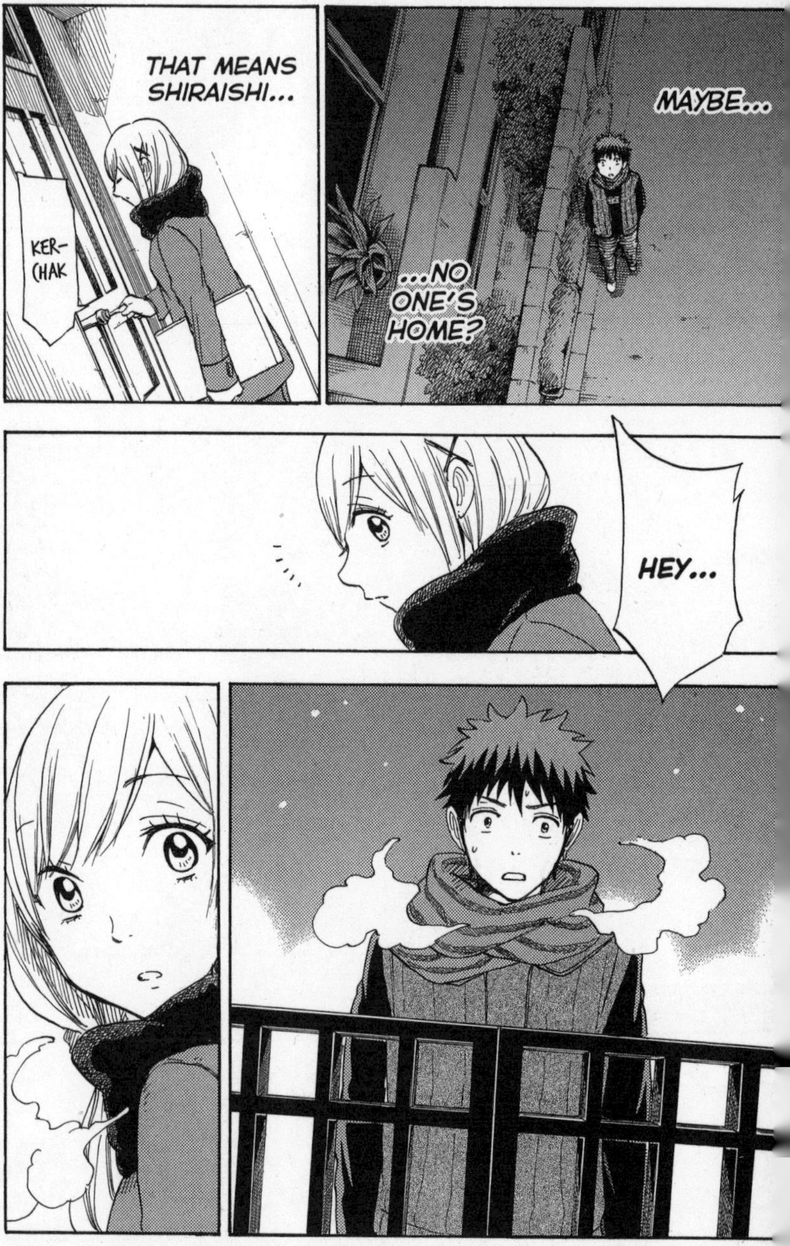
MAYBE...
...NO ONE'S HOME?
THAT MEANS SHIRAISHI...
KER-CHAK
HEY...

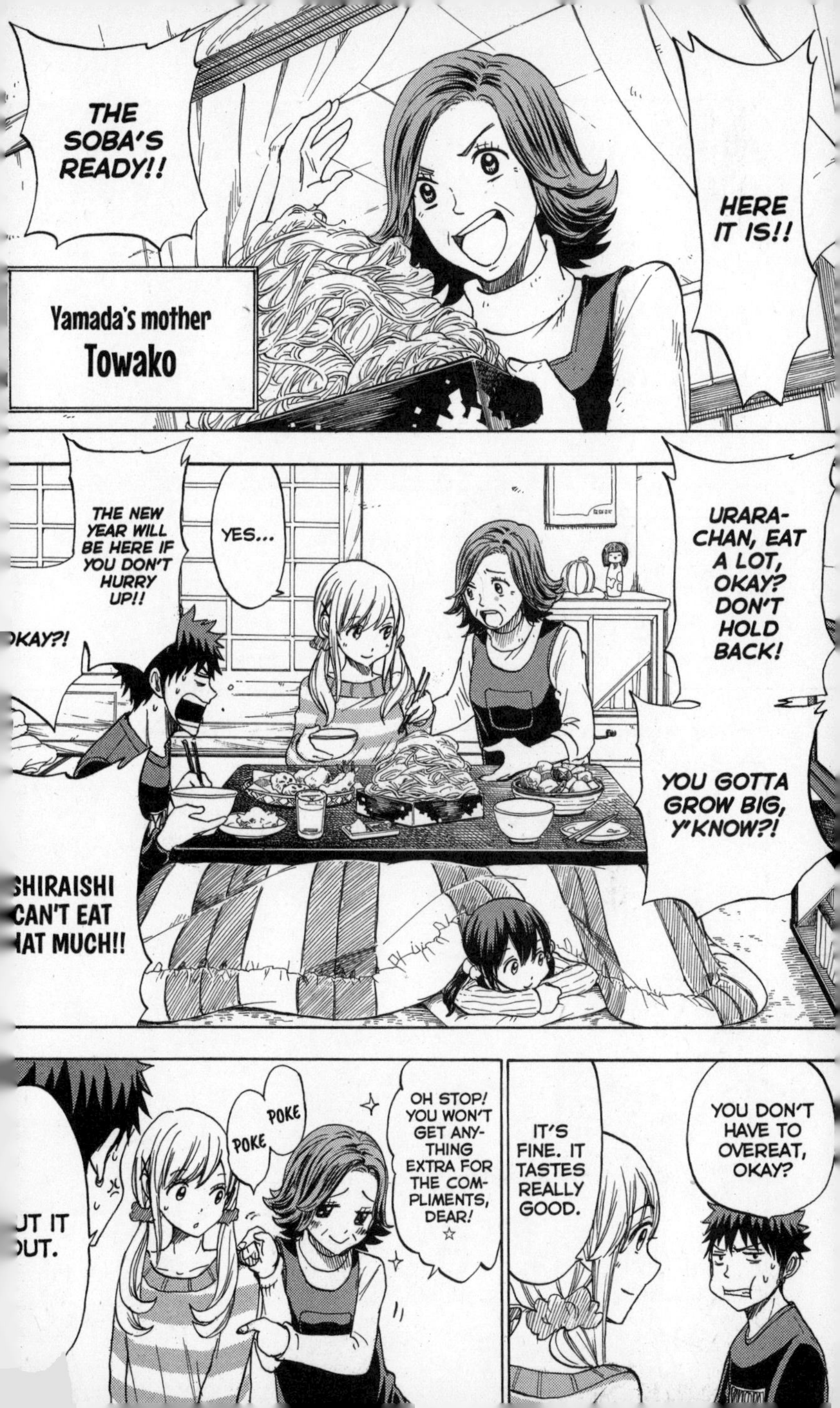

HERE IT IS!!
THE SOBA'S READY!!
Yamada's mother Towako
URARA-CHAN, EAT A LOT, OKAY? DON'T HOLD BACK!
YOU GOTTA GROW BIG, Y'KNOW?!
YES...
THE NEW YEAR WILL BE HERE IF YOU DON'T HURRY UP!!
KAY?!
SHIRAISHI CAN'T EAT HAT MUCH!!
YOU DON'T HAVE TO OVEREAT, OKAY?
IT'S FINE. IT TASTES REALLY GOOD.
OH STOP! YOU WON'T GET ANY-THING EXTRA FOR THE COM-PLIMENTS, DEAR! ☆
POKE
POKE
UT IT OUT.

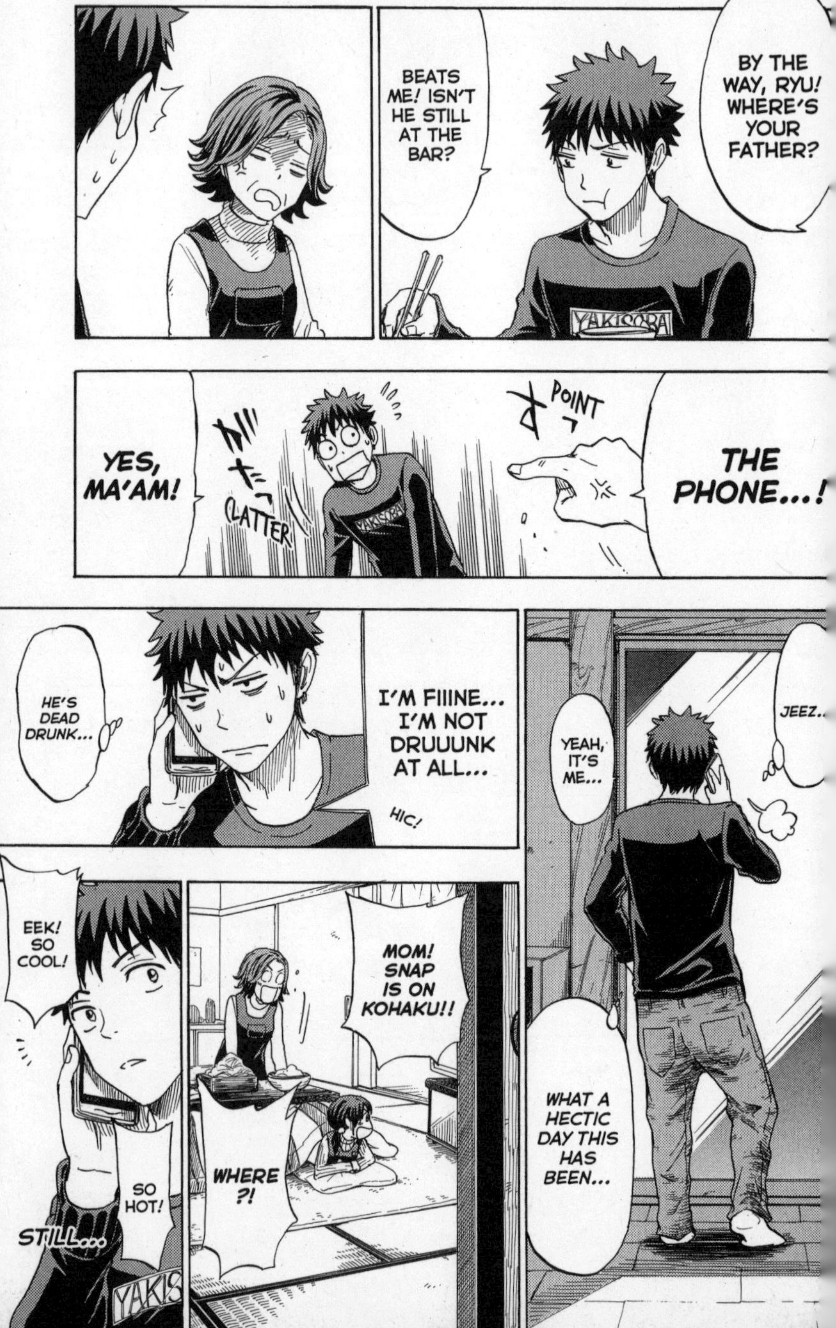
BY THE WAY, RYU! WHERE'S YOUR FATHER?
BEATS ME! ISN'T HE STILL AT THE BAR?
THE PHONE...!
POINT
CLATTER
YES, MA'AM!
JEEZ...
YEAH, IT'S ME...
WHAT A HECTIC DAY THIS HAS BEEN...
I'M FIIINE... I'M NOT DRUUUNK AT ALL...
HIC!
HE'S DEAD DRUNK...
MOM! SNAP IS ON KOHAKU!!
WHERE ?!
EEK! SO COOL!
SO HOT!
STILL...

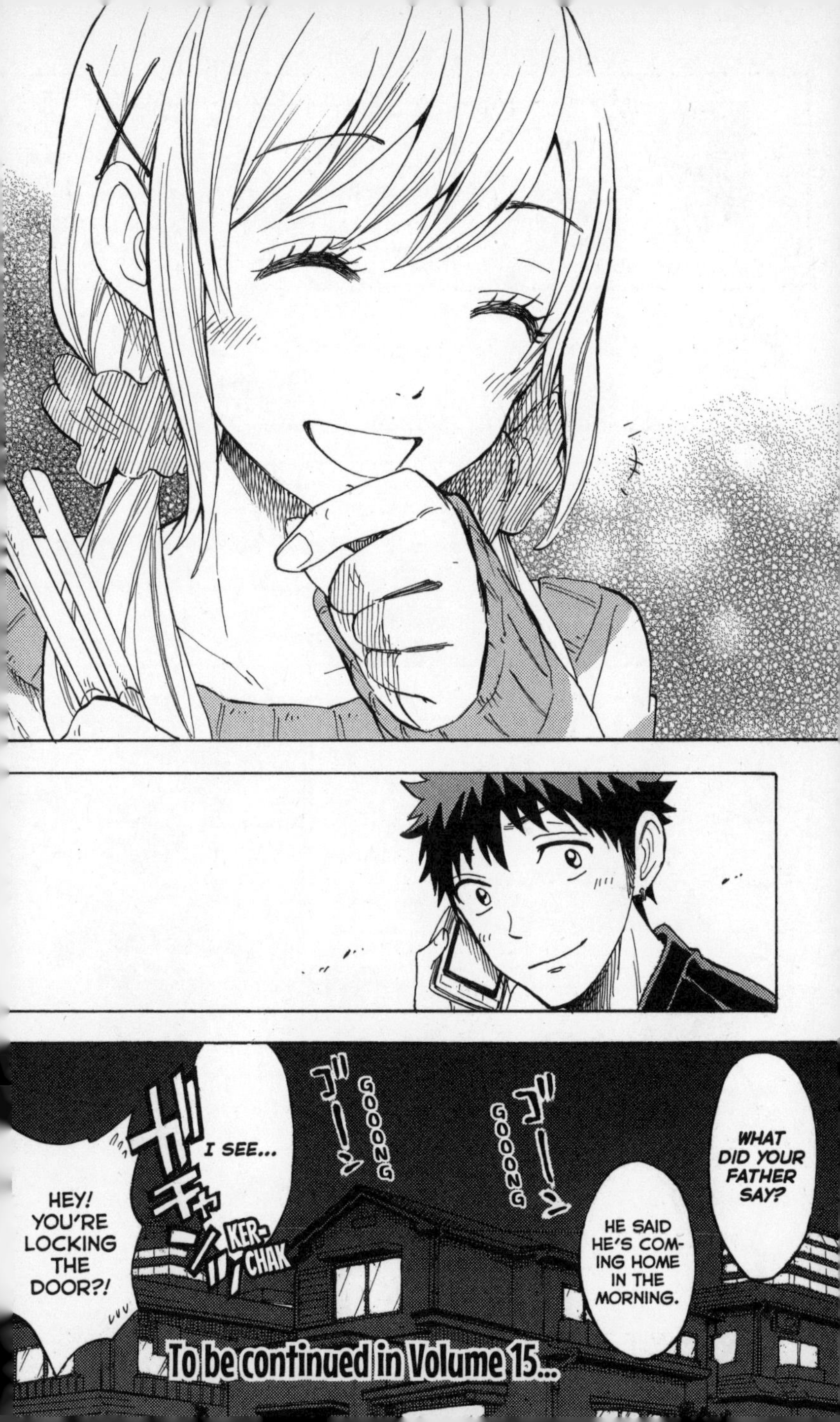

WHAT DID YOUR FATHER SAY?
HE SAID HE'S COMING HOME IN THE MORNING.
GOOOONG
GOOOONG
I SEE...
KER-CHAK
HEY! YOU'RE LOCKING THE DOOR?!
To be continued in Volume 15...

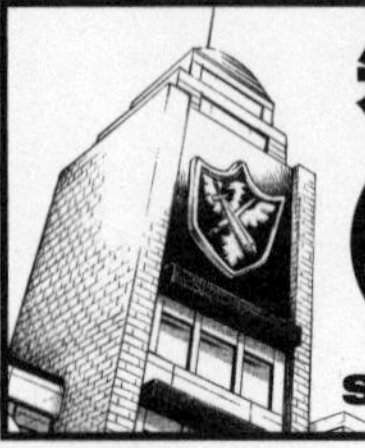

朱雀高等学校 裏ホームページ

SUZAKU HIGH SCHOOL UNDERGROUND WEBSITE

Let's get the 9th installment of our Q&A Corner started!

By the way, last time, we talked about Yamada's drawings of us. Well, we had them put up on the book's back cover!
Take a pic and use it for your own icons!
For a limited time, you can even download the data by scanning the QR code on the right with your cell phone!!

Now, let's check out the questions!

Q1. Where did Yamada-kun get the Sobasshi doll that's in his room?

Aichi Prefecture, H.N Riha-san

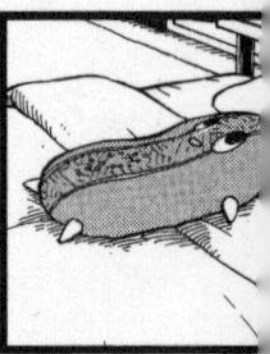

Oh, that! I was wondering about that too, so I asked him when I went to his house during the winter break.
And what do you think Yamada said?

"I got it from Tatsumi as a birthday present."

...is what he told me!!!!
Damn it! I wanna get a birthday present from a cute younger sister too!

I want that too!!

Tatsumi-chan gets annoyed with Yamada, but she actually really cares about him, huh?

Q2. Who hangs accessories (?) on the Supernatural Studies club sign? It changes from time to time!

Niigata Prefecture, H.N Sumio-san

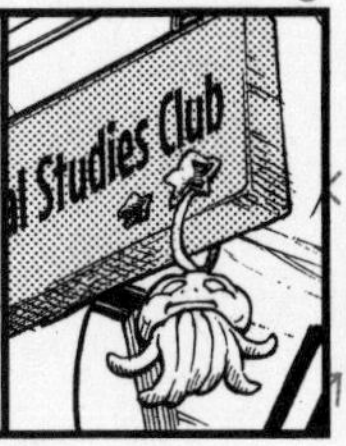
Studies Club

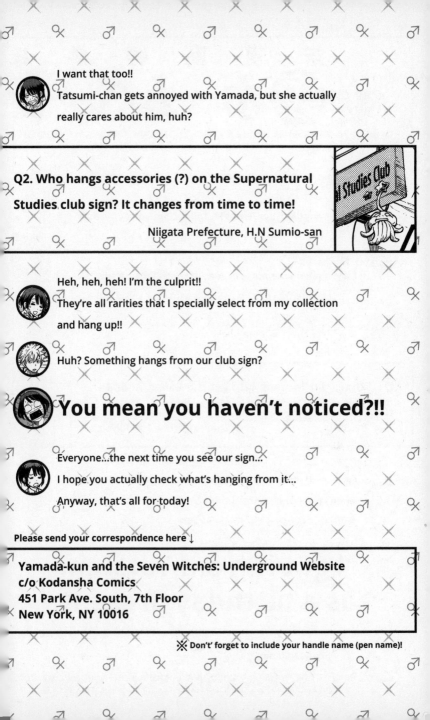

Heh, heh, heh! I'm the culprit!!

They're all rarities that I specially select from my collection and hang up!!

Huh? Something hangs from our club sign?

You mean you haven't noticed?!!

Everyone...the next time you see our sign...

I hope you actually check what's hanging from it...

Anyway, that's all for today!

Please send your correspondence here ↓

Yamada-kun and the Seven Witches: Underground Website
c/o Kodansha Comics
451 Park Ave. South, 7th Floor
New York, NY 10016

※ **Don't' forget to include your handle name (pen name)!**

Translation Notes

Shogi, page 15

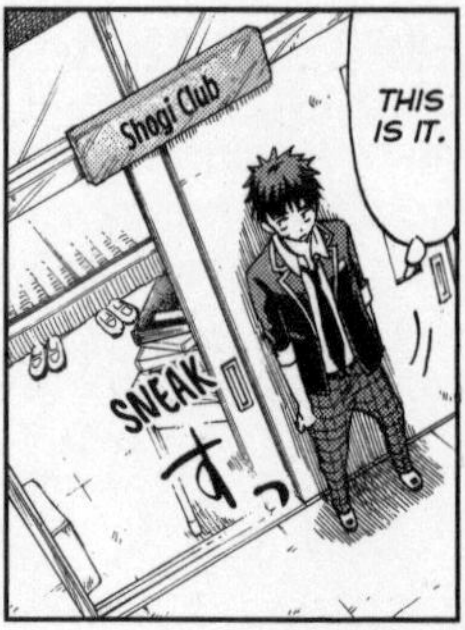
THIS IS IT.
Shogi Club
SNEAK
すっ

As mentioned in volume 11, shogi is Japanese chess. The literal translation of the name is "Generals' game" and the game's roots and can be traced back to the middle ages. It is similar to chess in its military-based strategy and rank-based pieces, but one major difference is something called the "drop rule." The drop rule allows for captured pieces to be played by the player who holds them.

Being single on Christmas Eve, page 71

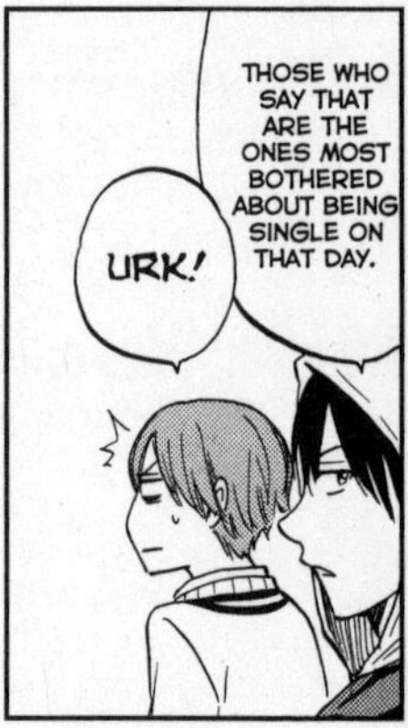
THOSE WHO SAY THAT ARE THE ONES MOST BOTHERED ABOUT BEING SINGLE ON THAT DAY.
URK!

In many Western nations, the Christmas holiday is a time for family. However, in Japan, though Christmas time can be spent with family, the more prominent tradition is to spend time with a love interest on Christmas Eve. Christmas Eve is known as a day for couples and is one of a few days during the year where most restaurants and love hotels (similar to motels in that they're often used for night activities of the physical variety) are fully booked. Because of this focus on dating and couples, being alone on Christmas Eve can be particularly sad for those without a date.

Christ's grave, page 83

Christ's grave likely refers to the Tomb of Jesus Christ in Shingo village, Aomori. Local legend has it that Jesus Christ's brother is the one who died on the cross in his place while Jesus escaped and eventually found himself in Japan. In Japan, he married a Japanese woman and lived out the rest of his life as a rice farmer. When he died, his remains were buried in a mound that is now called the Tomb of Jesus Christ.

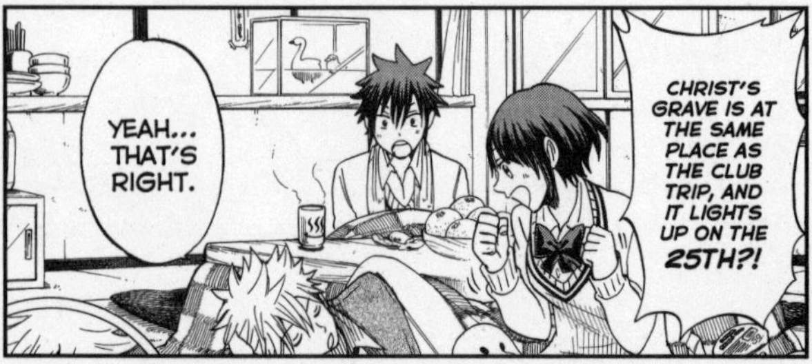
CHRIST'S GRAVE IS AT THE SAME PLACE AS THE CLUB TRIP, AND IT LIGHTS UP ON THE 25TH?!
YEAH... THAT'S RIGHT.

Shikishi, page 85

Also known as autograph boards, *shikishi* are thick, square pieces of paper that are traditionally used for calligraphy. *Shikishi* are also the primary medium for autographs from celebrities at press events and conventions.

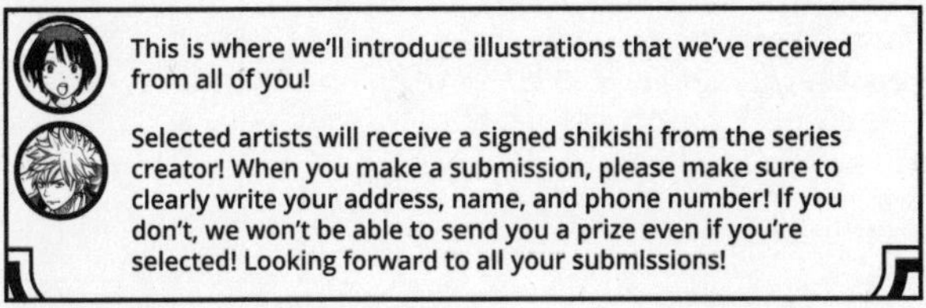
This is where we'll introduce illustrations that we've received from all of you!
Selected artists will receive a signed shikishi from the series creator! When you make a submission, please make sure to clearly write your address, name, and phone number! If you don't, we won't be able to send you a prize even if you're selected! Looking forward to all your submissions!

Yukata, page 84

Yukata are a type of casual kimono that is traditionally worn in summer by both men and women.

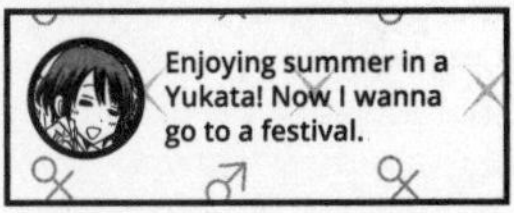
Enjoying summer in a Yukata! Now I wanna go to a festival.

Hundred Tales of Horror, page 143

The hundred tales of horror that Asuka starts in this scene appears to be based on the traditional parlor game called *Hyakumonogatari Kaidankai*. This game typically consisted of placing a mirror and 100 paper-covered lanterns called *andon* in a separate room, and having participants take turns telling scary stories and encounters with the supernatural. After a story-teller finishes their story, they must then go into the other room to look at the mirror and blow out a lantern. This continues until all the lanterns are out, after which the conditions will become perfect for the summoning of spirits. In most cases, people stop after the 99th story in fear that something spooky may actually make an appearance. Also, these types of games are usually played during summer as a Japanese way to cool off (in the way that getting scared makes one shiver or get chills), which explains why Yamada, and later, Odagiri, are so flummoxed that they're doing this on a cold day.

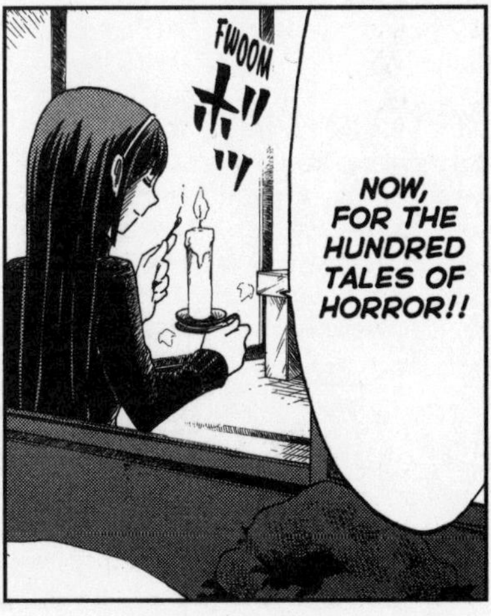
NOW, FOR THE HUNDRED TALES OF HORROR!!
FWOOM

Futons, page 149

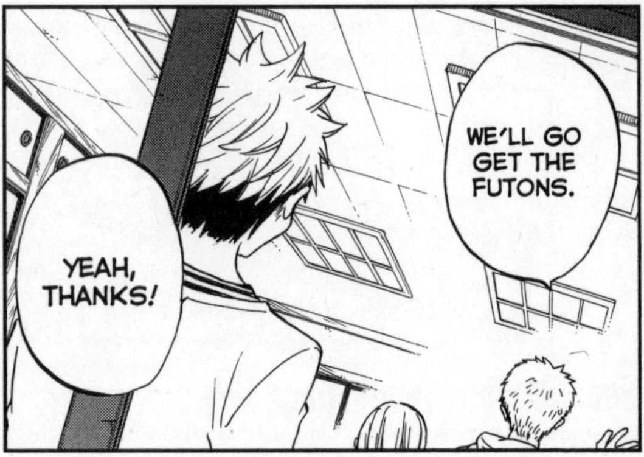
WE'LL GO GET THE FUTONS.
YEAH, THANKS!

In the U.S., a futon is a type of sofa that can be converted to a bed. It typically has a wooden frame with a thick mattress on top. The Japanese futon, which the Western one is based on, is the mattress itself, which is usually thinner and is laid on the floor as bedding at night and folded away during the day.

Laundry room, page 177

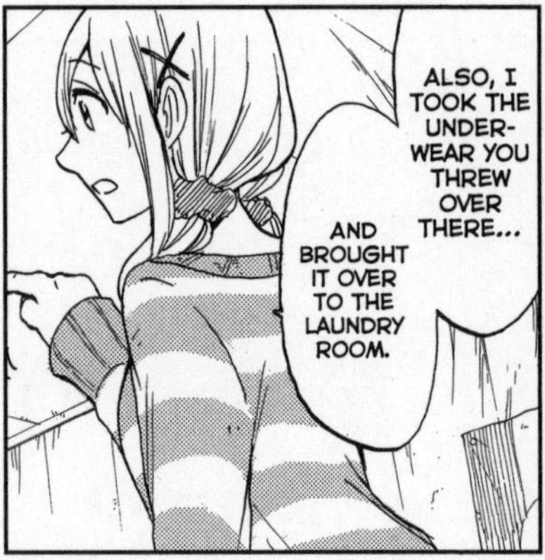
ALSO, I TOOK THE UNDER-WEAR YOU THREW OVER THERE...
AND BROUGHT IT OVER TO THE LAUNDRY ROOM.

In the original Japanese, the room in which Shiraishi places Yamada's underwear is technically the changing room (JP: *datsuijō*). In a standard Japanese house, this is the room where people change before going into the bathroom (in this case, a literal room for the bath, since the toilet is almost always its own separate room). This room usually has a sink, medicine cabinet, and other bathroom staples, but may also have a washing machine there, so it's usually where dirty clothes end up. The closest approximation in English would be the laundry room, so that's what was used as the translation.

Osechi, page 179

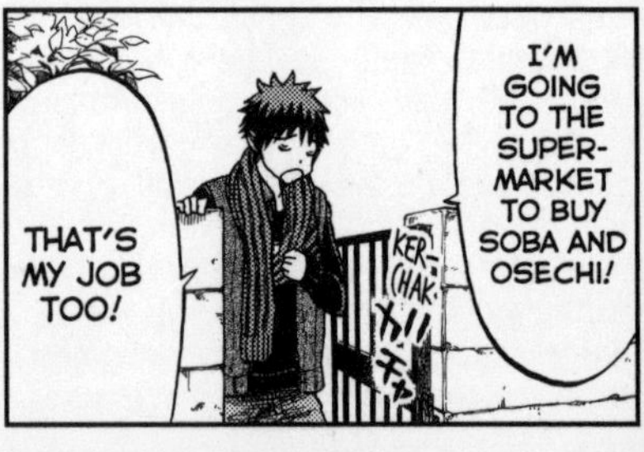
I'M GOING TO THE SUPER-MARKET TO BUY SOBA AND OSECHI!
KER-CHAK
THAT'S MY JOB TOO!

Osechi or *osechi-ryori* are traditional Japanese foods that are consumed for the New Year's holiday. They typically come in boxes similar to bento and are made up of several small dishes that each have special meanings.

HEIYU, page 180

This is most likely a parody of SEIYU, a large Japanese supermarket chain that has been wholly owned by the Walmart corporation since 2008.

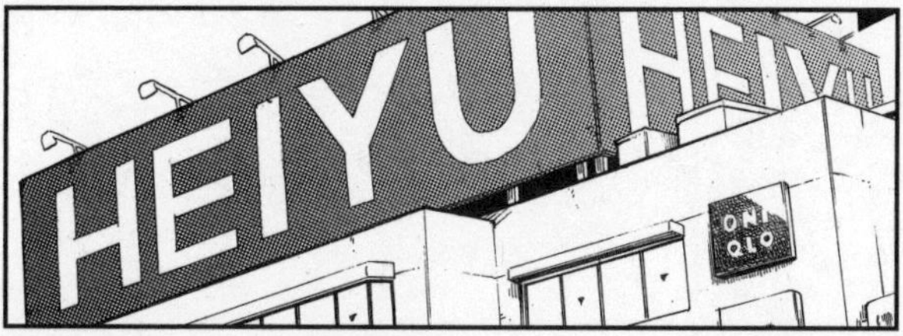
HEIYU
HEIYU
ONI QLO

Soba for New Year's, page 186

In addition to *osechi-ryori*, another traditional Japanese New Year's food is *soba* (Japanese buckwheat noodles). The holiday version of this dish is called *toshi-koshi-soba* (literally, year-crossing soba). Because soba is the easiest to cut of all Japanese noodles, *toshikoshi-soba* represents the cutting of old hardships from the previous year.

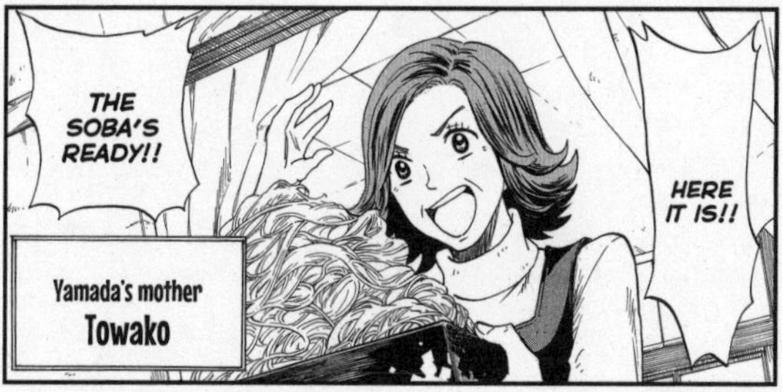
HERE IT IS!!
THE SOBA'S READY!!
Yamada's mother
Towako

SNAP and Kohaku, page 187

SNAP appears to be a parody of one of the most well-known, all-male bands in Japan, SMAP. As of 2017, the band is no longer together, but each of its members are famous enough to carry the same popularity that they once held as a unit. Kohaku is short for *NHK Kohaku Uta Gassen* (*NHK Red/White Song Battle*), a highly-rated singing competition that is shown on New Year's Eve in Japan. The contestants on the show are all top musicians, and the teams are divided into female vocalists (red team) and male vocalist (white team). The winning team is decided by a panel of celebrity judges with the help of a consolidated vote from audience members and viewers.

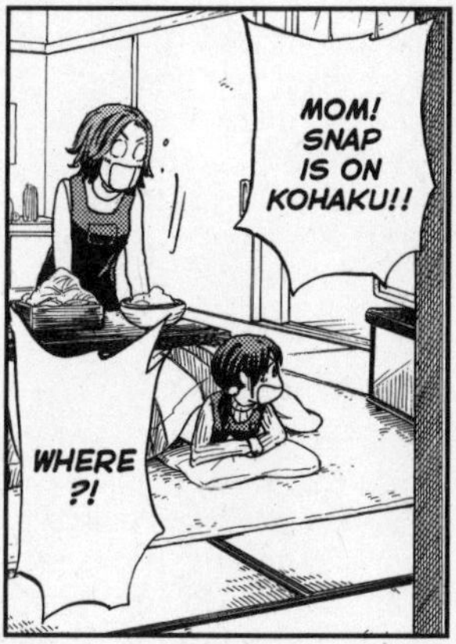
MOM! SNAP IS ON KOHAKU!!
WHERE ?!

KC KODANSHA COMICS

The award-winning manga about what happens inside you!

"Far more entertaining than it ought to be... wha kid doesn't want to think that every time the sneeze a torpedo shoots out their nose?"
–Anime News Networ

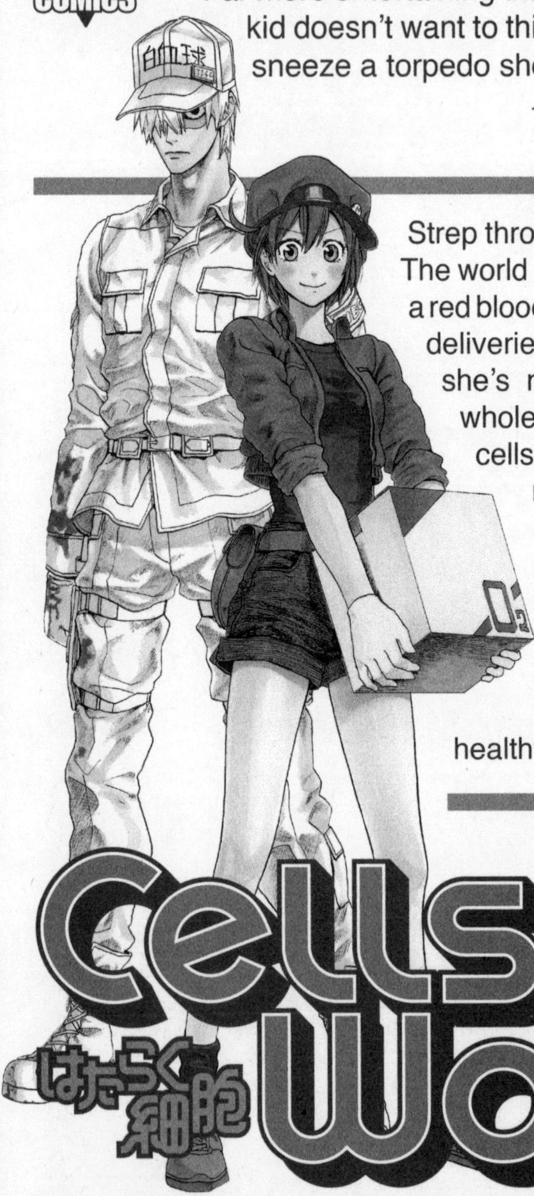

白血球

Strep throat! Hay fever! Influenza The world is a dangerous place fo a red blood cell just trying to get he deliveries finished. Fortunatel she's not alone...she's got whole human body's worth c cells ready to help out! Th mysterious white bloo cells, the buff and bras killer T cells, even th cute little platelets- everyone's got come together they want to keep yo healthy!

Cells at Work!

はたらく細胞

By Akane Shimi

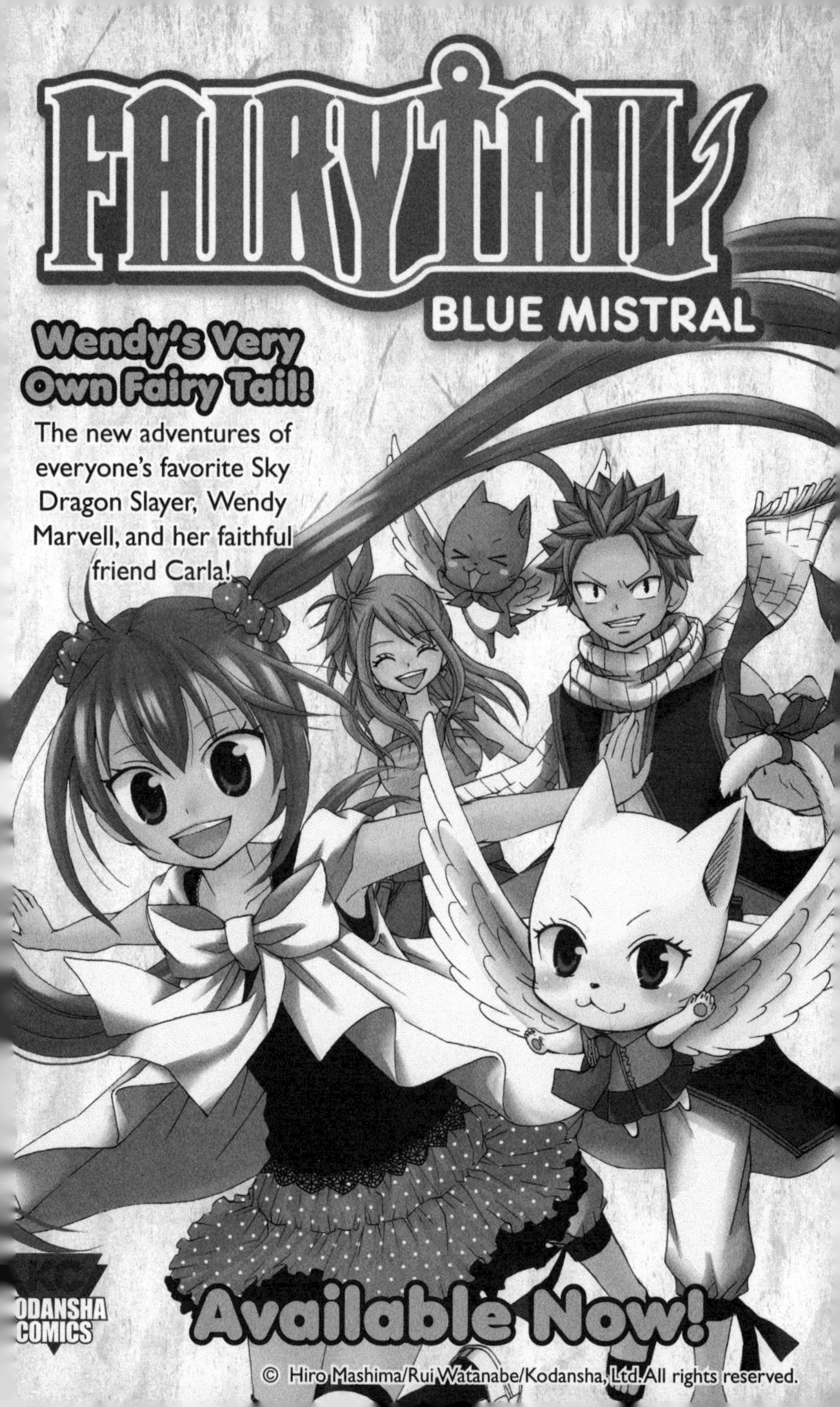

FAIRY TAIL
BLUE MISTRAL
Wendy's Very Own Fairy Tail!
The new adventures of everyone's favorite Sky Dragon Slayer, Wendy Marvell, and her faithful friend Carla!
KODANSHA COMICS
Available Now!
© Hiro Mashima/Rui Watanabe/Kodansha, Ltd. All rights reserved.

FINALLY, A LOWER-COST OMNIBUS EDITION OF FAIRY TAIL! CONTAINS VOLUMES 1-5. ONLY $39.99!

- NEARLY 1,000 PAGES!
- EXTRA LARGE 7"x10.5" TRIM SIZE
- HIGH-QUALITY PAPER!

KC KODANSHA COMICS

Fairy Tail takes place in a world filled with magic. 17-year-old Lucy is a wizard-in-training who wants to join a magic guild so that she can become a full-fledged wizard. She dreams of joining the most famous guild known as Fairy Tail. One day she meets Natsu, a boy raised by a dragon which vanished when he was young. Natsu has devoted his life to finding his dragon father. When Natsu helps Lucy out of a tricky situation, she discovers that he is a member of Fairy Tail, and our heroes' adventure together begins.

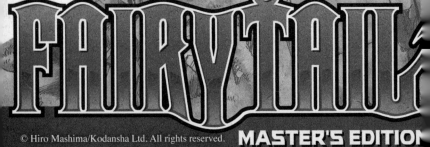

FAIRY TAIL

MASTER'S EDITION

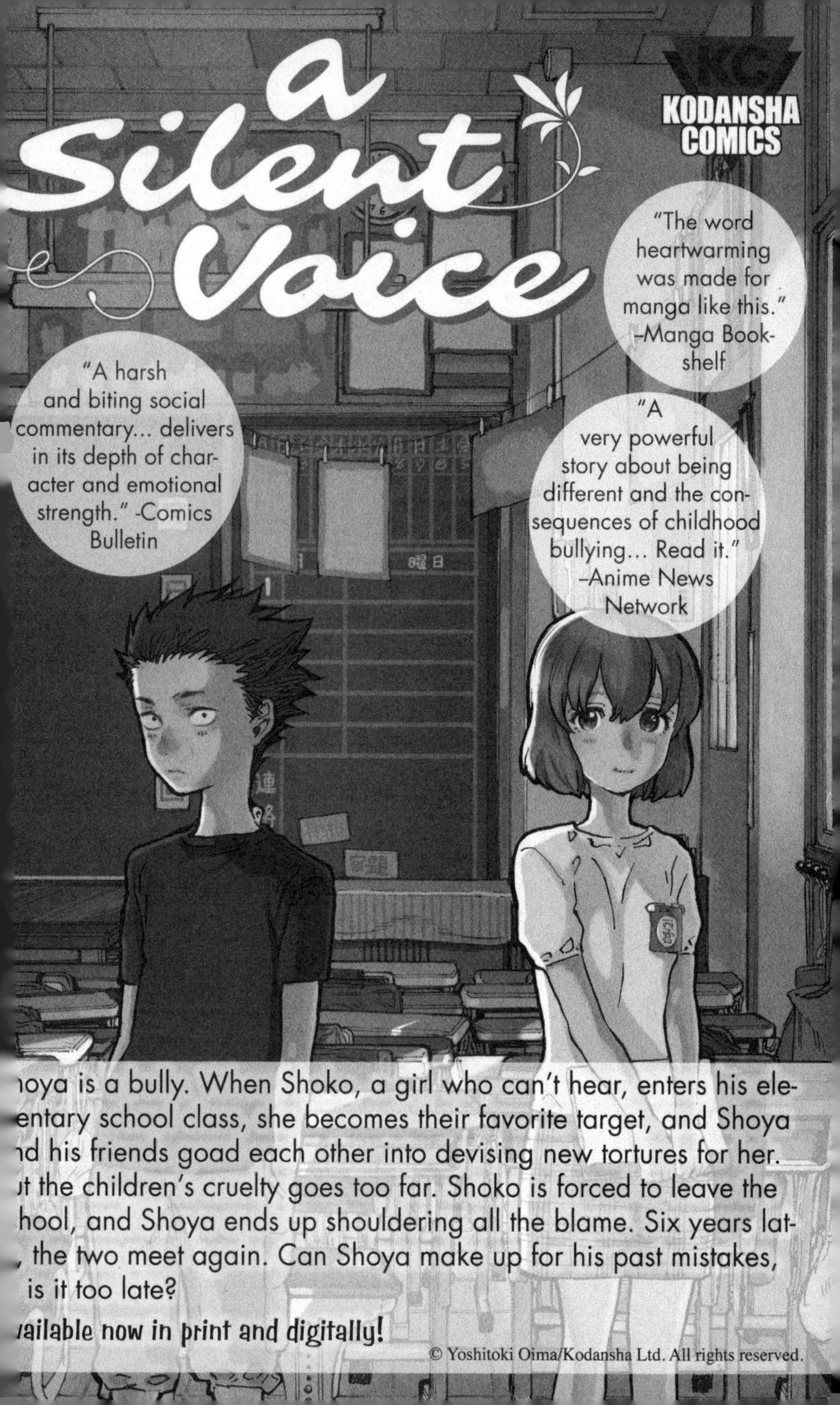
KODANSHA COMICS
a Silent Voice
"The word heartwarming was made for manga like this." –Manga Bookshelf
"A harsh and biting social commentary... delivers in its depth of character and emotional strength." -Comics Bulletin
"A very powerful story about being different and the consequences of childhood bullying… Read it." –Anime News Network
ıoya is a bully. When Shoko, a girl who can't hear, enters his ele-
entary school class, she becomes their favorite target, and Shoya
ıd his friends goad each other into devising new tortures for her.
ıt the children's cruelty goes too far. Shoko is forced to leave the
hool, and Shoya ends up shouldering all the blame. Six years lat-
, the two meet again. Can Shoya make up for his past mistakes,
is it too late?
vailable now in print and digitally!
© Yoshitoki Oima/Kodansha Ltd. All rights reserved.

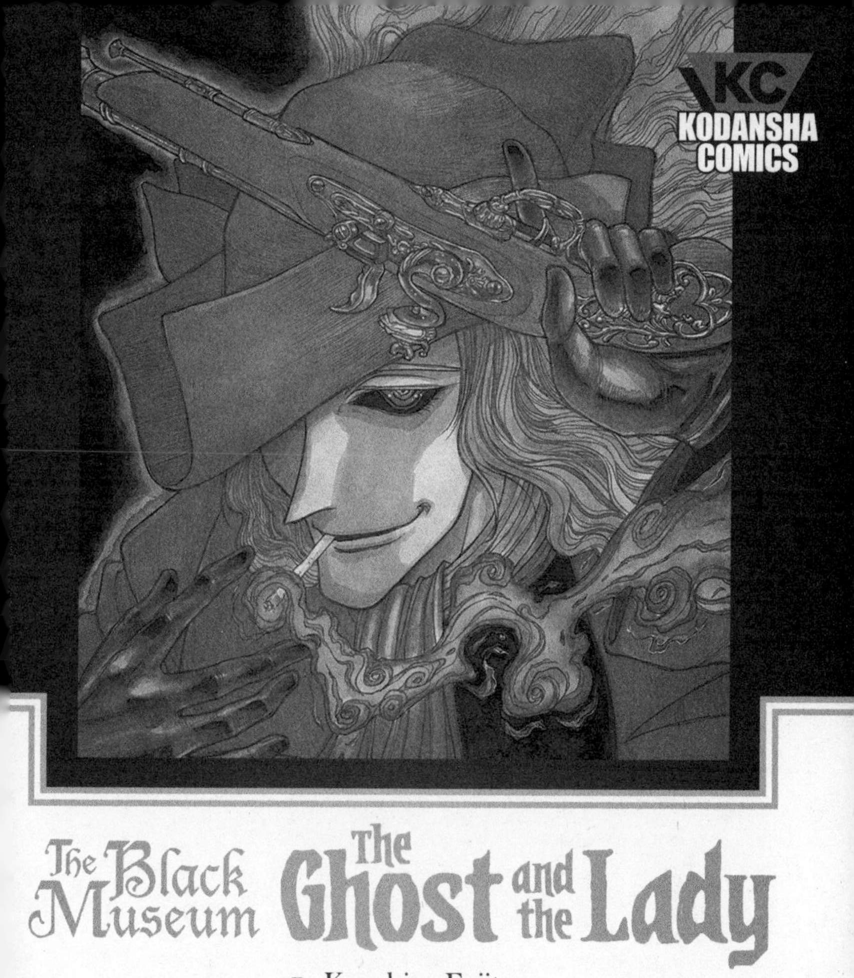
KC
KODANSHA COMICS

The Black Museum The Ghost and the Lady

By Kazuhiro Fujita

:ep in Scotland Yard in London sits an evidence room dedicated to the greatest 'steries of British history. In this "Black Museum" sits a misshapen hunk of d—two bullets fused together—the key to a wartime encounter between Florence ghtingale, the mother of modern nursing, and a supernatural Man in Grey. This ry is unknown to most scholars of history, but a special guest of the museum will ! the tale of *The Ghost and the Lady*...

Praise for Kazuhiro Fujita's *Ushio and Tora*

charming revival that combines a classic look with modern depth and pacing... **Essential viewing h for curmudgeons and new fans alike.**" — Anime News Network

REAT! The first episode of *Ushio and Tora* captures the essence of '90s anime." — IGN

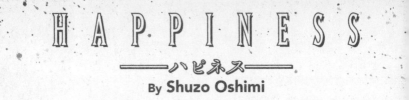

HAPPINESS

—ハピネス—

By Shuzo Oshimi

From the creator of *The Flowers of Evil*

Nothing interesting is happening in Makoto Ozaki's first year of hig school. HIs life is a series of quiet humiliations: low-grade bullie unreliable friends, and the constant frustration of his adolescent lust. Bu one night, a pale, thin girl knocks him to the ground in an alley and offe him a choice.

Now everything is different. Daylight is searingly bright. Food taste awful. And worse than anything is the terrible, consuming thirst...

Praise for Shuzo Oshimi's *The Flowers of Evil*

"A shockingly readable story that vividly—one might even say queasily—evokes the fe and confusion of discovering one's own sexuality. Recommended." —The Manga Critic

"A page-turning tale of sordid middle school blackmail." —Otaku USA Magazine

"A stunning new horror manga." —Third Eye Comics

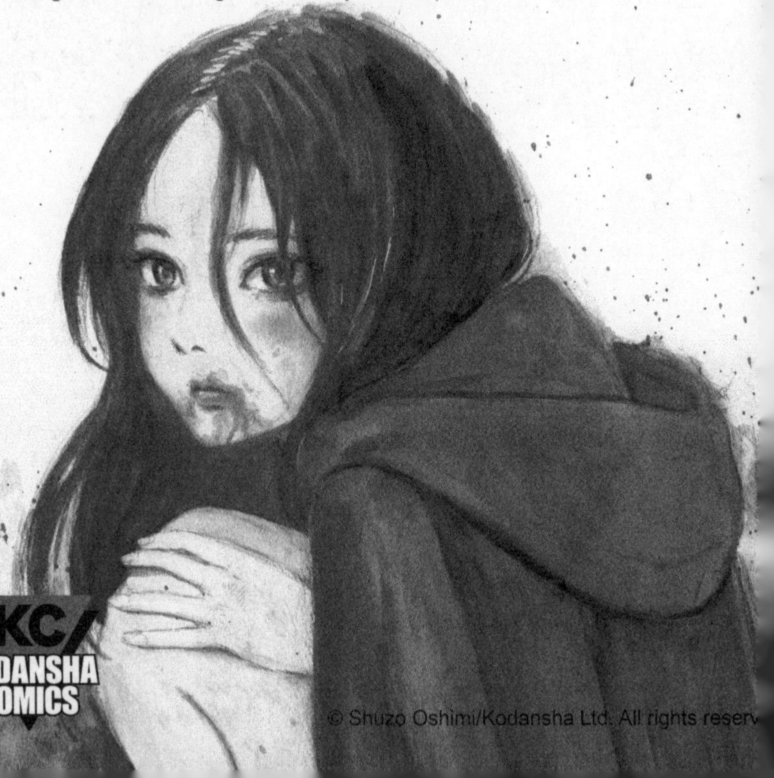

KODANSHA COMICS

INUYASHIKI

A superhero like none you've ever seen, from the creator of "Gantz"!

ICHIRO INUYASHIKI IS DOWN ON HIS LUCK. HE LOOKS MUCH OLDER THAN HIS 58 YEARS, HIS CHILDREN DESPISE HIM, AND HIS WIFE THINKS HE'S A USELESS COWARD. SO WHEN HE'S DIAGNOSED WITH STOMACH CANCER AND GIVEN THREE MONTHS TO LIVE, IT SEEMS THE ONLY ONE WHO'LL MISS HIM IS HIS DOG.

THEN A BLINDING LIGHT FILLS THE SKY, AND THE OLD MAN IS KILLED... ONLY TO WAKE UP LATER IN A BODY HE ALMOST RECOGNIZES AS HIS OWN. CAN IT BE THAT ICHIRO INUYASHIKI IS NO LONGER HUMAN?

COMES IN EXTRA-LARGE EDITIONS WITH COLOR PAGES!

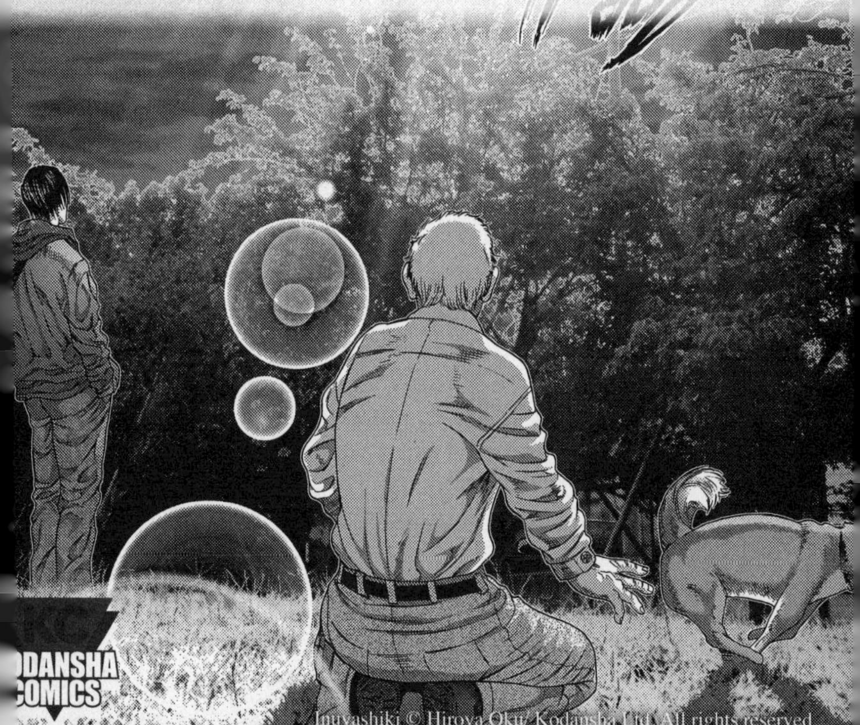

KODANSHA COMICS

KC
KODANSHA
COMICS

Japan's most powerful spirit medium delves into the ghost world's greatest mysteries!

Story by Kyo Shirodaira, famed author of mystery fiction and creator of *Spiral*, *Blast of Tempest*, and *The Record of a Fallen Vampire*.

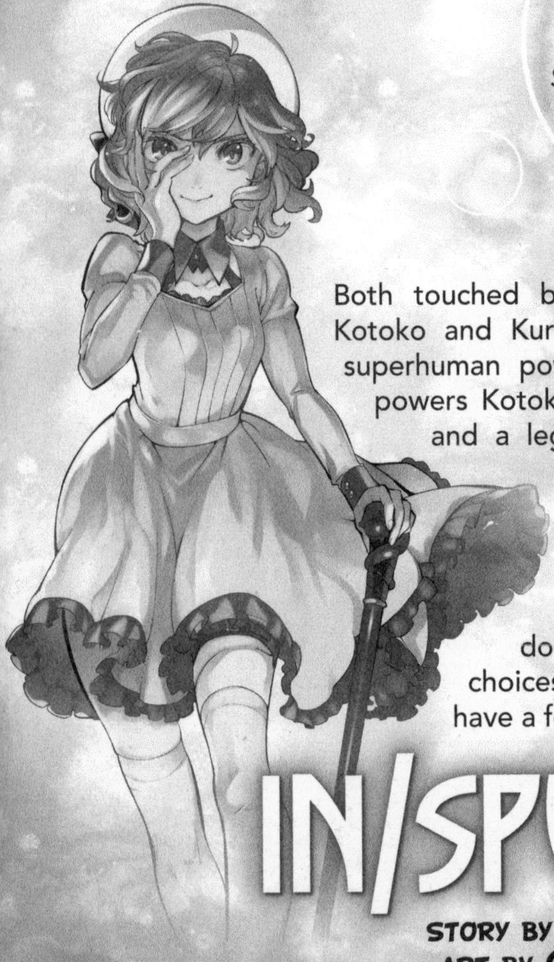

Both touched by spirits called yôka Kotoko and Kurô have gained uniqu superhuman powers. But to gain h powers Kotoko has given up an e and a leg, and Kurô's person life is in shambles. when Kotoko sugges they team up to de with renegades fr the spirit world, Ku doesn't have many oth choices, but Kotoko might j have a few ulterior motives...

IN/SPECTRE

STORY BY **KYO SHIRODAIR**
ART BY **CHASHIBA KATAS**

New action series from Hiroyuki Takei, creator of the classic shonen franchise Shaman King!

n medieval Japan, a bell hanging on the collar is a sign that a cat as a master. Norachiyo's bell hangs from his katana sheath, but he is onetheless a stray — a ronin. This one-eyed cat samurai travels across a ishonest world, cutting through pretense and deception with his blade.

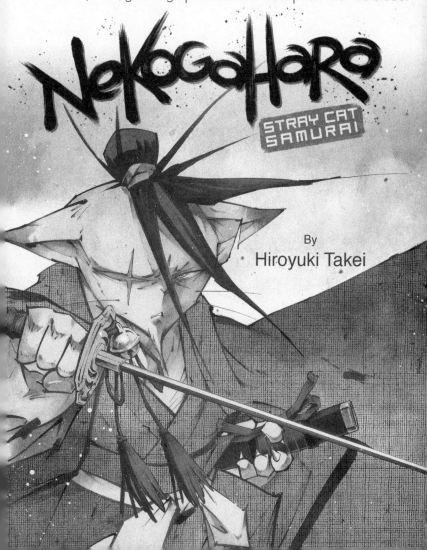

NEKOGAHARA

STRAY CAT SAMURAI

By
Hiroyuki Takei

Praise for the anime:

"The show provides a pleasant window on the highs and lows of young love with two young people who are first-timers at the real thing."

-The Fandom Post

"Always it is smarter, more poetic, more touching, just plain better than you think it is going to be."

-Anime News Network

Say I Love You.

Mei Tachibana has no friends — and says she doesn't need them

But everything changes when she accidentally roundhouse kicks the most popular boy in school! However, Yamato Kurosawa isn't angry in the slightest in fact, he thinks his ordinary life could use an unusual girl like Mei. But winnin Mei's trust will be a tough task. How long will she refuse to say, "I love you"?

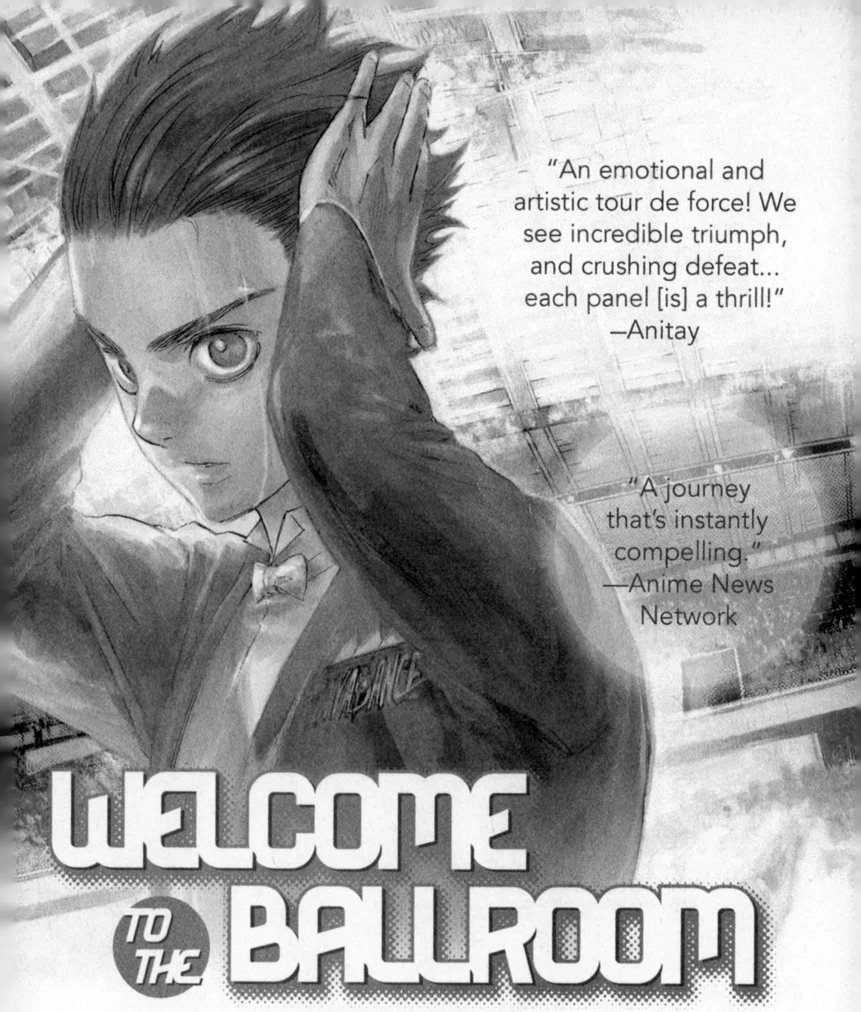
"An emotional and artistic tour de force! We see incredible triumph, and crushing defeat... each panel [is] a thrill!" –Anitay
"A journey that's instantly compelling." —Anime News Network

WELCOME TO THE BALLROOM

By Tomo Takeuchi

ckless high school student Tatara Fujita wants to be good at mething—anything. Unfortunately, he's about as average as a slouchy en can be. The local bullies know this, and make it a habit to hit him up cash, but all that changes when the debonair Kaname Sengoku sends em packing. Sengoku's not the neighborhood watch, though. He's a ofessional ballroom dancer. And once Tatara Fujita gets lled into the world of ballroom, his life will never be the ne.

KC KODANSHA COMICS

KC
KODANSHA
COMICS

A new series from the creator of *Soul Eater*, the megahit manga and anime seen on Toonami!

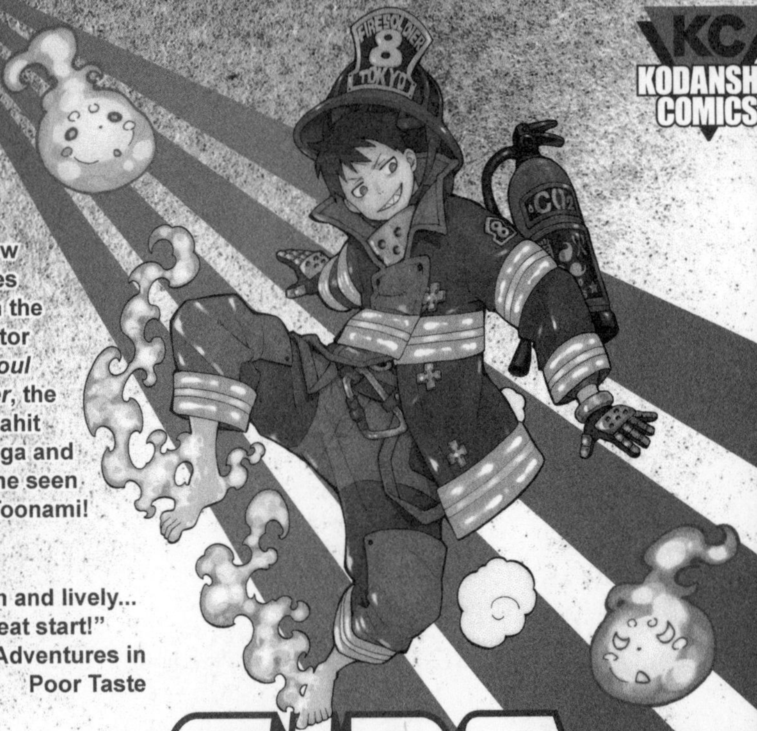

"Fun and lively... a great start!"
-Adventures in Poor Taste

FIRE FORCE

By Atsushi Ohkubo

The city of Tokyo is plagued by a deadly phenomenon: spontaneo human combustion! Luckily, a special team is there to quench t inferno: The Fire Force! The fire soldiers at Special Fire Cathedra are about to get a unique addition. Enter Shinra, a boy who possess the power to run at the speed of a rocket, leaving behind the famo "devil's footprints" (and destroying his shoes in the proces Can Shinra and his colleagues discover the source of this stran epidemic before the city burns to ashes?

Yamada-kun and the Seven Witches volume 14 is a work of fiction. Names, characters, places, and incidents are the products of the author's imagination or are used fictitiously. Any resemblance to actual events, locales, or persons, living or dead, is entirely coincidental.

A Kodansha Comics Trade Paperback Original.

Yamada-kun and the Seven Witches volume 14 copyright © 2014 Miki Yoshikawa
English translation copyright © 2017 Miki Yoshikawa

Published in the United States by Kodansha Comics, an imprint of Kodansha USA Publishing, LLC, New York.

Publication rights for this English edition arranged through Kodansha Ltd., Tokyo.

First published in Japan in 2014 by Kodansha Ltd., Tokyo, as *Yamada-kun to Nananin no Majo* volume 14.

ISBN 978-1-63236-354-1

Printed in the United States of America.

www.kodanshacomics.com

9 8 7 6 5 4 3 2 1

Translation: David Rhie
Lettering: Sara Linsley
Editing: Ajani Oloye
Kodansha Comics edition cover design: Phil Balsman